IMPLEMENTING EC LAW IN THE UNITED KINGDOM: STRUCTURES FOR INDIRECT RULE

Edited by
Terence Daintith

JOHN WILEY & SONS
Chichester · New York · Brisbane · Toronto · Singapore

First published in April 1995 by
Chancery Law Publishing Ltd
Baffins Lane
Chichester
West Sussex PO19 1UD

Published in North America by
John Wiley & Sons Inc
7222 Commerce Centre Drive
Colorado Springs CO 80919
USA

Typeset by
Photo·graphics, Honiton, Devon

Printed and bound in Great Britain by
Bookcraft (Bath) Ltd

This book is printed on acid-free paper responsibly manufactured from sustainable
forestation. At least two trees are planted for each one used for paper production.

ISBN 0 471 95225 7

A copy of the CIP entry for this book is
available from the British Library

Contents

CONTENTS

CONTENTS

7 Welcoming the Well and the Wealthy: Implementing Free Movement Rights in the United Kingdom   *167*

– Christopher Vincenzi

8 Television Without Frontiers   *213*

– Cecilia O'Leary and David Goldberg

9 Playing Safe: The United Kingdom's Implementation of the Toy Safety Directive   *239*

– Stephen Weatherill

CONTENTS

PART THREE: EFFECTS OF IMPLEMENTATION

Preface

Getting this book written has sometimes borne an uncomfortable resemblance to the complex processes of indirect, multinational and multicultural administration which it seeks to analyse. This has nothing to do with the behaviour of the contributors, whose co-operation has been exemplary. It derives from the fact that the research reflected here was originally conceived as the contribution of a United Kingdom team to a European Community-wide project with mixed Community and national funding. The task of first obtaining, and then maintaining, the necessary degree of alignment between the research and funding agendas of the relevant national and Community bodies has involved an almost continuous process of renegotiation, with one party or another, of the scope and ambitions of the work.

What has emerged from this very strenuous process is a book which is designed to function both as a straightforward analysis of the structures of indirect Community rule in the United Kingdom – structures which, to judge from coverage even in the serious press, are poorly understood save by Community law specialists – and as a critique and prospective on the functioning of indirect rule, based on detailed empirical research in some important substantive areas. That critique tries to take into account not only the internal situation of the United Kingdom, but the future needs of the Community as a whole: a topical and important concern as the 1996 European intergovernmental conference approaches.

Along the way our principal financial support has been a grant (L113251005) provided by the Economic and Social Research Council within the framework of its Single European Market Initiative. We have been most grateful for this, and in particular for the support and guidance of Professor David Mayes, the Co-ordinator of that Initiative during the period of our association with it. Other financial support, which we also acknowledge with gratitude, has been given by the Commission of the European Community and by the University of Huddersfield.

The people from government and industry who helped in a wide variety of ways with research for Chapters 5–9 are too numerous to thank by name here; I hope that they find in those Chapters a proper and accurate reflection of the views, information and commentary they so generously provided. Those Chapters depend heavily on the work of several research assistants, two of whom, Hilary Hiram and Cecilia O'Leary, joined the team of authors in the course of the work. Special thanks here, therefore, go to Jenna Brown, who participated in the early stages of work on Chapters 5 and 6 (a first experience of the law so inspiring that she left to obtain a professional qualification as a solicitor) and to Ian Phelps, who undertook research for Chapter 7.

It is not the purpose of this book to give a detailed picture of the state of the law at a given moment, but the reader may find it useful to know that we have tried, in revising and editing the material here, to reflect significant developments taking place up to 30 September 1994.

Terence Daintith
London, March 1995

Tables

REGULATIONS

DIRECTIVES

UK STATUTES

STATUTORY INSTRUMENTS

List of Contributors

Noreen Burrows is Professor of European Law at the University of Glasgow.

Terence Daintith is Professor of Law at the Institute of Advanced Legal Studies, and Dean of the School of Advanced Study, in the University of London.

David Goldberg is Senior Lecturer in Law at the University of Glasgow.

Hilary Hiram is Lecturer in Law at the University of Glasgow.

Imelda Maher is Lecturer in Law at the University of Warwick. In 1993 she was Visiting Fellow at the Institute of Advanced Legal Studies, University of London.

Cecilia O'Leary is Research Assistant at the Institute of Advanced Legal Studies, University of London.

Francis Snyder is Professor of European Law, European University Institute, Florence; Professor, College of Europe, Bruges; and Honorary Visiting Professor of Law, University College London.

John Usher is Professor of European Law and Director of the Centre of European Legal Studies, University of Exeter.

Christopher Vincenzi was, until September 1994, Principal Lecturer in Law at the University of Huddersfield. He is now Senior Research Fellow at Manchester Metropolitan University.

Stephen Weatherill is Reader in Law at the University of Nottingham.

Chapter 1
Introduction

1 The indirect administration of Community law

Stalin professed not to be afraid of the opposition of Rome – "The Pope?"
he said, "how many divisions has he got?"[1] – but many modern politicians
are more craven when it comes to Brussels, proclaiming their fear of a
group of bureaucrats who command neither armies, nor police, nor
extensive funds, nor even consciences. What these bureaucrats do have,
in profusion, are rules: rules for us and for our governments, in the shape
of laws to govern activities ranging from the framing of national budgets[2]
to the making of jam.[3] Yet having neither armies nor police, the Brussels
legislators have little or no capacity to enforce their laws themselves; for
this they rely on the resources of the States which are members of the
European Community. It is remarkable how rarely, over nearly half a
century of the life of the European Community institutions, those
resources have been explicitly withheld. Notwithstanding the frequency
with which each and every Member State has been at odds with Community policy, and hence in disagreement with the content of Community law, on one subject or another, the proclamation of a refusal to
comply with that law, or to co-operate in making it effective in the Member State's own territory, has been a rare event; and it has been all but
unknown for it to extend over a broad range of legal regulation, as
opposed to the specific law on which there is disagreement.[4] The rarity
of express refusal of compliance or co-operation of course says nothing
about possible unacknowledged deviance on the part of Member States,
and such deviance, and sheer inefficiency in enforcement, are today seen
as significant problems in the Community; but it is the expectation of

---

[1] Recorded in Churchill, *The Second World War: Vol 1, The Gathering Storm* 1st ed., 1948, 105.
[2] See EEC Treaty, as amended by the Treaty on European Union (1992), art 104c, and the
Protocol on the Excessive Deficit Procedure.
[3] See Council Directive 79/693/EEC on the approximation of the laws of the Member States
relating to fruit jams, jellies and marmalade and chestnut purée, OJ 1979 L205/5.
[4] Even the dramatic non-co-operation of the French "empty chair" policy in 1965 (which led to
the so-called "Luxembourg compromise") on majority voting does not appear to have been
accompanied by extensive French breaches of existing Community law: see Mason, "Luxembourg Compromise – Council of European Community ignores British attempt to exercise
implied veto power of Luxembourg Compromise," (1983) 13 *Georgia, J Int Comp L* 135, at n 13.

Member State enforcement, born of a rhetoric of loyalty, which gives such weight to the pronunciamentos of Brussels.

Given that the European Community machinery relies to such a remarkable degree upon laws, as opposed to other tools of government like money, people and organisation, it is also worth reflecting for a moment on the fact that in the majority of areas of its competence, these laws are designed to function indirectly. There are certain fields, like competition policy, agriculture, or transport policy, where the Community issues rules that are directly addressed to individuals and corporations, and are designed, so far as possible, to take effect without supplementation or detailing by further rules, and to be capable of immediate enforcement (by State authorities) through criminal penalties, civil liability, and otherwise. Elsewhere, the rules are addressed to Member States and require them to apply, or adjust, the substantive and procedural rules of their own legal systems so as to attain the results described in the Community's legislation. Community rules of this latter type, which may be contained in the Treaties themselves or be made by the Community authorities in the form of directives, cover a vast area of Community policy, including the achievement of the Single European Market. Such policy therefore relies on the Member States, not simply to provide enforcement tools like criminal and civil process, administrative inspection, and the like, but also to see to the transposition of the Community rules into the national legal system, by whatever adjustments to existing legal rules and other structures may be necessary. The Community, in other words, looks to the Member States for the implementation of its law, not just for its enforcement. While this double reliance multiplies opportunities for explicit and tacit non-compliance, it may paradoxically be a source of strength for the Community. Not only does it permit some national variation, some respect for local traditions and preferences, it also disguises, in varying degrees, the extent to which the national executive and judicial powers are engaged in the enforcement of rules of "alien" origin, by clothing those rules in the familiar forms of national law and regulation.

The advantages and disadvantages of such "internalisation" of Community law, the necessary and permissible degrees of divergence in its application, have been long-standing topics of discussion among professionals in the field.[5] These are vital issues from the standpoint of the Community policy-maker, but the intimate involvement of Member States in the process of implementation of Community law also raises questions

---

[5] *E.g.* Easson, "EEC directives for the Harmonisation of Laws: Some Problems of Validity, Implementation and Legal Effects" (1981) 1 YEL 1; Bermann, "The Single European Act: A New Constitution for the Community?" (1989) 27 Colum.J.Transnat'l Law 529, n 40; Schwarze, Govaere, Hélin and Van den Bossche (eds.), *The 1992 Challenge at National Level: Reports and Conference Proceedings 1989* (1990) 694–695; Potter, "Implications of the Single European Act on European Community Law-Making: a Modest Step Forward" (1993) 26 Vand.J.of Transnat'l Law 249 at 258.

of a more domestic character. These questions form the principal subject-matter of this book. Our concern, put briefly, is to ask how our own processes of law and administration are affected by their participation as essential elements in the implementation of Community law and policy. An increasing proportion of the activity of administrators (at both national and local level) and of judges is related to and shaped by the requirements of European Community law. How does this affect the nature of what they do and how they do it? Answers to such enquiries are not merely of national interest. They may contribute to the continuous process through which national administrations and legal systems within the Community learn from one another's actions and attitudes; more immediately, they should inform consideration of policy and process at Community level, by indicating how well – or badly – such policy and process, existing or projected, are absorbed or tolerated by a national system which functions as an essential part of such process.

2 United Kingdom trends, Community context

This question of the systemic impact of Community law and policy looks relatively straightforward, but as soon as one starts any detailed enquiry it becomes clear that Community impacts are tightly imbricated with the effects of domestically initiated changes to law and government. Since 1979 the United Kingdom has had a government strongly committed to radical public sector reform. It has brought a strong ideological commitment to such tasks as privatisation, and deregulation; its quest for economies in public spending has had a major impact on central-local government relationships; its desire for efficiency in central government has seriously challenged established conceptions of public accountability, notably the practice of Ministerial responsibility. Possibly coincidentally, possibly not, the use of judicial procedures as a means of calling government to account has increased dramatically over the same period. All of these trends encounter relevant Community impacts, particularly in the areas of economic regulation which are the Community's special concern. To set our more detailed work in context, therefore, this section briefly explores the relationship between these national trends and the demands of the Community structure, focusing on three trends where the association between national and Community-induced changes seems particularly intimate. These are first, the withdrawal of public authorities from tasks of substantive regulation; second, the centralisation of regulatory policy; and third, an increasing salience of private litigation in the policy landscape, in relation not only to the enforcement but even to the definition of policy, and the associated growth in the power of the courts.

(i) **The withdrawal of public authorities from tasks of substantive regulation**

This formulation is designed to describe without ambiguity a variety of moves whose nature is generally obfuscated by indiscriminate use of the labels "privatisation", "self-regulation", and "de-regulation". Each of these general terms has represented a significant domestic policy commitment over the last decade and more. Among Community members, the United Kingdom has led the way in the practice of privatisation, starting earliest in the process of selling off State enterprises, talking loudest about the ideological convictions underpinning its policy, and pursuing it furthest towards the transfer into private hands of all possible public functions, prisons and tax administration not excluded.[6] Simultaneously it has been committed to "deregulation" and "self-regulation", espousing with enthusiasm the policies of removal of regulatory distortions of competition pioneered in the United States by Presidents Carter and Reagan. While other States in the Community have also pursued deregulatory policies in recent years[7], the United Kingdom has again been notable for the ideological vigour of its commitment. Where other countries have tended to see deregulation as an apolitical exercise in reducing the mass and complexity of legal rules to which business is subject, ours has focused more strongly on substituting competition for rules, private enforcement for State enforcement, "self-regulation" (in the sense of industry regulation) for official regulation. Ideas of disburdening have also been present, but have been pursued somewhat fitfully; the 1994 Deregulation Act represents the most determined attempt so far to achieve a result – of eliminating unnecessary regulations – which has tended to elude earlier initiatives.[8]

There is certainly no basic contradiction between these policy drives and the demands of Community membership. While the EC Treaty takes care to be agnostic on the proper borderline between State and private property[9], its emphasis on avoidance of distortion of competition is sympathetic to privatisation, in so far as it inhibits, through provisions like those on State aids (Article 92) and State treatment of public enterprises

---

[6] On privatised prisons in the UK see Ryan, "Evaluating and responding to private prisons in the United Kingdom," (1993) 21 Int.J.Socio.Law 319–333; McDonald, "Public Imprisonment by Private Means," (1994) 34 Brit.J of Criminology (special issue) 29–48. On the "hiving-off" of certain tax services, see "Tax file squabble hits privatisation" *The Guardian*, March 31, 1994, 6; "US firm takes over tax records" *The Independent* May 23, 1994, 3.

[7] See Institut Français des Sciences Administratives, *Les Déréglementations* (1988).

[8] *E.g.* the post-war Labour Government's "bonfire of controls": see Pimlott, *Harold Wilson* (1993), 124–132; and the 1985 White Paper, *Lifting the Burden*, Cmnd. 9571, leading to the creation of the Enterprise and Deregulation Unit; and the new effort made in 1993, with the setting up of seven task forces of business people to review regulations: see 218 HC Deb., cols. 140, 472 (2, 4 February 1993), and Batchelor, "Small business welcomes untangling of red tape," *Financial Times*, 3 February 1993, 10, 24.

[9] Article 222: "This Treaty shall in no way prejudice the rules in member States governing the system of property ownership."

(Article 90), many of the uses of such enterprises which justify their continued existence. These and other provisions are capable of creating difficulties for particular aspects of privatisation policies[10], but not of a fundamental kind.

Deregulation deserves a closer look. As a domestic policy, it is again broadly in sympathy with the Community's goals of undistorted competition in a free market. Many of the substantive provisions of the EC Treaty, notably Article 30 forbidding measures of equivalent effect to quantitative restrictions, mandate the removal of those Member State regulations which erect barriers to trade. Complexity however develops where the Treaty acknowledges, in Article 36 (public policy justifications for restrictive measures), that national rules which inhibit trade between Member States (or the other economic freedoms of the Treaty) may serve important policy goals such as the protection of public health, or of the interests of consumers or workers, or the support of moral or ethical standards. Unless these goals are to be abandoned, the pursuit of free and undistorted trade, of free movement of labour, services and capital must be accompanied by measures to secure the harmonisation or mutual recognition of these national protective regulations.

It is this imperative which forces the Community into the paradox of regulating in order to deregulate. The United Kingdom government should be familiar with such paradoxes: despite its penchant for deregulation, it has found that its privatisation of public utilities with monopoly characteristics has required it to erect an entirely new structure of regulation to protect the users of such services. As integration has progressed, this paradox has become both more acute and more obvious. In its early years, the Community had an agenda set out with a fair degree of clarity in a legally binding Treaty. There was a single objective – economic integration – and an assumption that its attainment could in large measure be legally structured by straightforward legal prohibitions addressed mostly to Member States[11], linked to limited collective legislative competences, designed to create the essential conditions of harmonisation of policy for the prohibitions on restraints of trade to operate. The exercise of power under that system could effectively be policed by judicial means. As obvious barriers to trade, and discriminatory measures are steadily removed, however, so do the subtler barriers and distortions become apparent; and these, unlike tariffs and the grosser non-tariff barriers, reveal themselves as integral to the operation of distinctive national policies of economic regulation in pursuit of a variety of public interests. In consequence, continuing to pursue a policy of economic integration implies developing, at the European level, policies – for health and safety at work, for consumer protection, for environmental protection, for

---

[10] Daintith, "The Legal Techniques of Privatisation," in *International Privatisation: Strategies and Practices* (Clarke ed., 1994), 43–77, at 46–48; see also below Chapter 12, section 2.
[11] Exceptionally to individuals, as in EC Treaty, arts 85, 86.

employment relations – in substitution for those which, if pursued nationally, are doomed to produce distortions of trade. It is at this point, where European policy acquires a multitude of objectives to be held in some kind of balance, and hence totally ceases to be "programmable" through the legal structures adopted in the ECSC and EC Treaties, that the deregulation paradox assumes the additional form of the "democratic deficit" which presently troubles us, and the legitimacy of relying largely on judicial policing becomes suspect.

This process, and the need it engenders to engage in the making of new policy at the Community level, has occasioned tensions between the Community as a whole and individual Member States, among which the United Kingdom has been conspicuous. The government's ideology has led it to support with vigour the Commission's Single European Market programme[12], so long as that programme is eliminating straightforward barriers to trade and is opening markets, particularly in areas like financial services in which the United Kingdom enjoys comparative advantage; but that support has fallen away, and been replaced by suspicion or even hostility, when the Community has entered areas – like environmental policy – in which the Commission and other Member States feel that the avoidance of competitive distortion requires the acceptance of strict common regulatory standards. That hostility has been especially evident in all areas touching on labour markets, where the government profoundly fears the introduction of new market rigidities on a European scale, and where it has sought to insulate itself from this trend by its "opt-out" from the Social Chapter of the Maastricht Treaty.[13]

The very public proclamation of these differences should not distract attention from the fact that the Community itself is highly conscious of the risk of rigidities and has adopted approaches to regulation and to the definition of its own powers which are in broad sympathy, again, with the United Kingdom's own preferences. "Subsidiarity" is the main focus of attention in the 1990s, and we consider it in the following section; in the 1980s, the spotlight fell rather upon the idea of "mutual recognition" by Member States of their respective national regulatory regimes, as a means of combining free trade with regulatory protection of third parties without the need for detailed common regimes. Chapter 2 will examine the development of this concept and its legal articulation in the Community, and its significance will also be evident in several of our later Chapters. Here we need only try to relate it to the general notion of public withdrawal from detailed substantive regulation which forms the subject of this section.

---

[12] *Completing the Internal Market*, COM(85)310.
[13] See Treaty on European Union and Final Act, 7 February 1992: Protocol on Social Policy (1992) 31 ILM 247–373, at 357; and Agreement on social policy concluded between the Member States of the European Community with the exception of the United Kingdom of Great Britain and Northern Ireland, *ibid.*, at 358.

This kind of withdrawal may be effected in a number of ways, which may often, as already noted, be presented as applications of vague concepts of "privatisation", "self-regulation", and "de-regulation". First, and most obvious, is the simple repeal of regulations, an effort intermittently made in most Member States and currently represented in the United Kingdom by the Deregulation Act. We have already noted that the European integration project necessarily involves much deregulation of this type. A second alternative, for which the Deregulation Act also makes provision[14], is to contract out regulatory functions to private bodies. The effective delegation of regulatory functions (especially functions of inspection) to private bodies is already something of an administrative commonplace here: Ministry of Transport Vehicle Testing stations, and administration of exchange control by clearing banks, provide current and past examples. Definition of the rules, however, remains firmly in public hands. The device has affinities with a third alternative, that of drawing on the "self-regulatory" capacity of an industry or profession to secure regulation of its activities in the public interest. Here there will be some division of the function of rule-making between the public and private bodies involved. At one extreme government may be content to allocate competence and retain some supervisory capacity over its exercise[15], at the other, it may create a detailed structure of principles and procedures within which the "self-regulatory" bodies must work.[16] In all cases government will, to some extent, disburden itself of the task of laying down the detailed substantive rules which should govern conduct in the sector. A fourth approach consists in a change in the nature of regulation itself, whereby detailed prescriptive rules devised by government are replaced by general standards – often expressive of results rather than means – and procedures, within which private actors are expected to develop and monitor their own rules and practices: to regulate themselves, in fact. The United Kingdom government first took this approach in the field of employment health and safety with the Health and Safety at Work etc. Act 1974, and has since extended it to consumer safety[17], food safety[18], and offshore safety.[19] The approach to supervised industry

---

[14] See Deregulation and Contracting Out Act 1994, cls. 69–76 and Sched. 16.

[15] As with the regulation of the legal professions, under *e.g.* Solicitors Act 1974.

[16] As under the Financial Services Act 1986: see Page and Ferguson, *Investor Protection* (1992), especially Chapter 6.

[17] See the General Safety Requirement introduced by Part II of the Consumer Protection Act 1987.

[18] Through the general defence of "due diligence" to prosecutions under the Food Safety Act 1990, under which evidence of compliance with industry standards, or better individual practice, is needed.

[19] Offshore Installations (Safety Case) Regulations 1992 (SI 1992/2885), where the emphasis is on the preparation and operation of individual "safety cases" for each offshore installation, following the recommendations of the Cullen Report: *The Public Inquiry into the Piper Alpha Disaster*, Department of Energy, Cm. 1310, HMSO, 1990 (*reprinted* 1993).

regulation taken in the Financial Services Act 1986 likewise places considerable reliance on this kind of self-regulation by industry actors.

This fourth approach displays strong affinities with the Community concept of mutual recognition, especially as deployed in the so-called 'New Approach directives' in the field of technical harmonisation.[20] Both represent a shift, in regulatory style, towards simpler, general, performance-related standards and procedural safeguards, coupled with elaboration of detailed rules by private actors. In looking at specific examples later in this book we shall see that it may be difficult, even impossible, to determine whether United Kingdom practice has been shaping Community regulatory style or vice versa. The move to this kind of regulation has been widespread, and is not confined to Union Member States.[21] In given areas, some Member States have in practice long relied more heavily on general duties, while others have preferred specific rules.[22] At this stage only two remarks need to be made. First, it is clear that there is no basic tension between United Kingdom and Community views on this approach to regulation; but, second, there may well be specific implications of the application of the approach at Community level which can cut across other modes of State withdrawal from detailed regulation. Mutual recognition implies transparency in national enforcement, which may be hard to square with the delegations of regulatory functions which are involved, in the forms of "privatisation" of enforcement, and of "self-regulation", in the second and third approaches described above. This theme of enforcement is one which we have occasion to consider at a number of points in the Chapters that follow.

(ii) The centralisation of regulatory policy

Even within the United Kingdom, the delegations of regulatory power implicit in privatisation of enforcement, and in self-regulation, may seem to sit rather oddly with what we term here as a trend towards centralisation of regulatory policy. What may be going on, however, is a process of re-allocation of power from one set of decentralised entities to others: more precisely, from local authorities, traditional repositories of such power, to private enterprises and industry bodies. Reduction of the pow-

---

[20] See Council Resolution of 7 May 1985 on a new approach to technical harmonisation and standards: OJ 1985 C139/1. See Chapter 2, section 5.

[21] Thus the safety-case approach to offshore safety, espoused in the Offshore Installations (Safety Case) Regulations 1992, draws on earlier Norwegian practice: see Kaasen, "Safety Regulation of Off Shore Petroleum Activities: A Study of the Legal Frameworks for Safety Regulation on the Norwegian Continental Shelf" in *Sikkerhelsregulering: Petroleumsvirksomheten* (1984) at 557–599; and "Post-*Piper Alpha*: Reflections on Offshore Safety from a Norwegian Perspective," (1991) 9 *J.Energy & Nat.Resources L.* 281; Cullen Report, *op. cit.*, n 19, pp 278–79.

[22] In the field of health and safety at work, see the comparative study edited by Baldwin and Daintith, *Harmonization and Hazard* (1992), especially the contrast between Italian and Spanish approaches on the one hand, and German and British on the other.

ers and discretion of local authorities has been a constant of legislation since 1979[23]; the government has seen them as a threat to its attempts to reduce public expenditure, and more generally, as embodying attitudes, practices and assets whose control requires constant vigilance. In particular, it has seen in local authorities a serious obstacle to its project of "rolling back the frontiers of the State" through the policies of privatisation and deregulation it has pursued since 1979. While domestic attention has focused mostly on spending and service provision by local authorities, regulatory functions have also been affected, whether by way of transfers of regulatory power to the centre (that is, to government departments or other non-territorial bodies), of tighter central controls over local regulatory action, or the removal of regulatory powers altogether.[24] This impulse to centralisation, even if only in order to deregulate, has striking affinities both with the Community structure in general, with its strong focus on Member State responsibility[25], and with the requirements of mutual recognition for assurances of effective enforcement at Member State level. These requirements, as we shall see at a number of points below, may entail centralisation in relation not only to local authority, but also to other decentralised public powers[26], and may, as already suggested, hinder new forms of decentralisation.

Yet one of the Community's most stridently proclaimed commitments, in terms of governmental style, at the present time, is to subsidiarity. In the Maastricht Treaty itself this concept, it is true, seems to address only the relations between the Community and the Member States; as Article 3b(2) of the EC Treaty now puts it:

> "In areas which do not fall within its exclusive competence, the Community shall take action, in accordance with the principle of subsidiarity, only if and in so far as the objectives of the proposed action cannot be sufficiently achieved by the Member States and can, therefore, by reason of the scale or effects of the proposed action, be better achieved by the Community."

This certainly is the sense of subsidiarity to which the United Kingdom is most attached, but if we look to the intellectual pedigree of the concept, we find that its modern usage stems from the encyclical *Quadragesimo anno* promulgated by Pope Pius XI in 1931.

Here it referred to a principle invoked to protect individuals and social groups, and in particular the Catholic Church, against the totalitarian power of the State: the principle that public authorities should so far as possible refrain from intervening in any area of life in which groups and organisations of individuals are able to act and take care of matters in a

---

[23] See, *e.g.* Leach and Stoker, "The Transformation of Central-Local Government Relationships," in *Waiving the Rules: The Constitution under Thatcherism* (Graham and Prosser eds., 1988), 95–115.
[24] See Deregulation and Contracting Out Act 1994, ss 69–79.
[25] See below, Chapter 12, section 2.
[26] *E.g.* powers of national public agencies in relation to broadcasting: see below, Chapter 8.

11

sufficiently responsible way.[27] So understood it may serve as a protection of individual and collective freedom and responsibility from State intervention at all levels, and also as a basis for expectations that any movement of responsibilities from lower levels of government to higher ones will require justification, movement from the State to the Community level being just one example of this. These more general expectations appear to be expressed in Article A of the general part of the Treaty of European Union, which states:

> "...This Treaty marks a new stage in the process of creating an ever closer union among the peoples of Europe, in which decisions are taken as closely as possible to the citizen."

How, one may ask, can this principle be reconciled with the pressures for centralisation which, we have been suggesting, may be inherent in formal structure of the European Community and in its current regulatory style? How, indeed, is it to be related to an even more basic consideration: the difficulty of reconciling decentralised – particularly local – administration of regulation with an increasing scale of commercial and industrial activity? If, as is implicit in the Common Market project, firms are to be encouraged to outgrow the nation-State as a trading and even producing arena, ex hypothesi they will outgrow the local government level as well, and will complain of the inefficiency, and perhaps also the unfairness, of having their operations regulated on a local basis. There seems little point in striving to ensure that, in the interests of undistorted competition, the same production regulations apply in different Community countries, if significant differences persist within them by reason of local discretion. Such an argument has, it is clear, been loudly made to the United Kingdom government, which is actively seeking to respond to it.[28]

This type of argument, and the centralising measures we investigate later in Part Two of this book[29], may be seen as pointers to ambiguities in the concept of subsidiarity, and to its inability to provide any answer to key questions of division of competence. As expressed in Article 3b(2) of the amended EC Treaty, subsidiarity places the burden of proof on those who would argue for Community over Member State competence.

---

[27] See Cass, "The Word That Saves Maastricht? The Principle of Subsidiarity And The Division of Powers within the European Community," (1992) 29 CMLR 1107, at 1110–1128; van Kersbergen and Verbeek, "The Politics of Subisidiarity in the European Union," (1994) 32 J.Common Mkt.Stud. 215, especially at 221–226.

[28] See *Review of the Implementation and Enforcement of EC Law in the United Kingdom*, An Efficiency Scrutiny Report commissioned by the President of The Board of Trade, July 1993, which drew attention to difficulties faced by business because of divergent local regulatory practice, and recommended the establishment of what it was pleased to call FOCAL ("FOne Consultation and Advice Link") POINTS to provide business people with an opportunity to talk directly to officials) (pp. 5–6). Subsequently the Board of Trade announced, in January 1994, a review of the enforcement functions of local authorities, reported on September 30, 1994.

[29] See especially the case studies: Chapters 5, 6 and 8.

12

Yet in so far as subsidiarity is a reflection of a general idea of bringing government "nearer the people", it would appear to require that functions be exercised at higher levels as the scale of operation of "people" like food manufacturers is developed and enlarged, first beyond local, then beyond national boundaries. On this interpretation it calls seriously into question the very existence of local regulatory competences. But if the "people" we are worried about are not food manufacturers, but consumers of their products, then national, and even local, constituencies may be seen as the ones which are best capable of expressing distinctive tastes or needs. Subsidiarity, in other words, seems to point in different directions according to the priority one gives to the free trade, and the consumer protection, elements of policy.

(iii) **The increasing salience of private litigation**

The government's moves towards privatisation of regulatory enforcement, and industrial "self-regulation", imply some dilution of political responsibility for regulation, if only because these moves break the clear lines of public reporting and accountability on which such responsibility is traditionally based. Further weakening of these lines comes from government's general innovations in the sphere of public management, through the creation of executive agencies for the discharge of large blocks of public administration, operating not according to the political discipline of Ministerial responsibility, but rather to the business discipline of contractually framed performance targets and budgetary controls.[30] As political controls have waned, so judicial control has waxed in importance, thanks to the enlargement of possibilities for privately-initiated judicial review of administrative action.[31] The burgeoning popularity of this device in recent years suggests a growing preference among citizens for judicial vindication of rights over political advancement of interests.[32] This preference is echoed in the government's own programme for the commodification of its activities of public service and even public regulation through the Citizens' Charter programme.[33]

---

[30] See Lewis, "Reviewing Change in Government: New Public Management and Next Steps" [1994] *Publ L* 105.

[31] Convenient sources of reference are Cane, *An Introduction to Administrative Law*, 2nd ed (1992); Fordham, *Judicial Review Handbook* (1994, Wiley).

[32] JUSTICE-All Souls, *Administrative Justice: Some Necessary Reforms* (1988), 1–2; Woolf, "Judicial Review: A Possible Programme for Reform," [1992] *Publ L* 221–237. Others have questioned the significance of rising numbers of judicial review applications, pointing to a high degree of concentration of applications in a narrow range of subject areas: Sunkin, "What is Happening to Applications for Judicial Review," (1987) 50 *Mod L Rev* 432; Sunkin, "The Judicial Review Case-Load 1987–1989," [1991] *Publ L* 490; Sunkin, Bridges and Mészáros, *Judicial Review in Perspective* (1993).

[33] For a more extended argument in this sense see Daintith, "The Techniques of Government," in *The Changing Constitution* (Jowell and Oliver, eds. 3rd ed) (1994).

Again, basic harmonies exist between the domestic trend and its Community context. The style of Community administration is sympathetic to the increasing judicialisation of United Kingdom public policy. The Community Treaties are legalistic documents; today's rhetoric of a "Citizens' Europe" has long been prefigured in the legal sphere by the importance attached to private legal initiative as a means of securing Member State respect for Community obligations. From the initial acceptance by the European Court of Justice in *Van Gend en Loos*[34] that Article 177 of the EEC Treaty necessarily implied the possibility of direct enforcement in national courts of rights deriving from the Treaty, there has eventually developed, in the hands of the Court, a conscious policy of facilitating such enforcement, and in those of the Commission, a related policy of reliance on it as part of its general task of securing compliance.[35] National courts, as well as national administrations, thus find themselves cast as actors in the process of ensuring the faithful implementation of Community law. Suits for the vindication of Community rights can of course arise in a variety of ways. They may be prompted by national breaches of Treaty provisions themselves, or of regulations, whether the breach takes the form of a legislative rule or a specific act of administration.[36] Of more direct concern to us here, failure to transpose directives, the Community's main instrument of indirect rule, timeously, correctly, or at all, or failure to implement them properly once transposed, now accounts for a significant volume of litigation in the national courts of the Community, which continues to engender regular requests for interpretation from the European Court of Justice under the procedure of Article 177.

Reliance on Community rights in national courts may occur in litigation between private parties, in such areas as competition law where the Treaty imposes obligations directly on individual citizens.[37] This is not the case with directives, which, the Court of Justice has consistently held, can create direct obligations only for the Member State (or its "emanations", such as State-owned corporations).[38] Embarrassingly therefore, the appeal to the national court to participate in the implementation of directives is necessarily made in circumstances where the national administration is alleged to have failed, to the detriment of individual interests, to carry out its duties under Community law. Embarrassment is compounded where, as in the case of the United Kingdom, the faithful judicial application of Community law – whether expressed in directives

---

[34] Case 26/62 *NV Algemene Transport-en Expeditie-Onderneming Van Gend en Loos* v *Nederlandse Administratie der Belastingen* [1963] ECR 1.

[35] See generally Chapter 3, below.

[36] As in *Bourgoin SA* v *Ministry of Agriculture, Fisheries and Food* [1986] 1 QB 716; [1986] 1 CMLR 267 (CA).

[37] Most recently in Case C-91/92 *Paola Faccini Dori* v *Recreb Srl*, 14 July 1994, *The Times*, August 4, 1994. See *Current Survey*, [1994] Consum.L.J. CS57 and Chapter 12 below, text at n 68.

[38] See Maher, "National Courts as European Community Courts," (1994) 14 Legal Stud. 226, at 239–242.

or in other forms, and as interpreted by the Court of Justice – involves the adoption of new approaches to legislative interpretation, the assertion of new competences such as the non-application of Parliamentary legislation, and the invention of new, or expanded, remedies such as damages and interim relief against the government.[39] Nonetheless, as Chapter 11 demonstrates in some detail, United Kingdom courts, with understandable hesitations, have asserted these new capacities as against the executive, in a series of decisions which might be seen as marking a substantial shift in power, within British constitutional arrangements, in favour both of the courts and of the individuals who consequently enjoy enlarged opportunities for challenge to government action. Indeed, there are grounds for advancing a more radical argument, and suggesting that decisions on Community law such as *Factortame*[40], in which the House of Lords held that it could grant an interim injunction against the government to prevent the application of a statute which might be contrary to Community law, have had a spill-over effect on judicial thinking and decision-making on cases which have nothing to do with Community law, thus producing a general shift in favour of judicial, and in restriction of executive power.[41]

Chapter 11 certainly goes far to show that the assumption of duties as an agent of the Community has had a greater visible effect on the action of the courts than on the executive branch of government in the United Kingdom. That any effect should be more visible in the judicial sphere is not surprising: judges are constrained to give much fuller explanations of what they are doing and why they are doing it than are civil servants (or even politicians), and those explanations are less likely to be coloured and shaded by the need to avoid the giving of hostages to political fortune. Even making this allowance, accurate judgement of the extent of the "Community effect" on the judicial function, and in particular of its relationship with burgeoning judicial control of administration, remains difficult. The concentration of path-breaking domestic litigation in the field of sexual discrimination should be noted in this respect, and may reflect a rare combination of a distinctively framed Treaty provision (Article 119), relative unfamiliarity, in the United Kingdom, with the business of legislating for equality[42], and the presence of a vigorous independent enforcement agency. Elsewhere, the scope for private initiative in reinforcing compliance with Community law remains in principle curtailed by the structures of domestic law within which its requirements have been accommodated, and in practice largely untested by reason of the care with which the United Kingdom has seen to the proper transpo-

---

[39] *Factortame* v *Secretary of State for Transport* (No 1) [1990] 2 AC 85; (No 2) [1991] 1 AC 603.
[40] *Ibid.*
[41] See *M* v *Home Office* [1993] 3 All ER 537 (HL), *per* Lord Woolf at 564.
[42] The first legislation against discrimination in the civil sphere dates only from 1965: Race Relations Act 1965.

sition and implementation of those requirements. We explore this issue in detail in Chapter 10.

3 The structure of the book

This is the background against which we try to answer the question of how our own processes of law and administration are affected by their participation as essential elements in the implementation of Community law and policy. We try to do this in three stages, corresponding to the remaining Parts of this book.

(i) Indirect Rule: The Formal Structure

Part One is concerned with the structure and context of implementation of Community law at the national level. It first sets out, in Chapter 2, the formal structure for legal expression of policy at EC level. Starting from the basic Treaty provisions it builds up a picture of the legal instruments available to the Community for the articulation of its policy goals. The focus here is on what we have already described as the Community's principal governmental resource: its ability to make rules. The formal legal vehicles for decisions recognised by the Treaty of Rome – regulations, directives, decisions – may of course also be employed to express decisions about the use of other governmental resources, such as the funds which are at the disposition of the Brussels authorities[43]: financial instruments like these, and information-gathering and advice-dispensing agencies like the European Environment Agency, or the proposed European Agency for Safety and Health at Work[44], are of increasing importance to the operation of the Community as a whole.[45] Administration of Community funds, indeed, may create difficult problems of indirect administration analogous to those which arise from the implementation of Community law.[46] Within the compass of this work we are not able to

---

[43] On the funds see Lowe, "The Reform of the Community Structural Funds," (1988) 25 Common Mkt.L.Rev. 503–521; Gordon, "An Analysis of the EC Structural Funds," in *Tax Harmonisation in the European Community* (Kopits ed, 1992), 92–104; Klodt, Stehn *et al.*, *Die Strukturpolitik de EG* (1992).

[44] This will be situated in Bilbao. See Proposal for a Council Regulation establishing a European Agency for Safety and Health at Work, OJ 1994 C176; COM(94)233; Bull. EU 6–1994, 75. See also Baldwin and Daintith (eds), *op. cit.*, n 22 at 246–247; Chapter 12, section 3 (iv) and text accompanying n 113.

[45] See Streit and Mussler, *The Economic Constitution of the European Community from "Rome" to "Maastricht"*, Paper presented at Conference on "European Law in Context: Constitutional Dimensions of European Economic Integration", 14–15 April 1994, European University Institute, Florence.

[46] For examples relevant to the United Kingdom, see "Tories trip up in EC funds game ... regions pay the price of blocked grants row," *Financial Times*, 29 January 1992, 8; "Training hit in Euro-fund row," *The Guardian*, June 29, 1994, 13 (*tabloid*).

16

do justice to such issues, and Chapter 2 therefore does no more than to set such instruments in their legal context.

Within the field of formal rule-making, the Chapter first explains and develops the distinction between regulations and directives, and then proceeds to examine how approaches to the formulation of directives, in particular the degree of discretion they leave to Member States, have changed over time. It also examines the so-called New Approach to harmonisation through directives, and its relationship with the concept of mutual recognition of national regulatory standards as a tool for the construction of the single market. That concept has been developed on the basis of principles enunciated by the European Court of Justice in its *Cassis de Dijon* decision[47], and the Chapter also explains how, on the basis of its powers of Treaty application and interpretation, the Court has come to play an important law-making role; a role which, moreover, can be activated by private parties through the mechanism of litigation within their national judicial system.

The role of the European Court of Justice is a central concern of Chapter 3. Here the formal framework of rule-making competences, their exercise and interpretation, is clothed with material on the approach of the European Commission, as the Community's executive arm, to the task of assuring an adequate degree of compliance by Member States with the requirements of Community law. While this is in part a question of selecting the right kind or design of rule, it also involves finding an appropriate mixture of devices to ensure compliance once the rules have been promulgated. The Chapter argues that the Commission has placed considerable reliance on the law-making (or law-declaring) powers of the Court of Justice, as a tactical element in its compliance strategy.

In Chapter 4 we move into the United Kingdom domain. The role of the Chapter is to describe and analyse the formal structures which are available here for the transposition and implementation of the Community legal rules discussed in Chapter 2. The Chapter examines how the United Kingdom organises itself for participation in Community decision-making, and how it seeks to ensure that implementation issues are considered from the outset of the rule-making process; it looks at the legislative framework for transposition of Community law, and examines how government decides how to use it in individual cases; it considers the process of transposition itself, and the nature and degree of parliamentary involvement and control; and finally discusses in general terms our mechanisms for administrative and judicial enforcement.

We may sum up the function of Part One by saying that it is designed to show how the system of indirect implementation of Community law is supposed to work, particularly in the United Kingdom. Patient work by the Community authorities themselves and by the United Kingdom legis-

---

[47] Case 12/78 *Rewe-Zentral AG* v *Bundesmonopolverwaltung für Branntwein*: [1979] ECR 649, [1979] 3 CMLR 494.

lator, administrator and judge have over time created a complex and sophisticated system for a two-level polity, most of it articulated in the form of legal rules.

(ii) Some case studies

The second Part of the book looks at how this system actually operates, through five detailed case studies on the implementation in the United Kingdom of as many Community directives from a variety of fields, largely within the Single European Market programme.[48] These studies cover beer labelling (Chapter 5), food safety administration (Chapter 6), free movement of persons (Chapter 7), "television without frontiers" (Chapter 8), and toy safety (Chapter 9). Though each has been prepared by a different author (or authors) the studies follow a broad general pattern. Each focuses on a single Directive. It describes the background to the adoption of the Directive, in terms both of its economic or social environment and of surrounding Community measures, as well as the United Kingdom legal and administrative regime into which the Directive had to be inserted. It next briefly analyses the content of the Directive, and identifies the United Kingdom measures (if any) which have provided for its transposition, relating their content to that of the Directive, and to the regime background. The study then looks at post-transposition measures: the administrative arrangements made by government, the behaviour of the private actors affected by the measure, and any experience of enforcement of the measure. Each of the studies concludes by identifying features of the interaction between the United Kingdom and Community regimes which appear particularly salient within the field of the Directive.

Why study these particular directives, out of the very large number to which the United Kingdom has become subject over the past few years? The choice has been largely made not by ourselves, but within the framework of a Community-wide research project in which most of us have in one way or another been engaged over the period since 1989. This pro-

---

[48] The exception is the free movement Directive 90/364 examined in Chapter 7, which originated, along with its companion Directives 90/365 and 90/366, in a single draft general free movement Directive produced by the Commission in 1979 (see OJ 1979 C207/14), before the Single European Act.

ject, *The 1992 Challenge at National Level*, set out to compare the legal implementation of the Single European Market programme in the twelve Member States.[49] Co-ordinated from the European University Institute in Florence, and funded by the European Commission, its examination of national implementation law and practice was geared particularly to informing the Commission about what legislative methods, at Community level, were likely to work best in the Member States, providing the best "fit" with national styles and practices. With this in view the research agenda, in terms of specific directives for examination, was determined essentially by the Commission, and four of our studies, on beer labelling, food safety administration, television without frontiers and toy safety, were engendered in this way. The Florence project was abandoned at short notice in 1993, so that while the first two of the above studies have been able to draw on parallel experience elsewhere in the Community, the last two, begun only in that year, have not.

Given a free hand, we might have been led to produce a somewhat different set of cases, more overtly problematic from a specifically United Kingdom point of view. The selection presented here, however, has the great merit of randomness so far as domestic implementation difficulties, or the lack of them, are concerned. Moreover it offers a range of directives which cover all points of the spectrum of detail, from beer labelling (which prescribes precise words and symbols which have to appear), through to food safety administration and toy safety, which are directives of the 'New Approach' type concerned with general systems and standards of control. Economic and social contexts for the directives also present interesting contrasts: the actors who are the object of regulation under the directives range from the highly concentrated television industry, through the looser structures of the beer, food and toy industries, to the State itself (in the framework of the free movement of persons Directive discussed in Chapter 7, and also of food safety inspection discussed in Chapter 6). The interests protected are varied: consumer interests in safety and in honest labelling; "citizen" interests in freedom of movement; general public interests in moral and ethical standards, and in freedom of speech, alike raised by the regulation of television. These contrasts and variations produce, within the field of the case studies, a wide range of relationships between Community and national regimes, through which our core issue of the national effects of implementing Community law can be illuminated.

---

[49] Proceedings of the project have been published in three annual volumes, as follows: Schwarze, Govaere, Hélin and Van den Bossche (eds), *The 1992 Challenge at National Level: Reports and Conference Proceedings 1989* (1990); Schwarze, Becker and Pollack (eds), *The 1992 Challenge at National Level: Reports and Conference Proceedings 1990* (1991); Schwarze, Becker and Pollack (eds), *The 1992 Challenge at National Level: Reports and Conference Proceedings 1991/92 (1993)*.

(iii) Trends and problems

Such illumination is the task we set ourselves in Part Three. This contains three Chapters, which draw on the case studies and relate them to the general structure sketched in Part One, and to the set of issues raised in the earlier parts of this Chapter. Chapter 10 focuses on the issue of enforcement of regulatory policies, looking at changing United Kingdom preferences as between private and public initiative in such enforcement, and at the way in which Community policies, and their expression through directives, reinforce or inhibit these preferences. It demonstrates the interaction between public and private initiative, considering in particular the extent to which the individual may resort to the national courts to secure implementation of Community law where public action is lacking, using some of the concrete enforcement issues raised by the case studies to show how structures of the United Kingdom legal system may still operate to restrict such possibilities. Chapter 11 continues this reflection on judicial application and interpretation of Community law, and examines how the need to discharge these functions, as part of a composite Community legal apparatus, affects the general behaviour and position of the courts. Finally, Chapter 12 makes our studies of United Kingdom implementation the basis of a more general reflection on the viability of the system of indirect rule represented by the varied styles of Directive examined in the case studies. Is an approach which relies upon, yet constrains, Member State enforcement of policy adequate to the demands, and dangers, of unified product and service markets? Do the newer, less burdensome approaches to harmonisation launch the Community inexorably on the path of a de facto deregulation, or at least toward self-regulation, or are these tendencies simply a reflection of domestic preferences? Can an effective collaboration between Community-level and local regulators within the Community be mounted without creating a threat – equally dangerous, perhaps, whether real or only imagined – to the powers and competences of Member States?

One of the things which emerges consistently from the case studies is the extent to which day-to-day administrative decision-making in the United Kingdom, in the areas we examine, is influenced by European Community law. Lord Denning's striking image of Community law as a tide coming up our rivers[50] is today hardly adequate; a more accurate metaphor now is of a liquid which by capillary action is penetrating into every pore of the State, at least in its zones of economic and social action. One result of such interpenetration is that very real difficulty may arise in assigning responsibility for specific situations as between Community

---

[50] See *Bulmer* v *Bollinger* [1974] 2 All ER 1226, at 1231; *Shields* v *E. Coomes (Holdings) Ltd* [1979] 1 All ER 456, at 462.

and national decision-makers. In a country which is prone to believe the worst about all things foreign, this creates ample scope for political and journalistic mischief of the "Fishermen must wear hairnets, says Brussels" type, and more seriously, for misinterpretation and avoidance of responsibility. A number of examples have been collected and investigated by the Board of Trade's Efficiency Scrutiny Team for its 1993 *Review of the Implementation and Enforcement of EC Law in the United Kingdom*[51]; another reported on the day this is written arises in the aftermath of a minibus accident in which cub scouts were killed, when they might have been saved if wearing safety belts in the passenger seats. Representatives of minibus and coach operators said risks of legal liability prevented their fitting such belts without a legal requirement to do so; the Department of Transport claimed that to require this would be contrary to Community law; the Commission riposted that the Directive referred to, requiring belts only for the driver's and front row seats, was a minimum standard and in no way impaired the adoption of more demanding national standards.[52]

As the Efficiency Scrutiny Team recognised and demonstrated, to separate out misinterpretation, buck-passing, and rational decision-making in such situations demands careful case-by-case investigation. We believe, however, that considerable benefits can also flow from the attempt, undertaken here, to disentangle general trends in domestic approaches to regulation from the impacts of the Community legal system and Community policy. Clarification of this kind can both enhance our understanding of how law is implemented in the United Kingdom, and inform the Community's continuing attempts to equip itself with a structure of governance appropriate to the challenges of the 21st century.

4 **A note on terminology**

(i) **Implementation**

There are plenty of difficult and disputed terms in use in debates about Community policy (as well as some helpful ones whose use, for political reasons, has been practically outlawed in the United Kingdom, such as

---

[51] See Annexes A3 and J. Annex J also examines British "folklore" about lax standards of enforcement in other EU countries, finding that "nationalist fervour appears to account for a proportion of the myths that appear": p 198.

[52] Woodcock, "Seat belts could have saved him," *Daily Mail*, 17 May 1994, 1, 7; and for the linkage of this issue to the concept of pre-emption in Community law, below, Chapter 12, section (iv) (d) As further evidence of how firms demand to be regulated to protect their competitive position see HK Colebatch, "The Concept of Regulation in the Analysis of an Organised World," (1989) 11 Law and Pol. 71, 75–76 (on control of smoking on Australian airlines).

"federal"). We have begun to explore the idea of subsidiarity already; other concepts we can generally explain as and when necessary, but one further term, "implementation", deserves a very brief discussion here because it describes the central concern of the book, but is open to misinterpretation.

We use the term "implementation" to cover all parts and phases of the process of giving effect to a Community policy, from its incorporation into a Community legal instrument through to the taking of action by economic actors so as to put themselves into a position to comply with the policy. Some of these parts and phases attract distinctive terms. Thus "transposition" refers only to the process of expressing the substance of a Community legal instrument (or instruments) under national legal or administrative forms; "enforcement" refers to official action, whether *ex ante* or *ex post* in nature, designed to secure that the conduct of the relevant actors complies with the rules expressing the policy (or that non-compliance is sanctioned); "compliance" is used to refer to the behaviour of those on whom obligations are imposed as a result of Community policy (who may, of course, be public as well as private actors). It is, however, useful to remember that these distinct phases do not exhaust the process of implementation, and that there may be important activities (such as governmental consultations and distribution of information) for which only the generic term is appropriate.

(ii) European Community

A further note may be useful on the term "European Community". Though the term "European Union" has been introduced into the European lexicon by the Treaty of Maastricht (whose official title is indeed the Treaty on European Union), our references in this work will largely be to the European Community (or EC). This is now the legally-correct term for the European Economic Community established by the Treaty of Rome, which (as amended by the Single European Act[53] and by the Maastricht Treaty) contains the legal competences we are concerned to discuss. The Treaty of Rome, once the European Economic Community Treaty (EEC Treaty) is now simply the EC Treaty. "European Union" properly describes the whole complex of activities envisaged by the Maastricht Treaty, that is to say the new areas of political co-operation which fall outside the competence of institutions of the Community such as the

---

[53] [1987] 2 CMLR 741.

Court of Justice, along with the European Community, the Coal and Steel Community, and Euratom. Separation of "Community" elements from "Union" elements in European policy is certainly not watertight,[54] but these leakages are not crucial to our discussion.

TERENCE DAINTITH

---

[54] See Usher, "Maastricht and English Law" (1993) 14 Stat.L.R. 28, at 28–31.

Part One

National Implementation of EC Law: Structure and Context

Chapter 2
The Legal Articulation of Policy in the European Community

1 Introduction

This Chapter is designed to provide a description and commentary on certain aspects of rule making and policy making in the European Community. Whilst lawyers may be familiar with this material, it is unlikely that political scientists and economists will be so much at ease with both the focus and content of the Chapter. Its approach is, therefore, descriptive rather than analytic, although it does raise some important issues particularly on the role of the European Court of Justice in exercising its function of interpreter of Community law. Some commentators go so far as to describe the Court as being one of the political institutions, others have restricted their comments to its over-zealous activism whereas others again, notably lawyers themselves, have applauded the European Court of Justice for its overtly legislative role.[1]

Much of the Chapter relates to the nature and function of the Directive in the articulation of policy at Community level. There are several reasons for this focus, the most immediately apparent to the reader being the emphasis in our own case studies on the implementation of directives in the instances studied. However, the Directive is the preferred method of what is known as the harmonisation of laws within the Community and deserves full attention in that light. The Directive is also unique as a method of harmonisation[2] in the legal world.

---

[1] See Rasmussen, *On Law and Policy in the European Court* (1986), for a full discussion of the approach of various writers to the activism of the European Court.
[2] Harmonisation as a phenomenon in European Law has ceased to attract the attention which it did in the past. Current literature is thin on the ground. For readings see Close, "Harmonisation of Laws; use or abuse of powers under the EEC Treaty?" (1978) *E L Rev* 461; Ehlermann, "Harmonisation for harmonisation's sake?" (1978) *Comm Mkt L Rev* 4; Leleux, "Le rapprochement des legislations dans la CEE" (1968) C.D.E. 129; Megret, "La technique communautaire d'harmonisation des legislations" (1967) Rev.Marche Com. 181; Rodiere, "L'harmonisation des legislations europeennes dans le cadre de la CEE" (1965) Rev.trim.dr.euro. 336; Dashwood, "Hastening slowly: the Community's path towards harmonisation" in *Policy Making in the European Community* (Wallace, Wallace and Webb eds), 1st ed (1977). The controversies surrounding the

Furthermore, it provides a fascinating study of the way in which law makers believe that policy can be effected by the use of legal instruments (instrumentalism) and that the purpose of legal rules is to attain specific ends (functionalism). These issues are particularly important in a discussion of the various patterns of harmonisation of national laws within the European Community. The Community has developed in sophistication since its early days in the ways in which it has attempted to achieve an interrelationship between the systems of laws at the national level. These issues will be explored in the discussion of the definition and explanation of the function of harmonisation within the European Community.

The Chapter will also describe other types of legally binding acts adopted by the European Community, which may be conceived of, depending on disciplinary standpoint, as forms of governance, or as sources of European Community law. It is important to put into context the different ways in which the Community might choose to act in areas in which it has competence to do so, given the choice of legal base provided for by the Treaties, and given the range of subject matter covered by Community law.

The European Community can only act when, and if, there is a sufficient legal base for action contained in the Treaties. Without such a legal base, Community acts can be declared invalid by the European Court of Justice in an action for judicial review under Article 173 of the EC Treaty.[3] Such an action can be brought where the Community institutions have relied on an inappropriate legal base such as the wrong Treaty article.[4] Here the institutions, if they wish to proceed with the adoption of an act, must go back and follow the correct procedures outlined in the Treaty.[5] This issue has become very important in the life of the Community since the treaties now provide for six different ways of adopting directives, regulations or decisions, depending on the subject matter under consideration.[6] Some matters, such as health and safety at work, can be adopted by qualified majority vote, whereas others, such as workers' rights, require unanimity of the Council. The choice of an incorrect legal base could therefore lead to the Community institutions acting unlawfully. This approach, of course, stresses the legal result of such unlawful action. The political implications can be far more damaging in the sense that confrontation over the choice of legal base may lead to

power of the Community to harmonise national legislation have perhaps been settled since the days of the House of Lords' investigation, thus explaining the lack of interest. See House of Lords Select Committee on the EC, *The approximation of laws under Article 100 of the Treaty*, 22nd Report, 1977–78 HL 131.

[3] See Schermers and Waelbroek, *Judicial Protection in the European Communities*, 5th ed (1992).

[4] Case 45/86, *Commission v Council (Re GSP)* [1987] ECR 1493; Case 68/86 *United Kingdom v Council (Re Hormones)* [1988] ECR 855.

[5] See Case 68/86, *ibid*.

[6] For a succinct discussion of these methods see Craig, *Administrative Law*, 3rd ed (1994), 185–188.

one or more of the Member States refusing to accept particular aspects of legislation at all, destroying the necessary political will to take action on the part of the Community.

It should be noted that the term "regulation" will be used in different contexts throughout this book. For this Chapter, the style "Regulation" will be used in order to distinguish a European form of legislation from a domestic one and in order to distinguish the term from the sense it is used in the economic analysis of law.

2 Sources of Community law

(i) Treaty law

The primary sources of European Community law are the treaties which established the three original communities, *i.e.* the Coal and Steel Community, the European Economic Community and EURATOM. These Treaties have been amended on several occasions, for example by the Single European Act and the Treaty on European Union.[7] Each amendment has served either to clarify the earlier Treaties or to supplement them with additional provisions.

The Treaties can only be amended by following the procedures laid down in them – there is no other method of amendment. Therefore, any subsequent Community legislative act must conform to the Treaty provisions; otherwise these acts would be invalid. The Court of Justice has also held that laws in force in the Member States must conform to the Treaties otherwise the State concerned will be in breach of its Community obligations and, in particular, of Article 5 of the EC Treaty (the fidelity clause).[8] This includes any constitutional provisions, any Acts of Parliament (or equivalent in other Member States), any administrative act which has legal effects.[9] Finally, the Treaties cannot be amended by any political agreement to vary their terms, unless this is followed by a legal amendment.[10]

The nature of the Treaties as "the source of a new legal order of inter-

---

[7] The chronology of these amendments is outlined in Wyatt and Dashwood, *European Community Law*, 3rd ed (1993), Chapter 1.

[8] "This failure in the duty of solidarity . . . strikes at the fundamental base of the Community legal order". Case 39/72 *Commission* v *Italy* [1973] ECR 101. The Court has reiterated this formula on a number of occasions.

[9] Case 6/64 *Costa* v *ENEL* [1964] ECR 585; Case 106/77 *Simmenthal* [1978] ECR 629; Case 11/70 *Internationale Handelsgesellschaft* [1970] ECR 1125; Case C-213/89, *R* v *Secretary of State, ex p. Factortame* [1990] ECR I-2433.

[10] The Member States did thus try to alter the time limits laid down in Article 119 relating to equal pay for men and women. The European Court threw this out in the second *Defrenne* case; see Case 43/75 *Defrenne* v *Sabena* [1976] ECR 455.

31

national law" was first described by the European Court of Justice.[11] The Court distinguished European Law from international law and from the legal orders of the Member States. From these beginnings, the Court of Justice has begun to create a constitutional structure for the European Community with the introduction of concepts of direct effect of Community law, its supremacy over national law, the duties of the Member States in all their guises to implement Community rules and the doctrine of pre-emption which relates to the delimitation of the competences of the Member States and the Community itself.[12] All of these issues are discussed extensively in existing literature and this Chapter can do little more than explore the salient features of this constitutional order so as to describe the type and functions of the legal instruments used by the Community in pursuing the goal of completing the Single European Market.

3 Acts of the institutions

The Treaties do not confer a general legislative role on the European institutions. Instead, the institutions are given the power to adopt "acts" which have legal force sometimes in the Community legal order alone and sometimes within the legal orders of the Member States. These acts are defined in Article 189 of the EC Treaty:

> "In order to carry out their task and in accordance with the provisions of this Treaty, the European Parliament acting jointly with the Council, the Council and the Commission shall make regulations and issue directives, take decisions, make recommendations or deliver opinions.
>
> A regulation shall have general application. It shall be binding in its entirety and directly applicable in all Member States.
>
> A directive shall be binding, as to the result to be achieved, upon each Member State to which it is addressed, but shall leave the national authorities the choice of form and methods.
>
> A decision shall be binding in its entirety upon those to whom it is addressed.
>
> Recommendations and opinions shall have no binding force."

---

[11] Case 26/62 *Van Gend en Loos* v *Nederlandse Administratie der Belastingen* [1963] ECR 1.

[12] The term "constitutional" is frequently used in the literature on the work of the European Court. See, *e.g.* Weiler, "The Transformation of Europe" (1991) 100 Yale L.J. 2403; Cappelletti et al., *Integration Through Law*, (1986) Vol. I; Schermers, "The European Court of Justice: Promoter of European Integration" (1974) A.J.C.L. 444; Bebr, "The Reinforcement of the Constitutional Review of Community Acts under Article 177" (1988) Common Mkt.L.Rev. 667; Rasmussen, *The European Community Constitution* (1989).

(i) **Regulations and their defining features**

It can be argued that the definition of regulations in Article 189 of the EC Treaty, as general normative acts applying throughout the Community territory without the need for special enactment by the Member States[13], implies a delegated law-making power from the Member State legislatures to the Community institutions although such a delegation is not formally stated in the Treaties. To use an analogy from United Kingdom law, regulations are akin to delegated legislation and the Treaties are the enabling Act which prescribes the limits in which the institutions may adopt legislation. To continue this analogy further, it can be said that the legislatures of the Member States have collectively adopted the enabling Act, the Treaties, so that regulations, by dint of this delegation, do not require further legislative action on the part of the Member States to enable the Regulation to take force within their territories. Regulations, therefore, do not bind Member States as such, they are the law which applies in the territory of each Member State.[14]

As with delegated legislation in the United Kingdom, the vires of a Regulation can be tested before a court, this time the European Court of Justice, in a judicial review. Such judicial review is provided for by Article 173 which lays limits both on the standing of the persons who may challenge the validity of the legislation, and the grounds. This Chapter is not the place to discuss judicial review of Regulations[15] but it might be pointed out in passing that although the grounds of review are laid out in the Treaty, the Court of Justice has interpreted the meaning and extent of the grounds by reference to the administrative laws of all the Member States.[16] This is in keeping with the idea of collective delegation of powers to the Community institutions.

(ii) **Directives and their defining features**

In contrast to regulations, which are legally perfect instruments, directives, according to Article 189 of the EC Treaty, are binding only as to the result to be achieved upon each Member State to which they are

---

[13] The Court of Justice has described regulations as being "essentially of a legislative nature" in Cases 16 and 17/62 *Producteurs de Fruit* v *Council* [1962] ECR 471 at 478. The Court has stated that the direct application of a Regulation is independent of "any measure of reception into national law" in Case 34/73 *Variola* [1973] ECR 981 at 990. Of course, some regulations require Member States to take measures to put them into effect in full. Where this is the case, the Member States must not take any action which will jeopardise the aim of the Community act.

[14] The Court of Justice has never used this analogy but the force of its decisions do indicate that the legal nature of regulations arises from their legislative origin within the Community and not from any national action. See, *e.g.* the cases mentioned in footnote 13.

[15] For a discussion of Article 173 of the EEC Treaty and judicial review of Community acts, see Charlesworth and Cullen, *European Community Law* (1994), Chapter 7.

[16] See Schwarze, "Tendencies towards a Common Administrative Law in Europe" (1991) E. L. Rev. 320.

addressed. Directives leave to the Member States the choice of forms and methods of their implementation.

Directives, which are equally authentic in all the official languages of the Community, are the most frequently used form of Community legislation. The 1992 Single European Market programme[17] was introduced almost entirely by way of directives. The main benefit of directives is the flexibility which allows Member States to agree on a principle whilst leaving each state to work out the detail of implementation. This is, equally, their main drawback since it is not always clear how implementation can and should proceed.

(iii) **Problems of implementation of directives**

Failure to implement directives, or to implement them on time, incorrect or incomplete implementation, and the legal force of directives which have not been duly implemented, have been matters which have been addressed by the European Court of Justice. It is clear that the choice of form and methods lies in the discretion of the Member States but that that discretion is limited by general principles of Community law which have been articulated by the Court of Justice. In the adoption of the directive as a form of legislation, it is clear that the Member States intended to retain a legislative role and control. They did not delegate powers of legislating within the national legal orders to the institutions of the Community. They delegated a power to determine the shape and purpose of some aspects of national law but they reserved for their own legislatures the power to make national law in the area covered by the directive. To some extent the Court of Justice has replaced this definition of directive with a definition of its own, and by legal principles which seem to undermine the original demarcation of law-making power between the Community on the one hand and the Member States on the other, at least in so far as the wording of the Treaty goes.[18]

It is not surprising that the Court of Justice has held that Member States must implement directives within the time-limits laid down.[19] Nor is it surprising that the Court has held that directives must be implemented by national provisions of a binding nature which ensure effective application of the directive within the national legal order.[20] If the directive requires amendment to existing national law, then the measure implementing it must have the same legal force as the original legislation so that a mere administrative practice does not amount to

---

[17] *Completing the Internal Market*, COM(85)310 final.
[18] As we do not have access to the *travaux préparatoires* of the Treaties, this can only be conjecture.
[19] See Case 79/72 *Commission* v *Italy* [1973] ECR 667; Case 52/75 *Commission* v *Italy* [1976] ECR 277; Case 102/79 *Commission* v *Belgium* [1980] ECR 1473 and Case 301/81 *Commission* v *Belgium* [1983] ECR 467.
[20] Case 48/75 *Royer* [1976] ECR 497.

implementation.[21] Implementing measures must be precise, clear and transparent so that any person affected by the implementing legislation understands the Community background and must be fully aware of the intention on the part of the Community to create rights on his or her behalf. It must be open to the individual to rely on such rights in national courts.[22]

Failure to implement timeously and correctly means that a State is in breach of a Community obligation.[23] As such, the European Commission may institute proceedings against that State before the European Court of Justice (Article 169 of the EC Treaty). In the course of such proceedings, the Court will not accept "excuses" from the State relating to constitutional, administrative, legal or political problems it faced in the matter of implementation.[24] The Court of Justice has power to declare that a State is in breach of its Community obligations and the Treaty on European Union has now created the possibility of a financial penalty for such a breach.[25]

Therefore, there is a clear distinction to be drawn between regulations and directives. Regulations require no further action on the part of Member States whereas directives impose a positive duty to act to bring the purpose of the directive into the national legal order. However, the distinction between the two types of Community act, in terms of their legal effect within the national legal order, has been blurred by the Court of Justice, through the development of the concept of the direct effect of Community law. It is this concept, probably the most important which

---

[21] Case 102/79 *Commission* v *Belgium* [1980] ECR 1473; Case 96/81 *Commission* v *Netherlands* [1982] ECR 1791; Case 160/82 *Commission* v *Netherlands* [1982] ECR 4637; Case 300/81 *Commission* v *Italy* [1983] ECR 449.

[22] Case 29/84 *Commission* v *Germany* [1985] ECR 1661.

[23] Case 10/76 *Commission* v *Italy* [1967] ECR 1359. The failure of States to implement directives was recognised during the debates on the Treaty on European Union. A Declaration on the Implementation of Community Law was appended to the Treaty. This Declaration "stresses that it is central to the coherence and unity of the process of European construction that each Member State should fully and accurately transpose into national law the Community Directives addressed to it within the time-limits laid down therein . . . it [is] essential for the proper functioning of the Community that the measures taken should result in Community law being applied with as much rigour and effectiveness as in the case of application of their national law". The wording of the Declaration brings to mind the wording of the Court in the many cases which have come before it where States have failed to implement directives.

[24] Case 163/78 *Commission* v *Italy* [1979] ECR 771.

[25] Article 171 of the EEC Treaty was amended by the Treaty on European Union so as to allow the Commission to bring a State before the Court of Justice if that State has failed to comply with a judgement of the Court. In doing so, the Commission can specify the amount of the lump sum or the penalty payment to be paid by the Member State. If the Court finds that a Member State has not complied with its judgement, it can impose a lump sum or penalty payment. This is an action which takes place within the Community legal order. The State may also find that it is sued in damages in the national legal order if an individual can demonstrate loss owing to its failure to implement a Directive. On this issue see Cases C-6/90 and C-9/90 *Francovich and Bonifaci* [1993] 2 CMLR 66, discussed in Steiner, "From direct effect to Francovich: shifting means of enforcement of Community law" (1993) *E. I.. Rev* 3, and Chapters 3 (text at n 31 and section 4(iv)), 4 (text at n 13) and 11 (section 4) in this book.

the Court has developed, which introduced a point of similarity between the two major forms of Community secondary law.

It is an attempt by the Court to create an entirely new legal order of international law which creates rights and imposes obligations not only for and on Member States but also for and on individual citizens. The Court recognised very early on that individuals would be much more vigilant in protecting their rights than would be their governments. The concept of direct effect enables individuals to claim the rights granted by Community law in their own courts and as against their own State. In this respect Community law differs from any other species of international law since the direct effect of a Community provision arises from the specificity and autonomy of Community law and does not rely on the national constitutional orders of the Member States.[26]

Whether or not a Community provision can give rise to direct effect is entirely a matter for the European Court of Justice to decide since it is a question of interpretation of Community law in which the European Court has sole jurisdiction.[27] In the early days of the Community the Court applied the principle to Treaty provisions and regulations. The Court developed strict criteria for deciding whether or not a provision could have direct effect. The provision must be clear, unconditional, leave no discretion to the Member State or the European Institutions as to its implementation and it must be intended to confer rights on individuals. If these conditions were met then the Court was ready to recognise the direct effect of the provision.

Some debate arose as to whether directives could create similar effects within the national legal orders. Almost by definition it seemed that directives could not be directly effective, since they leave the choice of form and methods of implementation to the discretion of the Member States. To some, it appeared that they could create no effects in the national legal order without implementing legislation.[28] The Treaty seemed to foresee a two stage legislative procedure with the framework of legislation being adopted by the Community institutions and the detail being adopted by national legislatures. However, the Court of Justice rejected the idea of a two stage legislative procedure where in fact that second stage had been omitted by the Member States. Its reasoning was as follows: where a directive is properly implemented then an individual derives rights from the implementing legislation. Where the Directive is

---

[26] See Case 26/62 *Van Gend en Loos* [1963] ECR 1, in which the European Court declared the existence of the new legal order which creates rights and obligations for individuals as well as the contracting parties to the Treaty. The Court rejected the view that the courts of the Member States could determine the effects within the national legal order of Community provisions. Such a decision is traditionally one for the national courts.

[27] The Treaty provides in Article 177 that the European Court has jurisdiction in matters of interpretation of the Treaty as well as the interpretation of the acts of the institutions.

[28] This was the view of the French Conseil d'Etat and the German Finance Court, see *Minister of the Interior* v *Cohn-Bendit* [1980] 1 CMLR 543 and *Re VAT Directives (Bundesfinanzhof)* [1982] 1 CMLR 527.

not implemented, or it is implemented incorrectly, its "useful effect" (*effet utile*) would be destroyed if individuals were prevented from relying on it where it was intended to create rights on their behalf and national courts were not allowed to take the directive into consideration. The Court examined specifically the binding nature of directives for Member States and stressed that this consideration was of prime importance.[29] The Court thus held that a provision of a directive could create direct effect, providing that the criteria for direct effect were met and providing also that the time limit for its implementation had expired. This means that an individual may rely on a provision of the directive in the national court in order to assert his or her Community right.[30]

However, there is an important distinction to be made between the direct effect of a Treaty provision or a regulation on the one hand and the direct effect of a directive on the other. Since *Van Duyn*[31] it has been agreed that the State may not, as against individuals, plead its own failure to perform the obligations which the directive imposes. The rights created by the directive have correlative obligations on the State. This is known as "vertical" direct effect. However, Treaty provisions and regulations go further than this and may create obligations not only for the State but also as against other natural or legal persons. For example, Article 119 of the EC Treaty provides for equal pay of men and women. This Article itself imposes obligations on all employers, not only on the State when it is acting as an employer. This is called the "horizontal" direct effect of a Community provision.

To date, the European Court has declined to accept the horizontal direct effect of directives on the ground that the binding nature of directives arises only in relation to the State to which the directive is addressed.[32] An unimplemented directive cannot, therefore, impose new legal obligations on a private individual or corporation. However, the distinction between the horizontal and vertical direct effect of directives has raised anomalies as between the beneficiaries of Community rights leading to further questions as to whether the distinction is still required[33] and, if the distinction is valid, as to who is the "the State" for these purposes.[34]

If the direct effects of regulations and directives are a point of comparison between these two forms of legal instrument, then the indirect effect of directives is a point of contrast. The Court seems to have developed the concept of indirect effect to counteract the distinction it had itself drawn between horizontal and vertical effects of directives. The Court

---

[29] See Case 41/74 *Van Duyn* v *The Home Office* [1974] ECR 1337; Case 8/81 *Becker* [1982] ECR 53.
[30] Case 148/78 *Ratti* [1979] ECR 1629; Case 126/82 *Smit* [1983] ECR 73.
[31] *Op. cit.*, n 29.
[32] Case 152/84 *Marshall* v *South West Hampshire Area Health Authority* [1986] ECR 723.
[33] Advocate-General Lenz has recently argued against the distinction in his opinion in Case C-92/92, *Faccini Dori* v *RECREB*, judgment of 14 July 1994, see also Chapter 12, n 68.
[34] Beginning with Case C-188/89 *Foster* v *British Gas* [1990] ECR 3313.

has held that the courts of the Member States are under an obligation to consider the content and scope of a directive in order to review the lawfulness of national legal provisions with it irrespective of the capacity of the directive to create direct effects. An individual could not rely on the terms of the directive itself but the individual could ask the Court to take the terms of the directive into consideration in assessing the compatibility of national and Community law.[35] This obligation was reiterated in ever stronger terms by the European Court in a series of cases in which the obligation was imposed on the national courts themselves to interpret national law in such a way as to try to comply with the directive.[36] The obligation to find a concurring interpretation arises as soon as the directive comes into force rather than on the date of the expiry of the time limit laid down for implementation by national law.

The obligation to achieve such a concurring interpretation only arises in respect of directives. It does not arise in relation to regulations since they themselves form part of national law and must be applied by the national courts as being part of the national legal order.

(iv) Decisions and their defining features

Like regulations, decisions adopted by the Community institutions are legally binding instruments. However, the distinction to be drawn between regulations and decisions is in the limitation of the persons addressed. Regulations are general normative acts applying throughout the Community. Decisions are binding only on those to whom they are addressed. Decisions are frequently adopted by the Commission in the area of competition law where they set out the view of the Commission in respect of breaches of competition law. Such decisions may be reviewed by the European Court under Article 173.

A decision may also be addressed to one or more Member States requiring them to act in a particular way. Decisions could, therefore, have been the chosen instruments for the implementation of the Single Market Programme. The fact that they were not is probably the habit of harmonisation by way of directives developed under Article 100.[37] Also directives are more flexible instruments which provide the Member States with a

---

[35] Case 51/76 *VNO* [1977] ECR 113 and Case 38/77 *ENKA* [1977] ECR 2203.

[36] "National courts are required to interpret their national law in the light of the wording and purpose of the directive in order to achieve the result referred to in the third paragraph in Article 189" in Case 14/83 *Von Colson* [1984] ECR 1891, Case 79/83 *Harz v Deutsche Tradax* [1984] ECR 1921. In Case C-106/89 *Marleasing SA v La Comercial Internacional de Alimentacion SA* [1992] 1 CMLR 305, the Court stated that "in applying national law, whether the provisions in question were adopted before or after the Directive, the national court called upon to interpret it is required to do so, so far as possible, in the light of the wording and purpose of the Directive in order to achieve the result pursued by the latter and thereby comply with the third paragraph of Article 189 of the EEC Treaty". See also Chapter 3, section 4(iii).

[37] See section 4(i) below, on techniques of harmonisation.

degree of discretion which may be missing in the decision. Finally, in no case does the Treaty specify that decisions are the required form of Community act where harmonisation or approximation of laws is concerned. The Member States are not, therefore, accustomed to choosing the Decision as a technique for harmonisation and would be unlikely to make this choice where they are given an option on the form of Community law in the Treaties.

The decision could, in the future, become important in the implementation process since the Member States may wish to address a decision to a specific State which consistently fails to abide by its Single Market obligations. To date this mechanism has not been used in the context of the Single Market.

(v) **A Community hierarchy of norms?**

Within the system of Community law itself there is a clear hierarchical structure between the Treaties and Community acts in the form of regulations, directives and decisions. The Treaties are at the apex of this hierarchy with the result that all acts adopted by the institutions must comply with the provisions of the Treaties. It is not possible, therefore, to have a valid Community act which conflicts with a Treaty provision.[38]

As between regulations, directives and decisions there is so no such hierarchy. A regulation is not a superior rule or form of law to a directive or vice versa. Regulations and directives serve different functions and are used to attain slightly different goals. This issue was addressed during the debates on the Treaty on European Union but no agreement could be reached on determining an hierarchical structure. A Declaration attached to the Final Act of the Conference on the Treaty relating to the hierarchy of Community Acts indicated that this was one issue which would be discussed in the 1996 review of the Treaty.

4 Soft law

The Treaties also provide that the Community can adopt recommendations or opinions. Neither of these types of acts is legally binding but they do provide the opportunity for the Community to provide frameworks or guidelines for action. In the area of sexual harassment, for example, the Community decided against legislation but instead chose to adopt a resolution and a recommendation containing a code of good

---

[38] This is clear from the wording of Article 173 of the EC Treaty which provides for judicial review of acts of the institutions on the grounds of, amongst others, "infringement of this Treaty or of any rule of law relating to its application".

practice.[39] On other occasions, the institutions have chosen to adopt communications or notices setting out the meaning to be attached to Community law or policy. The adoption of notices is common in the area of competition law, whereas communications have been adopted in a number of areas.[40] One of the main discussions on the form of Community legislation in the run-up to the adoption of the Treaty on European Union was whether directives might be abandoned as a form of Community legislation in favour of the adoption of non-binding acts. Such a move would provide the Member States with greater freedom of action but would destroy the existing pattern of legislation. Soft law techniques have not been of special importance in relation to case studies in this book and they will therefore not be discussed further.[41]

It is also open to the Community to further its policies by the deployment of funds. Regional policy, for example, whilst established by legislation, is pursued largely at the discretion of the Commission in allocating quite substantial sums in partnership with Member States or local government.[42] These policies, again, have not formed part of the case studies contained in this book.

(i) Techniques of harmonisation

Within the context of the European Community, the harmonisation of laws is not an end in itself. It is not an objective of the Community to achieve uniform laws throughout the Member States. Harmonisation is a method by which the objectives of the Community can be achieved. From the cases studied in this book, it will be apparent that the directives and regulations serve as tools to enhance and support the fundamental pillars of the Community and the Single European Market: the free movement of goods, persons, services and capital. The harmonisation process could therefore be defined as one in which secondary rules support the primary Treaty rules to achieve certain goals. An example of this approach is the toy safety study (Chapter 9) in which the Community primary interest is in the free movement of goods, which can only be

---

[39] For the Resolution see OJ 1990 C157/3. For the Recommendation see OJ 1992 C27/4.
[40] For an explanation of the meaning of the term communication see Mattera, *Le Marché Unique Européen*, 2nd ed (1993). The European Court has been willing to declare both Notices and Communications susceptible to judicial review. The key point is the legal effects of the act rather than its legal form. For examples see Case 298/83 *CICCE* v *Commission* [1985] ECR 1105; Case 53/85 *AKZO* v *Commission* [1986] ECR 1965.
[41] See Schwarze, Govaere, Hélin, Van den Bossche (eds), *The 1992 Challenge at National Level: Reports and Conference Proceedings 1989* (1990), 694 *et seq.*; and in this book, Chapter 3, section 3(iii).
[42] See Armstrong, "Community Regional Policy" in *The European Community and the Challenge of the Future* (Lodge ed., 2nd ed, 1993) 131–151; Molle, "Regional Policy" in *Main Economic Policy Areas of the EC – After 1992* (P.Coffey ed, 4th ed, 1993); Scott and Mansell, "European Regional Development Policy: Confusing Quantity with Quality?" (1993) 18 E. L. Rev. 87.

achieved by ensuring that the toys traded in the single market are acceptable to consumers and meet certain standards of safety. There is a further need on the part of the Community to recognise the interests of manufacturers in having access to as wide a market as possible so that the minimum of Community regulation necessary to protect consumers is required. The harmonisation process is, therefore, a subtle and complex process requiring a balance of interests and it is understandable that there is so much criticism from Member States, from interest groups and from the press, when they see the Community institutions involved with the minutiae of daily life rather than becoming involved in great matters of state, particularly where the Community approach does not meet all their expectations.

The Treaties do not provide for definitions of terms in the area of harmonisation. There is, however, a distinction of terminology in the Treaties where different words are used to describe what is more generally known as the process of harmonisation. In the English version of the Treaties, three different terms are used – approximation, harmonisation and co-ordination of laws. In the German and Italian versions only two terms are used (*Angleichung* and *ravvicinamento* for approximation and harmonisation and *Koordinerung* and *coordinamento* for co-ordination). A comparison of the different language versions might suggest that there are really two types of activity at work in the whole harmonisation process: harmonisation in the sense of driving change in legal and administrative rules and structures, and co-ordination of policy goals without the concomitant changes in structures and rules. In harmonisation a Community process is at work; in co-ordination it is common action taken at the national level. The case studies in this book all fall under the heading of harmonisation rather than co-ordination.

The Treaties define the form which particular acts of the institutions must take in achieving harmonisation although in some instances the institutions – most often the Council – have a choice of legal form. In relation to the free movement of persons, for example, the Council may adopt regulations or directives to set out the measures required to bring about the free movement of workers (Article 49 of the EC Treaty). On a related matter, the question of social security for migrant workers, the Council may adopt "such measures as may be necessary" to provide for free movement of workers (Article 51 of the EC Treaty). No choice is given in matters of approximation of laws, regulations or administrative provisions of the Member States which directly affect the functioning of the common market. Here Article 100 of the EC Treaty requires the Council to adopt directives. As a derogation from this principle, in matters relating to the completion of the Single European Market, except for specified exemptions, the Council may adopt the measures required. This gives the Council a wider range of choices for the form in which legislation is adopted. It can be seen, therefore, that the form which legislation takes may be determined by the subject matter and defined by the

41

Treaties. On other occasions subject matter is only one of the factors to be considered in determining the form which legislation will take. Other factors are the purpose behind the measure and whether the need arises to amend national legislation.

For the most part, the Single European Market has required the amendment of national rules, regulations or administrative practices, and legislation has taken the form of directives. The Single Market Programme has, therefore, been a harmonisation programme rather than a programme of co-ordinated national effort. The Community has determined national policy and the Member States have been required to act to achieve this policy.

5 Patterns of harmonisation

(i) The Old and New Approaches

Before the Commission's White Paper on the completion of the Single European Market and the amendments to Article 100 of the Treaty of Rome, the harmonisation process had proved to be cumbersome and difficult. The approach taken by the Community had been to adopt specific legislation laying down detailed rules to be implemented into national regulations by each of the Member States. This "Old Approach" to harmonisation could be criticised as being too slow – by the time the Community had adopted some of the directives technology had advanced so far as to render the directives inappropriate. It could also be criticised as being an inappropriate method of regulation of industry, within the common market, since it attempted to impose common standards and did not allow for the diversity of acceptable standards defined by the European Court of Justice in its decision in the *Cassis de Dijon* case.[43] Here the Court had stressed that goods lawfully marketed in one Member State should not be prevented from entering another unless there were compelling national policy grounds, such as safety of consumers, for prohibiting their importation (the so-called "mandatory requirements"). The stress on "mutual recognition" in this decision rendered the "Old Approach" to harmonisation somewhat redundant and the Commission abandoned the detailed programme of regulation which it had formerly pursued.

The Commission's "New Approach" was based on the Court's judgment in the *Cassis de Dijon* case. It was also based on a different approach to

---

[43] Case 120/78 *Rewe-Zentral* v *Bundesmonopolverwaltung fur Brannwein* [1979] ECR 64. The *Cassis de Dijon* case has led to a subsequent inconsistent case law on the part of the Court. It has recently revised some of this jurisprudence, see Chalmers, "Repackaging the Internal Market – the Ramifications of the *Keck* Judgement" (1994) E. L. Rev. 385. See also Chapter 3, text at n 54 and Chapter 11, n 36.

regulation, one which was more in keeping with the internal patterns of regulation in the Member States themselves. In the Single Market White Paper, the Commission pledged itself to recommending harmonisation only in the area of mandatory requirements (the terminology of *Cassis de Dijon*) and only in the form of general levels or standards of protection, leaving the detailed rules to be drawn up by the European standardisation bodies. The involvement of private standards organisations reflects the growing importance of such bodies both internationally and nationally. The Commission also pledged that it would not introduce harmonisation legislation in areas which could not be described as mandatory: these areas would be subject to mutual recognition, so as "to achieve a better balance between the roles of the legislator and the standards bodies, and between consumer/environmental protection and consumer choice".[44]

What is not clear in the New Approach is whether the Community institutions have delegated powers to national standards bodies and to CEN and CENELEC, the European standards organisations or even to sectors of industry. Furthermore, it is not clear from the Treaties whether the Community institutions have the power to delegate. Article 100a, which is the legal base for the toy and food safety legislation discussed in this study, does allow the Council to adopt measures for the approximation of the provisions laid down by law, regulation or administrative action in Member States. It could be argued that the Member State intended this as a general power of delegation and the measures need not necessarily only be those which seek to amend national law. It could be argued that Article 100a creates the power to be exercised by the Council to delegate the function of harmonisation to private bodies as this is necessary for the attainment of the Single Market programme.

Community law does provide for certain principles where powers are delegated. These principles have been developed in the context of delegation of powers within the Commission and delegation to bodies outside the Community institutions.[45] The Commission is entitled to delegate part of its functions to one of its number to act in the name of the Commission, for example, in competition matters, providing always that such delegation does not replace the overall power of the Commission.[46] Secondly, the Commission may not delegate policy decisions but only administrative or executive functions. Any such delegation must be necessary to enable the Commission to act effectively in a way in which it otherwise could have acted. As far as delegating powers to outside agencies is concerned, the general principles remain as those laid down in the *Meroni* case.[47] Here the Court held that "delegation of a discretionary power, *i.e.*

---

[44] See Burrows, "Harmonisation of technical standards: reculer pour mieux sauter?" (1990) Mod. L. Rev. 597.
[45] See Lenaerts, "Regulating the regulatory process: 'delegation of powers' in the European Community" (1993) *E. L. Rev.* 23.
[46] Case 5/85 *AKZO Chemie* v *Commission* [1986] ECR 1965.
[47] Case 9/56 *Meroni* v *High Authority* [1957] ECR 133.

other than a clearly defined executive power, to bodies established entirely outside the framework of Community law is contrary to the principle of institutional balance and hence illegal".[48] The Court of Justice has not had occasion to determine the question as to whether the New Approach is in fact delegation and, if so, whether it is a permissible delegation in the sense that the national standards bodies have only an executive rather than a policy making function. The balance is finely drawn between the two. Certainly the Old Approach suggested that harmonisation of standards was a legislative function rather than a purely technical one and Article 100a does not distinguish the two processes except to state that "any measures" might be taken in place of the adoption of directives as envisaged in Article 100. As stated above, it could be argued that the Community institutions might, by way of a directive, delegate technical matters to bodies established outside the framework of Community law.

The Commission has argued that the New Approach does not involve any measure of delegation. It points out that the framework directives contain the only essential requirements required by Community law. Setting European industry standards is not a matter for the Community institutions. Such standards are voluntary codes and are independent of Community law. To follow this argument through, provided a toy matches the standards contained in the toy safety directive then it need not comply with the standards setting bodies and need not obtain the CE mark. States would not be able to prohibit importation of such goods and indeed this is the case. As Weatherill points out, the application of the CE mark to a toy merely attests that the manufacturer or importer believes that the toy conforms to the criteria laid down in the directive; it does not guarantee that it does so.[49] If the Commission is right, therefore, and the Community institutions have not delegated decision-making or any other powers to private standards bodies, then the New Approach is merely an exercise in simplification of harmonising legislation and signifies the withdrawal of the Community from legislating for technical standards except in the most general of terms. The New Approach, however, also forbids Member States from introducing new technical rules without the agreement of the Commission. Taken together with the doctrine of preemption which requires the Member States to withdraw from the "regulatory space"[50] where the Community has acted, the New Approach may mean that the Single European Market will see a regulatory gap with the potential influx of sub-standard products. In such a situation consumers will have little protection in the form of national or Community regulation.

One weakness of the New Approach is, of course, that the more general

---

[48] Toth, *The Oxford Encyclopedia of European Community Law* (1993), Vol I, 605.
[49] Chapter 9, section 3(i).
[50] Hancher and Moran, *Capitalism, Culture and Economic Regulation* (1989), 271–99.

the terms, the more latitude there is for avoidance and the more difficult is the policing. Industry must be trusted to comply and self-regulation by industry assumes greater importance than under the Old Approach. Regulation at the level most appropriate to the subject of regulation may be more effective and efficient. At the end of the day, self-policing and self-regulation will be as efficient and effective as required by the market, but in the market there will be scope for "rogues" as well as well ordered sectors.

Regulation at the level of industry may also be a correct interpretation of the principle of subsidiarity. The Treaty on European Union does not seem to foresee this definition of subsidiarity but it is one which is in keeping with the concept as it has been used in the Community since the days of the Jenkins' presidency.[51]

(ii) **Vertical and horizontal directives**

The change in approach to harmonisation has led to a new distinction as between vertical and horizontal harmonising directives. This distinction relates to the content of the directive and seems to describe the group of persons who are to be regulated by a particular Community directive. A horizontal directive is one which applies throughout an industry. It sets out general principles rather than specific rules and leaves a wide latitude for interpretation. The Control of Foodstuffs Directive is a horizontal directive of this type.[52] In contrast, vertical directives are specific to identifiable groups within an industry and tend to be more detailed. Such directives control the very details of a product's development, such as composition, manufacture, labelling, and even package size of the product. The Beer Labelling Directive is such an example.[53] As noted by Lister, rather than standards, they prescribe formulae.[54]

Industry tends to prefer horizontal directives which avoid over-prescription and allow industry to adapt to the rules in a variety of different ways. Control rests in its own hands rather than in the hands of the Commission. As knowledge or practices develop so too can industry react to changed circumstances. The down-side of this approach is, however, that industry may assume that competitors do not comply with the rules to the same extent as themselves and, as control is decentralised, they have no proof that competitors are acting within the limits of Community law. In this sense industry must develop trust both in competitors and in

---

[51] Cappelletti et al, *Integration Through Law*, Vol. 1: *Methods, Tools and Institutions*, (1986) Book II, 40.
[52] See Chapter 6.
[53] See Chapter 5.
[54] Lister, *Regulation of Food Products by the European Community* (1992), 197.

enforcement officials across the Community. Industry must then begin to develop its own networks, as indeed must enforcement agents.

The move towards horizontal directives may be as a result of what has been described as the crisis of harmonisation.[55] Vertical directives are time consuming in terms of implementation by national authorities and they may, therefore, not be implemented at all. The proliferation of vertical directives in the area of food law shows how this might come about. Vertical directives (sometimes also known as recipe type directives[56]) exist in matters of composition, in labelling and in manufacturing processes of a variety of goods. Some of these vertical directives include numerous specific exemptions, derogations and cumbersome procedures for amendments. They very often require further, even more detailed, directives. Directive 77/94/EEC,[57] for example, on compositional and labelling criteria needed the adoption of specific further legislation on permitted colours, antioxidants, emulsifiers, stabilisers and preservatives in order to define categories of flavours and additives. In the area of food law, this confusion and proliferation has led the Commission to call for a single piece of legislation laying down the principles of food law in the Community.[58]

It is not always easy to distinguish the approaches of the Commission by using such terms as old and new approaches and horizontal and vertical directives. A straightforward analysis of the texts of directives leave an impression that the New Approach is tempered with the Old and that the Commission only reluctantly cedes to the Member States in matters of detail. However, the important feature of the New Approach is the reliance on the Member States in developing and implementing Community policy whilst at the same time leaving the Community legislator the task of balancing any conflicting Community goals, for example between the objectives of free trade and consumer protection.

The New Approach implicitly recognises that the achievement of absolute identity between regulatory regimes of Member States within particular sectors is, in practice, impossible. Methods of enforcement and the type of regulatory regime remain within the hands of the Member States. The New Approach is, by definition, subsidiarity in action. Notwithstanding the advantages of the New Approach, difficulties have emerged. Whereas the Old Approach and vertical directives created problems for Member States in agreeing to particular prescriptions, the New Approach raises problems of agreement of what constitutes equivalence across the

---

[55] Dehousse, "Some Reflections on the Crisis of the Harmonisation Model" in *A Regulatory Framework for Foodstuffs in the Internal Market* (Snyder ed., EUI working paper LAW No. 94/4, 1994), 43–49.

[56] For a discussion of "recipe" type directives see, Lister, *op. cit.*, n 52, chapter 7.

[57] OJ 1977 L26/55.

[58] Commission recommendation of 11 March 1994 concerning a coordinated programme for the official control of foodstuffs for 1994, OJ 1994 L80/25; for a debate on the possibility of such a framework, see Snyder, *op. cit.*, n 53, pp 113–121.

Community, in terms of both the standards set and the methods by which those standards are to be monitored and enforced.

The case studies which form Part Two of this book take up the issues of the form of Community legislation and its function in the completion of the Single Market Programme. Directives and their implementation form the major part of the case studies, all of which demonstrate the importance of law making in the completion of the Single Market Programme.

NOREEN BURROWS AND
HILARY HIRAM

Chapter 3
The Effectiveness of European Community Law: Institutions, Processes, Tools and Techniques[1]

1 Introduction

Law has always been a central symbol and a basic instrument of European integration. Yet today the effectiveness of European Community law increasingly seems in issue. Even in ordinary circumstances, this state of affairs would raise serious questions of law, policy, politics and social theory. Stimulated by the Maastricht Treaty on European Union, however, it has converged with and fuelled an emerging debate on the future of western Europe. Two important strands in this debate concern, on the one hand, the merits of different ways of ensuring the effectiveness of Community law, and, on the other hand, the institutional structure of future European society and the relations between its component parts. This Chapter focuses mainly on the first strand, but it also seeks to contribute to the wider debate.

The Chapter has three specific purposes. First, it considers some of the principal means which are currently used to ensure the effectiveness of Community law. "Effectiveness" is taken to mean the fact that "law matters: it has effects on political, economic and social life outside the law – that is, apart from simply the elaboration of legal doctrine."[2] By its emphasis on the social context in which law operates, as well as in its interdisciplinary character, this definition is broader than the legal doc-

---

[1] The author wishes to thank Jason Coppel, Terence Daintith, Renaud Dehousse, Nathalie Habbar, Christian Joerges, Emir Lawless, Giandomenico Majone, Emile Noël, Anna Papaioannou, Richard Rawlings, several past and present officials of the EC Commission and an anonymous reader for the *Modern Law Review* for their contributions to this Chapter. A slightly longer version of this Chapter originally appeared in (1993) 56 *Mod. L. Rev.* 19. In the interim several changes have been made in the text and some additional references have been included in the footnotes. Like the original version, however, this Chapter is concerned only with European Community law; it does not consider the effectiveness of the law of the European Union in the broader sense, which also embraces the Common Provisions and Titles V and VI of the Maastricht Treaty.
[2] Snyder, *New Directions in European Community Law* (1990), 3.

trine of "effectiveness", either "procedural" or "substantive".[3] It includes – but is not limited to – implementation, enforcement, impact and compliance.[4]

This Chapter is concerned not only with the nature of effectiveness but also with its legal and institutional preconditions.[5] The European Community has a complex institutional structure. The effectiveness of Community law depends on Community institutions, Member States, corporatist arrangements, pluralist politics, policy networks, and individuals.[6] This Chapter focuses on two Community institutions, the Commission and the Court of Justice. Consequently, its second purpose is to present a systematic reinterpretation of these institutions, including their basic processes, tools and techniques, with regard to the task of ensuring the effectiveness of Community law.[7] For this purpose, it is necessary to draw on both law and other disciplines. In addition to charting the development of certain aspects of legal doctrine, this Chapter thus may illustrate some of the ways in which our understanding of Community law, and in particular of Community institutions, may be enriched by a contextual method.[8]

On the basis of this discussion of different institutional arrangements for ensuring the effectiveness of law, the third purpose of the Chapter is to pose several normative questions. What division of labour should prevail among Community institutions in ensuring the effectiveness of Com-

---

[3] On procedural effectiveness see, *e.g.* Case 33/76 *Rewe-Zentralfinanz eG and Rewe-Zentral AG* v *Landwirtschaftskammer für das Saarland* [1976] ECR 1989; Case 45/76 *Comet* v *Producktschaap voor Siergewasen* [1976] ECR 2043; Case C-213/89 *R.* v *Secretary of State for Transport, ex parte Factortame* [1990] 3 CMLR 1; Case C-208/90 *Emmott* v *Minister for Social Welfare* [1991] 3 CMLR 894. On substantive effectiveness, see *e.g.* Case 14/83 *von Colson and Kamaan* v *Land Nordrhein-Westfalen* [1984] ECR 1891; Case 222/84 *Johnston* v *Chief Constable of the RUC* [1986] ECR 1651. For the argument that "procedural" and "substantive" effectiveness are two sides of the same coin, see Mead, "The obligation to apply European law: is Duke dead?" (1991) 16 *E. L. Rev.* 490, 492–495.
[4] In other words, effectiveness may include both the effects of legal norms and the following of legal norms. See Teubner, "Regulatory Law: Chronicle of a Death Foretold" in *The Crisis of Law in the Welfare State* (Lenoble ed 1992), 451 n 2, citing Rottleuthner, *Einfuhrung in die Rechtssoziologie* (1987), 54 *et seq.*
[5] The extent to which efficiency is a prerequisite of effectiveness, in the sense either of a specific relation between costs and benefits or of a particular quality of decisions, lies outside the scope of this Chapter.
[6] Although these different forms of organisation are crucial determinants of the extent of the effectiveness of Community law, they have attracted little attention from legal scholars. Useful work by political scientists includes Cawson (ed), *Organized Interests and the State: Studies in Meso-Corporatism* (1985); Lehmbruch and Schmitter, *Patterns of Corporatist Policy-Making* (1982); Streeck and Schmitter, "From National Corporatism to Transnational Pluralism: Organized Interests in the Common Market" (1991) 19 Pol.& Soc'y 133; Marin and Mayntz (eds), *Policy Networks: Empirical Evidence and Theoretical Considerations* (1991).
[7] The relations between institutions, rules, ideologies and processes may be considered to be of the four key areas of EC law in context: see Snyder, *op. cit.*, n 2, chapter 1. For different approaches to the analysis of institutions, see Komesar, "In Search of a General Approach to Legal Analysis: A Comparative Institutional Alternative" (1981) 79 Mich.L.Rev. 1350; Komesar, "Taking Institutions Seriously: Introduction to a Strategy for Constitutional Analysis" (1984) 51 U.C.L.R. 366; Keohane and Hoffmann (eds), *The New European Community* (1991); Sbragia (ed), *Euro-Politics: Institutions and Policymaking in the 'New' European Community* (1992).
[8] See generally Snyder, *European Community Law*, 2 vols. (1993).

munity law? Are existing institutions adequate? If not, what gaps exist, and how might they be filled? What is our vision of future western European society? Do we have any criteria and any processes by means of which choices about the future can be made? These questions direct our attention to the connections between the purposes of the Community, its rules and processes, and its institutional structure. They help us to consider whether the institutions of the present are adequate for the future. This Chapter aims to put these questions on the legal and political agenda.

The remainder of the Chapter is divided into three main parts. The first of these identifies the nature of non-compliance in the contemporary Community legal system, and then considers the effectiveness of Community law as a problem of policy and theory. The following two parts discuss different responses to non-compliance with Community law: administrative negotiation of effectiveness by the Commission, and the development of a judicial liability system by the Court of Justice. Each of these two parts presents a heuristic model, designed not to give a comprehensive account of the institution, but instead to identify some of its main features in the light of the issue of the effectiveness of Community law. In conclusion, a systematic comparison is proposed between the two sets of institutions, processes, tools and techniques. It is also argued, however, that administrative negotiation and improved adjudication should not be envisaged as alternatives. Instead they should be developed in tandem, if necessary following appropriate modifications in the two institutions and changes in the institutional structure of the Community. It is further suggested that neither the Commission and the Court of Justice taken together as institutions, nor negotiation and adjudication taken together as processes, despite their merits, are sufficient alone to ensure the effectiveness of Community law. Instead, further changes in both the institutions and the processes of the Community are necessary in order to ensure the effectiveness of Community law in the future.

2 Compliance, implementation, enforcement and effectiveness

(i) The new challenge of compliance

The deadline for the completion of the internal market passed at the beginning of 1993. The deadline was not legally binding, but this does not mean that it has had no effect. On the contrary, its practical consequences stand as a tribute to the brilliance of specific individuals and organisations in elaborating strategies for further integration, as well to the instrumental and symbolic use of law by organisations without recourse to legal force.[9]

In addition, the mere fact that the 1992 deadline was stated in the Single European Act, and consequently in Article 8A of the EEC Treaty, focused a fierce spotlight on the effectiveness of Community law.[10] It led to a concentration by politicians, administrators, judges, lawyers and academics on implementation, impact and compliance.[11] This in turn highlighted many achievements but also revealed numerous problems. The latter centred on the transposition of Community directives and national compliance with Community law, including Court of Justice decisions. These concerns were to culminate in a Declaration on the Implementation of Community Law, annexed to the Maastricht Treaty. The Declaration enjoined Member States to transpose Community directives fully and adequately into national law within the specified deadlines; it also stated that, while Member States might take different measures to enforce Community law, these measures should result in Community law being applied with the same effectiveness and rigour as national law.[12]

These concerns reflect the transformation of the legal, economic and political configuration of western Europe since the late 1950s. This new context gives a different character to non-compliance with Community law today.[13] Withdrawal from the Community is now ruled out as an option for national policy. As a result, it has been argued, in order to avoid the rigours of closer integration, Member States may resort increasingly to a new political and legal strategy. This strategy consists in the

---

[9] Compare Maravcsik, "Negotiating the Single European Act: National Interests and Conventional Statecraft in the European Community" (1991) 25 Int'l Organiz. 19; Streeck and Schmitter, *op. cit.*, n 6; Sandholtz and Zysman, "1992: Recasting the European Bargain" (1989) 42 World Pol. 95; and Ehlermann, "The Internal Market Following the Single European Act" (1987) 24 *Comm. Mkt. L. Rev.* 361.

[10] For earlier studies, see Ciavarini-Azzi, *L'Application du Droit Communautaire par les Etats membres* (1985); Siedentopf and Ziller (eds), *Making European Policies Work: The Implementation of Community Legislation in the Member States*, 2 vols. (1988).

[11] Beginning in 1985, the Commission issued periodic progress reports on the enactment and transposition of internal market legislation. Formal reports were also required under Art. 8B of the EC Treaty. The Commission also issued occasional reports; see *e.g. National Measures for the Implementation of the White Paper on the Completion of the Internal Market: Situation as at 1.10.1990* (1990). Beginning in 1984, it has also made an annual report to the European Parliament on the monitoring of the application of Community law, of which the most recent are the Eighth Annual Report, COM(91)321 final (October 16, 1991), OJ 1991 C338/1 and the Ninth Annual Report, OJ 1992 C250/1. See also Schwarze, Govaere, Hélin and Van den Bossche (eds), *The 1992 Challenge at National Level: Reports and Conference Proceedings 1989* (1990); Schwarze, Becker and Pollack (eds), *The 1992 Challenge at National Level: Reports and Conference Proceedings 1990* (1991); Schwarze, Becker and Pollack (eds), *The 1992 Challenge at National Level: Reports and Conference Proceedings 1991/92* (1993). See also Editorial Comments, "How to strengthen the effectiveness of Community law" (1991) 28 *Comm. Mkt. L. Rev.* 711.

[12] Declaration 18, para 1. The same Declaration asks the Commission to report regularly to the Council and the Parliament on its monitoring activities. Previously, the report was addressed to the European Parliament alone.

[13] See Weiler, "The Transformation of Europe" (1991) 100 Yale L.J. 2403, 2463–2464.

selective application of Community law. Such a state of affairs could, without exaggeration, be described as the "new challenge of compliance".[14]

(ii) **Effectiveness as a policy problem**

The effectiveness of Community law is, first of all, an issue of public policy. The issue is not, however, unique to the Community: instead it is common to most if not all contemporary states. The same is true of the tension between centralised steering and decentralised action, even though in the Community this tension may take specific forms, and even if it is sometimes manifested publicly in the lack of effectiveness of law.[15]

Yet the Community system has specific features. Despite the importance of centralised institutions, such as the Commission, the Council, the European Parliament, the Court of Justice and the Court of First Instance, both intergovernmental and decentralised decision-making have always been part of the Community system. The European Council, composed of the Heads of State and Government, plays an essential role in European integration[16], while the importance of decentralised decision-making is legally expressed by the principle of subsidiarity in the Maastricht Treaty. The implementation and the enforcement of Community law are carried out partly by the Commission, the Court of Justice and the Court of First Instance, but it is done primarily by the Member States through national administrations and national legal systems.[17] The Community operates mainly by means of indirect administration, in which Community policies and laws, enacted by the Council or the Commission, are implemented by national authorities. These features pose specific problems with regard to the effectiveness of Community law.[18]

---

[14] See Weiler, *op. cit.*, n 13. See also Weiler, "The White Paper and the Application of Community Law" in *1992: One European Market? A Critical Analysis of the Commission's Internal Market Strategy* (Bieber, Dehousse, Pinder and Weiler eds 1988). Compare the same author's earlier discussion, which concluded that unilateral withdrawal would be preferable to inactive membership, over-active membership or selective membership: Weiler, "Alternatives to Withdrawal from an International Organization: The Case of the EEC" (1985) 20 Israel L.Rev. 282.

[15] The tension between central decision-making and decentralised implementation is common to most contemporary states. See Teubner, "Substantive and Reflexive Elements in Modern Law" (1983) 17 L.& Soc.Rev. 239; Teubner, "Autopoiesis in Law and Society: A Reply to Blankenburg" (1984) 18 L.&Soc.Rev. 291; Handler, "Dependent People: The State and the Modern/Postmodern Search for the Dialogic Community" (1988) 35 U.C.L.A.L.Rev. 999; Handler, *The Conditions of Discretion: Autonomy, Community, Bureaucracy* (1986).

[16] See Werts, *The European Council* (1992).

[17] See Rideau, "Le rôle des états membres dans l'application du droit communautaire" (1985) 18 A.F.D.I. 864.

[18] As to the ways in which the European Court has dealt with such problems, see Case 103/88 *Fratelli Costanza SpA* v *Comune di Milano* [1989] ECR 1839 (all levels of the national administration are bound by the duty of Community loyalty in Article 5 of the EEC Treaty) and Case C-8/88 *Re Suckler Cows Germany* v *EC Commission* [1992] 1 CMLR 409 (the Commission is not entitled to interfere in the distribution of powers established by national law, but may verify whether the supervisory and inspection procedures established according to the arrangements within the national legal system are in their entirety sufficiently effective to enable the Community requirements to be correctly applied).

Commentators agree that the effectiveness of Community law has become increasingly problematic. An empirical study published in 1986 distinguished different types of non-compliance.[19] Though the categories were not discrete, they included lack of implementation (incorporation or transposition), lack of application, lack of enforcement, pre- and post-litigation non-compliance, legislative, executive and judicial non-compliance, defiance, evasion and benign non-compliance.[20] The authors concluded that, even though most non-compliance was benign, being due to factors of political or administrative paralysis rather than deliberate political decisions, there was a "growing problem of compliance"[21] and that "non-compliance has ... become an issue high on the Community agenda".[22]

It is difficult to evaluate the extent of non-compliance satisfactorily. Our knowledge concerning the implementation and enforcement of Community law by Member States has been described recently as a "black hole".[23] Apart from the specific numbers, however, two types of non-compliance, or instances of the ineffectiveness of Community law, have a particular symbolic importance. First, it is clear that in the past decade the number and proportion of instances in which Member States fail to comply with a judgment of the Court of Justice has increased significantly.[24] As the Commission pointed out in 1989, "[t]his situation gives rise for concern as it undermines the fundamental principles of a Community based on law".[25] Secondly, there is the failure of Member States to transpose directives adequately or at all. One commentator has remarked that this "represents not only a drain on the Commission's limited enforcement capacity, but also an obstacle to the credibility of EEC law as a whole and to the creation of the internal market in particular".[26]

---

[19] See Krislov, Ehlermann and Weiler, "The Political Organs and the Decision-Making Process in the United States and the European Community" in *Integration Through Law. Methods, Tools and Institutions*, Vol.1, Book 2: *Political Organs, Integration Techniques and Judicial Process* (Cappelletti, Secombe and Weiler eds 1986), 61–85.

[20] *Ibid.*

[21] *Ibid.* 68, 87.

[22] *Ibid.* 77; see also Weiler, "The White Paper and the Application of Community Law" *op. cit.*, n 14, p 345.

[23] Weiler, *op. cit.*, n 13, p 2463. See also Krislov, Ehlermann and Weiler, *op. cit.*, n 19, p 77.

[24] Compare Krislov, Ehlermann and Weiler, *op. cit.*, n 19, pp 74–77 [28 cases]; and Commission of the European Communities, *Seventh annual report to the European Parliament on Commission monitoring of the application of Community law – 1989*, OJ 1990 C232/1 at C232/5 [82 cases]. As of 1988 this increase may have been roughly in proportion to the increase in the number of judgments delivered: Anderson, "Inadequate Implementation of EEC Directives: A Roadblock on the Way to 1992?" (1988) 11 Boston Coll.Int'l & Comp.L.Rev. 91, 96, n 25. However, from 1989 to 1990 the number of judgments delivered fell from 94 to 77 while the number not complied with rose from 12 to 25: see Commission, Eighth Annual Report, *op. cit.* n 11 at II, 102–119.

[25] Seventh Annual Report, *op. cit.*, n 24 at C232/5. See also European Parliament Resolutions of April 11, 1984, OJ 1984 C127/67, and 19 March 1990, OJ 1990 C68/172.

[26] Anderson, *op. cit.*, n 24, p 96.

The Commission's contributions to the 1991 Intergovernmental Conferences included a staff paper, which canvassed potential sanctions to ensure compliance with the judgments of the Court of Justice and the effectiveness of Community law more generally.[27] The list included countermeasures against a recalcitrant Member State[28]; financial sanctions, to be imposed by the Court of Justice in an action for failure to comply with a previous judgment of the Court of Justice[29]; and more explicit requirements flowing from Article 5 of the EEC Treaty. The paper also canvassed an extension of the jurisdiction of the Court of Justice, including (a) the power for the Court to take its own decision, with direct effect, on the measures needed to transpose Community law into national law[30], (b) the power to declare national law incompatible with Community law or to annul it, and (c) the power to issue injunctions. Finally, the Commission proposed recognition of the financial liability of a Member State towards persons suffering harm from the failure of the State to meet its Community law obligations.[31]

In addition to contributing to the formulation of Community policy, the debate on the effectiveness of Community law has had more general implications. On the one hand, it has confirmed the well-known truth that the implementation and enforcement of law are often highly political, in the sense that they require the exercise of power and a choice between competing values. Indeed the very definitions of effectiveness, implementation and compliance frequently involve sensitive institutional and political questions. Compared with national legal and political systems, the Community system is complex, novel and lacking in legitimacy. As a result, it may be suggested, these observations as to the political nature of the effectiveness of law hold with stronger force in the Community system, though this has not always been recognised. Consequently the discussion concerning the effectiveness of law, which might have seemed initially to be primarily of a technical character, has begun to open the Community system to a salutary discussion of the politics of law, and politics more generally, at Community level.

---

[27] "Commission Opinion of 21 October 1990 on the proposal for amendment of the Treaty establishing the European Economic Community with a view to political union", 81; and *Contributions by the Commission to the Intergovernmental Conference*, (Document drawn up on the basis of COM(90)600 and SEC(91)500), 151–155: both published in *Intergovernmental Conferences: Contributions by the Commission* EC Bull.Supp.2/91.

[28] Dismissed immediately: *ibid.* 151. The possibility of such countermeasures under the ECSC Treaty is provided by Article 88(3)(b) of the ECSC Treaty, but this has never been used: *ibid.*

[29] See now Articles 169, 171 of the EC Treaty, as amended by the Maastricht Treaty.

[30] Ruled out on political grounds: *op. cit.* n 27, p 153.

[31] See now Joined Cases C-6/90 and C-9/90 *Francovich and Bonifaci* v *Italy* [1992] IRLR 84, noted Szyszczak (1992) 55 Mod. L. Rev. 690; Duffy (1992) 17 E. L. Rev. 133; Curtin (1992) 21 I.L.J. 74. See also Ross, "Beyond *Francovich*" (1993) 56 Mod. L. Rev. 55; Steiner, "From Direct Effect to *Francovich*: Shifting Means of Enforcement of Community Law" (1993) 18 E. L. Rev. 3; Temple Lang, "New Legal Effects resulting from the Failure of States to Fulfil Obligations under European Community Law" (1992–93) 16 Fordham Int'l L.J. 1. See also Chapter 4, text accompanying n 13.

On the other hand, the debate has stimulated a renewed interest in the advantages and disadvantages, not only of the role of law in European integration, but also of different strategies and indeed different degrees of economic and political integration. The effectiveness of Community law, different forms of economic and political integration, and the Community's institutional integrity are seen increasingly to be closely related. We have only to recall the recent Opinions of the Court of Justice concerning the draft Agreement on the European Economic Space.[32] The Opinions made it clear that questions concerning the nature, role and effectiveness of Community law are fundamental to the future legal and institutional architecture of western Europe. They concern not only the existing Member States of the Community. They are also of great importance to the members of EFTA and the countries of eastern Europe which have recently negotiated, or are currently seeking, closer ties with the Community.

Ensuring the effectiveness of Community law involves basic questions concerning the political bases of the Community, its legitimacy, the scope for institutional change and hence its likely future development. It is suggested that any serious discussion of how to improve the effectiveness of Community law leads on to a consideration of the potential for development of Community institutions, the relation between the Community and the Member States, and hence the purposes of the Community and the possible and desirable alternatives for the shape of western Europe in the future.

(iii) **Effectiveness as a theoretical issue**

The effectiveness of Community law needs also to be conceived as a theoretical issue. Effectiveness may refer not only to compliance but also to implementation, enforcement and impact. These terms are often taken to denote distinct phenomena, though sometimes they represent different perspectives on the same phenomena, and sometimes the meanings of the terms overlap. There is no universally accepted definition of these terms, in particular with respect to Community law. Nor is there much empirical research with regard to Community law on these topics.

A commonly used approach to the effectiveness of Community law is that of implementation theory. The political process is defined as "a process of problem-solving by the politico-administrative system".[33] This process consists of three phases: policy formulation, implementation and

---

[32] Opinion 1/91 *Re the Draft Treaty on a European Economic Area* [1992] 1 CMLR 245, noted Burrows (1992) 17 E. L. Rev. 352; Opinion 1/92 *Re the Draft Treaty on a European Economic Area (No. 2)* [1992] 2 CLMR 217.
[33] Siedentopf and Ziller, *op. cit.*, n 10, p 3.

impact.[34] Based on this approach, the study by Krislov, Ehlermann and Weiler distinguishes between four phases: adoption, implementation (incorporation), application and enforcement.[35] This conception is based on the traditional hierarchy of administrative organisation, used in implementation theory, and the formal stages of the legal process in the Community system. It can be extremely useful in analysing the effectiveness of law as a problem of policy, in particular in identifying points of non-compliance with hierarchically superior rules.

Yet, even as a means to identify potential solutions to problems of policy, this kind of approach has substantial shortcomings. First, it reflects the top-down perspective of the policy-maker.[36] Consequently it tends to minimise the extent to which the implementation and enforcement of law, whether by administrative means or by courts, might involve processes of negotiation, in which the specific characteristics of the various parties concerned are extremely important. This feature is likely to be especially prominent, and hence the shortcoming particularly great, in systems with divided powers. In the Community, we can observe, several levels of government have decision-making powers and responsibility for the implementation and enforcement of law. Horizontal as well as vertical relations between them are crucial, and, as will be shown later, a fundamental role in ensuring the effectiveness of law is played by negotiation.

Secondly, as applied in the Community context, the term "effectiveness" has a wide variety of meanings. We can distinguish at least seven types of effectiveness: (1) the enactment of Community policy into legislation by Community institutions; (2) the implementation of Community regulations by the Member States; (3) the transposition of Community directives into national law; (4) the implementation of Community secondary legislation, or of national transposing or implementing legislation, within or by the national civil service; (5) the use of Community law by economic undertakings, other organisations and individuals, in the sense, following Weber[37], that they orient their behaviour in relation to Community law; (6) recourse to litigation in a national court based on Community law, including a directive which has been recognised as having, or is argued to have, direct effect; and (7) the enforcement of Community law by national courts, including the interpretation of

---

[34] *Ibid.* p 3, citing Mayntz (ed), *Implementation politischer Programme* (1980), 238–239.

[35] Krislov, Ehlermann and Weiler, *op. cit.*, n 19, p 62.

[36] For a useful evaluation of traditional implementation studies, see Ham and Hill, *The Policy Process in the Modern Capitalist State* (1984). Theoretical statements which appear potentially fruitful for analysing the effectiveness of Community law include, for example, Elmore, "Organizational Models of Social Program Implementation" (1978) 26 Publ.Pol. 185; Richardson, Ogus and Burrows, *Policing Pollution: A Study of Regulation and Enforcement* (1982); and Majone, *Evidence, Argument and Persuasion in the Policy Process* (1989).

[37] Rheinstein (ed), *Max Weber on Law in Economy and Society*, trans. Shils (1966), 3–5.

national legislation in the light of Community law. Implementation the-ory does not always distinguish between these different situations.[38]

Thirdly, for the purposes of this Chapter, the effectiveness of law is conceived of in relatively broad terms, so as to emphasise the social mean-ing of law as well as positive norms. Seen from this perspective, the effec-tiveness of law is not easily contained within legal doctrinal or administrat-ive categories. In every legal system there is a gap between law in the books and law in action. It would be remarkable if Community law were any different. The mere existence of such a gap should not necessarily be a cause for concern.[39] With respect to the effectiveness of Community law, what is more important is to concentrate on those gaps which are (a) especially problematic and (b) capable of being at least partially resolved or closed. This requires us to identify the gaps which exist; to explain why they exist; to identify and distinguish those gaps which are likely to be long-term features of the Community system; and, if possible, to focus on those (ideally less-enduring) gaps which pose real difficulties for the operation and development of the Community. This in turn requires a more multi-faceted, open-ended enquiry than is consistent with implementation theory.

Thus, a different approach is necessary in order eventually to elaborate a theoretical conception of the effectiveness of Community law. Though completing this task lies beyond the scope of this Chapter, let us begin by conceiving of effectiveness as including implementation, enforcement and compliance. We may define implementation as "the process and art of deliberately achieving social change through law."[40] This definition appears at first glance to start from the viewpoint of the policy-maker, but it is sufficiently broad to encompass perspectives at different levels of a divided-power system. It also conceives of implementation as a con-tinuous process, not as a fixed state of affairs. The implementation of law involves conflict, negotiation, compromise and mutual adjustment. Even though implementation may be characterised by patterns and relative stability in the long term, it is not one-way but rather is recursive and cir-cular.[41]

Compliance can then be seen as "a series of reactive behaviours through which the targets of state action seek to accommodate the new

---

[38] Situations of non-compliance are clearly distinguished, however, in Krislov, Ehlermann and Weiler, *op. cit.*, n 19, pp 62–77.

[39] See Abel, "Law Books and Books about Law" (Review Essay on Rheinstein, *Marriage Stability, Divorce and the Law* [1972]), (1973) 26 Stan.L.Rev. 175.

[40] Clune and Lindquist, "What 'Implementation' Isn't: Toward a General Framework for Implementation Research" (1981) Wis.L.Rev. 1044, 1045. More specifically, "it is the study of governmental organizations trying to influence [mainly] other organizations to do something that is difficult enough to require a great deal of interaction": Clune, "A Political Model of Implementation and Implications of the Model for Public Policy, Research, and the Changing Roles of Law and Lawyers" (1983) 69 Iowa L.Rev. 47, 51.

[41] See Clune, *op. cit.*, n 40, p 78. See also Snyder, *op. cit.*, n 2, pp 8, 32–62, 169–171.

incentives and disincentives with existing imperatives."[42] Such behaviour often takes place within organisations, such as national administrations. Consequently, it is essential to take account of the priorities, structures, incentives and ideologies of these organisations, in short, bureaucratic politics.[43] This concept of compliance focuses less on ultimate outcomes and more on ongoing negotiations, political and legal processes and organisational change. The latter are potentially both forms of implementation and forms of compliance, and they may (but often do not) involve means of enforcement, such as incentives, recourse to courts, or the threat or use of sanctions. For present purposes, implementation, enforcement and compliance, defined in this way, will be deemed to be different facets of effectiveness. This theoretical conception may seem very different from the conception of effectiveness which underpinned the discussion of the effectiveness of Community law as a problem of policy. Its utility for policy should emerge, however, during the course of this Chapter.

3 Administrative negotiation of effectiveness

(i) Introduction

We may begin with the Commission. The principal means which the Commission itself has used to ensure the effectiveness of Community law are three-fold: litigation, in particular infringement proceedings under Article 169 of the EC Treaty; so-called "soft law"; and structural reform involving national administrations. Legally speaking, all are based on the powers of the Commission as set out in Articles 4 and 155 of the EC Treaty. Each, it will be suggested, is best conceived of as part of a process of administrative negotiation.

(ii) Litigation as negotiation

As is well-known[44], Article 169 provides in formal terms that an infringement proceeding is to have two stages: first, an administrative stage including (a) the Commission invitation to a Member State to submit observations on the alleged breach and (b) delivery by the Commission of a reasoned opinion; and, secondly, a judicial stage, in which, if necessary, the Commission brings the matter before the European Court. As

---

[42] Clune and Lindquist, *op. cit.*, n 40, p 1068.
[43] *Ibid.* p 1068; see also Peters, "Bureaucratic Politics and the Institutions of the European Community" in Sbragia (ed), *op. cit.*, n 7.
[44] See generally, Mattera, *Le marché unique européen: Ses règles, son fonctionnement* (2nd ed, 1990), 681–719; Dashwood and White, "Enforcement Actions under Articles 169 and 170 EEC" (1989) 14 E. L. Rev. 388.

in most if not all legal systems, however, most disputes are settled (or otherwise disposed of) in the early phases of the process. The following Table shows the general trend in the use of the procedure.

Though showing only rough orders of magnitude rather than precise figures, the table indicates clearly the decline in the number of outstanding cases as the procedure moves through the administrative stage towards the judicial stage and then to judgment.

It also suggests three more interesting hypotheses regarding the Commission's use of the procedure to ensure the effectiveness of Community law. First, the importance of the Commission's reasoned opinions, sometimes been called the "hidden jurisprudence" of Community law, may be in decline. Current statistics indicate an increasing termination of infringement procedure at the formal notice stage. Secondly, the last point suggests, in turn, that the informal request for further particulars may be playing an increasingly important role in the settlement of infringement disputes. Thirdly, if this is the case, it may represent a significant change since the mid-1980s in the dominant mode of settling infringement disputes. Informal requests are dealt with today mainly via the Committee of Permanent Representatives of the Member States (COREPER: the ambassadors [and their deputies] of the Member States to the Community), or in "package meetings" between the Commission and national administrative authorities; in both settings a specific legal obligation may be merely one element among many in a particular negotiation.[45]

We usually think of negotiation and adjudication as alternative forms of dispute settlement.[46] It may be suggested, however, that, in the daily practice and working ideology of the Commission, the two are not alternatives but instead are complementary. The main form of dispute settlement used by the Commission is negotiation[47], and litigation is simply a part, sometimes inevitable but nevertheless generally a minor part, of this process. The Commission has a distinctive role in the Community litigation system. It is the ultimate "repeat player"[48] in Community litigation.

---

[45] These observations require further development in the light of a theory of litigation behaviour: see Griffiths, "The General Theory of Litigation: A First Step" (1983) 2 Z.Rsoz. 145.

[46] See the classic statement in Gulliver, *Disputes and Negotiations: A Cross Cultural Perspective* (1979).

[47] With regard to competition matters, see van Bael, "The Antitrust Settlement Practice of the EC Commission" (1986) 23 *Common Market Law Review* 61; Wilks, "The Metamorphosis of European Competition Policy" in Snyder (ed), *op. cit.*, n 8, Vol. 2. More generally, see Dashwood and White, *Enforcement Actions under Articles 169 and 170 EEC* (1989) 14 ELR 388, 400.

[48] See Galanter, "Why the 'Haves' Come Out Ahead: Speculations on the Limits of Legal Change" (1974) 9 L.& Soc.Rev. 95, 98–100; Galanter, "Afterward: Explaining Litigation" (1975) 9 L.& Soc.Rev. 347. Member States are also repeat players in Community litigation, though litigation rates vary from country to country and no Member State uses the Luxembourg courts nearly as much as does the Commission. The few repeat players among non-privileged applicants under Article 173 of the EEC Treaty use the Court of Justice or the Court of First Instance even less, not to mention the fact that in such cases the defendant is frequently the Commission: see Harding, "Who Goes to Court in Europe? An Analysis of Litigation against the European Community" (1992) 17 *European Law Review* 105.

Table 1 *Article 169 Infringement Proceedings for All Member States 1975–1990*

	Total Complaints*		Letter of Formal Notice		Reasoned Opinion		Reference to ECJ		Judgement	
	No	%	No	%	No	%	No	%	No	%
1975	+		60	+ +	23	+ +	2	+ +	1	
1976	+		90	+ +	38	+ +	6	+ +	2	+ +
1977	+		68	+ +	28	+ +	8	+ +	4	+ +
1978	+		100	+ +	46	+ +	15	+ +	6	+ +
1979	+		200	+ +	79	+ +	18	+ +	7	+ +
1980	208	100	240	**	82	39.4	28	13.5	19	+ +
1981	353	100	256	72.5	147	41.6	50	14.2	17	9.1
1982	464	100	335	72.2	157	44.5	45	9.7	31	4.8
1983	591	100	289	48.9	83	14.0	42	7.1	18	6.7
1984	621	100	454	73.1	148	23.8	54	8.7	17	3.0
1985	929	100	503	54.1	233	25.0	113	12.2	26	2.7
1986	1084	100	516	47.6	164	15.1	71	6.5	30	2.7
1987	1110	100	572	51.5	197	17.7	61	5.5	41	3.7
1988	1444	100	569	39.4	227	15.7	73	5.1	50	3.5
1989	1547	100	664	42.9	180	11.6	96	6.2	26	1.6
1990	1535	100	960	62.5	251	16.4	77	5.0	38	2.4

* Includes both complaints and infringements detected by the Commission's own inquiries
** Reported figures; discrepancy due to slightly different counting methods
\+ Not available
\+\+ Not calculated because of lack of availability of number of total complaints

Sources:
(a) Complaints:
1975–79: not available
1980–81: Commission of the European Communities, *First Annual Report to the European Parliament on Commission Monitoring of the Application of Community Law – 1983*, COM(84)181 final (1984), p 7
1982–90: Eighth Annual Report, *op. cit.*, n 11, p 133 (Table 12)

(b) Letters of Formal Notice:
1975–80: Krislov, Ehlermann and Weiler, *op. cit.*, n 19, p 69 (Table 9)
1981–90: Eighth Annual Report, *op. cit.*, n 11, p 91 (Table 1)

(c) Reasoned Opinions:
1975–80: Krislov, Ehlermann and Weiler, *op. cit.*, n 19, p 69 (Table 9)
1981–90: Eighth Annual Report, *op. cit.*, n 11, p 91 (Table 1)

(d) References to ECJ:
1975–80: Krislov, Ehlermann and Weiler, *op. cit.*, n 19, p 69 (Table 9)
1981–90: Eighth Annual Report, *op. cit.*, n 11, p 91 (Table 1)

(e) Judgments:
1975–81: Krislov, Ehlermann and Weiler, *op. cit.*, n 19, p 69 (Table 9)
1982–84: Seventh Annual Report, *op. cit.*, n 24, p C232/37 (Table 7)
1985–90: Eighth Annual Report, *op. cit.*, n 11, p 97 (Table 7)

It is in a position to use litigation in a continuous, proactive as well as reactive way, so as to create counters, lay down conditions or establish frameworks for negotiation. In other words, it can convert litigation into a resource for structured bargaining.[49] In the context of what is essentially litigation between governments, frequently involving unresolvable conflicts and indeterminate conclusions[50], the Commission can use litigation as an aspect of its negotiating strategy.[51]

(iii) **Soft law**

A second means used by the Commission is "soft law", rules of conduct which, in principle, have no legally binding force but which, nevertheless, may have practical effects. Such measures are frequent in Community law.[52] In using soft law, the Commission also follows a practice which has been employed for some time by national administrations.[53] To give one example, beginning in 1980 after the *Cassis de Dijon* case, the Commission developed the quasi-legal form of the communication.[54] In its 1985 White Paper it announced an intention to make greater use of this device.[55]

---

[49] On law, including litigation, as a political resource, see Snyder, "Anthropology, Dispute Processing and Law" (1981) 8 J.L.& Soc. 141, 154–155; Kenis and Schneider, "The EC as an International Corporate Actor" (1987) 15 Europ.J.Pol.Res.437; von Benda-Beckmann and van der Velde (eds), *Law as a Resource in Agrarian Struggles* (1992). On structured bargaining, or bargaining with legal entitlements, see *e.g.* Clune, *Law and Public Policy: Map of an Area*, Working Paper No. 6, Robert M.Lafollette Institute of Public Affairs, University of Wisconsin-Madison, 1991, 10–11.

[50] See Hudec, "'Transcending the Ostensible': Some Reflections on the Nature of Litigation between Governments" (1987) 72 Minn.L.Rev. 211.

[51] A good example is Case 232/78 *Commission v France* [1979] ECR 2729, which was part of the lengthy negotiations leading to Council Regulation 1837/80 on the common organisation in sheepmeat and goatmeat. The use or threat of litigation in this way may be facilitated by the Maastricht Treaty revision of Articles 169 and 171 of the EEC Treaty to provide for fines or penalty payments as a result of infringements of Community law.

[52] For general discussions of Community soft law, see Wellens and Borchardt, "Soft Law in European Community Law" (1989) 14 ELR 267; Thurer, "The Role of Soft Law in the Process of European Integration" in *L'avenir du libre-echange en Europe: vers un Espace économique européen?* (Jacot-Guillarmod ed 1990); Snyder, "Soft Law and Institutional Practice in the European Community", European University Institute (EUI) Working Paper, (1993). See also Dehousse and Weiler, "EPC and the Single Act: From Soft Law to Hard Law?" in *The Future of European Political Cooperation* (Holland ed 1991); Snyder, "European Community Law and International Economic Relations: The Saga of Thai Manioc" in *Essays in Honour of Professor Wang Tieya: A Festschrift* (Macdonald ed 1993).

[53] See, *e.g.* Ganz, *Quasi-Legislation* (1987); Cliquennois, "Que reste-t-il des directives? A propos du vingtième anniversaire de l'arrêt Crédit foncier de France" (1992) 20 Act.Jur.D.A. 3; Chiti, "Circolare I: Circolare amministrattiva", *Enciclopedia Giuridica*, Vol. VI (Rome, 1988).

[54] Case 120/78 *Rewe-Zentral AG v Bundesmonopolverwaltung für Brantweinn ("Cassis De Dijon"):* [1979] ECR 649. For the Commission's interpretation of this judgement, see Commission of the European Communities, Communication from the Commission concerning the Consequences of the Judgement given by the Court of Justice on 20 February 1977 in Case 120/48 ("*Cassis de Dijon*"), OJ 1980 C256/2. See also Chapter 2, section 5(i).

[55] Commission of the European Communities, Completing the Internal Market (White Paper from the Commission to the European Council, Milan, 28–29 June 1985) COM(85)310 final, 39, para 155.

From the standpoint of the Commission, communications have several advantages.[56] They are systematic rather than piecemeal, resembling legislation rather than litigation. They are under the control of the Commission, thus in effect bypassing the Council. They are also proactive rather than reactive, enabling the Commission, without waiting for the Council or the Court of Justice, to present its interpretation and stake out its position concerning entire economic sectors. Communications play a vital role today in Commission efforts to ensure the effectiveness of Community law. They identify what is settled and what is in dispute, circumscribe the arena for debate, and define the agenda for negotiation and, if necessary, litigation. In other words, they aim to provide guidelines for negotiating the implementation of Community law.

Can this soft law become "hard" law? Communications refrain from asserting that they have legal force.[57] However, the translation from quasi-legal to legal form could occur directly by Community legislation, assuming the Member States agreed, or it could be accomplished indirectly by judicial recognition. In the latter event, two avenues are conceivable. The first involves the positive invocation of soft law. It might comprise either an action by the Commission under Article 169, using soft law as a "sword", or an action by a private party in a national court, involving the use of soft law as either "sword" or "shield", with recourse to the Court of Justice by means of Article 177. In either event, legal force could be given to a previously quasi-legal act. The second avenue might consist of an Article 173 action to annul the Commission's act. Such an action is most likely to be brought by a Member State.

Commission soft law thus is enacted and operates in the shadow of Community law. It may be used in matters concerning which the Commission has legal authority to act, within the limits of Commission discretion, and so long as it does not impose on Member States any new legal obligations. Though specific procedures, forms and conditions of publication may increase the likelihood that Soft law will be effective, these same elements risk translating soft law into hard law, if and when the soft law is contested before the Court of Justice. Exercising its power of judicial review, the Court of Justice may decide that the putatively soft law has hard legal consequences, and thus transgresses the boundary between negotiation and legislation.[58] In this event, the advantages of soft law are

---

[56] The remainder of this paragraph is drawn from my contribution to the "United Kingdom Report" in Schwarze, Govaere, Hélin and Van den Bossche (eds), *op. cit.*, n 11, p 611.

[57] See the Community framework on State aid to the motor vehicle industry, OJ 1989 C123/3, and the German reaction, which led the Commission to issue Decision 90/381 amending German aid schemes for the motor vehicle industry, OJ 1990 L188/55.

[58] An excellent illustration of this distinction, though the converse of soft law, is the PVC case concerning, *inter alia*, the legal status of the rules of procedure of the Commission: see Joined Cases T-79/89 et al, *Re the PVC Cartel: BASF and Others* v *Commission* [1992] 4 CMLR 357. See also Hill, "Court ruling imperils work of Commission" *Financial Times*, February 28, 1992; see also Case C-292/90 *British Aerospace plc and Rover Group Holdings plc* v *Commission* [1992] 1 CMLR 853.

negated, and the Commission then has little recourse except inaction or the Community legislative process.

(iv) Structural reform

A third, more general technique by which the Commission tries to ensure the effectiveness of Community law is structural reform. Structural reform means the reform or reshaping of legal, economic and political structures[59], including those of the Community or the Member States. It is a type of social, usually institutional adjustment, involving the reallocation of power. In the Community setting, such reforms are likely to affect the distribution of power between the Community and the Member States, among Community institutions and among various parts of the national governmental systems. Some of these reforms increase the effectiveness of Community law; others do not; some may possibly be neutral.

Structural reform may be undertaken by the judiciary, the administration or other parts of government. Legal scholars in Europe and the United States have concentrated mainly on the courts.[60] However, structural reform in the Community has occurred at least as much, if not more, by administrative means, in particular by relations between bureaucratic organisations. Such relations have been referred to variously as bureaucratic interpenetration[61], structural coupling[62], or inter-organisational exchange.[63] In Commission jargon they are now often called *parténariat* (partnership), a term which has recently been consecrated in Community legislation.[64]

The general legal framework of structural reform by administrative means is the duty of Community loyalty or principle of sincere co-oper-

---

[59] On the meaning of structures, see Snyder, *op. cit.*, n 2, Chapter 2. Structures have a dynamic as well as a static aspect. For the present purposes, it is useful to emphasise that structures "represent outcomes of processes that have previously occurred; they are configurations of interests, congealed at least temporarily in the form of institutionalised sets of social relations" (*ibid.* at 42). They are "simultaneously representations of previous outcomes as well as frameworks, influences and sometimes determinants of continuing conflicts and compromises" (*ibid.* at 61).
[60] See the sources cited in n 117 and n 129 below.
[61] See Scheinman, "Some Preliminary Notes on Bureaucratic Relationships in the European Economic Community" (1966) 20 Int'l Organiz. 750. See also Cassese, "Theoretical Sketch of the Cooperative and Multidimensional Nature of Community Bureaucracy" in *Community Bureaucracy at the Crossroads* (Jamar and Wessels eds 1985) and Cassese, "La costituzione europea" (1991) 11 *Quaderni Costituzionali* 487.
[62] See Teubner, "The Two Faces of Janus: Rethinking Legal Pluralism" (1992) 13 Cardozo L.Rev. 1443.
[63] See Levine and White, "Exchange as a Conceptual Framework for the Study of Interorganizational Relationships" [1961] Admin.Sci.Q. 583.
[64] For example, see Council Regulation 2052/88, art. 4(1), OJ 1988 L185/9, which provides, *inter alia*, for "une concertation étroite, entre la Commission, l'Etat membre concerné et les autorités compétentes désignées par celui-ci au niveau national, régional, local ou autre, toutes les parties étant des parténaires poursuivant un but commun. Cette concertation est ci-après denommée 'parténariat'." This example illustrates only one type of partenariat in a broader sense.

ation, the so-called "fidelity clause": Article 5 of the EC Treaty. The potential scope of this principle as applied to the Commission is illustrated by *Zwartveld*.[65] In this case the Court held that the Commission was obliged to give active assistance to a national judge who was acting in the prosecution of offences under Community law, in casu, alleged fraud against the fish marketing regulations, and who required the disclosure of information connected with the offences. It stated that the Commission was not entitled, on the basis of the 1975 Protocol on the Privileges and Immunities of the European Communities, to refuse to disclose documents which might otherwise be confidential or to permit its officials to refuse to give evidence as witnesses in national proceedings. Such refusals would breach Article 5 unless they were based on an order issued by the Court of Justice.

Conversely, Member States are also governed by Article 5. According to Temple Lang[66], the "fidelity clause" affects their participation in four different ways. First, Member States may have a legal duty, in certain circumstances, to consult the Commission, especially if there is any doubt as to whether a national measure is contrary to Community law, in particular to avoid the risk of infringing Community rules. Secondly, Member States may have a duty to provide information if the Commission believes it needs certain information and requests it. Thirdly, the Commission and the Member States have a reciprocal duty of co-operation in the Community sphere, that is, "when Member States are implementing Community measures or policies, are acting on behalf of the Community, or are using powers which are regulated by the Community".[67] Fourthly, Article 5 may conceivably be invoked to prevent a Member State from insisting on "linkage" between unrelated measures in Council discussions; it is at least arguable that a similar rule might apply to negotiations in the form of inter-organisational exchange.

Some forms of inter-organisational exchange are initiated by the Commission, acting on the basis of Articles 4 and 155. Current examples include dialogue with Member States in the preparation of transposing legislation, sectoral or "package" meetings, and horizontal meetings between the Commission and national administrations to review progress in the application of directives.[68] Also important are exchanges of staff between the Commission and national departments responsible for applying Community law. Inter-organisational exchange is not necessarily lim-

---

[65] Case C-2/88 *J.J. Zwartveld and Others* [1990] 3 CMLR 457; see also Emiliou, Sharpston and Snyder, "European Community Law" in *Current Legal Problems 1992*, Vol. 45, Pt. 1: *Annual Review* (Pettet ed 1992), 58.

[66] Temple Lang, "Community Constitutional Law: Article 5 of the EEC Treaty" (1990) 27 *Comm. Mkt. L. Rev.* 645.

[67] *Ibid.* 655. See also Case C-33/90 *Re Toxic Waste in Campania EC Commission v Italy* [1992] 2 CMLR 353.

[68] See Commission, *op. cit.*, n 24, p C232/6, Commission, *op. cit.*, n 11, p *iv*. With regard to environmental matters, see Macrory, "The enforcement of Community Environmental Law: Some Critical Issues" (1992) 29 *Comm. Mkt. L. Rev.* 347, 348 n 5, 362 n 35.

ited, however, to national administrations. The Commission has long maintained close continuing contacts with non-governmental organisations concerned with development, and it has recently initiated contacts with other groups, such as environmental organisations.[69]

Neither the fluidity of the setting nor the importance of negotiation, however, serves to expand the legal power of the Commission, at least if this power is contested in the Court of Justice. In the French case involving the Code of Conduct[70], the Commission argued that it was entitled to take certain informal measures, having no legal force, within the framework of its parténariat with national administrations.[71] It suggested that Article 189 did not prevent the conclusion of consensual arrangements with Member States concerning the scope of a provision of Community law: the consensus itself guaranteed legal certainty for the parties, who in practice were perfectly aware of their obligations, while the arrangement did not affect third parties.[72] However, the Commission's argument was rejected by the Court of Justice, which, without examining whether the measure in question had been negotiated and agreed, concluded that the Commission lacked the power to adopt any such acts.

As a technique for ensuring the effectiveness of Community law, these types of structural reform are largely incremental. Other types, however, may occasionally be dramatic, at least when viewed in the longer term. These are forms of inter-organisational exchange which are broader in scope, often initially unforeseen or even unintended. The most striking examples are the changes in national administrations which have resulted from the practical requirements of Community membership. These changes can be grouped into five categories.[73]

First, Community membership has led in some countries to changes in the relationship between the executive and the legislature. For example, in Italy and France the need to ensure the transposition of EC directives has resulted recently in a much greater delegation of legislative power by the parliament to the executive.[74] Secondly, Member States with divided-power systems have had to reconsider, and sometimes clarify, the constitutional allocation of powers with regard to the enactment, transpo-

---

[69] See Commission of the European Communities, Proposal for a Council Directive on packaging and packaging waste, COM(92)278 final – SYN 436 (15 July 1992), 70. See also Harlow, "A Community of Interests: Making the Most of European Law" (1992) 55 Mod. L. Rev. 331.

[70] C-303/90 *France* v *Commission*, judgment of November 13, 1991; see also (1991) 5615 *Agence Europe* 15 (23 November 1991).

[71] *Ibid. Rapport d'audience*, 20, para 18.

[72] *Ibid.* 20, para 19.

[73] Some of these categories are also identified in Meny, "Variation sur un thème donné: l'application des directives par les Etats membres" (1985) 34 Rev.Fr.Admin.Publique 179, 182.

[74] See Boulouis, "La incidencia del Derecho comunitario en la organizacion administrativa francesa" (1992) 9 *Administracion de Andalucia, Revista Andaluza de Administracion Publica* 51; Gaja, "New Developments in a Continuing Story: The Relationship between EEC Law and Italian Law" (1990) 27 *Comm. Mkt. L. Rev.* 83, 89–93; Grottanelli de Santi, "The Impact of EC Integration on the Italian Form of Government" in *Italy and EC Membership Evaluated* (Francioni ed 1992), 184–186.

sition and implementation of Community law. This has occurred, for example, in Spain, Belgium, Italy and Germany.[75] Indeed, the origin of the term "subsidiarity" in Community law is widely ascribed to a spring 1988 meeting between Commission President Jacques Delors and representatives of the German Länder.[76] Third, Community membership has required all Member States, not only to establish representatives in Brussels, known collectively as COREPER[77], but also to maintain continuing links between COREPER and national administrations. With the increasing development of the Community, these links have tended to give less prominence to ministries concerned with general diplomatic matters and more to technical ministries.[78]

Fourth, special administrative bodies dealing with Community matters have been established, special sections within some existing departments have been created and the substance of work in numerous departments has changed. In the United Kingdom, for example, accession to the Community required the establishment of the Intervention Board for Agricultural Produce, as well as major changes in the work of the Ministry of Agriculture and Fisheries, Customs and Excise and the Department of Trade and Industry.[79] Fifth, in virtually all Member States Community membership has led to the development of mechanisms to co-ordinate participation in the making and implementing of Community law. Among the most well-known examples are European Secretariat of the Cabinet Office in the United Kingdom[80], the SGCI in France[81] and the *Dipartimento per il coordinamento delle politiche comunitarie* in Italy.[82] These institutions are especially important for the present purposes, since a lack of co-ordination within national administrations has been among the major reasons for delays in the implementation of Community law.[83]

---

[75] See, *e.g. Bayerische Staatsregierung* (Bavarian Government) v *Bundesregierung* (German Federal Government) (Case 2 BvG 1/89) before the *Bundesvergassungsgericht* (German Federal Constitutional Court): [1990] 1 CMLR 649.

[76] See Wilke and Wallace, *Subsidiarity: Approaches to Power-sharing in the European Community*, RIIA Discussion Papers 27 (London: The Royal Institute of International Affairs, 1990), 3–4.

[77] See Tortora de Falco, *Il Comitato dei Rappresentanti permanenti dai Trattati istitutivi alla prassi Comunitaria* (1980).

[78] See Hayes-Renshaw, Lequesne and Mayor Lopez, "The Permanent Representatives of the Member States to the European Communities" (1989) 28 J.C.M.S. 119; Lesquesne, "L'adaptation des administrations nationales à l'existence des Communautés européennes: Le cas des ministères francais" (1987) 42 Rev.Fr.Admin.Publique 275.

[79] See also Bender, "Whitehall, Central Government and 1992" (1991) 6 Publ.Pol.& Adm. 13.

[80] See Le Sueur and Snyder, "La incidencia del Derecho de la Comunidad europea en la organizion administrativa del Reino Unido" (1992) 9 *Administracion de Andalucia, Revista Andaluza de Administracion Publica* 67.

[81] *Secrétariat général du comité interministériel pour les questions de co-opération économique européenne*: see Meny, "France" in Siedentopf and Ziller (eds), *op. cit.*, n 10, pp 285–294; Boulouis, *op. cit.*, n 74.

[82] See Chiti, "Il Coordinamento delle Politiche Comunitarie e la Riforma degli Apparati di Governo" (1989–90) 1 *Associazione per Gli Studi e le Ricerche Parlamentari* 235; Chiti, "La creacion y ejecucion del Derecho comunitario en los Estados compuestos: Italia" (1992) 9 *Administracion de Andalucia, Revista Andaluza de Administracion Publica* 11.

[83] See Commission of the European Communities, "Implementation of the Legal Acts required to build the Single Market" COM(90)473 final (1990), 2, 7, paras 5, 23.

For both the Commission and national administrations, structural reform serves useful purposes. The Commission is able to fulfil its functions only by entering into relations with national administrations, and vice versa. For example, each needs clients (*e.g.* national administrative support for Commission proposals), labour services (*e.g.* experts of different types) and other resources (*e.g.* information). Indeed, despite continuing problems concerning the delineation of organisational domains, whether in terms of legal competence or political terrain, such inter-organisational exchanges have become indispensable, both to segments of the Commission on the one hand and parts of national bureaucracies on the other.

In addition, inter-organisational exchange has been concerned increasingly with the effectiveness of Community law. Recent Commission monitoring reports note that "contacts between Commission departments and national authorities concerning the implementation of Community law have been stepped up".[84] As the Commission pointed out:

> "Beyond the formal incorporation of Community Directives into national law, there is the problem of how the rules are actually applied by the national authorities. Private individuals very rarely come into contact with Community law or the Community authorities, such contacts generally being established via national legislation or a national department. It is for this reason that consistency in application is important. As this is a matter of administrative practices rather than of legal rules, consistency can be guaranteed only by exchanges of experience. This was the approach adopted by the Mattheus programme in the customs field, and it is an approach which the Commission proposes to extend to other areas covered by a body of Community rules".[85]

In such exchanges the meaning of compliance – the effectiveness of Community law – is negotiated or "constructed" by the Commission and its national counterparts.[86] At the same time these negotiations contribute to the gradual reshaping of both Community and national institutions.

4 The development of a judicial liability system

(i) Introduction

Among the central problems of the effectiveness of Community law has been the failure of Member States to transpose Community directives into national law. During the past twenty-five years, the Court of Justice

---

[84] Seventh Annual Report, *op. cit.*, n 24, p C232/6; Eighth Annual Report, *op. cit.*, n 11, *iv.*
[85] Seventh Annual Report, *op. cit.*, n 24, p C232/7.
[86] See also Clune, *op. cit.*, n 40, p 65.

'TRULY OUTSTANDING'

So said Professor Van Gervan, former Advocate General at the Court of Justice, Luxembourg about **Remedies in EC Law: Law and Practice in the English and EC Courts,** by Mark Brealey and Mark Hoskins.

It has proved to be a highly successful and truly ground-breaking work, providing both authoritative commentary on the substantive law and expert guidance on how to apply it in practical situations.

This book enables you to gain a full understanding of:

- how EC law applies in the English courts
- the remedies available in English courts for breach of EC law
- the remedies available in EC courts for breach of EC law

■ Practical treatment

The authors combine authoritative legal information with practical treatment, including relevant case law, hands-on procedural guidance and a full set of precedents and sample pleadings. This means that the advice they provide can be quickly translated into a series of practical measures. You may even come across otherwise undiscovered ways of protecting or defending your clients' interests.

■ What some of the Reviewers have said ...

"The authors display impressive insight." **European Law Review**

"Those who are looking for a book which can be clutched with confidence in court and cited if necessary to the judge will ... be particularly grateful for Brealey and Hoskins."
International and Comparative Law Quarterly

"Practitioners should reach for this book as soon as they spot an issue of Community law."
The Law Society's Gazette

"Written in an accessible manner, it is not only pleasant to read but also a reliable reference book to be consulted in daily practice." **International Insurance Law Review**

**REMEDIES
—— IN ——
EC LAW**

Mark Brealey
and
Mark Hoskins

Foreword by Judge David Edward

FT
LAW & TAX

Remedies in EC Law provides practical information on:

1. Application of EC Law in the English Courts
Sources of EC Law
Supremacy of EC Law
Direct Effect
Interpretation

2. Remedies in English Courts for Breach of EC Law
Effective Protection of EC Law Rights
Damages
Injunctions
Restitution
Judicial Review

3. Preliminary References
References to the Court of Justice for a Preliminary Ruling

4. Remedies in EC Courts for

Breach of EC Law
Proceedings Against Member States for Breach of EC Law
Judicial Review of EC Acts—Article 173 of the EC Treaty
Plea of Illegality—Article 184 of the EC Treaty
Judicial Review of Failure to Act—Article 175 of the EC Treaty
Suing the Community in Damages
Interim Relief—Articles 185 and 186 of the EC Treaty
Procedure Before the EC Courts

5. Precedents

6. Appendices
Rules of Procedure of the EC Courts

Please send me **Remedies in EC Law** by Brealey and Hoskins on 21 days' FREE approval
If I am not satisfied with the book, I will return it in good condition and owe nothing.

I would like _____copy/ies of
REMEDIES IN EC LAW: LAW AND PRACTICE IN THE ENGLISH AND EC COURTS
Published: May 1994 Price: £82.95
(prices include p&p and may change without notice)
ISBN: 085121 9551

NAME _____
TITLE _____
FIRM _____
ADDRESS _____
_____
_____
POSTCODE _____
TEL NO. _____
NATURE OF BUSINESS
_____

☐ Please invoice my firm
☐ Cheque enclosed for:
£ _____
(Please make payable to Pearson Professional)
Please charge to my:
Access /MasterCard/Visa /Carte Bleu
Diners Club/Amercian Express

CARD NO. _____
EXPIRY DATE _____
SIGNATURE _____
DATE _____

RETURN TO: FT Law & Tax
FREEPOST
21-27 Lamb's Conduit Street
London, WC1N 3BR

OR CALL FREEPHONE: 0800 289 618
(please quote reference EP/068 when ordering)

FT Law & Tax, formerly Longman Law, Tax & Finance
is a Division of **Pearson Professional**
Registered address: Maple House, 149 Tottenham Court
Road, London, W1P 9LL Registered Number: 2970324

has responded to this problem, not by negotiation, as in the case of the Commission, but in processes of adjudication. In seeking to fulfil its role – set out in Article 164 of the EC Treaty – of ensuring "that in the application and interpretation of this Treaty the law is observed", the Court of Justice has created a judicial liability system. By "judicial liability system" is meant a set of institutional arrangements in which "a liability rule is established providing that one person or organization can seek relief from a government agency for specified conduct".[87] The system is triggered by complaints brought by injured parties; the government agency need not of course be a court.[88] The judicial liability system of the Community has been elaborated by the Court of Justice less by design than in an ad hoc, reactive and unsystematic manner. As a result, its constituent elements are often viewed merely as individual cases and discrete, though related, principles. If one seeks to compare Community institutions with regard to ensuring the effectiveness of Community law, however, these elements can be seen to be interconnected, interdependent, forming a coherent whole and in this sense systematic.

Directives typically lay down a deadline for transposition, and it is assumed in Article 189 of the EC Treaty that they will be transposed before or by the deadline. Article 189 also assumes that once a Directive has been transposed into national law, an individual upon whom the Directive has conferred rights will rely, not on the Directive, but on the national transposing legislation. By virtue of its unique characteristics, a Directive is ideally suited to a federal or confederal system. In principle, it provides a Community umbrella which allows for national diversity and variation within the range and scope permitted by the terms of the Directive.

Two features of a directive thus are especially pertinent from the standpoint of ensuring the effectiveness of Community law. On the one hand, directives involve a two-phase legislative procedure, in which, following the enactment of the directive at Community level, Member States must transpose the directive into national law. On the other hand, directives are designed to harmonise national legislation rather than to make it absolutely uniform, with the result that national transposing legislation may differ in each Member State. Each of these features raises a well-known problem of effectiveness. On the one hand, Member States may not fulfil their legal obligation to transpose a directive into national law, either by failing to enact the transposing legislation, or by transposing a directive inadequately or partially. On the other hand, uniform application of Community law depends partly upon mutual recognition, partly upon national administrations, and partly upon litigation in national courts; its effectiveness may thus often depend upon national political and legal systems.

---

[87] Clune and Lindquist, *op. cit.*, n 40, p 1083.
[88] *Ibid.* pp 1083–1084.

These problems are, for three reasons, especially serious in the Community now and in the near future. First, the Directive is the main legislative act for completing the Single Market. Secondly, by virtue of its structure and purpose it is, of all Community acts, the one that is the most consistent with the principle of subsidiarity. Thirdly, though the question whether the Directive should be replaced as a Community act has long been discussed[89], the 1991 Intergovernmental Conference on Political Union rejected a proposal for the incorporation into the treaty of a "Community law"[90], a new act of the Community under Article 189 that would have been adopted by the co-decision procedure. Instead it settled for a Declaration on the Hierarchy of Community Acts[91], annexed to the Maastricht Treaty, according to which the Member States agreed to reconvene the Intergovernmental Conference in 1996 to examine to what extent it might be possible to review the classification of Community acts with a view to establishing an appropriate hierarchy between the different categories of act.[92] As a result, the most frequently used type of Community act in the near future is likely to remain the directive.

The Court of Justice has elaborated the elements of the judicial liability system in four overlapping stages. They concerned the direct effect of directives, the interpretation of national legislation, the availability of compensation and the potential harmonisation of national remedies.

---

[89] See Boulouis, *Droit institutionnel des Communautes europennes* (1st ed, 1984), 14. The European Parliament's pre-SEA Draft Treaty for a European Union provided for the directive to be replaced by a "law", a legislative act having the character of framework legislation: see Article 34(1), OJ 1984 C77/41–42.

[90] The original proposal for a revised Article 189 provided, *inter alia*, that:

"A Community law shall have general application. Its provisions may either be binding in their entirety and directly applicable in all Member States or may be binding, as to the result to be achieved, upon the Member States, but shall leave to the national authorities the choice of form and methods. . ."

The Community law was designed to establish, in the Community legal order, a hierarchy of norms similar to that found in national legal systems. It was to be used to establish basic principles and general policies; in addition, certain matters would be reserved for determination by a Community law. Among its stated advantages was that "en particulier, il devient possible, dans ce schéma, de faire désormais l'économie de l'instrument hybride, et de statut ambigu, que constitue, à l'heure actuelle, la directive" (Commission, Document de travail SG(91)4021, février 27, 1991, 3). On the Luxembourg Presidency's revised draft of Articles 189 and 189a of the proposed Treaty, see: "Draft Treaty of the Union" (1991) 1722/1723 *Agence Europe* (July 5, 1991), 17–18.

[91] The reference to a new Community law was eliminated in the Dutch Presidency's second draft. In its place, a Declaration was drafted for inclusion in the Final Act of the Conference, and this Declaration was agreed with the final draft of the Treaty: see "Draft Union Treaty (Dutch Presidency's Working Document)" (1991) 1746/1747 *Agence Europe* (20 November 1991), 14–15.

[92] Declaration on the Hierarchy of Community Acts (Declaration 16); reprinted in (1992) 1 CMLR 719, 785.

(ii) **The direct effect of directives**

Though the direct effect of directives was implicit in *Grad*[93], it was not held expressly to be possible until *SACE*.[94] The European Court first held a Directive on its own to be directly effective in *Van Duyn*.[95] The rationale for these decisions was the principle of effet utile. In *Ratti*[96] the Court held that a Directive may have direct effect, if at all, only after the expiration of the deadline for transposition. In contrast to the earlier cases, this decision was based on a type of Community estoppel, the idea that a Member State should not be allowed to profit from its own failure to fulfil its Community obligations.[97]

All of these cases involved claims by individuals against governments. The question whether a Directive could be invoked by one individual against another was settled in the *Marshall* case.[98] The Court held that a Directive could not be invoked horizontally, that is, by one individual against another. It considered that according to Article 189, and consistently with the idea of estoppel, a Directive is binding only on Member States. Consequently, "a Directive may not of itself impose obligations on an individual".[99]

In elaborating these principles, the Court of Justice addressed a central problem with regard to the effectiveness of Community law. Article 189 of the EC Treaty assumes that Member States will transpose directives into national law by the specified deadline. Member States failed increasingly to do so. Individuals were therefore not able to invoke rights conferred upon them by Community directives. The Court of Justice filled this gap by recognising that a directive could have vertical direct effect. This recognition formed the first plank in the judicial liability system.

(iii) **The interpretation of national legislation**

Nevertheless, important problems remained. Indeed, each successive judicial decision both resolved outstanding questions and opened up new areas of controversy. Three issues proved especially difficult. First, a direc-

---

[93] Case 9/70 *Grad* v *Finanzamt Trautstein* [1970] ECR 825.
[94] Case 33/70 *SpA SACE* v *Ministry for Finance of the Italian Republic* [1970] ECR 1213.
[95] Case 41/74 *Van Duyn* v *Home Office* [1974] ECR 1337, see also Chapter 2, text accompanying n 31.
[96] Case 148/78 *Publicco Ministero* v *Ratti* [1979] ECR 1629.
[97] This was the first time the European Court used the idea of Community estoppel, according to Pescatore, "The Doctrine of 'Direct Effect': An Infant Disease in Community Law" (1983) 8 ELR 155, 169. See also Curtin, "The Province of Government: Delimiting the Direct Effect of Directives in the Common Law Context" (1990) 15 E. L. Rev. 195.
[98] Case 152/84 *Marshall* v *Southampton & Southwest Hampshire Area Health Authority (Teaching)* [1986] ECR 723.
[99] *Ibid.* at 749, para 48. On the procedural implications of this case, see Prechal, "Remedies after *Marshall*" (1990) 27 CMLR 451. As to the definition of the State, see Case C-188/89 *Foster* v *British Gas* [1990] ECR 3313.

tive could not be enforced by one private party against another. Second, once a directive had been transposed into national law, the relationship between the directive and the national transposing legislation was not entirely clear.[100] Third, this confusion was acute in the case of directives which did not have direct effect, but which were eventually transposed into national law.[101]

Confronted with these problems, the Court of Justice was to employ the technique of judicial interpretation. In order to settle the last two issues, it relied on the doctrines of effet utile and estoppel, together with the Article 5 of the EC Treaty "fidelity clause".[102] In *von Colson*[103] and *Harz*[104], the Court laid down certain rules of construction, which were to be used by national courts for interpreting national legislation designed to implement Community directives. Even when a directive did not have direct effect, a national court, in applying the provisions of a national law specifically introduced to implement the directive, was required to interpret its national law in the light of the wording and the purpose of the directive.[105]

However, some national courts continued to interpret national legislation according to national methods of interpretation, even if the directive was enacted prior to the national legislation. This difficulty arose especially in the United Kingdom, with its distinctive tradition of statutory interpretation.[106] In addition, the guideline from the Court of Justice did not seem to cover the situation in which the Community directive was not directly effective and the national legislation appeared to be perfectly clear; this view was held for example in France.[107]

---

[100] The Court of Justice has held, however, that if a directive has been correctly implemented, individuals must rely on national transposing legislation, not on the directive: Case 270/81 *Felicitas Rickmers-Linie KG & Co.* v *Finanzamt für Verkehrsteuern, Hamburg* [1982] ECR 2771; see also Case C-208/90 *Emmott* v *Minister for Social Welfare* [1991] 3 CMLR 894, 915.

[101] For more detailed discussion, see my section on directives and national law in Emiliou, Sharpston and Snyder, *op. cit.*, n 65, pp 59–61.

[102] See Temple Lang, *op. cit.*, n 66; Constantinesco, "L'article 5 CEE, de la bonne foi à la loyauté communautaire" in *Du droit international au droit de l'intégration: Liber Amicorum Pierre Pescatore* (Capotorti, Ehlermann, Frowein, Jacobs, Joliet, Koopmans, and Kovar [eds], 1987).

[103] Case 14/83 *von Colson and Kamann* v *Land Nordrhein-Westfalen* [1984] ECR 1891.

[104] Case 79/83 *Harz* v *Deutsche Tradax* [1984] ECR 1921.

[105] *von Colson, op. cit.*, n 103; *Harz, op. cit.*, n 104. This rule of construction is subject to the general principles of legal certainty and non-retroactivity: Case 80/86 *Criminal Proceedings against Kolpinghuis Nijmegen* [1987] ECR 3969; see also Case C-262/88 *Barber* v *Guardian Royal Exchange* [1990] ECR I-1889.

[106] See *Duke* v *Reliance* [1988] 1 All ER 626; *Finnegan* v *Clowney Youth Training Programme* [1990] 2 All ER 546. For discussion, see Howells, "European Directives – The Emerging Dilemmas" (1991) 54 *Mod. L. Rev.* 456, 461–463.

[107] See Galmot and Bonichot, "La Cour de Justice des Communautés européennes et la transposition des directives en droit national" (1988) 4 Rev.Fr.Dr.Admin. 1, 22. As to the subsequent change in the case law of the Conseil d'Etat, see *Application of Raoul Georges Nicolo*, October 20, 1989, [1990] 1 CMLR 173, noted in (1990) 15 *E. L. Rev.* 267.

In November 1990 the Court of Justice decided *Marleasing*[108], which expanded and clarified the scope of its guidelines for the interpretation of national legislation in the light of Community directives. *Marleasing* was an Article 177 reference from a Spanish court. The parties in the main action were both private parties; the Community directive in question had not been transposed into national law; and the directive omitted basic substantive rules embodied in the national legislation. The Court of Justice restated that a directive could not have horizontal direct effect. Nevertheless, it stated that national courts, called upon to determine a dispute in a matter falling within the sphere of application of a directive, are required to interpret their national legislation, as far as possible, in the light of the wording and the purpose of the Directive. In contrast to previous cases, this obligation was stated expressly to apply to national legislation enacted either before or after the directive. According to the Court of Justice, the obligation flows from two sources: first, the obligation imposed on Member States by Article 189 of the EC Treaty to achieve the results provided for in directives, and, second, the obligation of Community loyalty stated in Article 5 of the EC Treaty.

This broad guideline was the second plank in the development by the Court of a judicial liability system. It bears especially heavily on national courts. Not only does it enlist their co-operation in referring cases to Luxembourg for preliminary rulings. It also requires them to confront expressly the distinctive judicial techniques of Community law. Moreover, it may go even further by requiring them to re-appraise, modify or even abandon, in the light of Community law, some of the time-honoured techniques of their national legal systems. *Marleasing* may enable private parties inter se to rely on Community directives, at least provisionally and in some circumstances. However, given the diversity of the legal systems of the Member States, *Marleasing* is likely to be only a short-lived solution to the problem of the effectiveness of Community law that is posed by the nature of directives.

(iv) **The availability of compensation**

A Community directive may confer rights on individuals, but be too imprecise to have direct effect. If a Member State fails to transpose the directive into national law, it in effect deprives individuals of otherwise enforceable Community rights. The failure is the more flagrant if the Member State continues not to transpose the Directive even after a suc-

---

[108] Case C-106/89 *Marleasing* v *La Comercial International de Alimentacion SA* [1990] ECR 1, noted Stuyck and Wytinck (1991) 28 *Comm. Mkt. L. Rev.* 205–223, Mead (1991) 16 E. L. Rev. 490; see also Curtin "Directives: The Effectiveness of Judicial Protection of Individual Rights" (1990) 27 *Comm. Mkt. L. Rev.* 709; De Burca, "Giving Effect to European Community directives" (1992) 55 Mod. L. Rev. 215.

cessful infringement proceeding by the Commission. It may also be the case that no national legislation falls within the ambit of the directive, so, unlike *Marleasing*, the dilemma cannot be resolved by judicial interpretation. An opportunity to formulate a solution to this conundrum arose in *Francovich*.[109]

Briefly, Council Directive 80/897 sought to ensure employees throughout the Community a minimum level of protection in case of insolvency of their employer. Specific guarantees were provided for the payment of unpaid remuneration. Member States were required to implement the Directive by October 1983. In *Commission* v *Italy*[110] the Court of Justice held that the Italian Republic had failed to comply with its obligation. Subsequently various employees of undertakings which became insolvent, leaving substantial arrears of salary unpaid, brought proceedings in Italy against the Italian Republic. They sought payment of the compensation provided for by the Directive or, alternatively, damages. By means of the Article 177 procedure the Court of Justice was asked, inter alia, whether the State was liable to pay compensation for harm suffered by an individual as a result of its failure to transpose the Directive.

In a bold judgment the Court of Justice accepted the principle of State liability. It stated that the full effectiveness of Community rules might be called into question, and the protection of enforceable Community rights would be weakened, if individuals could not obtain compensation where their rights were infringed by a breach of Community law for which a Member State was responsible. The possibility of compensation was particularly important where the effectiveness of Community rules was subject to action by the State and where, if the State failed to act, individuals could not vindicate their Community rights before national courts. According to the Court, the principle of liability of the state in such a case was inherent in the scheme of the Treaty and also followed from the Article 5 of the EC Treaty "fidelity clause".

The principle of State liability is a new development in Community law.[111] It was not previously recognised by the Court of Justice, though the Commission had considered for some time that Article 5 of the EC Treaty, together with the general principles of Community law, required Member States to provide a compensation scheme for private individuals whose interests are prejudiced by government acts conflicting with Community law.[112] The precise scope of Member State liability remains of

---

[109] Joined Cases C-6/90 and C-9/90 *Francovich and Bonifaci* v *Italy* [1992] IRLR 84. For further discussion, see Duffy, *op. cit.*, n 31; Szyszczak, *op. cit.*, n 31; Curtin, *op. cit.*, n 31.

[110] [1989] ECR 143.

[111] For a summary of the previous position, see Bronckers, "Private enforcement of 1992: Do Trade and Industry Stand a Chance Against the Member States?" (1989) 26 *Comm. Mkt. L. Rev.* 513, 519–520; Barav, "Damages in the Domestic Courts for Breach of Community Law by National Public Authorities" in *Non-Contractual Liability in the European Communities* (Schermers, Heukels and Mead eds, 1988).

[112] See Bronckers, *ibid.* 519–520; see also Mattera, *op. cit.*, n 44, pp 700–704, and the text at n 31 above.

course to be determined. It is not clear, for example, whether it extends to all directives which meet the conditions stated by the Court[113]; whether it applies to Community acts other than directives; and whether national courts, as well as the European Court, are entitled to determine a breach of Community law leading to liability.[114]

Even as it stands, the *Francovich* principle, though not exactly "a charter for private sector employees"[115], is likely to give individuals, organisations and their lawyers a significant instrument to use in national courts in enforcing Community law against their national governments, with eventual recourse to the Court of Justice under Article 177.[116] Of equal importance for the effectiveness of Community law is the broader impact of the judgment. First, the principle of State liability may prove a powerful political and legal symbol. A declaration of liability

> "creates an abstraction, an absolute claim on public resources. Through its visibility and its authoritative source, it commands central attention on the crowded public agenda. A judicial declaration demands responsive action, and it stirs political actors to prepare such a response."[117]

Secondly, the *Francovich* case is likely to have an effect on relations between the Community and the Member States. The principle of State liability is embodied in a complex judgment, yet its generality and ambiguity may help to create an expectation that the principle might be enforced. Thirdly, this expectation in itself is likely to be an element, implicit if not explicit, in bargaining processes between the Commission and Member States, especially concerning the implementation of Community law.[118] The principle of State liability represents the third plank in the judicial liability system elaborated by the Court of Justice.

(v) Towards the harmonisation of national remedies?

In *Francovich* the Court of Justice recalled that, in the absence of Community provisions, it was for national legal systems to lay down the pro-

---

[113] Liability was said to be subject to three conditions. First, the result laid down by the directive must involve rights conferred upon individuals. Secondly, the content of those rights must be identifiable on the basis of the provisions of the directive. Thirdly, there must be a causal link between the Member State's failure to fulfil its obligations and the damage suffered by the persons affected.

[114] See also the sources cited in n 31 above.

[115] "Highlights: February 1992", (1992) 21 IRLR 53.

[116] It has been argued that individuals should be able to seek the grant of an injunction or the award of damages against a Member State which adopts a measure in breach of a directly effective rule of Community law, and also that in principle they should be able to rely on these rules even in the case of Community rules which are not directly effective: see Temple Lang, *op. cit.*, n 66, p 653.

[117] Diver, "The Judge as Political Powerbroker: Superintending Structural Change in Public Institutions" (1979) 65 Virg.L.Rev. 43, 80.

[118] See also Elmore, *op. cit.*, n 36, pp 220–221.

cedural steps for legal action to ensure the full protection of Community rights.[119] These "conditions of substance and form" were not to be less favourable than those governing national remedies, and they were not to make the enforcement of Community rights impossible.[120] While thus recognising that Community rights are to be enforced primarily in national courts[121], the Court's jurisprudence has none the less impinged increasingly on national legal remedies. At the same time as national administrative law is being influenced considerably by general principles of Community law, such as proportionality[122], the Court of Justice is beginning to contribute to the restructuring of national procedural systems.[123]

In the celebrated *Factortame* case the Court of Justice set aside the rule of English constitutional law that an injunction cannot be granted against the Crown, at least where the rule prevents the enforcement of a right conferred by Community law.[124] In *Emmott* it declared that, where an individual wishes to rely as against a Member State on rights contained in a directly effective Directive, time does not begin to run, and therefore the individual cannot be time-barred even under the normal domestic rules on limitations of actions, until such time as the Directive has been properly transposed into national law.[125] More recently, in *Zuckerfabrik*[126] the Court held that interim measures should be available when the legality of Community law was being questioned before a national court, and a national court has a duty to consider granting such relief if requested by a party to do so.[127] These steps towards the gradual reshaping of national remedies can be viewed as a fourth element in the Community judicial liability system.

The four elements in this system need to be appreciated as a whole from two different perspectives. Seen from the bottom up, they help to provide judicial protection for the individual. Seen from the top down,

---

[119] Joined cases C-6/90 and C-9/60 *Francovich and Bonifaci* v *Italy op. cit.*, n 31 at 93, para 42.
[120] See Case 45/76 *Comet* v *Produktschap voor Siergewassen*: [1976] ECR 2043.
[121] See Green and Barav, "Damages in the National Courts for Breach of Community Law" (1986) 6 Y.E.L. 55; Oliver, "Enforcing Community Rights in English Courts" (1987) 50 Mod. L. Rev. 881; Steiner, "How to make the action suit the case: Domestic Remedies for Breach of EEC Law" (1987) 12 E. L. Rev. 102; Ward, "Government Liability in the United Kingdom for Breach of Individual Rights in European Community Law" (1990) 19 Anglo-Am.L.Rev. 1.
[122] See Schwärze, *European Administrative Law* (1991).
[123] See Duffy, *op. cit.*, n 31, pp 137–138.
[124] Case C-221/89 *R.* v *Secretary of State for Transport, ex p Factortame Ltd and Others* [1991] 3 CMLR 589.
[125] Including where the directive has been implemented but in terms which vary from the directive such that the implementing measure does not fully represent the rights contained in the directive: Case C-208/90 *Emmott* v *Minister for Social Welfare* [1991] 3 CMLR 894, 916, para 23.
[126] Joined Cases C-143/88 and C-92/89 *Zuckerfabrik Suderdithmaschen and Zuckerfabrik Soest* v *Hauptzollamt Itzehoe* [1991] ECR I-415, noted Schermers (1992) 29 *Comm. Mkt. L. Rev.* 133.
[127] In addition, the conditions for suspending Community acts could not vary from one Member State to another. See further Oliver, "Interim Measures: Some Recent Developments" (1992) 27 *Comm. Mkt. L. Rev.* 7, 24–25; Barav, "Enforcement of Community Rights in the National Courts: The Case for Jurisdiction to Grant Interim Relief" (1989) 26 Comm. Mkt.L.Rev. 369.

they perform an essentially political function of social control.[128] These two perspectives are complementary, one representing the view of individual actors or organisations, and the other representing a conception of the Community legal system as a whole. Both perspectives are essential in order to understand the contribution and the limits of the judicial liability system in ensuring the effectiveness of Community law.

Seen from the second perspective, the judicial liability system embodies a type of structural reform, not by administrative negotiation but by adjudication. In the United States constitutional lawyers have focused on the Supreme Court. In the late 1970s they identified a new kind of public law litigation, "institutional litigation", which

> "typically requires the courts to scrutinize the operation of large public institutions. The suits are generally brought by persons subject to the control of the institutions who seek as relief some relatively elaborate rearrangement of the institution's mode of operation".[129]

Views have differed as to the novelty of institutional litigation.[130] All agree, however, that, in institutional litigation, "[l]itigation inevitably becomes an explicitly political forum and the court a visible arm of the political process".[131]

It is tempting to apply these observations to the Court of Justice. After all, in the Community, as in the United States, the institutional vacuum resulting from executive and legislative inaction led to an increased role for the judiciary. In both systems, the appropriateness of such a judicial response has been the subject of intense controversy.[132]

It is suggested, however, that the precise analogy is misplaced. First, the Court of Justice is activated by individuals and organisations who, in contrast to plaintiffs in American institutional litigation, are not inmates of institutions in any specific sense. Secondly, the judicial liability system in the Community has been developed by the Court of Justice mainly

---

[128] This point is argued forcefully with regard to appeal courts in general in Shapiro, "Appeal" (1980) 14 L.& Soc.Rev. 629. Note that a similar dual role in the Community legal order is played by the concept of institutional balance: see the Opinion by Advocate-General Van Gerven in Case 70/88 *European Parliament* v *Council* [1990] ECR I-2041. Whether such a duality of function is characteristic of other basic concepts of Community constitutional and administrative law remains to be seen.

[129] Eisenberg and Yeazell, "The Ordinary and the Extraordinary in Institutional Litigation" (1980) 93 Harv.L.Rev. 465, 467–468. See also, *e.g.* Chayes, "The Role of the Judge in Public Law Litigation" (1976) 89 Harv.L.Rev. 1281; Cox, "The New Dimensions of Constitutional Litigation" (1976) 51 Wash.L.Rev. 791; Diver, *op. cit.*, n 117.

[130] Chayes and Cox argue that its procedures and remedies depart significantly from the model of traditional litigation: see Chayes, *op. cit.*, n 129 ; Cox, *op. cit.*, n 129. In contrast, Eisenberg and Yeazell, *op. cit.*, n 129, suggest that the only new features are its substance, especially new rights, and its power.

[131] Chayes, *op. cit.*, n 129, p 1304; Diver, *op. cit.*, n 117, p 65.

[132] With regard to the Community, see Pescatore, "La carence du législateur et le devoir du juge" in *Rechsverglechung, Europarecht und Staatenintegration, Gedachtnisschrift für L.-J. Constantinesco* (1983) and Rasmussen, *On Law and Policy in the European Court of Justice* (1986).

through the Article 177 procedure: the reach of the Court into the operation of national public institutions, including administrations, is restricted by the fact that its jurisdiction is limited in principle to interpreting (or ruling on the validity of) Community law. Thirdly, and consequently, Community litigation does not involve the negotiation by the Court of Justice with defendant institutional parties of detailed rules regarding the internal organisation of national institutions.

In the United States it has been argued that:

> "The demands of structural reform have magnified the explicitly political dimensions of litigation. Parties have used litigation less as a method for authoritative resolution of conflict than as a means of reallocation of power. Rather than an isolated, self-contained transaction, the lawsuit becomes a component of the continuous political bargaining process that determines the shape and content of public policy. This transformation in the character of litigation necessarily transforms the judge's role as well. . ."[133]

In the Community, it is suggested, the role of "political powerbroker"[134] in this strong sense has been resisted thus far by the Court of Justice. None the less, there are common features, and this brief comparison with the United States Supreme Court is instructive. It enables us to begin to situate Community law litigation in the political process, at both the Community and the national levels, and it illuminates the political dimension of the Community judicial liability system. By elaborating the elements of this system, rather than by institutional litigation in the American sense, the Court of Justice has played a central role in organising and reshaping relations among Community institutions and between the Community and the Member States.

5 Conclusion

This Chapter has explored the nature and preconditions of the effectiveness of Community law as well as some of the principal means of ensuring it. In doing so, it has focused on two of the main Community institutions, the Commission and the Court of Justice. For this purpose it has treated each of these institutions as part of a distinctive configuration of elements, each comprising particular processes, tools and techniques. We can now draw these strands together more systematically, identify some of the advantages and disadvantages of each institutional configuration and point to some possible future developments.

The Commission has sought to ensure the effectiveness of Community

---

[133] Diver, *op. cit.*, n 117, p 45.
[134] *Ibid.*

law mainly by the process of negotiation. It has relied essentially on three tools: the Article 169 procedure, soft law and structural reform. Its techniques have included efforts to increase its powers to implement Community law and to expand the legal competence of the Community; these have often employed in conjunction.

It has been suggested here that the three tools used by the Commission to ensure the effectiveness of Community law are all best viewed as different forms of negotiation. Among them, however, structural reform has assumed a special significance. For three reasons, this should not be surprising. First, the increasing role of the Member States in the Community system has constrained the Commission, with the result that the other tools available to it are relatively ineffective or increasingly fragile. Secondly, the effectiveness of Community law, at its making, depends primarily on negotiation. Of all the tools used by the Commission, structural reform represents negotiation in the purest form. Consequently, and thirdly, structural reform seems to be the most appropriate tool for dealing with problems of effectiveness which result from recalcitrance or administrative incapacity. Potentially at least, it can focus directly on the lowest or most problematic levels of the system.[135] In addition, it may involve a broader range of interests and can be more finely tuned.[136] It has thus been especially well-adapted to (though not always successful in dealing with) the problems of effectiveness which up to now have appeared to be the most typical of the Community system.

But administrative negotiation as a means of ensuring the effectiveness of Community law also has shortcomings. First, though allowing potentially for a broad representation of interests, it may be limited in practice to those subjective interests expressed by governments or by powerful organisations.[137] Hence it may tend to favour objective interests which are crystallised in everyday assumptions or which are embodied in largely implicit, organisational constraints.[138] The same generalisation may hold true of courts[139], though the use of courts by weaker parties to assert their interests in the *Francovich* case is instructive. In the process of administrative negotiation, however, the risk that other interests may be neglected is increased by the lack of publicity, the informal nature of any agreement and the relative lack of procedural safeguards.

Secondly, litigation, soft law and structural reform need to be assessed, not simply as part of Commission strategy for implementing Community law, but also with regard to the effectiveness of Community law in the broad social sense, including its legitimacy. Litigation and structural reform may be used solely to elaborate legal doctrine. Usually, however,

---

[135] See also Elmore, "Backward Mapping: Implementation Research and Policy Decisions" (1979–80) 94 Pol.Sci.Quar. 601.
[136] See also Clune and Lindquist, *op. cit.*, n 40, p 1088.
[137] See Streeck and Schmitter, *op. cit.*, n 6.
[138] See Snyder, *op. cit.*, n 2, Chapter 2.
[139] But see Chayes, *op. cit.*, n 129.

in common with the use of soft law, they are deployed as forms of negotiation to achieve broader social, political or economic aims. The aims, the means of achieving them and the eventual results are frequently unknown to the general public. In addition, the legal framework within which these tools are deployed is ambiguous or uncertain. European administrative law is currently being developed.[140] This, it may be suggested, could enhance the legitimacy of the Commission, perhaps facilitate an increase in its powers to adopt delegated legislation, and hence increase the efficacy of its tools and techniques for ensuring the effectiveness of Community law.

Thirdly, the use of structural reform as a means of increasing the effectiveness of Community law must also be assessed at a more general level. The increasing inter-penetration of Community and national administrations risks accentuating an already great orientation in the Community towards administrative means of policy-making, techniques of problem-solving and political culture. More than twenty years ago Scheinman warned of the danger that "the technical ministries and services will become the dominant actors along with their Commission counterparts in the direction and management of major economic sectors, if not the entire economy".[141] Since then, political choices have often been treated as if they were ideologically neutral.[142] It has been argued recently that the Community has already ventured too far down this road.[143] Regardless of the merits of this argument, it is crucial – for citizens, national governments and the integrity of the Community itself – that political values be expressed in the Community system *and* at the level of the Community. For this reason, it is imperative that structural reform not be the only, or even the principal, means of ensuring the effectiveness of Community law.

In contrast to the Commission, the Court of Justice has aimed to ensure the effectiveness of Community law by means of adjudication. In dealing with the problem of non-transposition of directives, the basic tool of the Court of Justice has been the gradual, piecemeal development of a judicial liability system. As a means of supervision and control, the creation of a judicial liability system is not unusual. However, the system which has been developed by the Court of Justice has distinctive features. First, it has been established by the process of adjudication, that is, gradually by the judiciary, rather than in a single act by the legislature. Secondly, it has been directed mainly at governments, not at private organisations. Thirdly, its primary target has been the failure of Member States to fulfil their Treaty obligations, in particular by failing to transpose Com-

---

[140] See Schwärze, *op. cit.*, n 122.
[141] Scheinman, *op. cit.*, n 61, p 769.
[142] Weiler, *op. cit.*, n 13, pp. at 2476–2477; see also Duhamel, "Le traité de Maastricht: La dérive néo-nationaliste" *Le Monde*, dimanche 16-lundi 17, février 1991, 6.
[143] See Kennedy and Specht, "Austria and the European Communities" (1989) 26 *Comm. Mkt. L. Rev.* 615.

munity directives into national law. Fourth, and consequently, its aim has been limited in scope: to enforce the correct transposition of directives, that is, to ensure the effectiveness of Community law in this limited (but none the less important) formal sense. Fifth, the branch of Community-level government from which complainants seek relief, in the last instance, is the same branch which is the source of the rules, that is, the Court of Justice. Sixth, the system depends on one of the key relationships in the Community, namely the relationship between the Court of Justice and national courts.

The Court of Justice has also used two other tools which are characteristic of the Community judicial process. One is individual litigation, typically beginning in a national court and reaching the Court of Justice on an Article 177 reference. This tool determines a reactive, *ad hoc* working method. The second tool is the judicial decision, which in the Court of Justice is embodied in a single written judgment. For present purposes, the judgment has two features of special importance. On the one hand, it usually contains two related but distinct decisional parts: the *dispositif*, which is narrowly formulated and refers only to the particular case at hand; and significant principles, which, expressed in key paragraphs of the judgment, encompass not only the particular case but also potential future situations. On the other hand, the Court of Justice is not bound by precedent and, though it tends of course to follow a jurisprudence constante, it can change its mind. Together with the nature of individual litigation, these features of the judgment give the Court of Justice considerable flexibility in testing its ideas, developing its "courteously didactic method"[144] or modifying its strategies for ensuring the effectiveness of Community law.

The main techniques employed by the Court of Justice include the constitutionalisation of the founding treaties[145], the interpretation of legal texts, and judicial creativity, particularly with regard to basic Community law principles. On the one hand, the Court of Justice has given great emphasis to the doctrine of *effet utile*, explicitly or implicitly. As if following Pescatore[146], it has presumed that any rule of Community law is meant to have an effect. On the other hand, the Court of Justice has gradually "hardened" the duty of Community loyalty expressed in Article 5 of the EC Treaty. In fact, Article 5 of the EC Treaty may be viewed as the cornerstone of the Court of Justice's judicial liability system.

The use of a judicial liability system to ensure the effectiveness of Community law has several disadvantages. These disadvantages, as the advan-

---

[144] Mancini, "The Making of a Constitution for Europe" (1989) 26 *Comm. Mkt. L. Rev.* 595, 606.
[145] See, in particular, Weiler, "The Community System: The Dual Character of Supranationalism", (1981) 1 Y.E.L. 267; Easson, "Legal Approaches to European Integration: The Role of Court and Legislature in the Completion of the European Common Market" (1989) 12 J.Europ.Integr. 102; Mancini, *op. cit.*, n 144.
[146] See Pescatore, "The Doctrine of 'Direct Effect': An Infant Disease in Community Law" (1983) E. L. Rev. 155, 177.

tages, flow from a particular configuration of institutions, processes, tools and techniques. The first disadvantage stems from the judicial origins of the system. The system has been developed by means of the process of adjudication, that is, by the judiciary in response to *ad hoc* claims. Consequently, almost by definition, it is likely to be less normatively coherent and less comprehensive than a legislative scheme.

A pertinent example concerns the judicial harmonisation of national remedies. The general principles of law, elaborated by the Court of Justice on the basis of Articles 164, 173 and 215 of the EC Treaty, surely include the right to an effective remedy.[147] Differences in national remedies affect the extent to which individuals can rely in practice on rights derived from Community law. It is however open to question whether the institutions, processes, tools and techniques which are currently being used to harmonise remedies are entirely adequate for this purpose. Achieving a harmonisation of national remedies sufficient to ensure effective enforcement of Community rights, while simultaneously respecting the legitimate differences among Member States, is a difficult task. The judiciary, litigation, Article 5 of the EC Treaty and treaty interpretation all have inherent limits.[148] Consequently, it is suggested, serious consideration should be given to enacting legislation designed to harmonise selected elements of national systems of remedies for the enforcement of Community rights.[149] Such elements might include, for example, time limits and the availability of interim relief. Otherwise Member States may fail adequately to fulfil their obligations under Article 5 of the EC Treaty[150], and individuals may find Community law to be ineffective.

In the Community context, moreover, the structure of the judicial liability system has broader implications for institutional development. By

---

[147] See Case 222/84 *Johnston v Chief Constable of the Royal Ulster Constabulary* [1986] ECR 1651; see also Curtin, "Directives: The Effectiveness of Judicial Protection of Human Rights" (1990) 27 *Comm. Mkt. L. Rev.* 709.

[148] On the use of Article 5 of the EC Treaty by the European Court of Justice in reforming national procedural systems, see Temple Lang, *op. cit.*, n 66, p 647. Summarising the case law, he argues that national procedures and national remedies must be adapted as far as possible to protect fully the rights given by Community law (*ibid.* at 651); Member States are required to legislate to create sanctions and to provide administrative and enforcement procedures and personnel (*ibid. passim*); but that the Commission cannot use Article 5 of the EC Treaty to create new kinds of obligations for Member States (*ibid.* at 650). See also Constantinesco, "L'article 5 CEE, de la bonne foi a la loyante communautaire" in *Du droit international au droit de l'integration: Liber Amicorum Pierre Pescatore* (Capotorti *et al.* 1987).

[149] See also Oliver, "Enforcing Community Rights in the English Courts" (1987) 50 Mod. L. Rev. 881, 894–897. Aspects of remedy systems in the Member States have already been harmonised to some extent by Community legislation; see for example, Council Directive 76/207, art. 6, OJ 1976 L39/40 (equal treatment for employed persons); Council Regulation 1430/79, OJ 1979 L175/1 (payment or remission of import or export duties); Council Regulation 1679/79, OJ 1979 L197/1 (post-clearance recovery of import or export duties); Council Directive 89/665, OJ 1989 L395/33 (public procurement).

[150] The Commission staff paper to the 1991 Intergovernmental Conference proposed that Article 5 of the EEC Treaty be amplified to state which types of remedies are required for the effective enforcement of Community rights: see *Contributions by the Commission to the Intergovernmental Conference, op. cit.*, n 27, pp 152–153.

breathing new life into the form of judicial co-operation envisaged by Article 177, it strengthens the vertical relations of collaboration within the judicial branch at two levels of government. However, it does not involve directly any other national institutions, such as parliaments. In addition, it does not necessarily strengthen existing relations between Community institutions, nor does it create any new horizontal links between them, as might have been the case if, for example, the judicial liability system had been enacted by the Council, following a Commission proposal and in co-operation with the Parliament. Such implications for the potential development of institutions need to be considered in evaluating alternative processes, tools and techniques for ensuring the effectiveness of Community law.

A second shortcoming of the judicial liability system with regard to ensuring the effectiveness of Community law derives from the fact that it relies on *ad hoc* claims. On the one hand, in general, there is a real question whether the effectiveness of law can be ensured adequately by a system triggered solely by individual claims.[151] This deficiency is accentuated by the absence of framework legislation. On the other hand, a judicial liability system of the Community is inevitably more complex than in any national system. For example, litigation rates throughout the Community are influenced by diverse legal cultures, and, for this reason among others, they differ substantially among the Member States.[152] This alone would make it unlikely that individual litigation by itself could result in the uniform effectiveness of Community law. More generally, however, we simply know too little about the sociological features of Community law or litigation involving Community law to rely heavily on a judicial liability system as a principal means for ensuring effectiveness.

Thirdly, any judicial liability system is only a very diffuse, extensive form of supervision. It represents one end of a continuum, the other end of which is occupied by direct regulation. In developing the judicial liability system, it may be suggested, the Court of Justice so far has been concerned more with ensuring the formal enactment of national transposing legislation, and less with guaranteeing any particular legislative content; this is because the content is mainly determined already by the Community directive. The judicial liability system has been mainly a means to enforce this Community law obligation. Its main strength so far has been the articulation of legal principles. Correlatively, its principal weakness lies in the fact that its most public result has been the creation of political symbols. The extent to which these symbols are likely to coerce Member States for other purposes, let alone whether they appeal or are even known to the wider public, is open to question. Symbolic action is

---

[151] See Griffiths, *op. cit.*, n 45; Whitford, "Structuring Consumer Protection Legislation to Maximize Effectiveness" (1981) Wis.L.Rev. 1018, 1043, 1026–1027.
[152] See Plett and Meschievitz (eds), *Beyond Disputing: Exploring Legal Culture in Five European Countries* (1991).

significant, but it may fail to make any real impact on the effectiveness of Community law, especially if by "effectiveness" we refer to effects in addition to the elaboration of legal doctrine.

Fourthly, the European Community system involves complex and delicate relations, not only among Community institutions, but also between the Community and the Member States. Some room for manoeuvre for Member States is essential. It may be suggested that if one means of preserving such a political space is denied, others will be found. Therein lies the difficulty of an increasingly extensive interpretation of Article 5 of the EC Treaty. The Court of Justice has increasingly deduced specific practical duties from its general words.[153] In these circumstances, it would not be surprising if Member States were to seek other strategies.

Such strategies may be illegal, such as various forms of non-compliance; or they may be legal, such as systematic recourse to subsidiarity[154], creative compliance with the letter but not necessarily the spirit of the law[155], or opting out.[156] In addition, Member States may resort to devices which can play a role analogous to that of directives, as originally intended, that is, to encourage, facilitate or permit decentralised decision-making. Such devices include techniques of statutory interpretation, national legal remedies, or instances in which central governments take refuge behind national constitutional structures to preserve regional or local decision-making.[157]

In this context, the increased use by the Court of Justice of Article 5 of the EC Treaty is a double-edged sword. It tends to restrict or close off some of these avenues, but at the same time it suggests the existence of underlying problems which currently cannot be dealt with by the Community by any other means. As part of the process of enforcing Community law, it may be effective both in elaborating legal doctrine and in stimulating changes in specific cases. At the same time, however, when used as a tool to achieve major institutional changes, such as the harmon-

---

[153] More than half of the cases in which Article 5 of the EEC Treaty (now EC) and the corresponding Articles 86 of the ECSC Treaty and 192 of the EAEC Treaty were cited up to 1990 have occurred since 1 January 1985: Temple Lang, *op. cit.*, n 66, p 645.

[154] See Constantinesco, "La Subsidiarité comme Principe Constitutionnel de l'Intégration Européenne" (1991) 46 *Aussenwirtschaft* 439; Kapteyn, "Community Law and the Principle of Subsidiarity" Speech to the United Kingdom Association for European Law, London, November 2, 1990; Emiliou, "Subsidiarity: An Effective Barrier against the 'Enterprises of Ambition'?" (1992) 17 E. L. Rev. 383; Constantinesco, "Who's Afraid of Subsidiarity?" (1991) 11 Y.E.L. 33.

[155] See McBarnet and Whelan, "The Challenge of Creative Compliance" presented at the Economic and Social Research Council Workshop, *Compliance and the Single European Market Programme*, Institute of Advanced Legal Studies, London, June 29, 1992.

[156] See the various protocols to the Maastricht Treaty. With regard to differentiation in the Community generally before the Maastricht Treaty, see Nicoll, "Paths to European Unity" (1985) 23 JCMS 199; Ehlermann, "How Flexible is Community Law? An Unusual Approach to the Concept of 'Two Speeds'" (1984) 82 Mich.L.Rev. 1274.

[157] See also Rasmussen, "Les Etats membres et l'inexécution des obligations communautaires" (1989) 48 *Pouvoirs* 39; for historical analogies, see Snyder and Hay, "Comparisons in the Social History of Law: Labour and Crime" in *Labour, Law and Crime: An Historical Perspective* (Snyder and Hay eds. 1987), 24–26.

isation of national remedies, the increasingly broad interpretation of Article 5 may have reached its limits. Its further extension may jeopardise the legitimacy of the Court of Justice without necessarily achieving more general social and political results. Adjudication and a judicial liability system may be less adequate than other processes and tools, whether at Community level, through the European Council, by intergovernmental means or by the Community in conjunction with the Member States.

The basic question is not which set of institutions, processes, tools and techniques is to be preferred absolutely to the other. Instead, it concerns the types of policies, issues or participants for which each is more suitable. Viewed from this standpoint, the preceding discussion of the Commission and the Court of Justice pinpoints certain institutional gaps in the Community system.

With regard to ensuring the effectiveness of Community law, the Community system seems to have worked best so far in creating legal principles and dealing with national administrations. Adjudication and negotiation have been sufficient, first, to establish the Community legal order vis-à-vis those of the Member States and, secondly, to cope with the ineffectiveness of Community law stemming from recalcitrance or administrative incapacity. But judicial and administrative processes do not occur in a political vacuum. Neither the Commission and the Court of Justice taken together as institutions, nor negotiation and adjudication taken together as processes, despite their merits, are sufficient alone to ensure the effectiveness of Community law in the broader social sense, in particular in so far as it entails the commitment of citizens, popular participation and political legitimacy. For this purpose, it may be suggested, other institutions, processes, tools and techniques are also required.

The legal and political future of the Community is now on the agenda. A debate is emerging as to the Community's institutional and political configuration. At the top of the agenda must be the creation of effective democratic political institutions at Community level, together with the establishment of processes for the public expression of choices concerning Community politics and Community law within the Community system. These and other measures could help to develop political participation, together with negotiation and adjudication, as one of the basic processes in the Community system. Such changes, or similar reforms, in the institutions and the processes of the Community are likely to be essential in ensuring the effectiveness of Community law in the future.

FRANCIS SNYDER

Chapter 4
The Legal Framework for Implementation in the United Kingdom

1 Introduction

While this Chapter is essentially concerned with the formal mechanisms for the transposition of Community[1] legislation into the legal systems of the United Kingdom, it starts with an examination of the way in which domestic scrutiny may be exercised over Community legislation before its enactment. It concludes with a discussion of the use of domestic judicial remedies to give effect to Community legislation, in particular in those instances where the public authorities in the United Kingdom have failed, whether wholly or in part, to transpose Community law into the domestic systems.

2 The Law-making stage

While it may seem a statement of the obvious, membership of the European Communities has meant that the enactment of legislation binding within the United Kingdom is no longer the sole concern of United Kingdom institutions. Certain acts of the Community institutions become law simply by being adopted by the relevant Community institution, namely decisions under the ECSC Treaty, regulations under the EC and Euratom Treaties, and decisions under the EC and Euratom Treaties, in so far as they may be regarded as law rather than as the mere application of the law. When these acts emanate from the EC Commission, as will be the case with decisions under the ECSC Treaty, no United Kingdom minister will normally have participated in the legislative process, and when they emanate from the EC Council, or from the Council and Parliament

---

[1] This Chapter is not concerned with the areas of non-Community inter-governmental co-operation (Foreign and Security Policy, Home Affairs and Justice) under the Maastricht Treaty on European Union.

jointly under Article 189b of the EC Treaty, although a United Kingdom minister and MEPs elected in the United Kingdom will have participated, the normal United Kingdom parliamentary processes will be bypassed.

Steps have therefore been taken by both Houses of Parliament at least to scrutinise proposed Community legislation[2], and to control the activities of United Kingdom ministers when they participate in the work of the Council. The House of Commons Select Committee on European Legislation was established in 1974, and its terms of reference were altered in 1990.[3] It considers draft proposals by the Commission for legislation, other documents published for submission to the Council of Ministers or to the European Council, other documents published by one Community institution with a view to submission to another, and any other document relating to European Community matters deposited in the House by a Minister. It reports its opinion as to whether such proposals or other documents raise questions of legal or political importance; it reports what matters of principle, policy or law may be affected thereby, and to what extent they may affect the law of the United Kingdom, and makes recommendations for the further consideration of such documents by the House. Such consideration in principle takes place before one of the three European Standing Committees created in the 1990 reforms[4], dealing respectively with (1) Agriculture and the Environment, (2) Trade, Industry and Transport, and (3) other matters (most particularly Finance and Taxation).

Correlative to this scrutiny procedure, a ministerial undertaking was given to the House in 1974 not to agree in Council to matters pending debate in the Commons. This was later formalised into a resolution of the House and an amended version was agreed in October 1990. Under this, no minister of the Crown should give agreement in the Council of Ministers to any proposal for European legislation which has been recommended by the Select Committee on European Legislation for consideration, or is still subject to scrutiny, unless that committee has indicated that agreement need not be withheld, or the minister considers the proposal to be confidential, routine or trivial, or substantially the same as a proposal on which scrutiny has been completed, or the minister concerned decides that for special reasons agreement should not be withheld. In the latter case the minister should, at the first opportunity thereafter, explain the reasons for his decision to the Select Committee, and, if the proposal is awaiting consideration by the House, to the House. It would appear that although it cannot totally block ministerial action at the EC level, the spirit of this resolution has been observed. Nevertheless, its utility may be questioned following the increased use of qualified

---

[2] See Lord Fraser of Tullybelton, Scrutiny of Community Legislation in the United Kingdom Parliament, in *In Memoriam JDB Mitchell* (1983) pp 29–37.
[3] *Hansard*, col. 397, 24 October 1990.
[4] *Hansard*, cols. 393–395, 24 October 1990.

majorities which resulted from the Single European Act, and it may be wondered how far this procedure is compatible with the amended version of Article 146 of the EC Treaty resulting from the Maastricht Treaty, which requires that a minister at a Council meeting should be "authorised to commit the government of that Member State".

The House of Lords Select Committee has always had wider terms of reference, being appointed to consider Community proposals, whether in draft or otherwise, to obtain all necessary information about them, and to make reports on those which, in the committee's opinion, raise important questions of policy or principle, and on other questions to which the committee considers that the special attention of the House should be drawn. Hence, unlike the Commons Scrutiny Committee, the Lords Committee is not limited to consideration of documents submitted to the Council or the European Council; moreover it does inquire into the merits of proposals or other questions and has produced a number of "own initiative" reports. It has also issued reports as a response to judgments of the European Court of Justice.[5]

The Lords Committee is aided by a system of Sub-Committees. Sub-Committee E (Law) is chaired by a Lord of Appeal[6] and includes a number of Lords of Appeal among its members, having as its terms of reference to consider and report to the committee on (a) any Community proposal which would lead to significant changes in United Kingdom law, or have far-reaching implications for areas of United Kingdom law other than those to which it is immediately directed; (b) the merits of such proposals as are referred to it by the Select Committee; (c) whether any important developments have taken place in Community law; and (d) any matters which it considers should be drawn to the attention of the committee concerning the vires of any proposal.

The reports drawn up on these criteria have in fact become widely used legal source materials.

3 Mechanisms for the implementation of Community law in the United Kingdom legal system

The mechanism for the introduction of Community law into the legal system of the United Kingdom is contained in the European Communities Act 1972. The Act contains definitions of "the Communities" and "the Treaties" for the purposes of the Act, the latter definition including not only the basic Community treaties and the successive Treaties of

---

[5] See, *e.g.* HL Select Committee on the European Communities, *Direct Applicability of Directives* (10th Report, 1974–75 HL 85), responding to Case 41/74 *Van Duyn* v *Home Office* [1974] ECR 1337.
[6] The current incumbent, Lord Slynn, is in fact a former judge of the European Court of Justice.

Accession but also any treaty entered into before 22 January 1972 by any of the Communities (with or without any of the Member States) and ancillary treaties entered into by the Member States. For the period after 22 January 1972, provision is made for a treaty to be specified as a Community treaty by Order in Council, distinguishing between treaties entered into by the Communities, which may simply be specified, and treaties entered into by the United Kingdom itself, where the specification order must be approved by resolution of each House of Parliament.

However, this should be read with the European Parliament Elections Act 1978 implementing the EC Council decision on direct elections to the European Parliament, which states that no treaty which provides for any increase in the powers of the European Parliament is to be ratified by the United Kingdom unless it has been approved by an Act of Parliament.[7] In the light of this, it may be observed that the amendment of Section 1(2) of the European Communities Act to include the Single European Act was effected by separate legislation, the European Communities (Amendment) Act 1986, which did not in fact incorporate Part III of the Single Act, on political co-operation, into United Kingdom law. The same technique was used in the European Communities (Amendment) Act 1993 to add the Maastricht Treaty to the list; there only the titles amending the Community treaties were incorporated, to the exclusion, *inter alia*, of the titles on Foreign and Security Policy and on Cooperation in the field of Justice and Home Affairs. The Protocol on Social Policy was also specifically excluded.

The fundamental provision of the European Communities Act 1972, conveying the particular nature of Community law, is its recognition in Section 2(1) of enforceable Community rights and obligations. Such rights and obligations appear essentially to be those which arise by virtue of the Treaty concept of direct application and the caselaw concept of direct effect. Under the EC and Euratom Treaties the Council and the Commission may issue regulations expressed to be directly applicable in all Member States[8]; and the Court of Justice has developed the concept of direct effect by which, subject to certain conditions, certain obligations imposed on individuals, on Member States or on Community institutions by provisions of Community law may give rise to correlative rights enforceable by individuals before national courts.[9] This principle was very well established by the time of the accession of the United Kingdom; hence the terms of the European Communities Act 1972 that all such rights, powers, liabilities, obligations and restrictions from time to time

---

[7] Section 6(1).
[8] EC Treaty art. 189.
[9] For the original statement of the concept in Community law, see Case 26/62 *NV Algemene Transport en Expeditie Onderneming van Gend en Loos* v *Nederlandse Tarief Commissie* [1963] ECR 1. See further Chapter 2, n 26 and Chapter 12, section 1(iv)(f).

created or arising by or under the Treaties, and all such remedies and procedures from time to time provided for by or under the Treaties, as in accordance with the Treaties are without further enactment to be given legal effect or used in the United Kingdom are to be recognised and available in law, and be enforced, allowed and followed accordingly. Putting it very crudely, it could be said that the European Communities Act provides that if as a matter of Community law a provision is to be law in the United Kingdom, it shall be law in the United Kingdom.

By providing for the enforcement and recognition of rights, powers, and obligations which are without further enactment to be given legal effect or used in the United Kingdom, the Act uses a formula which is apt to cover legislation directly binding on individuals, directly applicable legislation and the principle of direct effect, without expressly using these terms. Be that as it may, the Community Treaties are not alone in purporting to confer rights on individuals, but in the case, for example, of the European Human Rights Convention, the absence of any provision equivalent to this provision of the European Communities Act 1972 has led the English courts to hold that convention does not confer on individuals direct rights justiciable in an English court, and that such direct rights are available only in relation to the commission and court established under that Convention.[10]

The fact that rights and obligations arising directly under Community law are transformed into enforceable Community rights and obligations under the European Communities Act 1972 has consequences in domestic law. It would appear that in so far as a Community obligation gives rise to rights in favour of individuals, breach of that Community obligation becomes in English law a breach of a statutory duty imposed for the benefit of private individuals to whom loss or damage is caused by a breach of that duty. Thus a breach of a provision of Community law giving rise to individual rights may constitute a cause of action in English private law under the established heading of a breach of a statutory duty.[11] Even in the context of public law, an injunction may be granted to prevent a Minister breaching enforceable Community rights.[12]

It may however be wondered how far this emphasis in the English case-law on "enforceable" (i.e. directly effective or directly applicable) Community rights is compatible with the decision of the European Court in Cases C-6 and 9/90 *Francovich* v *Italy*[13] where it held that there are circumstances under which a Member State may be liable in damages for harm caused by its failure to implement a Directive even where the provisions of the Directive do not give rise to directly effective rights against the

---

[10] *Malone* v *Metropolitan Police Comm'r* [1979] Ch. 344, [1979] 2 All ER 620, *per* Megarry V-C.
[11] *Garden Cottage Foods Ltd* v *Milk Marketing Board* [1984] AC 130, [1983] 2 All ER 770, HL, *per* Lord Diplock.
[12] Case C-213/89 *R* v *Secretary of State for Transport, ex p. Factortame* [1991] 1 All ER 70.
[13] Joined Cases C-6/90 and C-9/90 *Francovich and Bonifaci* v *Italy* [1992] IRLR 84. 19 November 1991; examined at some length in Chapter 3, text at n 31 and section 4(iv).

State. Italy had failed to give effect to Council Directive 80/987 on the protection of employees in the event of the insolvency of their employer, and the Italian government was therefore sued for damages by a number of people who had been employed by firms which had become insolvent and who had not received the payments guaranteed to them under the Directive. On the question of direct effect, the Court held that while it was clear that the Directive imposed a guarantee of payment and how much was to be paid, it was not clear that the State itself was the debtor against which the guarantee could be enforced. Nevertheless, the Court went on to hold that the full effect of Community law rules could be undermined if individuals whose rights were harmed by a Member State breaching Community law could not obtain damages, and reparation was indispensable where the full effect of Community law depended on the action of Member States, as is the case with directives. The Court invoked the principle of Community solidarity in Article 5 of the EC Treaty, stating that it imposed an obligation on the Member States to wipe out the illegal consequences of a breach of Community law. It concluded that there was a liability to pay damages to compensate for the harm caused by failure to implement a Directive subject to three conditions: the Directive should require rights to be conferred on individuals, the content of these rights should be identifiable from the provisions of the Directive, and there should be a causal link between the obligation imposed on the Member State and the harm suffered by the applicant. While the procedural rules for such an action for damages are left to national law, and should not be less favourable than those relating to parallel national remedies or make the action virtually impossible[14], it may be wondered whether the concept of breach of statutory duty is the appropriate method of providing compensation for harm caused by a breach of Community law where there is no directly effective Community law right to breach, and the duty is rather that of the national court to follow the case-law of the European Court under Section 3(1) of the European Communities Act.

The recognition of rights and obligations arising directly from Community law in Section 2(1) of the European Communities Act 1972 is reinforced in further provisions of that Act. Section 2(4) provides, inter alia, that any enactment passed or to be passed is to be construed and have effect subject to the foregoing provisions of that section, *i.e* the rights recognized under Section 2(1). The effect is as if a clause to that effect were read into the subsequent Act.[15] It represents an attempt to ensure, within the limits of United Kingdom parliamentary legislation, the primacy of Community law in relation to later United Kingdom legislation. However, in the present context, it appears to be generally con-

---

[14] Repeating Case 199/82 *San Giorgio* [1983] ECR 3595.
[15] *Factortame* v *Secretary of State for Transport* [1989] 2 All ER 692.

ceded that Section 2(4) prevents at least any accidental unilateral alteration of rights and obligations arising directly under Community law.

Further provisions[16] require any question as to the meaning or effect of any of the Treaties or as to the validity, meaning or effect of any Community instrument to be treated as a question of law. They require judicial notice to be taken of the Treaties, of the Official Journal and of any decision of, or expression of opinion by, the European Court of Justice on any such question, and require courts in the United Kingdom to determine such questions in accordance with the principles laid down by, and any relevant decision of, the Court of Justice, unless a reference is made for a preliminary ruling. In effect, decisions of the Court of Justice are treated much as decisions of the House of Lords, except that they are binding even on the House of Lords itself, and extensive discussion of the caselaw of that court may be found in the earliest English cases[17] reported after accession. The options available to a United Kingdom court are, therefore, to make up its own mind in clear matters, to follow decisions of the Court of Justice, to distinguish those decisions, or to make a reference for a preliminary ruling either where there is no precedent or where it is sought to persuade the Court of Justice to change its mind. What is of particular relevance here, however, is that in so far as the concepts of direct effect, of the primacy of Community law, and of the duty to compensate for harm caused by a failure to give effect to a Directive[18] are creatures of the caselaw of the Court of Justice, the obligation imposed by Section 3(1) of the European Communities Act 1972 on United Kingdom courts to follow the decisions of the Court of Justice would appear to produce the same practical result as Section 2(1) and Section 2(4) of that Act.

4 Formal implementation

With regard to such Community law that does not fall within Section 2(1) and thus requires specific national implementation in the United Kingdom, Section 2(2) of the Act enables Orders in Council to be made. It also enables designated ministers or departments to make regulations for the purpose of implementing any Community obligation of the United Kingdom, or enabling any such obligation to be implemented, or of enabling any rights enjoyed or to be enjoyed by the United Kingdom under or by virtue of the Treaties to be exercised. Such Orders or regu-

---

[16] Sections 3(1), 3(2).

[17] *Minnesota Mining and Manufacturing Co* v *Geerpres Europe Ltd* [1973] CMLR 259, *per* Graham J. For an early attempt to synthesise decisions of the Court of Justice, see *Lowenbrau Munchen* v *Grunhalle Lager International Ltd* [1974] 1 CMLR 1, *per* Graham J.

[18] See the *Francovich* judgment above, n 13.

lations may also be made for the purpose of dealing with matters arising out of, or related to, any such obligation or rights. This power is reinforced by what is popularly referred to as a "Henry VIII clause", the first phrase of Section 2(4) enabling such Orders in Council or regulations to make any such provision as might be made by Act of Parliament.

Nevertheless, the powers under the European Communities Act 1972 do not preclude the use of parallel powers in other legislation or the implementation of Community obligations by separate Act of Parliament. This is particularly the case with regard to company law harmonisation, where, after the First Directive had been implemented in the European Communities Act 1972 itself, the Second Directive on the protection of share capital was implemented by the Companies Act 1980, and the Fourth Directive on company accounts was implemented in the Companies Act 1981. By way of contrast, the Third Directive on agreed mergers was implemented by statutory instrument in the Companies (Mergers and Divisions) Regulations 1987, and implementing legislation for the EC Regulation creating the new legal form of the European Economic Interest Grouping was also enacted in a statutory instrument.[19] However, in reversion to previous practice, the Directive on auditors was implemented in the Companies Act 1989.

Obviously statutes may also be used where it is necessary to go beyond the limits imposed by the European Communities Act 1972[20], for example to impose taxation or to produce a retroactive effect, and, even before accession, the provisions of the Finance Act 1972 introducing value added tax were drafted so as to implement the directives on value added tax. Statute has also been used where a Community obligation arises from a judgment of the European Court of Justice which does not indicate the precise limits of that Community obligation. Hence, the Importation of Milk Act 1983 was enacted in response to a judgment of the Court of Justice[21] holding that United Kingdom restrictions on the import of UHT milk were contrary to the Community rules on the free movement of goods. On the other hand, when the President of the European Court ordered the United Kingdom, as an interim measure, to suspend the application of certain provisions of the Merchant Shipping Act 1988 in Case 246/89R *Commission* v *United Kingdom*[22], the necessary amendments to the Act were made by a statutory instrument issued under Section 2(2).

Following ministerial undertakings given at the time of accession, it would appear to be regarded as preferable to use a specific power to implement a Community obligation rather than the general power of implementation. Indeed, the European Communities Act 1972[23] itself

---

[19] SI 1989/638.
[20] See Schedule 2.
[21] Case 124/81 *Commission* v *United Kingdom* [1983] ECR 203.
[22] [1989] ECR 3125.
[23] *I.e.* under the European Communities Act 1972, s. 2(2).

created a number of these specific powers relating to food, seeds and other propagating material, fertilisers and feeding stuffs, animal health, plant health and certain aspects of road transport.[24] Use of these parallel powers may be subject to different conditions and may, for example, allow heavier penalties to be imposed than under the general power. Pre-existing independent powers may also be used, for similar reasons[25], or a parallel power may be used in conjunction with the general power. For enforcement reasons, again, provisions in such statutory instruments made under the general power may be deemed to be made under the parallel power.[26] So far as the general power under the European Communities Act 1972 is concerned, it requires the designation of a minister or department (unless the implementation is to be by Order in Council), the existence of a Community obligation or a right enjoyed by the United Kingdom under the Community Treaties[27], and it is subject to a list of exceptions.[28]

Although the distinction may seem highly technical, unless the implementation of Community legislation is itself to be by Order in Council, the minister or department wishing to make regulations must be designated for that purpose by an Order in Council. Such designation orders may be broad in scope, such as those designating the Commissioners of Customs and Excise with regard to customs matters of the European Communities[29] or the Minister of Agriculture, Fisheries and Food with regard to the common agricultural policy.[30] Others are extremely specific, such as that designating the Treasury with regard to measures relating to credit and financial institutions and to the taking of deposits or other repayable funds from the public.[31] Orders in Council, requiring no designation order, have, however, been used for such matters as the implementation of freedom of establishment and freedom to supply services for professions[32], and generally with regard to free movement of

---

[24] See *ibid.* Sched. 4.

[25] See *e.g.* the Measuring Instruments (EEC Requirements) (Gas Volume Meters) Regulations 1983 (SI 1983/1246), made under the Gas Act 1972, s. 39(6)(a), (b).

[26] See, *e.g.* the Packaging and Labelling of Dangerous Substances Regulations 1978 (SI 1978/209), made under the European Communities Act 1972, s. 2, and the Health and Safety at Work etc. Act 1974, ss. 15, 82, Sched. 3. The Regulations state that in so far as any provision of them is made under the European Communities Act 1972, s. 2, that provision is to be enforced as if it were a health and safety regulation made under the Health and Safety at Work etc. Act 1974, s. 15: Packaging and Labelling of Dangerous Substances Regulations 1978, reg. 7 (1).

[27] European Communities Act 1972, s. 2(2).

[28] See *ibid.* Sched. 2.

[29] European Communities (Designation) Order 1977 (SI 1977/980).

[30] European Communities (Designation) Order 1972 (SI 1972/1811).

[31] SI 1990/1304.

[32] See, *e.g.* the European Communities (Services of Lawyers) Order 1978 (SI 1978/1910); the Veterinary Surgeons Qualifications (EC Recognition) Order 1980 (SI 1980/1951); and the Nursing and Midwifery Qualifications (EC Recognition) Order 1983 (SI 1983/884).

workers.[33] The detailed arrangements for the enforcement of judgments of the European Court of Justice are also laid down by Order in Council.[34]

As might be expected with regard to secondary legislation, the scope for Parliamentary control is limited. Any statutory instrument containing an Order in Council or regulations made in the exercise of a power conferred by the European Communities Act 1972 is subject to annulment by resolution of either House of Parliament, if it is made without a draft having been approved by resolution of each House.[35]

Whether use can be made of Section 2(2) depends essentially on the existence either of a Community obligation of the United Kingdom, or of a right enjoyed or to be enjoyed by the United Kingdom under or by virtue of the Treaties. With regard to Community obligations, it has long been established that a directly applicable Regulation does not need substantive re-enactment into national law. Indeed, the Court of Justice has held that it must not receive national re-enactment[36] since the origin of the legislation in Community law might thereby be disguised, and those affected might not realise that Community law remedies were available in relation to the legislation. Nevertheless, many regulations by their terms do actually require Member States to take implementing measures, such as the EC Regulation introducing the European Economic Interest Grouping. Indeed, the specific enabling powers created by the European Communities Act with regard to food, the grading of horticultural produce, and road transport, do confer specific powers to issue subordinate legislation relating to the administration, execution and enforcement of directly applicable Community provisions. It is, however, clear that the role of a statutory instrument here is to provide machinery to help the application of the Community law, and not to disguise the directly applicable provisions.

Furthermore, although a directly applicable provision of Community law may, as a matter of Community law, render automatically inapplicable any conflicting provision of national legislation, there may still be a Community obligation formally to repeal such national provisions, since their apparent maintenance in force may give rise to a state of uncertainty as to the possibility of relying on Community law.

On the other hand, the Community obligation to enact into domestic law directives (the legal instruments archetypically used in the internal market programme) which are not directly applicable in terms of the EC Treaty is not affected by the fact that provisions in a Directive may be capable of direct effect. This is explained partly by the wording of the Treaty which expressly envisages national implementation of directives,

---

[33] See, e.g. the Immigration (Revocation of Employment Restrictions) Order 1972 (SI 1972/1647).

[34] European Communities (Enforcement of Community Judgments) Order 1972 (SI 1972/1590).

[35] s. 2(2), Sched. 2, para 2(1), (2).

[36] Case 34/73 *Variola SpA* v *Amministrazione italiana delle Finanze* [1973] ECR 981.

and partly by the fact that the direct effect of a directive is a residual concept, which may in general only be invoked against the defaulting Member State whereas the directive itself may well require obligations to be imposed by that Member State on other subjects of the law.

The "rights" enjoyed by the United Kingdom to which effect may be given under Section 2(2) would appear to extend to certain express powers, such as the power in the Lawyers' Services Directive to reserve certain defined activities to prescribed categories of lawyers, and to require lawyers from other Member States to work in conjunction with the local lawyers, and to require lawyers from other Member States to work in conjunction with the local lawyer when representing a client in legal proceedings. However, the view seems to have been taken (at least in some Departments) that a bare permission or mere toleration in Community law would not justify the use of Section 2(2), the example of such a permission might be EC legislation declaring payments, that would normally be unlawful state aid, to be compatible with the Common Market.

The European Court has for many years held that Community obligations may not be implemented by simple administrative practice since, by their nature, administrative practices may be altered at the whim of the authorities. Despite the espousal of the cause of deregulation by the present British government, it would in fact appear to have been general practice of successive British governments to give effect to the Community obligations through formal legislation. There do, nevertheless, appear to be examples of non-legislative action. In a rather technical area, the open systems interconnection information aspects of the public procurement provisions in Council Decision 87/95, on standardisation in the field of information technology and telecommunications, appear to have given rise in this country to circulars from the Department of Trade and Industry and more detailed documentation produced by the Central Communications and Telecommunications Agency.[37] On the other hand, it may be suggested that there is no legal need to use formal legislation to implement a mere permission accorded to a Member State by Community law provided any correlative obligations may be enforced by other means. So, for example, the power under Article 4(1) of Council Regulation 857/84, for a Member State to grant compensation to producers undertaking to discontinue milk production definitively was at first implemented in the United Kingdom by contracts with individual producers on a non-statutory basis.

Express limitations on the use of Section 2(2) to give effect to Community obligations and rights in the United Kingdom are set out in Schedule 2 to the European Communities Act. Schedule 2 prohibits the making of any provision imposing or increasing taxation; this explains,

---

[37] Another example, possibly justified by the wording of the Directive itself, is to be found in the administrative enforcement of the European content provisions of the "Television without Frontiers" Directive, discussed later by O'Leary and Goldberg in Chapter 8.

101

for example, why the Value Added Tax Directives have been implemented in the United Kingdom by Act of Parliament, though it may be doubted whether it explains why the European Economic Interest Grouping (Fees) Regulations 1989 were made under Section 56 of the Finance Act 1973 rather than under Section 2(2) of the European Communities Act, which was the provision used for the basic European Economic Interest Grouping regulations, when the fees at issue appeared to be payments for services such as registration. Similarly, there is no power to issue retrospective legislation, and the absence of any suitable parallel enabling power meant that, in one well-known instance, a retrospective change in the period of application of United Kingdom guaranteed prices for pigmeat, following our accession, was effected by Regulation 1822/75 issued by the EC Commission, thus taking advantage of the direct application within the legal systems of the United Kingdom of EC regulations. It is not permissible to confer any further power to legislate by subordinate instrument other than in the form of rules of procedure for any court or tribunal, and, finally, there are restrictions on any punishment that may be imposed when a new criminal offence is created by statutory instruments under Section 2(2).

5 Administrative machinery and co-ordination

Although there is no Minister for Europe as such in the United Kingdom government, it is clear that it is the Foreign and Commonwealth Office which performs the lead role with regard to the link between the Community decision-making process and the domestic political process. Within the Foreign Office there are two European Community departments, one concerned with the external policy of the Community, the other concerned with the internal policy of the Community, and within the latter department Community activities are reputedly divided into about nine different areas of responsibility. Within the domestic political system, the Cabinet structure does provide some relatively complex machinery for the co-ordination of policy. However, the precise roles of current Cabinet sub-committees and of their personnel are still not treated as matters of public information. In administrative terms, however, it may be said that there is a European Secretariat within the Cabinet Office, and this is divided into two main units. The larger of these units is headed by a Grade 2 civil servant (the old rank of Deputy-Secretary), acting under the Cabinet Secretary, and assisted by a Grade 3 (Under-Secretary), a Grade 5 (Assistant Secretary) and four Grade 7s (Principals) each of whom has been attributed a number of defined areas of responsibility with regard to Community policy. The second unit is the Legal Section, divided into two sub-units, one concerned with legal advice, and the other concerned with litigation. The Litigation Department is, of course, particularly concerned with enforcement proceedings involving the United Kingdom, and with the co-ordination of observations and references for preliminary rulings, but it should also be said that there is an underlying assumption that departments will have their own legal advice. The operational significance of the committees serviced by the European Secretariat of the Cabinet Office can be judged from the fact that those committees apparently meet two or three times a week throughout the whole year, with the possible exception of August. Within each domestic department of the United Kingdom Civil Service, there are now a number of departmental contact persons with specific responsibilities in the area of European Community policy, and it seems that these names are circulated amongst those concerned by means of a regularly updated list. By way of example, it may be observed that the Department of Trade and Industry, which of course has a particular interest in the single market legislation, apparently lists about seventy separate areas of interest for which there is a named departmental contact. The degree of specialisation involved may be deduced from the fact that, for example, consumer affairs are sub-divided into a number of different subjects.

In conclusion, it may be suggested that whilst the United Kingdom system of central co-ordination is very elaborate, and appears at the technical level to be reasonably efficient, nevertheless it cannot ensure compliance with Community obligations if the relevant political will is not there.

The United Kingdom has in fact usually appeared in a good light in successive general Commission Reports on the enforcement of Community law and in the special Reports on the implementation of the 1992 programme. In the latter context, the United Kingdom has usually appeared in the top three of the league table with Denmark and France. However, it would appear from a Commission Report in December 1992[38] that the position changed in the second half of 1992. According to this, the United Kingdom had fallen to third from the bottom of the league, having failed to implement 46 of the 215 single market instruments which should by then have been implemented. Only Italy and Spain had (marginally) worse records. There would appear to have been delays even in areas where the United Kingdom had a particular interest, such as financial services.

Whether there were political reasons – possibly connected with domestic problems over the internal implementation of the Maastricht Treaty – is not for this lawyer to say. However, during the course of 1993, the United Kingdom would appear to have regained its usual position.

---

[38] *Agence Europe* No. 5870, 3 December 1992.

6 The use of national remedies in Community law

Given that the administration of most substantive aspects of Community law is the responsibility of national authorities, the availability of national remedies which may be used by or against national authorities forms an essential element in the proper application and enforcement of Community law within each Member State, and is considered in more detail elsewhere in this book.[39] The availability of national remedies is also vital in so far as Community law may directly give rise to rights and obligations for and between individual subjects of the law.

With regard to the enforcement of Community law by (as distinct from against) national authorities, the basic principle is that, in the absence of specific Community rules, the national authorities must enforce Community law by national methods, including, if necessary, the use of criminal penalties.[40]

Where an individual or trader wishes to enforce Community law against national authorities before national courts, the basic principle remains that, in the absence of any relevant Community rules, normal national remedies should be used provided that they do not make it practically impossible to exercise enforceable Community rights[41], and that these national rules are non-discriminatory.[42] National rules are subject to the overriding obligation on national courts to protect directly effective rights under Community law.[43] Hence the relevant national limitation periods apply[44] if they comply with these conditions. On the other hand, where a Member State fails correctly to implement a Directive, the view has been taken that private citizens cannot be expected to know their rights until proper implementation occurs, and therefore time does not begin to run against them until this has happened.[45] Similarly, the effective implementation of Community law was held to require United Kingdom courts to ignore a national rule which was thought to preclude interim relief being granted against the Government.[46] It may therefore be suggested that at the level of judicial remedies, rights derived from Community law may be more effectively protected than those arising under domestic law alone.

Turning from these general rules to their operation in the United Kingdom, in areas effectively taken over by Community law, such as customs legislation, many prosecutions will in reality be for the enforcement of Community law. However, despite a number of reported prosecutions relating to the tachograph required to be installed in certain vehicles by

---

[39] See Chapters 3 and 10.
[40] Case C-68/88 *Commission* v *Greece* [1989] ECR 2965.
[41] Case 33/76 *Rewe-Zentralfinanz eG* v *Landwirtschaftskammer für Saarland* [1976] ECR 1989.
[42] Case 130/79 *Express Dairy Foods Ltd* v *Intervention Board for Agricultural Produce* [1980] ECR 1887.
[43] Case 61/79 *Amministrazione delle Finanze dello Stato* v *Denkavit Italiana Srl* [1980] ECR 1205.
[44] Case 33/76 *Rewe-Zentralfinanz eG* v *Landwirtschaftskammer für Saarland* [1976] ECR 1989.
[45] Case C-208/90 *Emmott* [1991] ECR I-4269.
[46] Case C-213/89 *R.* v *Secretary of State for Transport ex p. Factortame* [1991] 1 All ER 70.

Community legislation[47], the fact remains that in the reported criminal cases where questions of Community law have arisen, the point has usually been taken by the defence.[48] Another classic function of the public authorities is revenue collection which, in the case of customs duties and agricultural levies, for example, is carried out on behalf of the Community. Enforcement of Community law by public authorities may also take the form of a civil action. Thus the Attorney-General, pursuant to his general power to enforce public rights, or duties owed to the public at large, may, for example, seek an injunction to require an undertaking to admit inspectors sent by the EC Commission to investigate an alleged breach of the Community competition rules.

A similar enforcement power may be exercised at the local level by local authorities under the Local Government Act 1972, which provides that a local authority may institute proceedings in its own name for the promotion or protection of the interests of the inhabitants of its area.[49] This has been held to mean that a local authority may bring an action to protect public rights.[50] It now appears that if the defendant in such an action alleges that the national legislation which the local authority is trying to enforce is in breach of Community law, the local authority will not be required to give an undertaking in damages, in part on the basis that the liability to compensate for loss caused if there is such a breach will be that of central government.[51] However, that statement is not as simple as it seems, because the authorities required under Community law to apply directives as such include even, for example, autonomous local authorities as in Case 103/88 *Costanzo* v *Milan*[52], where the city of Milan was held liable to give effect to the terms of an EC public works Directive rather than the incorrect Italian national implementation of that Directive, when inviting tenders to build a new football stadium. If that is the case, it is at the least arguable that not only national authorities but also local authorities may be liable in damages if they do not give effect to their Community obligations. Unfortunately, it would appear that *Costanzo* was not discussed in the *Kirklees* case.

With regard to the enforcement of Community law against public authorities in England, the introduction of the procedure for judicial review and the subsequent line of cases holding that this form of action must be used in disputes subject to public law[53], but may only be used in such cases, have made it essential to distinguish between public law and private

---

[47] *E.g.* the prosecution which led to the reference by the House of Lords in Case 133/83 *R.* v *Thomas Scott & Sons Bakers Ltd* [1985] 1 CMLR 188.
[48] See, *e.g. R* v *Goldstein* [1983] 1 All ER 434, [1983] 1 WLR 151, [1983] 1 CMLR 244, a case which did not lead to a reference to the Court of Justice.
[49] Local Government Act 1972, s. 222(1)(a).
[50] *Solihull Metropolitan Borough Council* v *Maxfern Ltd* [1977] 2 All ER 177, [1977] 1 WLR 127.
[51] *Kirklees BC* v *Wickes* [1992] 3 All ER 717.
[52] [1989] ECR 1839.
[53] See, *e.g. O'Reilly* v *Mackman* [1983] 2 AC 237, [1982] 3 All ER 1224; and *Cocks* v *Thanet District Council* [1983] 2 AC 286, [1982] 3 All ER 1135.

law in the context of the enforcement of Community law before English courts.

In practice, the most frequently used form of direct judicial control over public authorities in England in the context of the enforcement of Community law has been the action for a declaration. However, if the declaration is construed as relating to rights and duties arising under public law rather than to the enforcement of the private law rights of the plaintiff, the declaration must be sought by way of an application for judicial review.[54] Subject to this, with regard to the enforcement of Community law, actions for a declaration have been used in two separate ways: either to challenge the validity of United Kingdom acts in the light of Community law, or to challenge the validity of Community acts. In the first category was the first reference from an English court, where a declaration was sought that Miss Van Duyn was entitled to enter and stay in the United Kingdom.[55] Similarly, in Case 118/78 *Meijer* v *Department of Trade*[56] a declaration was sought that the United Kingdom was no longer authorised to control the importation of potatoes from other Member States. The second category includes the English *Isoglucose Cases*[57], where declarations were sought that certain regulations were void and of no effect and that the United Kingdom government was not entitled to implement them. Hence, an action for a declaration may provide a very attractive method of avoiding the restrictions on actions for the annulment of regulations brought by private individuals under Article 173 of the EC Treaty.

Although a claim for damages against a public authority may be attached to an application for judicial review, claims based on normal principles of tortious liability have been held to involve private rights arising under the common law.[58] That a breach of Community law giving rise to rights enforceable by individuals before national courts may constitute a breach of statutory duty under English law as was indicated by the House of Lords in the *Garden Cottage Foods* case[59], has already been mentioned. The same approach was followed at first instance when damages were claimed in respect of the revocation by a ministry of a general licence to import turkeys from France[60], held by the Court of Justice to constitute a breach of Article 30. On appeal, however, it was held that, in the absence of abuse of power, the only remedy was judicial review. It was further held that for a minister (or other official) to do something which he had no power to do under Community law, where he knew that

---

[54] *O'Reilly* v *Mackman* [1983] 2 AC 237, [1982] 3 All ER 1224.
[55] Case 41/74 *Van Duyn* v *Home Office* [1974] ECR 1337.
[56] [1979] ECR 1387.
[57] Cases 103 and 145/77 *Royal Scholten Honig* v *Intervention Board* [1978] ECR 2037.
[58] *Davy* v *Spelthorne BC* [1984] AC 262.
[59] *Garden Cottage Foods* v *Milk Marketing Board* [1984] AC 130, for discussion of this case see Chapter 11, text at n 77.
[60] *Bourguoin* v *MAFF* [1985] 3 All ER 585.

he had no power so to act and that his act would injure the plaintiff (in this case French turkey producers and traders), could also give rise to a cause of action for misfeasance in public office. However, the House of Lords has now recognised that this approach needs reconsideration in the light of the *Francovich* judgment.[61]

In principle, and by virtue of the European Communities Act 1972, points of enforceable Community law may be taken in litigation between individuals in the same way as points of domestic law. For example, numerous actions claiming equal pay from private employers have been founded upon Article 119 of the EC Treaty.[62] Similarly, injunctions have been sought and obtained[63] to prevent breaches of the competition rules of the Treaty, and the principle enunciated by the House of Lords in the *Garden Cottage Foods* case[64] – that a breach of Community rules giving rise to rights enforceable by individuals before national courts constitutes a breach of statutory duty giving rise to liability in damages under English law – would appear to be equally applicable where the defendant is a private trader or undertaking.

On the other hand, provisions of Community law, and particularly of competition law, have been invoked as defences in disputes between private parties from the time of accession. Indeed, there are instances where, in actions begun before accession, the defendant was granted leave to amend his defence so as to allege a breach of Articles 85 and 86 of the EC Treaty.[65] Articles 30 to 36, prohibiting measures equivalent to quantitative restrictions in trade between Member States, have also been frequently invoked as a defence in civil proceedings[66], particularly in so far as they restrict the use of industrial and intellectual property rights to prevent parallel imports from one Member State to another.

Questions of Community law have even arisen in the context of probate proceedings. In one such case the point at issue was whether probate in England could be granted to the Bank of Ireland, an Irish corporation.[67] Rules implementing Article 52 of the EC Treaty expressly allowed a corporation constituted under the law of any Member State to act as a custodian trustee, but further required that such a corporation should be empowered by its constitution to undertake trust business in England and Wales. In an earlier case it had been held that the Irish statute constitut-

---

[61] *Kirklees BC* v *Wickes* [1992] 3 All ER 717.
[62] E.g. *Shields* v *E. Coomes (Holdings) Ltd* [1978] ICR 1159, [1979] 1 All ER , 3 CMLR 44; *Jenkins* v *Kingsgate (Clothing Productions) Ltd* [1981] 1 CR 715, [1980] 1 CMLR 81, EAT; *Worringham* v *Lloyds Bank Ltd* [1982] 1 CR 299, [1982] 3 All ER 373, to take some early examples.
[63] See *Budgett* v *British Sugar Corpn* (1979) February 16 (unreported, but noted in [1979] *European Law Review* 417); *Engineering and Chemical Supplies (Epsom and Gloucester) Ltd* v *AKZO Chemie UK Ltd* (1979) December 6 (unreported, but noted in Commission Decision 83/462 [1983] 3 CMLR 694 [ECS/AKZO]); *Cutsforth* v *Mansfield Inns* [1986] 1 All ER 577.
[64] *Garden Cottage Foods, op. cit.*, n 58.
[65] E.g. *Aero Zipp Fasteners* v *YKK Fasteners (UK) Ltd* [1973] CMLR 819.
[66] Case 51/75 *EMI Records Ltd* v *CBS United Kingdom Ltd* [1976] ECR 811.
[67] *Re Bigger* [1977] Fam. 203, [1977] 2 All ER 644.

ing the Bank of Ireland could not give it power to undertake trust business in England and Wales, but in *Re Bigger*[68] it was held that, as a result of the Treaty, the bank could be enabled by Irish legislation to act in England and Wales.

Perhaps the most striking impact of the proper implementation of Community law has been on courts and tribunals of limited jurisdiction. After the view had been expressed in the Employment Appeal Tribunal that the industrial tribunals and their jurisdiction were pure creatures of statute, as was the appeal tribunal, and the tribunals could exercise no powers other than those conferred on them by statute[69], it was accepted that such tribunals should apply any relevant Community law within their sphere of competence.[70] In the light of this, it may be observed that the Value Added Tax Tribunal has had little difficulty in giving effect to provisions of the Sixth VAT Directive despite the provisions of United Kingdom legislation, as in *Parkinson* v *Commissioners of Customs & Excise*[71], and the Immigration Appeal Tribunal in the *Giangregorio* case[72] stated clearly that the United Kingdom is not able to invoke rules which are contrary to the clear and unconditional provisions of a Directive.

However, such tribunals often have not only substantive but also financial limits on their jurisdiction, and following a judgment of the European Court which held that certain provisions of the Equal Treatment Directive gave rise to enforceable individual rights, the Industrial Tribunal in *Marshall* v *Southampton AHA (No. 2)*[73] held that the statutory limit on compensation did not provide an adequate remedy as required by the EC Directive, and awarded a higher sum. The matter went to the House of Lords, which referred it to the European Court. The European Court held that the requirement under the Directive to give full and adequate compensation meant that a predetermined limit of the amount of compensation to be awarded by a tribunal should be ignored if it prevented proper compensation.[74]

The amounts subsequently awarded by tribunals to women who were required to leave the armed services on the grounds of pregnancy indicate very clearly the real impact of the proper implementation of Community law.

JOHN A. USHER

---

[68] *Ibid.*
[69] *Amies* v *Inner London Education Authority* [1977] ICR 308, [1977] 2 All ER 100, [1977] 1 CMLR 336.
[70] *Shields* v *E. Coomes (Holdings) Ltd* [1978] ICR 1159 at 1167, [1979] 1 All ER 456 at 461, 462; *Macarthys Ltd* v *Smith* [1979] ICR 785 at 788, [1979] 3 All ER 325 at 328, [1979] 3 CMLR 44 at 45.
[71] [1986] 3 CMLR 1.
[72] [1983] 3 CMLR 472.
[73] [1988] IRLR 325.
[74] Case C-271/91 *Marshall* v *Southampton AHA (No. 2)* (2 August 1993); for further discussion of *Marshall* see Chapter 11, text at n 32.

Part Two

Implementation in the United Kingdom: Case Studies

Chapter 5
Showing Your Strength: Alcohol Content Labelling and the Beer Industry

1 Introduction

The directive whose implementation is the subject of this first case study requires that all beverages containing more than 1.2 per cent of alcohol by volume must indicate their strength on the label, simultaneously visible with the product name.[1] This is not legislation which will change the world; indeed, some might think it so banal that only a mind fuddled by the absorption of alcohol at significantly higher concentrations could have thought it worthy of investigation. This would be unfair. The very simplicity of this requirement, the ease with which, one would assume, it might be transposed into, and applied within, any legal system, its apparently technical character, all make it an excellent case for an examination of the sorts of legal issues that might arise out of routine implementation of Community policy. Once such an examination gets under way, it does not take long to find out that differences of tradition, economic structure, language, law and administrative practice between countries of the European Union bring complexity to the realisation even of such mundane aims as telling drinkers the strength of what they are drinking.

At the stage of introducing this study, a single example will suffice. How should you spell "alcohol"? This "Alcohol Content" Directive, as we shall call it, is an amendment of the general Food Labelling Directive, made in 1979[2], part of whose purpose is to ensure that while national labelling requirements do not impede the free flow of trade, consumers can fully understand the labelling information they are given. This information must therefore appear "in a language easily understood by purchasers."[3] Applying this simple rule in multi-lingual jurisdictions, especially those where language is an acute political issue, is far from

---

[1] Directive 86/197 (OJ 1986 L144/38).
[2] Directive 79/112 (OJ 1979 L33/1).
[3] Article 14(2).

easy[4], but it has an impact even in a country like the United Kingdom, where it has been suggested that beer drinkers may be dangerously misled by the description "Diat" on some German lager labels, which signifies not to the fact that the beer is low in calories or alcohol, but that it comes from particular areas in Germany.[5] Now it might be thought that language could not possibly be a problem when it came simply to specifying percentages, but even here difficulties arose in Denmark, where the implementing order required the abbreviation "alk." (from the Danish alkohol), not the "alc." indicated by Community law.[6] Protests from the national organisation representing wine and spirits sellers led the Danish authorities to concede that "alc." might nonetheless be used since the use of foreign languages for labelling purposes was permissible where their spelling differed only insignificantly from Danish.[7]

There is good reason, then, to be suspicious of claims that the implementation of a directive such as this must be plain sailing. This Chapter explores its application to the brewing industry in Britain. While it will show, on the basis of our investigations in central and local government, and in the industry, that the implementation process *was* in this case felt to be unproblematic, it is important to start by sketching the background to that process, first in terms of Community policy, and next in terms of the United Kingdom beer market, so that the significance of this finding can be appreciated, and related to the findings of other case studies. As we go along we shall see, moreover, that the smoothness of the implementation process does not necessarily signify the absence of lessons about British implementation of Community law, or of impacts on British administration, or of possibilities for improvement.

2 Background to the study

(i) General Community food labelling policy

Food labelling measures form part of the general foodstuffs policy of the European Community. That policy is driven by two principal objectives:

---

[4] See Case C-369/89 *Piageme ASBL, Evian and others* v *Peeters* [1990] ECR 2971; [1993] 3 CMLR 725, concerning Belgian language requirements for the labelling of mineral water. It is also worth noting that in this case, an alleged breach of Belgian labelling regulations was invoked not by consumers, but by trade rivals: on the interests protected by labelling rules, see below, section 2(i); See further, on language issues, Van Bunnen, "L'emploi des langues dans l'étiquetage et le droit communautaire" (1988) Journ.Trib.com. 41. After the *Peeters* case, the Commission published its Communication (93/C 345/03) concerning the use of languages in the marketing of foodstuffs in the light of the judgment in the *Peeters* case: OJ 1993 C345/3. This runs to 45 paragraphs.

[5] See Food Advisory Committee, *Report on Review of Food Labelling and Advertising* (FdAC/REP/10) (1991), para 122.

[6] See Commission Directive 87/250 providing for technical implementation of the alcohol content Directive, art. 2(2): OJ 1987 L113/57.

[7] See Rasmussen, "Denmark" in *The 1992 Challenge at National Level: Reports and Conference Proceedings 1990* (Schwarze, Becker and Pollack eds, 1991), 82–83; and EC Commission, Communication concerning the use of languages, *op. cit.*, n 4, para 41.

114

the creation of a single European market in foodstuffs as in other products, and the protection of the health of consumers. It is this latter objective which underlies (or should underlie) national regulations governing the preparation and sale of foodstuffs; and it is inconsistencies in such national regulations which may be the major cause of barriers to cross-frontier trade in foodstuffs within the single market. As we have seen[8], the reconciliation of the two broad objectives of Community policy in this, as in other product standards fields, can be attempted in two ways. The first is through the elaboration of common Community standards for the regulation of foodstuffs, in substitution for inconsistent national standards; once this has been achieved, goods meeting the standard can move with complete freedom with no risk to consumer health or other interests. The alternative is the so-called New Approach, under which distinct national standards may remain in place so long as they respect basic principles designed to protect relevant consumer or other interests, and Member States are bound to admit products from other States whose standards comply with such principles, even if the products do not conform with the importing State's own rules.

In practice, there is no bright line between these two approaches. In particular, it would be a major mistake to assume that prior to the adoption of the New Approach, all harmonisation involved the elaboration of a fully-detailed Community product standard. The very use of the device of the Directive, which requires to be transposed into the Member State's legal order by national legislation, regulation, or other action, ensures that at least a formal element of national regulation remains; and most harmonisation directives were drafted so as to leave some room for national variations of substance. Unlike the Directive on Official Control of Foodstuffs[9], the general scheme of the Community food labelling directives dates from this earlier period: the main Directive was adopted in 1979. While the Directive lays down specific and binding rules which labels must satisfy, it nonetheless describes itself as "horizontal", operating across the entire range of foodstuffs, and allows for a variety of derogations in particular circumstances and leaves a variety of discretions to Member States.[10] This approach, as we shall see, still leaves room for genuine debate as to the compatibility of particular national labelling rules with the Community requirements.

How does the regulation of food labelling assist in the achievement of the Community's objectives in this field? Honest and clear labelling of processed foodstuffs is essential if the consumer is to know what he or she is eating or drinking. Of itself it does not secure a given quality or composition of food, but by adding to the information in the possession

---

[8] See Chapter 2.
[9] Below, Chapter 6.
[10] See for example Article 4, allowing for different provisions in Community provisions applicable to specific foodstuffs, and Article 12, leaving to Member States the enactment of detailed rules for the labelling of foodstuffs which are not prepackaged – for example, draught beer: see below, sections 4(iii), 5(ii).

of the consumer, it facilitates consumer judgments about the relationship between quality and price and about the satisfaction of personal tastes or requirements (*e.g.* for "healthy" foods) and thus makes it harder to sell bad food. Member States may of course seek to secure these desirable information goals to different degrees and in different ways, and such differences may themselves be barriers to trade, quite independently of any issues of food composition or quality. If the same foodstuff has to be labelled differently for home consumption and for export to each of the Community countries, higher costs will clearly be incurred, and trade inhibited. This is true regardless of whether a State's labelling rules are in any sense discriminatory, for example by imposing more onerous requirements upon imports than upon home products.

Labelling's link with the key interest of protecting consumer health and safety is thus somewhat indirect, enabling the consumer to identify foods which would not be safe for him or her, rather than controlling their production or import directly. Some of its importance, of course, flows from the way national labelling policies tend to reflect and reinforce their direct controls on quality and composition of food (notably, on additives to food), which are capable of functioning as distinct barriers to trade and which are the subject of distinct Community regulation.[11] There are, however, other kinds of consumer interest that might be advanced by the regulation of labelling, notably the avoidance of misleading presentation of products: thus the beer consumers' group CAMRA (the Campaign for Real Ale) has expressed concern about "badge brewing", where a beer is sold under one or several names implying that it comes from small specialist breweries – a practice particularly widespread in Belgium, but not unknown in Britain.[12]

Against this background, we can see that the proper implementation of food labelling rules laid down by the Community is prima facie of concern to a variety of interests. First come consumers and consumer groups, for whom effective labelling regulations, whether of national or Community origin, represent a guarantee of product information and an enhancement of market power. Next come exporters and importers of foodstuffs across member State borders, for whom Community directives should function as an assurance of market access. Third, producers for the domestic market have a double interest: first, in the workability of their national regulations as amended, restricted, or stiffened by Com-

---

[11] See for example ECJ Case 178/84 *Commission* v *Germany* [1987] ECR 1227, [1988] 1 CMLR 780, in which the European Court of Justice invalidated, as contrary to Article 30 and not justified by any health risk, the application of the German *Reinheitsgebot* to prevent the importation of any foreign-produced beers containing additives. For commentary see Note, "The Free Movement of Goods and Regulation for Public Health and Consumer Protection: The West German 'Beer Purity' Case" (1988) 28 Virginia Jl.Int'l Law 753. For the Community rules on additives see directives 2645/62 (OJ 1962 L279/1); 64/54 (OJ 1964 L16/64); 88/388 (OJ 1988 L184/61); and 89/107 (OJ 1989 L40/27).

[12] See CAMRA document sc 29–3–93.

munity requirements – an interest which is the analogue of that of consumers, and exists independently of whether there is any significant cross-border trade in their product; second, in the proper enforcement of the Community standard with respect to imports, where these exist. Finally, it is worth mentioning the interest of national enforcement agencies, who will be concerned to see that the Community standard is indeed enforceable, whether at point of importation or of sale.

(ii) The beer market

(a) *The European market*

Among major trading blocs and nations, the European Community has the largest beer production, and this production forms a significant proportion of the Community's economy.[13] Whilst the European beer market is the most diverse in the world, with a high proportion of independent brewers in most Member States offering a high level of consumer choice, the national markets remain relatively self-contained with only 4 per cent of all beer consumed in the Community crossing a national border.[14] This has been reflected in – and perhaps in turn reinforced by – historically highly diverse rates of excise duty on beer[15]; harmonisation is now under way, though significant disparities still remain.[16]

Northern Europe beer markets (Belgium, Germany, France, Luxembourg, Netherlands and the United Kingdom) are characterised by a tied house system, under which the owner (or more often, tenant) of a beer outlet is obliged to purchase all of the outlet's beer and related drink requirements from a particular brewery. The arrangement is generally linked with ownership of the premises by the brewery. While Southern markets, with no history of beer drinking, are expanding, fuelled by Northern European groups such as Heineken, BSN and Guinness[17], these Northern markets are presently static or in a state of decline. European brewers do not, however, see the tied-house system as preventing pen-

---

[13] Production was 293.9 m hectolitres in 1991, out of a world total of 1170m hectolitres; North America, at 259.4 m hectolitres, was the next largest producer: Brewers' Society, *Statistical Handbook* (1993), 65.

[14] Elland, *Beer Supply Agreements* (1991), 3.

[15] At the beginning of 1992, United Kingdom excise duty on beer was 77.71 Ecu per hectolitre, as compared with 2.8 Ecu per hectolitre in France, a multiple of 28: Commission of the EC, *Excise Duty Tables*, (DOC XXI-720/92-EN). See also Bruning, "Brewers step up campaign for reduction in beer excise duty" *Brewers' Guardian*, September 1993, 23–25.

[16] See Directive 92/84 on the approximation of the rates of excise on alcohol and alcoholic beverages (OJ 1992 L316/29), following Directive 92/83 on the harmonisation of the structures of excise duties on alcohol and alcoholic beverages (OJ 1992 L316/21). The United Kingdom will still be subject to relatively high rates of duty as compared to its nearest neighbour, France (the difference being 32 p per pint). See also House of Commons Agriculture Committee Fourth Report, *Effects of the Beer Orders on the Brewing Industry and Consumers* (1992–93) HC 402, Evidence, 119.

[17] Economist Intelligence Unit, (1993) 362 *Marketing in Europe*, 70.

etration of new products to these markets; they attribute this to the general decline in the beer market, together with consumer brand loyalty.

(b) *The United Kingdom market: structure*

In the United Kingdom, beer holds a declining share of an alcoholic drinks market which has commanded a more or less constant share of personal disposable income – about 3.5 to 4 per cent – over the last thirty years. Despite its relative decline, expenditure on beer remains massive: about £10bn. in 1988, which still represents well over half the spending on all alcoholic drinks.[18] Since 1988, however, the volume of production has fallen, to 36.3 million barrels in 1992, the lowest figure for over twenty years.[19]

The structure of the industry has changed significantly in recent years. One element of this, the steady shift from on-sales (in public houses, clubs and restaurants) to off-sales (in off-licences, supermarkets, grocers, for home consumption), may be seen as a reflection of long-term socio-economic trends.[20] This shift has special significance in relation to labelling, since the great bulk of on-sales (70 per cent)[21] are of draught beer, sold in kegs or casks, and not requiring a label. The more off-sales mount, the greater the proportion of sales caught by EC labelling rules.

Another element represents a response to governmental intervention. The Monopolies and Mergers Commission concluded in 1989 that concentration in brewing, coupled with the effects of the tied-house system, meant that "the integrated businesses of the brewers are not subject to the test of free competition at the manufacturing, wholesaling or retailing stages in respect of on-licensed outlets."[22] To repair this situation the government issued two Beer Orders[23], the first of which provided that national brewers owning more than 2,000 licensed premises had to dispose, or release from tie, half their premises in excess of that number by 1 November 1992. In 1989 the beer industry was certainly concentrated; there were six national brewers holding 80 per cent of the market, the remainder being divided between eleven regional brewers, 41 local brewers, some 160 small brewers, and three brewers without tied estates.[24] The effect of the Tied Estate Order, however, was to set off a series of mergers and redistributions of assets. These, while creating one or two large retailing groups with large numbers of public houses, reduced the num-

---

[18] (1993) 2 *Mintel Leisure Intelligence*, p 5, fig. 2.
[19] House of Commons Agriculture Committee, *op. cit.*, n 16, p x.
[20] Off-sales, as a proportion of the total, rose from 18 per cent in 1989 to 21 per cent in 1991, and are expected to reach 28 per cent in 2001: House of Commons Agriculture Committee, *op. cit.*, n 16, Evidence, p 166.
[21] See (1993) 34 *Euromonitor*, p 13, table 13.
[22] *The Supply of Beer: a report on the supply of beer for retail sale in the United Kingdom*, Cm 651 (1989), para 11.92.
[23] The Supply of Beer (Tied Estate) Order 1989 (SI 1989/2390); The Supply of Beer (Loan Ties, Licensed Premises and Wholesale Prices) Order 1989 (SI 1989/2258).
[24] Monopolies and Mergers Commission, *The Supply of Beer, op. cit.*, n 22, para 1.11.

ber of national brewers to five (Bass, Carlsberg-Tetley, Courage, Scottish and Newcastle, Whitbread) with a combined market share of 82 per cent. The number of regional brewers was down to seven, with 11 per cent of the market; local brewers held 6 per cent, and small brewers 1 per cent.[25]

(c) *The United Kingdom market: imports and exports*

While the high bulk and low value characteristics of beer are not conducive to high levels of international trade[26], there has nonetheless been a steady increase in United Kingdom imports and exports of beer during the period 1987–1991. Imports increased 25 per cent from 409 m litres in 1987 to 633 m litres in 1991, representing about 10 per cent of total consumption.[27] 94 per cent of these imports came from the Community – mainly from Ireland, the Federal Republic of Germany and the Netherlands[28] – and the great majority of these imports were undertaken by brewers themselves.[29] The United Kingdom export market is far less developed than the import market, but still growing. Exports increased from 100 million litres in 1987 to 180 million litres in 1991. The United States and the Irish Republic were the major destination markets in that year, with 53.1 and 48.4 million litres respectively, whilst the rest of the Community accounted for 32.5 million litres.[30]

We may summarise the industry background against which the implementation of the Labelling Directive took place as one of highly concentrated production; very wide variation in the size of producers (including a significant number of very small producers); a steadily growing emphasis on labelled beers; a high degree of producer control of imports; and a very small European Community export market (less than 1 per cent of the domestic market). Against this background it is not surprising to find that Directive 86/197 has been seen much more as the imposition of a new domestic labelling standard than as an instrument for guaranteeing access between Community markets. The Directive, however, contains both elements, and we turn now to examine its context and content.

---

[25] Monopolies and Mergers Commission, *Report on the proposed joint venture between Allied-Lyons PLC and Carlsberg A/S*, Cmnd. 2029 (1992), table 3.3.
[26] Fishwick and Denison, *The Geographical Dimension of Competition in the European Single Market* (Cranfield School of Management for the Commission of the European Communities, 1992), 145, point to long-distance transport costs and brand loyalties as important market barriers not affected by single market legislation.
[27] *Euromonitor, op. cit.*, n 21, table 5 and p 7. The quantity of beer imported would be higher were it not for the fact that some foreign beers (*e.g.* Carlsberg and Fosters), representing about 17 per cent of all beer consumption, are brewed in the United Kingdom under licence and are therefore counted as home produced.
[28] *Ibid.* p 6, table 6.
[29] 70 per cent according to the Monopolies and Mergers Commission, *op. cit.*, n 22.
[30] *Euromonitor, op. cit.*, n 27.

119

3 The Directive

(i) The "Parent" Directive, 79/112

Directive 86/197 is an amendment of the basic Food Labelling Directive, 79/112, which contains the rules for the information that must accompany the labelling, presentation and advertising of foodstuffs for sale to the ultimate consumer. The 1979 Directive, which applies to food-stuffs in their final packaged form, pursues the twin aims of liberalisation of trade, and consumer protection, already identified.

The Directive makes a basic distinction between misleading labelling, packaging and advertising of foodstuffs, which are prohibited by Article 2, and minimum standards for labelling.[31] Article 3 gives a list of those particulars which it is compulsory to indicate on the label of all foodstuffs. These are (1) the name of the product, (2) its ingredients (this does not apply to alcoholic beverages), (3) net quantity, (4) date of minimum durability, (5) special conditions of use and storage, (6) a contact name for the manufacturer, packager or vendor in the Community, (7) parti-culars of its place of origin (when omission would mislead the purchaser), and (8) instructions for use, where necessary. Articles 5–13 amplify these requirements and provide exceptions.

Article 7 specifies that claims of high or low content of a certain ingredient must be accompanied by that ingredient's minimum or maximum quantity in absolute or percentage terms. No provision is made for the indication of alcoholic content or for the listing of the ingredients in alcoholic beverages, but reference is made to their indication in the future, by additional provision to be made within four years (by 1983) (Article 6(3)).

The Directive requires Member States to amend their law as necessary, and to apply that amended law so as to permit trade in all products com-plying with its terms no later than December 1980 (two years after its notification to Member States), and so as to prohibit trade in non-com-plying products no later than December 1982 (four years after notification) (Article 22). It leaves to Member States all questions of enforcement, and penalties.

(ii) Directive 86/197

Directive 86/197, which was notified to Member States in May 1986, amended Directive 79/112 in partial implementation of its Article 6(3). The amendment stated that all beverages containing more than 1.2 per cent by volume of alcohol must indicate their strength on the label, simul-

---

[31] This distinction is also basic to United Kingdom law: see below, section 4(i).

taneously visible with the product name. Trade in products complying with this amendment was to be permitted from May 1988, and trade in products which did not comply by May 1989 was to be prohibited. The amendment did not, however, provide for the listing of ingredients of alcoholic drinks, as foreshadowed by Article 6(3). The Commission promised this in its Communication on the Free Movement of Foodstuffs of 1989[32]; and in 1992 brought forward the "QUID" (QUantitative Ingredient Declarations) proposal, which would, *inter alia*, provide for this listing of ingredients of alcoholic drinks.[33] The original intention of the Commission was that the proposal should be implemented into national legislation so as to prohibit trade in products which did not conform to its provisions by 30 June 1994, but disagreement among Member States as to whether ingredient listing for alcoholic drinks should be legislated for within specific regimes for types of drinks (spirits, wines etc), or through the "horizontal" approach of the 1979 labelling Directive, has delayed progress. The principle of fuller labelling of alcoholic drinks is, however, not contested by governments, though there is likely to be significant industry opposition, both within the United Kingdom[34] and elsewhere in the Community, on grounds of over-crowding of labels, and possible needs to invest in new labelling machinery.[35]

4 Transposition into United Kingdom law

(i) The law prior to the Directives

The first comprehensive piece of legislation in England and Wales regarding the fitness of food for human consumption was the Adulteration of Food and Drink Act 1860. That Act prohibited the sale of food to which substances had been added rendering it injurious to health; and more generally, prohibited the sale of any impure foodstuff. A supplement to this Act in 1872 provided for the appointment of public analysts and the use of local enforcement officers to take samples and prosecute offenders. For the more general protection of the consumer, the Sale of Food and Drugs Act 1875 prohibited the sale of food not of the nature, quality or substance demanded. In the same year the Public Health Act empowered enforcement officers to take pre-emptive measures to ensure

---

[32] OJ 1989 C271/9, para 18.
[33] Proposal for a Council Directive amending Directive 79/112/EEC on the approximation of the laws of the Member States relating to the labelling, presentation and advertising of foodstuffs (presented by the Commission) – COM(91)536 final – SYN 380 – Brussels, 7 April 1992. The proposal was approved, with amendments, by the European Parliament on October 27, 1993 (Minutes, PV36, pp 21–29), and now awaits further consideration by Commission and Council.
[34] Telephone conversation with Ministry of Agriculture, Fisheries and Food, 13 September, 1993.
[35] On German concerns see Schwarze, Becker and Pollack, eds., *op. cit.*, n 7, p 117–119, and Rees, *Signpost to European Food Trading* (1989), 149.

that unfit food did not reach the consumer; this was done by introducing powers of inspection and, where necessary, of seizure of food and its presentation to a justice of the peace. The main aims and scheme of these Acts – notably, nationally determined rules enforced by local authorities and their statutory officers – have endured through subsequent Food Acts of 1928, 1938 and 1955 and are still apparent in the current (1990) Act. Food safety, including labelling, is now covered, in England, Wales and Scotland, by the Food Safety Act 1990.[36]

At the time of the making of the 1979 Directive, general food labelling rules were contained in the Labelling of Food Regulations 1970[37], made under the Food and Drugs Act 1955, Section 7. Like Community law, the Act distinguished false or misleading labelling, an offence under Section 6, from the general regulation of the contents of labels. The general labelling requirement under these Regulations did not, however, apply to "intoxicating liquor", which was the subject of a separate regulation (reg. 16). This provided that all intoxicating liquor was to carry a label stating the packer or labeller of the drink and their business address, or those of the company on whose behalf it was packed or labelled; the name or description, or both, of the drink, sufficiently specific to indicate its true nature to the intending purchaser; and its country or countries of origin. Alcoholic strength had also to be indicated for spirits and certain other drinks, but not for beer, cider, perry and grape wines.

The regulations provided for their enforcement by food and drugs authorities (reg. 30(2)), which comprise "unitary" local authorities[38], upper tier authorities (county councils), and the larger lower tier authorities, together with port health authorities.[39] The authorities act through "authorised officers" (s. 86) equipped with powers of taking food for sampling (s. 91) and of entry on premises (s. 100). Breaches were to be prosecuted as minor criminal offences, subject to a fine or up to three months' imprisonment (reg. 30(1)). Preventive powers were not provided by the Act, save in respect of imported food, where restrictions on movement could be imposed by port health authorities (s. 104).

(ii) The transposition of the 1979 Directive

Transposition of the 1979 and 1986 Directives was thus greatly facilitated by the fact that they fell within the framework of existing primary legis-

---

[36] For full discussion of that Act (which does not extend to Northern Ireland: s. 60(5)), see Chapter 6 below.
[37] SI 1970/400. Separate labelling regulations for 19 specific food categories existed then and continue to exist. Food labelling law for England and Wales is currently contained in 64 different sets of regulations and amendments. There are separate regulations for Scotland (60 sets) and Northern Ireland (61 sets).
[38] *I.e.* those that discharge the full range of local government functions for their area.
[39] See ss. 83, 88(1).

lation, in the form of the Food and Drugs Act 1955. There was no necessity either to enact new primary legislation, or to use the powers provided by Section 2 of the European Communities Act 1972[40]; instead, adequate implementation could be achieved through the promulgation of new regulations under the 1955 Act. This was the task of the Ministry of Agriculture, Fisheries and Food (MAFF), the Department with general – though not exclusive – responsibility for food safety.[41]

The first of the implementing regulations were the Food Labelling Regulations 1980[42], largely transposing the contents of the 1979 Directive, in largely identical wording. They differed mainly in arrangement rather than content, but were more detailed and specific in defining some of the terms used in the Directive[43], and in substantially developing the Directive's provisions relating to "Claims and Misleading Descriptions".[44] They also omitted, without explanation, the Directive's requirement to indicate the net quantity of the food.[45]

The Directive leaves to the discretion of Member States the labelling of items sold without prepackaging, so long as the consumer receives sufficient information (art. 12). Under the 1980 Regulations, food sold for immediate consumption, and not prepackaged – like draught beer – need not carry a label (reg. 27(1)).

An additional requirement found in the regulations but not in the Directive related to alcoholic beverages. It stated that alcoholic drinks with a 1.2 per cent strength by volume or strength by mass must be so marked using "per cent vol." or "per cent mas" (reg. 30). Beer, however, along with the other alcoholic beverages exempted from strength labelling under the 1970 regulations, was excluded from this requirement (reg. 30(2)).

The regulations entered into force on January 1, 1983, two weeks after the date set by the Directive. The enforcement arrangements of the 1970 Regulations were not changed. They were replaced in September 1984, for England and Wales, by the Food Labelling Regulations 1984[46], made under the consolidating Food Act 1984, but without substantive changes.

(iii) The transposition of the 1986 Directive

This was effected by way of amendments to the 1984 Regulations.[47] MAFF consultations, both during the legislative process at Community level and

---

[40] See Chapter 4, sections 2, 3.
[41] The Department of Health, for example, is generally responsible for port health functions.
[42] SI 1980/1849.
[43] Compare reg. 2 with art. 1(3) of the Directive.
[44] Compare regs. 35–37 with art. 2 of the Directive.
[45] This requirement was met by the Weights and Measures Act 1963 (Intoxicating Liquor) Order 1984, (SI 1984/1314), later consolidated and amended by the Weights and Measures (Intoxicating Liquor) Order 1988 (SI 1988/2039).
[46] SI 1984/1305.
[47] The Food Labelling (Amendment) Regulations 1989 (SI 1989/768).

at the stage of transposition, disclosed little or no opposition to the proposals. The amendments remove from the Regulations all reference to alcoholic strength by mass, as this was not the form specified by the Directive. A new regulation 31 requires the indication of the strength by volume of all drinks with a strength of 1.2 per cent or more and gives the form that the marking is to take as "alcohol (or alc.)... per cent vol" (to no more than one decimal place), while new regulations 31A (and 33(1)(c)) make provision for non-prepackaged drinks (like draught beer), for which the strength indication was to be provided by means of a convenient notice at point of sale (or a menu or wine list). The amendments also implement Commission Directive 87/250[48], laying down the technical procedures (measurement temperature, tolerances, precision) for the operation of the 1986 Directive.

The reformulation of Regulation 31, and its extension to beer, cider and so on, and to dispensed drinks, took effect from 17 July 1989, a couple of months later than the Directive required.[49]

(iv) **Measures subsequent to the 1986 Directive**

There have been further changes both to United Kingdom and Community food safety and labelling law since the transposition of the 1986 Directive. The legal framework in which the labelling provisions operate has changed by reason of the adoption of the Food Safety Act 1990.[50] This introduced major changes into United Kingdom food safety law, but did not affect the substance of alcoholic drinks labelling requirements. Such change has, however, come about as a result of Council Directive 89/395[51], which among other labelling provisions restricts the use of the description "low alcohol" to drinks having an alcoholic strength of between 0.05 and 1.2 per cent by volume, and which was given effect in the United Kingdom by the Food Labelling (Amendment) Regulations 1990[52], coming into force in January 1991.

Difficulties with Community food labelling law have followed from a related United Kingdom measure. The Licensing (Low Alcohol Drinks) Act 1990 lowers from 1.2 per cent to 0.5 per cent the minimum alcohol content at which a drink is treated as intoxicating and is subjected to alcohol licensing law. As a corollary the Government proposed to lower

---

[48] OJ 1987 L11/57.
[49] Regulation 1, and compare 1986 Directive, art. 2(1) (1 May 1989).
[50] The 1984 Labelling Regulations, as amended, now operate as if made under s. 16(1)(e) of the 1990 Act. This seems to involve no substantive change, but the enforcement bodies are now food authorities, as defined by s. 5 of the 1990 Act, and the exercise of their powers is now subject to the functioning of the Codes of Practice provided for by s. 40 of the Act: see below, section 5(iv)(b), and generally, Chapter 6 below.
[51] OJ 1989 L186/17.
[52] SI 1990/2488, regs. 14 and 15. The regulations apply to England and Wales only.

to 0.05 per cent the level above which the Food Labelling Regulations would require the declaration of alcohol content. This was clearly inconsistent with European law, setting the threshold at 1.2 per cent save in those cases (covered by Directive 89/395 above) where a "low alcohol" or similar claim is made: in other words, where there was an issue of misleading labelling, rather than of providing a necessary minimum of information. Draft regulations circulated in October 1992 by MAFF sought to deal with this by creating a defence that the offending drink had been imported from a Community country in which its sale, as labelled, would have been lawful, but were withdrawn after the EC Commission objected that, even if thus applied only to domestic production, they would breach Directive 86/197 by imposing a more stringent standard.[53] The extension of the strength marking provisions to all alcoholic drinks had been thought necessary in order that consumers were not misled or confused about the strength of drinks and to help prevent sales staff from selling intoxicating drinks to those under 18 years old, but Ministers felt able to defer to Commission objections on the ground that the relevant information was commonly provided anyway.[54] This deference is noteworthy, given that the United Kingdom had just won approval in the European Court of Justice – contrary to the arguments of the Commission – for its policy of imposing stricter labelling requirements on domestic cigarettes than those provided by the relevant Community Directive.[55]

(v) The United Kingdom's performance in transposition

In transposing the general labelling Directive and the beer labelling Directive with a high degree of accuracy, and within brief periods after the time limit set by the Council, the United Kingdom has outperformed at least some of its European partners. Transposition came two years late in France, and had not taken place by late 1990 in Italy, Luxembourg or Portugal, while in Spain it was said that no express transposition was necessary, since the national labelling law was already consistent with its requirements.[56] It is worth noting that several other countries which were as prompt or prompter in transposition also enjoyed the advantage of pre-existent primary legislation broad enough to authorise the changes

---

[53] See *Developments*: "low alcohol labelling," (1993) 10 Trad.L. 54; [1993] Cons.L.Bull., no. 86, pp 6–7.
[54] Letter of MAFF of October 14, 1993. The draft regulations also proposed repeal of rules requiring a minimum alcohol content for shandies; this raised no problem for the Commission.
[55] Case C-11/92 *R. v Secretary of State for Health, ex parte Gallaher Ltd* [1993] ECR n.y.r.; *The Times*, June 28, 1993. See critical comments by Weatherill, "Regulating the internal market: result orientation in the Court of Justice," (1994) 19 E. L. Rev. 55; and Stapleton, "Minimum directives: Do Not be Misled," (1994) 111 L. Q. Rev. 213.
[56] See Schwarze, Becker and Pollack eds., *op. cit.*, n 7 at 208–209, 224, 305, 337, 411.

required by the Directives.[57] Another relevant factor is the complexity of the transposition process in different countries: jurisdictions such as Belgium, Germany, Italy and Spain all have to cope with the issue of the allocation of regulatory competence between national and regional authorities, from the standpoint both of rule-making and of rule-enforcement.[58] The United Kingdom is spared these difficulties, though as we shall see, its arrangements for local enforcement are highly relevant to the implementation of the Directive.[59]

5 The domestic implementation of the Directive

(i) General considerations

The Directive which is the subject of this study embodies the simplest kind of legal provision: one which lays down a mandatory rule of behaviour – here, that alcoholic drinks labels include a particular kind of information. The multi-level character of Community law means, however, that even such a simple requirement involves obligations and actions for a variety of agencies in addition to the producers and packagers of beer who would appear to be its primary addressees. We have already noted the general obligation on the State to bring the Directive into effect in domestic law, discharged in the United Kingdom by the promulgation of the Food Labelling (Amendment) Regulations 1989. This effectively timely transposition makes it unnecessary to consider what the position might have been in regard to the possible direct enforceability of the Directive by interested parties in the absence of such measures.[60]

Beyond transposition, the Directive engenders other duties for public authorities. The State has a duty to permit the sale of beverages from other Community countries whose labelling complies with the Directive, which will effectively fall on the customs authorities and port health authorities – at the stage of importation – and on the general enforcement authorities – at the point of inspection or sale.[61] This duty of course requires abstention, rather than action, from these authorities. Positive obligations relevant to the effective operation of the Directive relate to exports rather than domestic sales, and are imposed by the Official Control of Foodstuffs Directive of 1989[62], with a view to ensuring, consistently

---

[57] E.g. the Netherlands: *ibid.* pp 360–370. See also above, section 4(ii).
[58] For indications of how these issues bear on the transposition process, see *ibid.* pp 26–29 (Belgium), 205–208 (Spain); *The 1992 Challenge at National Level: Reports and Conference Proceedings 1991/92*, (Schwarze, Becker and Pollack eds., 1993) pp 11–27 (Germany), 219 (Spain).
[59] Below, section 5.
[60] See further, Chapter 10 below.
[61] See Case 94/82 *De Kikvorsch* [1983] ECR 947; Case 182/84 *Miro BV* [1985] ECR 3731; Cases C-13/91 and C-113/91 *Michael Debus* [1992] ECR 3617.
[62] Directive 89/397 (OJ 1989 L186/23). See in general Chapter 6 below.

with the "new approach",[63] that Member States can have confidence in each others' food law enforcement arrangements, and avoid burdensome import checks. Article 2(2) of the Directive requires Member States to "ensure that products intended for consignment to another Member State are inspected with the same care as those intended for marketing in their own territory". This obligation has been implemented in the United Kingdom in the Code of Practice of Food Standards Inspections No. 8, made under Section 40 of the Food Safety Act 1990, which provides:

> "Authorised officers should inspect products intended for sale anywhere within the European Community with the same care as they inspect products intended for sale in the United Kingdom. When inspecting manufacturing premises they should check that products intended for sale within the EC are manufactured *and labelled* either in accordance with United Kingdom legislation or in accordance with the legislation of the Member State where the food will be sold" (emphasis supplied).

There is no evidence that the performance of these various duties in the United Kingdom has been controversial or has given rise to litigation. The same appears to be true of other Member States, with the exception of Germany[64] and the Netherlands, whence several cases of enforcement of domestic drink labelling requirements in regard to imports have been referred to the European Court of Justice under Article 177 of the EEC Treaty.[65]

Significantly more difficult is the question of what positive duties of enforcement of the Directive's provisions, in regard to domestic production and imports alike, fall on the relevant authorities. In markets like that for beer, where imports are relatively small, lax enforcement may not only impair the consumer protection objectives of the Directive, but may constitute a significant source of discrimination in favour of domestic producers, if they are able to ignore the Directive's requirements and are thereby spared costs which other more scrupulous countries' producers are bearing. Such costs have been alleged to exist even in relation to the beverage labelling Directive.[66] On this point the terms of the Directives are elaborate but not unambiguous, requiring that national legislation, amended to comply with their provisions, "shall be applied in such a manner as to permit", or "to prohibit", trade in products which respect-

---

[63] Above, Chapter 2, section 5(i).
[64] See note 11, *supra*.
[65] See the *De Kikvorsch* and *Miro* cases, *op. cit.*, n 61 above, and Case 27/80 *Fietje* [1980] ECR 3839, [1981] 3 CMLR 722.
[66] See the complaints of small German brewers, reported in Schwarze, Becker and Pollack eds, *op. cit.*, n 7, p 117. More generally, Trading Standards Officers surveyed on enforcement questions often pointed to difficulties for small food and drinks companies arising out of frequent changes in labelling regulations.

ively comply, or fail to comply, with their requirements.[67] It is assumed
that an obligation to prohibit is not tantamount to one of extinguishing
trade in non-complying products; but how much effort towards extinction
does a Member State have to deploy? Is a simple declaration or prohibition, with no official enforcement effort, enough? The European Court
of Justice has said no more than that Article 5 of the EC Treaty requires
Member States to take all measures necessary to guarantee the application and effectiveness of Community law. This has recently led it to
hold that the level of a penalty prescribed by legislation was insufficient
because it had no real deterrent effect.[68] What level of enforcement effort
might fail to satisfy Article 5 is a much more difficult question. Before
looking at United Kingdom practice relevant to this issue, we should give
a sense of its likely importance by examining how the transposed Directive was received and implemented by the brewing industry itself.

(ii) **The reactions of the brewing industry**[69]

The United Kingdom brewing industry is organised in two national associations, the Brewers' Society (which represents all national and regional
brewers and most of the large local brewers, and whose members account
for 95 per cent of domestic production)[70], and the Small Independent
Brewers' Association (which represents the majority – about 100 – of
brewers in this category who, however, only account for about 1 per cent
of production).[71]

While the former organisation was heavily involved in consultation with
MAFF before the passage of the Directive and its transposition, and was
able to consult its members for their opinions, SIBA was not consulted
by government – a perhaps understandable omission given the size of its
members' market, its relatively recent foundation in 1980[72], and the fact
that most of its members produce only draught beer, on which the label-

---

[67] See *e.g.* Directive 86/197, art. 2(1). Here the French text has "la législation . . . est appliquée
de manière à admettre (interdire) le commerce," which leaves the same question open.
[68] Cases C-382–3/92 *Commission v United Kingdom* [1994] ECR n.y.r.
[69] Information in this section is based on interviews with representatives of the Brewers' Society,
and of the Small Independent Brewers' Association (SIBA); and on a questionnaire administered
to 19 brewers, drawn proportionally from the different categories identified by the Monopolies
and Mergers Commission (*op. cit.*, n 22).
[70] In January 1994 the Society changed its name to the Brewers' and Licensed Retailers' Association (BLRA), reflecting the changes noted in section 2(ii)(b) above: Large, "A New Spirit in
Portman Square" *Brewers' Guardian*, February 1994, pp 10–11.
[71] There are also regional organisations, such as the Yorkshire Brewers' Association and the
Northern Independent Brewers' Association.
[72] SIBA however reported that it has been obtaining increased recognition from government,
and is now being consulted on EC proposals that directly affect the brewing industry, but has
to find out for itself about those with indirect impact.

ling regulations impinge less directly.[73] Neither organisation felt that the Directive had given or would give any economic problems to its constituents; but while the Brewers' Society was confident that its members were fully consulted and informed about the Directive and Regulations, SIBA was less sure that its own information efforts, by way of notification of new legal requirements, including these labelling rules, in its monthly newsletter to members, necessarily produced an adequate level of awareness.

Enquiries among a group of 19 brewers, including members of both organisations, suggested that while the fact of change in legal requirements was effectively communicated by the organisations, ascertaining the precise content of the requirements was much more troublesome. For more than half the group (11), press coverage and the SIBA were the sole sources for this information. Of the remaining eight, all of whom also used SIBA/Brewers' Society and press coverage, one used a legal consultant, one used its packaging department, two contacted their local Trading Standards office, and four had spoken to MAFF. There was a general feeling, among the eight brewers in the group supplying in bottles or cans and hence directly affected by the Directive and Regulations, that their having been able to comply in time (if they had: one brewer had not) owed something to chance; first intimation of the need for change had usually come by word of mouth.

The brewers experienced no substantive problems in complying with the new regulatory requirements. Prior to their introduction, all those who supplied labelled products showed the name of the product, its net quantity, place of origin and their own name or address or both, along with the alcoholic content in original gravity (og). In consequence the only change the brewers had to make was to use alcohol by volume measurements instead of original gravity. Even among the small brewers contacted, the switch to a new measurement method and the amendment of labels appears to have gone off without difficulty, though one respondent noted that it would not have changed labels while existing stocks lasted, even if this had been necessary to achieve timely compliance. Experience from other Member States is similar, either because no substantive change was needed at all, or because (as with Ireland)[74] adequate warning was given by government. Only German breweries complained of relabelling costs.[75]

It is fortunate that compliance was painless, since with one exception

---

[73] Casks of draught beer must be supplied with details of the manufacturer and its alcoholic content in the form of alcohol by volume, but this need only be given in the form of notification to the retailer, who must then show the alcohol content in accordance with the Food Labelling Regulations 1984, reg. 31A and 32(1)(c) (as amended): for example, by means of a notice in the bar of a public house, or by inclusion on the label clipped to the beer pump. Casual observation suggests that compliance with this requirement is poor.

[74] Schwarze, Becker and Pollack eds., *op. cit.*, n 7, pp 260–262.

[75] See note 66, *supra.*

brewers saw little or no positive benefit flowing from the new requirements. Most viewed them purely in consumer protection terms, and felt
that no significant additional protection was given. Producing for the
domestic market only, they hardly perceived the free trade objectives of
the Directive, and were indifferent both to the threat and the opportunity
of increased European competition. The exception was a brewer who
did export, and thought harmonisation very important for this reason.
Experience since this survey, notably with retailer imports of beer labelled
for consumption in other Member States[76], suggests that the general attitude to imports may have been too complacent.

(iii) Consumer opinion

United Kingdom consumer associations are grouped for purposes of European issues and representation in the Consumers in the European Community Group (CECG). The Group enjoys full consultative status with
MAFF on food issues, including labelling issues, and also has direct contacts with the Community's Economic and Social Committee, with the
European Parliament and with the umbrella organisation for European
consumer groups, the Bureau Européen des Unions de Consommateurs
(BEUC). It expressed itself as happy with Directive 86/197, but – not
surprisingly – favours enactment of the "QUID" proposals.[77]

In addition to consulting CECG, MAFF has also recently commissioned
a survey on food labelling.[78] While this suggested a considerable awareness among shoppers of labelling issues, including interest in ingredients,
it found at the same time that 75 per cent of respondents were satisfied
with the information given on labels, and that half were swayed in their
purchasing decisions mainly by brand name. No information specific to
beer – or even to alcoholic beverages generally – was reported, but it
would be surprising if beer buyers showed themselves to be more sensitive
to labelling issues than shoppers generally. There has been no evidence
of any kind from other sources to suggest consumer dissatisfaction with
beer labelling arrangements.

(iv) Official enforcement[79]

We have noted that the structure of Directives 79/112 and 86/197 is such
that no administrative steps are necessary, beyond transposition of their

---

[76] Personal imports of beer under enlarged duty-free concessions have received greater publicity
(see Tett, "EC backs Customs duty-free rule," *Financial Times*, March 3, 1994), but their legality
does not depend on labelling harmonisation, since the Food Labelling Regulations relate only
to the *sale* of incorrectly labelled items, not import, possession or use.
[77] Above, section 3(ii).
[78] MAFF, *Food Labelling Survey England and Wales* (HMSO, 1990).
[79] See generally Jukes, "Regulation and enforcement of food safety in the UK" (1993) 18 Food
Pol. 131–142.

rules, to make them effective as legal obligations upon producers. Official enforcement could therefore simply take the form of action post hoc, in the form of warnings, prosecution or penalties following discovery of breach of the rules. Enforcement officers might, indeed, adopt a passive attitude in relation to discovery, and await complaints from aggrieved consumers – or trade rivals – before undertaking any investigation. A more interventionist, preventive approach would involve occasional or systematic inspections at the production or retail stage or both, with a view to detecting breaches in advance of any impact on consumers.

(a) *Before 1990*

It appears clear from our inquiries that food authorities are not content simply to adopt a reactive attitude and await consumer complaints about labelling. Beyond that, it is difficult to generalise about United Kingdom practice. Prior to the enactment of the Food Safety Act 1990, no attempt was made centrally to promote uniformity of practice among local authorities with food responsibilities, in relation to labelling as in relation to other food control matters. Local authorities with such responsibilities vary greatly in size, structure and resources[80]; moreover, the type of professional officer who discharges these responsibilities varies according to the type of authority. In unitary and lower-tier authorities this has normally been the Environmental Health Officer (EHO), in upper tier authorities the Trading Standards Officer (TSO). Given the historic primary concern of EHOs with health and of TSOs with dishonest dealing, policy divergence between authorities on enforcement matters would not be surprising. We made inquiries of some 20, mainly upper-tier, food authorities about their practice. The EHOs who responded stressed health risk to the public as the key indicator for the allocation of scarce inspection and enforcement resources. Since mis-labelling in itself (as opposed to the fraudulent concealment of adulteration) did not represent such a risk, labelling would only be checked in the course of routine inspection of major food producers and food importers, and on the occasion of checks on smaller producers prompted by concern about possible infringement of other food regulations which might result in risk to the public. TSOs, on the other hand, placed heavy emphasis on proper labelling, seeing it as a bulwark against adulteration leading to health risks, as well as against fraud. Labelling appeared to play the lead role, rather than an accessory one, in their programmes or projects of inspection, sampling, and advice. Both groups of officers laid the main emphasis on preventive inspection at the premises of producers; policy on retail inspection, both generally and for mis-labelling, appeared to vary considerably. So too did attitudes to prosecution, with one EHO taking the

---

[80] See section 4(i) above, and for the statutory allocation, Food and Drugs Act 1955, s. 83, now replaced (without significant alteration) by Food Safety Act 1990, s. 5. The structure of local government is currently (September 1994) under review.

view that its time and cost had never been justified for a labelling contravention, while some TSOs appeared to prosecute regularly, and routinely to follow up infringements.

While there may be a difference of emphasis between authorities according to which type of official discharges labelling-related functions, it is clear that major disparities of practice also exist within these groups. A notable example of this relates to record-keeping. There are no national figures for the number of investigations and infringements of the food labelling regulations. There was at one time a requirement for local authorities to pass such data to the relevant Department on a regular basis, but as the data were never put to any use, the requirement was abandoned. Individual authorities now show no consistency in the way they collect and present their own data on infringements and prosecutions: some have statistics on labelling infringements (but none specific to beer labelling, or even to alcoholic beverage labelling); others only have figures relating to food law contraventions in general.

Quite aside from any standards of enforcement implicit in European Community law, it is clear that there were before 1990 pressures to reduce the adverse effects, for food producers, of this diversity. Local authorities sought themselves to provide a framework for harmonisation of practice in the general area of trading standards, including labelling, by the creation in 1978 of the Local Authorities Co-ordinating Body on Trading Standards (LACOTS), which has promoted the exchange of information (including information about practice elsewhere in Europe) and the development of policies for the harmonisation of regulatory approaches by different food authorities. Notable among these is the "home authority" principle, identifying the "home authority" of a food company, as a primary contact for it and source of official information about it.[81]

(b) *The effect of the Food Safety Act*

The "level playing field" concept within the Single European Market of course provides a new reason for national concern with local enforcement practice, in food labelling as elsewhere. The Food Safety Act embodies a major shift of discretion and control from the local to the national level, inspired in part by the need for qualitative and quantitative harmonisation of food inspection practice posed by Directive 89/397 and its sequel, the so-called Additional Measures Directive.[82] A major programme of standardisation of practice has been initiated by central government through the promulgation of a number of Codes of Practice under Section 40 of the Act.[83] These address both issues of co-ordination between two-tier authorities (Code of Practice No. 1) and of the content of inspections (Code No. 3). These Codes are binding on the relevant

---

[81] LACOTS, *Home Authority Principle* (April 1994). See further Chapter 9, section 5(iii).
[82] Council Directive 93/99 (OJ 1993 L290/14); see also Chapter 6, text accompanying n 27.
[83] The 16 Codes presently in force are noted at Chapter 6, n 48.

local authorities, which in exercising their statutory functions must have regard to the relevant provisions of the Codes and must comply with any Ministerial direction in the Codes which requires them to take specific steps (s. 40(2)).[84] Of particular importance is paragraph 2(f) of Code No. 3, which states that inspection should include the "inspection of labels, labelling requirements and advertising material." Both EHOs and TSOs have noted that the Directives are being invoked by MAFF to secure more uniformity in enforcement practice and in the collection of statistics. Under the Control of Foodstuffs Directive, central government is required to report to the Commission[85]; and in its turn, it has now taken, under the Food Safety Act (s. 41), power in very general terms to require reports and returns from local authorities.

While the discipline of the Control of Foodstuffs Directive has undoubtedly been significant, it is important to realise that in this respect it simply confirmed and reinforced a strong and pre-existent domestic trend. A review of food safety was initiated by government at the time of the passage of the consolidating 1984 Act; worries in the 1980s about outbreaks of salmonella and listeria poisoning reinforced the questioning of the enforcement system; and more generally there has been an impatience on the part of industry and commerce with variations in local authority enforcement practice, and a desire in government to respond to these concerns.[86]

6 Conclusions

What may we learn, from this mundane micro-history, about the larger issues of legal implementation of Community law and policy? Perhaps we should start by noticing that, in the application of the Alcohol Content Directive to the beer industry in Britain, we have an example of European Community law working very largely in the way that it is supposed to. The Directive was a straightforward piece of rule-harmonisation, effective in removing a potential barrier to trade (in that pre-existing national modes of calculating and labelling for alcohol content did in fact differ) and in increasing consumer protection.[87] Though it laid down a specific rule, it left sufficient latitude to cope with variations in national con-

---

[84] *Ibid.* n 48 and accompanying text.
[85] Article 14, Directive 89/397/EEC (OJ 1989 L186/23), see further Chapter 6, section 5(iii)(b).
[86] See for example the complaints about variations in local authority inspectors' practice in health and safety matters (especially as compared with Health and Safety Executive inspectors) noted in Department of Trade and Industry, *Review of the Implementation and Enforcement of EC Law in the United Kingdom* (1993), Annex B (health and safety case study), pp 98–101; see also Chapter 6, section 5(i).
[87] One TSO noted that "alcoholic content labelling of drink is an important tool in controlling the practice [of] ... adulteration or substitution of alcoholic drinks": letter of Cornwall TSO, 15 May 1994.

ditions: so that, for example, it could be applied to draught beer production and retailing by means of more detailed national regulations.[88] National regulations implemented the Directive in a timely and accurate way; the industry was made sufficiently aware of the Directive and regulations, by government and trade bodies, to be in a position to comply. The genuinely normative effect of the Directive is demonstrated by the government's withdrawal of the 1992 draft regulations which would have unilaterally lowered the threshold for declarations of alcohol content from 1.2 to 0.05 per cent.

The textbook appearance of events here reinforces the relevance of this example as a basis for putting some more fundamental questions about Community law of this type and its national implementation. The first basic question might be put in this way: can the Community have an effective policy for preventing conflicting regulatory standards from functioning as trade barriers, other than at the cost of significant intrusion into national administration?

Within the economy of the EC Treaty, the removal of measures of equivalent effect to quantitative restrictions is supposed to have real, not just formal, effects. Viewed from close up, it is doubtful how far a measure like this, harmonising substantive rules of conduct, can go in this direction. It can render illegitimate any State obstruction of complying imports; such negative obligations should be relatively easily policed by the vigilance and self-interest of importers, traders and retailers. But to secure equality of conditions of competition there needs to be some assurance that the harmonised rule will be applied with broadly approximated enthusiasm and effectiveness in all Member States. Achieving this demands a number of conditions which, our beer story shows, are not easily satisfied. Member States need to have similar interests in the relevant consumer protection goals – not to say, as did the Greeks, that rapid implementation of this Directive could hardly be expected because alcoholism was not a Greek problem.[89] National enforcement systems need to be capable of central control and policing, which has in the past clearly not been the case with that of the United Kingdom in this area (though some other national systems are more centralised).[90] Alternatively they need to be consumer driven (which would at least relate enforcement intensity to local market conditions); but this is not the case either with beer labelling or labelling

---

[88] See regs. 31A and 33(1)(c) of the amended 1984 regulations, above, section 4(iii), implementing a general requirement of "adequate information" in art. 12 of the 1979 Directive. These are, it is worth noting, among the most complex of the current UK food labelling regulations, and MAFF has specifically asked for comment on their operation in it recent consultation on the consolidation and review of the 1984 regulations: MAFF, "Interested Parties" letter of 30 March 1994.

[89] Schwarze, Becker and Pollack eds., *op. cit.*, n 7, pp 190–191.

[90] Schwarze, Becker and Pollack eds., *op. cit.*, n 7, pp 26–29 (Belgium), 81–85 (Denmark); Schwarze, Becker and Pollack eds., *op. cit.*, n 58, pp 245–255 (France), 270 (Ireland).

in general, since if consumers generally had the information to challenge the accuracy of labelling, labelling regulations would hardly be needed.[91]

Most fundamental, however, is the problem of achieving a given intensity of enforcement of a legal rule. A rule in the form of a simple mandatory requirement – the wording on a beer label – carries no explicit, nor even implicit, instruction to the authorities as to the rigour with which they should enforce it. Prosecutorial discretion is a common feature of Community legal systems, even of those which claim to restrict it, such as Germany.[92] As we have seen[93], the labelling Directives themselves make no attempt to give such instructions. It is, indeed, difficult to imagine how an enforcement standard – which would be bound to tolerate something less than 100 per cent compliance – could be so expressed as itself to be capable of effective policing in the Community interest. The emergence of such a standard is, however, a necessary element of the "New Approach" to removal of trade barriers, which relies on importer State confidence in exporter State standards and their enforcement. Chapter 9, on toy safety, amply demonstrates this point. As already noted here, however, the same effects arise under the Control of Foodstuffs Directive, not only, or even mainly, in relation to foodstuffs destined for intra-Community export, but in relation to all foodstuffs, including domestic control of domestic production for the domestic market. While creation of mutual confidence in domestic standards may be seen under the "New Approach" as an alternative to new harmonised rules, it is important to note that where such rules already exist, over quite large areas of the food industry including labelling, the measures to create confidence will be added to the harmonising power of the rules; indeed, that they may need to be added if rules of the kind we have been examining in this Chapter are to be applied consistently across the Community. This is especially the case, perhaps, in markets like beer where most producers and enforcers alike may find it hard to perceive the Community relevance of labelling practice and enforcement. The veiling of the Community rules through transposition in domestic regulations can only accentuate this difficulty.

As already indicated, and as Chapters 6 and 9 develop in more detail, assuring harmonisation of enforcement levels or approaches involves a considerable degree of intrusion into domestic administrative procedures. Such intrusion can hardly be avoided if common ideas about methods and intensity of enforcement are to be disseminated across Member States. It is notable that the Government's push for greater uniformity of approach among food authorities, and for comprehensive reporting, has followed the 1989 Directive and the Food Safety Act; it was

---

[91] For more general treatment, see Chapter 10, below.
[92] See Herrman, "The German prosecutor" in *Discretionary Justice in Europe and America* (Davis ed 1976), 16–74.
[93] Above, section 5(i).

not triggered earlier by the labelling Directives. Perhaps it may seem odd that the Government in the Community which has most loudly vaunted the virtues of deregulation and the need for observation of the principle of subsidiarity should be thus vigorously carrying forward the implementation of a Community food safety regime which combines detailed substantive rules and intrusive procedural requirements. The beer labelling case shows, however, that Community requirements can provide convenient extra leverage in aid of the quite distinct governmental project of restricting the independence of action of local authorities, in their regulatory no less than in their other functions. We explore further, in our final Chapter, the broader issues – of how regulatory competence is scaled to market scope and structure – of which beer labelling gives some tantalising hints.

TERENCE DAINTITH

Chapter 6
The Official Control of Foodstuffs

1 Introduction

Within a book whose prime concern is the nature of the implementation process in relation to European Community law, the random inclusion of a study of the Official Control of Foodstuffs Directive[1] is serendipitous.[2] In being primarily concerned with enforcement and, therefore, with an important aspect of implementation[3], this particular Directive offers the opportunity for a study of the implementation of implementation. The main provisions of the Directive are concerned with the scope, manner and frequency of inspections of food premises as a means of enforcing EC regulations on foodstuffs, with the overall aim of providing verification of compliance with them. The manner, style and overall context of its implementation within the United Kingdom may, therefore, be capable of revealing much about not only the implementation of EC legislation into United Kingdom law *per se*, but also about the relationship between EC and United Kingdom regulatory styles, particularly within the current de-regulatory climate. This, in turn, may allow some predictions as to the direction the SEM programme may take.

These aims may appear somewhat ambitious. To begin with, it is indeed a dubious claim that such a generalisation can be founded on the study of a single directive. Further, the implementation of the Directive is so recent that the full extent of its impact on either foodstuffs regulation itself or the SEM programme as a whole are, as yet, largely unknown, and although the study includes an element of empirical research, much of it involves theoretical or speculative enquiry. It can only, therefore, present a limited and somewhat contingent view. Notwithstanding these opening caveats, however, the study does present evidence that despite its apparently unproblematic, and apparently welcome, implementation,

---

[1] Directive 89/397/EEC (OJ 1989 L186/23).
[2] On the manner in which the case studies, which form Part Two of this book, were selected, see Chapter 1, section 3(ii).
[3] This is to adopt the view of implementation as a continuous process which includes enforcement and compliance in its elements. See Clune and Lindquist, "What Implementation Isn't: Toward a General Framework for Implementation Research" (1981) Wis.L.Rev. 1044–1116; Snyder, Chapter 3 in this book.

the structure of the Directive itself and the structure of the national regime in which it is implemented, combine to present a good example of current, state-of-the-art regulatory style.

What then is its structure and what are its effects? The emphasis on the *Official* Control of Foodstuffs implies that the Directive is concerned with enforcement by officials, as opposed to enforcement by private individuals themselves; prima facie, so it is. But as this Chapter goes on to show, an examination of the forms and structures of its implementation yields little evidence that this is in fact the case. Instead, implementation of the Directive may be seen as encouraging control not primarily by officials charged with enforcing foodstuffs legislation, but by industry operating within a strongly centralised regulatory framework. This may be seen as contributing to the further developing of systems of self-regulatory control which increasingly have their parallels in other sectors of economic life.

2 Background to Directive 89/397/EEC within EC food policy

The food industry represents the largest sector of European manufacturing and trade[4] and is, therefore, a major target of regulatory controls. Since the market between Member States of the EC must be "made free", legal regulations have been developed into the chief liberating instrument. Thus, if trade barriers are not to be erected on health grounds, so as to constitute an effective quantitative restriction of the free movement of goods between Member States, any justification for excluding certain categories of food imports has to be eliminated. But whilst barriers to trade in food products should be eliminated and products lawfully produced and marketed in one Member State should not face any national restrictions to import or export[5], a major concern of government, the food industry, and consumers, is that the quality and safety of such products may be uneven within the twelve Member States. If consumers are to feel confidence in products from other Member States and governments of Member States are not to restrict free movement as a result, the efficient functioning of the market requires that health and safety standards are satisfied. This is, of course, to assume that the satisfaction of consumer safety standards is a prerequisite of efficient market functioning.

-----

[4] In June 1994, the United Kingdom alone had 403,000 employees in the food industry: (1994) 102 *Employment Gazette*, p. S9, table 1.3. An estimated £45 billion was spent on household food in 1992, just under 12% of total consumer expenditure: HMSO, *National Food Survey 1992* (1993), and 9.52% of total consumers expenditure in 1992 was on meals eaten out: *Retail Business Market Surveys*, July 1994, p 4.

[5] Decision in Case 120/78 *Cassis de Dijon* OJ 1980 C256/2. For a discussion of the *Cassis de Dijon* case, see Chapter 2, section 5(i).

On the assumption that free movement of goods and consumer protection were in conflict, rather than running in parallel, the European Court of Justice, in its interpretation of Articles 30 and 36 of the EC Treaty[6], attempted to reconcile them. In its caselaw, the Court has emphasised the need to restrict the powers of the Member States to introduce or enforce any measures which might hamper the flow of trade; this approach has caused some disquiet in certain Member States and has raised concerns amongst consumer groups[7], since unregulated trading could result in the elimination of acceptable food standards along with the elimination of trade barriers. Nonetheless, the Commission has accepted a modified version of the Court's approach in its own legislative framework.[8]

Directive 89/397/EEC on the Official Control of Foodstuffs falls into the category of horizontal regulation. It lays down general rules to be followed by national enforcement authorities in inspecting the production and distribution of foodstuffs but does not specify exactly how implementation of substantive rules is to be enforced.[9] Rather, it seeks to ensure that the general principles governing the carrying out of official controls are harmonised. Indeed, the Preamble states that Member States

---

[6] Since *Cassis de Dijon* the Court has developed its position in a number of cases including Case 286/81 *Oosthoek's Uitgeversmaatschappii* [1982] ECR 4575; Case 407/85 *Drei Glocken* v *USL Centro-Sud* [1988] ECR 4233; Case C362/88 *GB-INNO-BM* v *Confederation du Commerce Luxembourg* [1990] ECR 1–667; Cases C-1 and C176/90 *Aragonesa de Publicidad Exterior SA (APESA)* v *Departamento de Sanidad y Seguridad Social de la Generalitat de Cataluna (DSSC)*, Judgment of 25 July 1991 and Case 94/82 *De Kikvorsch Groothandel* [1983] ECR 947. The recent decision of the Court in *Keck* and *Mithouard* (Cases C-267 and 268/91 Judgment of 24 November 1993) can be seen as having limited the application of the *Cassis* principle so that Member States have greater capacity to exercise local controls; see Chalmers, "Repackaging the Internal Market" (1994) 19 Eur.L.Rev. 385–403. See also Micklitz and Weatherill, "Consumer Policy in the European Community: Before and After Maastricht" (1993) 16 J.Consumer Pol. 285–322, where the authors note that the Court's application of "negative law" in these cases (that is, provisions of Community law directed at removing obstacles to cross-border trade) to defeat national law "involves a preference for the consumer advantages of free trade over the advantages for the consumer of national regulation which impedes trade" (p 289).

[7] It has been commented that the approach taken by the ECJ has been to the detriment of consumers and that the freedom to regulate food safety within the EC is much more limited than in the USA, where individual states may exercise a far wider discretion. See von Heydebrant, "The Free Movement of Foodstuffs: Has the Court of Justice Got it Wrong?" (1991) 16 E. L. Rev. 391–415.

[8] The Commission's White Paper, *Completing the Internal Market* (COM(85)310), set out its new approach to harmonisation in relation to foodstuffs. Legislation is required where the life and health of humans is involved and where there is a need to satisfy mandatory requirements for fair trading and protection of consumers to provide for official checks. This is the so-called "mutual recognition" approach, which the Commission has defined as "where a product suitably and satisfactorily fulfils the legitimate objective of a Member State's own rules . . . the importing country cannot justify prohibiting its sale in its territory by claiming that the way it fulfils the objective is different from that imposed on domestic products" (Communication from the Commission on the consequences of *Cassis de Dijon* OJ 1989 271/3).

[9] For a more detailed discussion of distinctions between the regulatory styles of the EC, see Chapter 2.

should be allowed a certain degree of freedom as to the practical means of carrying out inspections, in order not to interfere with systems of proven worth which are best suited to their particular situation.[10]

The significance of the Directive lies in its being central to the implementation of the entire EC food policy strategy; without harmonisation of systems and procedures at every stage in the food chain, substantive EC regulations can neither be seen to be policed nor effectively enforced at national level. It thus purports to institute a framework of food control mechanisms in which consumers can have confidence in the quality of any product, regardless of origin – and, as a corollary, to promote the effective functioning of the foodstuffs market within the SEM. The Directive is based on the premise that Member States actually have systems in existence in relation to food standards and the health of consumers. Indeed, if they did not, there would be few rules to harmonise and many to create afresh. Given that the problem that the Directive seeks to address is a ubiquitous mistrust between Member States, of both the adequacy of those standards and the degree of thoroughness with which they are enforced, acceptance of one another's standards is clearly vital.

The effects of Directive 89/397/EEC are to place the onus of control on the exporting, rather than the importing, Member State and to institute a once-and-for-all inspection regime at the point of production; a product produced in Manchester and subject to United Kingdom controls cannot therefore be excluded from the market in Munich on health grounds. Free movement of goods requires that equivalence as to both the enforcement of standards and the standards of enforcement must be presumed.

A third effect arises from the horizontal form of the Directive; if implementation between Member States is to be consistent, the same must be true for implementation *within* Member States. Central governments, in order to give substance to a framework Directive, must therefore play a significant part in ensuring the uniform application of controls at local level. Whilst the United Kingdom asserts that the recommendations, made in the Sutherland Report,[11] which argue for consistency in the implementation of EC law through the centralisation of enforcement methods are inefficient and costly, it accepts the recommendations which seek to promote a partnership between actors in the harmonisation pro-

---

[10] Thus, Azzi notes in *Making European Policies Work*, Vol. I (Siedentopf and Ziller eds 1988), that it is the "vocation" of Community law to be absorbed into national law as naturally as possible (p 199).
[11] *The Internal Market After 1992: Meeting the Challenge*, Sutherland Report to the EEC Commission by the High Level Group on the Operation of the Internal Market, October 1992.

cess – the "co-operative approach".[12] One focus of this study is whether, in United Kingdom practice, such a distinction has been maintained.

3 Directive 89/397/EEC

In its draft form, the Directive used the term "inspection" rather than "control" in its title.[13] In the event, however, official control is defined as inspection by the competent authorities of compliance with provisions relating to foodstuffs, food additives and materials and articles intended to come into contact with foodstuffs which are aimed at preventing risks to public health, guaranteeing fair commercial transactions and protecting consumer interests.[14] Control comprises one or more of inspection, sampling and analysis; inspection of staff hygiene; examination of written and documentary materials; and examination of any verification systems set up by the undertaking and of the results obtained.[15] Such control methods apply to virtually any object or process involved in the manufacture and distribution of foodstuffs.[16]

The real substance of the Directive is contained in Article 4. Inspections are to be carried out regularly and, where non-compliance is suspected, means proportionate to the end to be observed should be used in carrying them out. Inspections should cover all stages of production, manufacture, import into the Community, processing, storage, transport, distribution and trade and it is for the inspector to decide at what stage, or stages, inspections shall be carried out. As a general rule, they should be carried out without prior warning[17]; inspectors must be granted adequate powers to carry out their duties[18] and have the right to take the requisite measures if they discover, or suspect, an irregularity.[19] Any person (natural or legal) concerned shall be obliged to undergo any inspection and assist inspectors in the accomplishment of their tasks.[20] Undertakings (*i.e.* manufacturers, distributors, carriers, wholesalers, retailers etc.) should not have the right to oppose inspectors but, at the

---

[12] See DTI, *Review of the Implementation and Enforcement of EC Law in the United Kingdom*, (1993) p 20.
[13] See Proposal for a Council Directive on the Official Inspection of Foodstuffs, (OJ 1987 C20/6).
[14] Article 1.
[15] Article 5.
[16] Article 6 sets out what the control methods in Article 5 apply to: premises, transportation and machinery; raw materials, technological aids and other products used for the preparation and production of foodstuffs; finished and semi-finished products; materials and articles intended to come into contact with foodstuffs; cleaning and maintenance products and processes and pesticides; processes used for the manufacture and processing of foodstuffs; labelling and presentation of foodstuffs; and preserving methods.
[17] Article 2.
[18] Preamble.
[19] Article 10.
[20] Article 11.

same time, their legitimate rights must be preserved, in particular the right to manufacturing secrecy and the right of appeal. Thus, a balance is to be struck between effective enforcement and infringement of civil and commercial rights.[21]

Member States are obliged to report on measures taken to implement the Directive and the effectiveness of those measures.[22] First, they must ensure that the competent authorities draw up forward programmes laying down the nature and frequency of the inspections to be carried out. Secondly, they have the further obligation to send information on implementation to the Commission by 1 May of each year, specifying the criteria applied in drawing up these programmes, the number and type of inspections carried out and the number and type of infringements established.

4 Transposition into United Kingdom law

Directive 89/397 was transposed into United Kingdom law, as part of a broader process of reform of food law, by the Food Safety Act 1990. There was thus no need to resort to either dedicated primary legislation nor to the provisions contained in the European Communities Act 1972.[23] The provisions of the Directive are not set out in their entirety within the Act itself. Rather, the Act sets up structures and mechanisms of responsibility and enforcement which allow the obligations imposed by the Directive to be operative.

Two legal mechanisms were used. First, under Section 17, Ministers may make such regulations as they consider necessary or expedient for the purpose of executing, administering or enforcing any Community obligations in relation to food, food sources or contact materials. Since the coming into force of the 1990 Act, several statutory instruments which implement aspects of the Directive have been adopted in relation to

---

[21] It should be emphasised that the EC does not have authority to compel any Member States to take punitive measures against its own citizens or the citizens of other Member States, either in principle or in terms of specifying the particular form that sanctions ought to take. Directive 89/397/EEC cannot, therefore, require Member States to impose criminal sanctions in respect of any food control obligations and the choice of the form and methods of enforcement are left to individual Member States. The lack of uniformity of sanctions between them in this respect was a problem addressed by the Sutherland Report (*op. cit.*, n 12) and again by the Commission in its Green Paper: *Access of Consumers to Justice and the Settlement of Consumer Disputes in the Single Market* (COM(93)576 final).

[22] Article 14.

[23] For further discussion, see Sections 2 and 3, Chapter 4.

exports and sampling and the qualifications of inspectors.[24] Secondly, under Section 40, Ministers may issue Codes of Practice in relation to the execution and enforcement of the Act. Provisions of the Directive, relating to the nature, manner and scope of food standards and hygiene inspections, the requirements for forward planning of inspections and that inspections of products intended for consignment to another Member State must be carried out with the same care as those intended for the United Kingdom market, have been transposed in this way.[25]

In addition, food officers must complete statistical returns, under Section 41, in relation to official action taken as a result of inspections, in accordance with the requirement imposed on the United Kingdom to report on an annual basis to the Commission in relation to food control.

The Directive has now been supplemented by an Additional Measures Directive[26] which relates to the availability of suitably qualified personnel in, and standards of, laboratories. It requires Member States to ensure that competent authorities have sufficient technical and administrative competence to carry out inspections. They must also ensure that laboratories entrusted with control functions adopt generally acceptable and accredited systems of quality control. In view of the importance of the food industry to the European market as a whole, the Directive also recognises the need for co-ordination of foodstuffs control between the competent authorities of the Member States and between them and the Commission by requiring them to co-operate with designated Commission officials. The function of these officials is to monitor the equivalence and effectiveness of national official control systems.

The transposition of the Directive was apparently unproblematic in that it was transposed timeously.[27] In addition, by avoiding the "copy out" method of transposition[28] the obligations of the Directive have been inte-

---

[24] The Food Safety (Exports) Regulations (SI 1991/1476), and Food Safety (Exports) Regulations (Northern Ireland) 1991 (SR 1991/344), extend existing legislation to cover exports to implement Articles 2 and 3 of the Directive. Article 7 (on the qualifications for inspectors and analysts) was implemented by the Food Safety (Sampling and Qualifications) Regulations 1990 (SI 1990/2463), and Food Safety (Sampling and Qualifications) Regulations (Northern Ireland) 1991 (SR 1991/198). The Infant Formula and Follow-on Formula Regulations 1995 (SI 1995/77) have recently come into force.

[25] The Codes of Practice reproduce the requirements of the Directive in similar but not identical language. Code of Practice No. 3 defines "inspection" and specifies that, as a general rule, inspections should be carried out without prior notice; Codes of Practice Nos. 8 and 9 stipulate that forward programmes, in relation to food safety and hygiene inspections, should be drawn up by food authorities and that officers must inspect products intended for export to other Member States with the same degree of care.

[26] Directive 93/99/EEC (OJ 1993 L290/14).

[27] The Directive was implemented in general terms through the Food Safety Act 1990 which came into force 1 January 1991. The target date for the Directive's implementation was 20 June 1991.

[28] The "copy out" approach has been described by the DTI as where the implementing legislation simply refers to or literally adopts the same, or virtually the same, language as the Directive itself. It can be contrasted with "elaboration", which involves completely rewriting the Directive into the style associated with traditional domestic legislation. The DTI feels that the elaborative method increases the risk of over-implementation and that copy-out, accompanied by notes of

grated within the language and context of domestic primary legislation and regulations made under it.[29] However, the implementation of the Directive cannot be examined outside of its transpositional context. Since it was transposed within the 1990 Act, this is, clearly, the Act itself. But, at the more general level, it is also the overall regulatory climate in which the Act appeared; accordingly, the style and content of the 1990 Act can be seen as the product of the environment in which it was conceived.

It is in relation to both the regulatory structures in which the Directive's provisions are placed and in relation to the broader aims of the Directive, as a whole, that the issues arising from its implementation may be seen. Whether the aims of Directive 89/397 are truly co-extensive with the aims of the government's overhaul of food regulation and food control or whether, instead, the Act provided the opportunity effectively to shape the Directive into a mould required by its own agenda,[30] is the fundamental question underlying the implementation of the Directive. We must now turn to the background and structure of the Food Safety Act 1990, to provide the means of examining the effects of the chosen method of transposing the Directive.

5 The Food Safety Act 1990

(i) Background

In the same year that the Food Act 1984 was passed[31], a government review of food law was initiated. A five year programme of consultations with the foodstuffs industry, consumers and enforcement authorities, with the declared aim of ensuring safety throughout the food chain ensued, in order to deal with increased consumer choice, new technological developments in food production and manufacture, and changing retail patterns. What was required was a comprehensive food policy and effective system of enforcement which would allow adequate control of foodstuffs in the interests of the consumer without imposing undue restrictions on the industry. Added to this was the additional obligation to implement EC foodstuffs Directives. A general Food Advisory Committee was set up, together with several other committees to look at specific aspects of food safety. The composition of these committees of experts

---

practice and guidance, ought to be considered where possible. Whichever method is used, "the least burdensome approach for business should be employed": DTI *Review of the Implementation and Enforcement of EC Law in the United Kingdom, op. cit.* n 13.

[29] On the "vocation" of EC law, see G.Azzi, *op. cit.*, n 11.

[30] The elaborative method of transposition would seem to facilitate this; in addition, there would seem to be implications arising from it in terms of the transparency debate.

[31] The 1984 Act did not apply in Scotland, where the Food and Drugs (Scotland) Act 1956 continued in force. See Chapter 5, Section 4(i).

has not, however, been uncontroversial, since some 75% of their members were connected with either the government, the food industry or both.[32]

Media campaigns arising from the salmonella, listeria, botulism and bovine spongiform encephalopathy "scares" in the late 1980s, reflecting public concern about food safety, may be seen as accelerating the legislative timetable in this area. The incidence of reported food poisoning tripled between 1982 and 1989 from about 15,000 cases to 55,000 and publicity in relation to salmonella and problems with yoghurt, soft cheeses and eggs heightened public awareness of potential risks. The Audit Commission examined this problem and indicated that there was, indeed, cause for concern. 12 per cent of a sample of 5,000 food related premises were found to display "high risks" in regard to food safety. Take-away outlets showed the highest percentage (18.6% presenting a high risk), closely followed by food manufacturers (18%) and restaurants (17.5%).[33] The passing of the 1990 Act can be seen, therefore, as motivated both by the necessity to respond to media and consumer-led demands, as well as to obligations resulting from membership of the EC. The Directive was not therefore the immediate, or only, reason for the introduction of the 1990 Act; rather, the introduction of the 1990 Act presented a useful and timely legislative opportunity for the Directive to be implemented.

A White Paper, *Food Safety – Protecting the Consumer*[34] was produced, outlining the current state of food law and enumerating the government's legislative proposals. These were to ensure safe methods of food technology and distribution methods, ensuring that food is not misleadingly labelled or presented, reinforcing present powers and penalties against law-breakers, ensuring that new EC directives can be implemented and streamlining legislation by combining the Acts which apply in England and Wales and Scotland. The aims, therefore, were to consolidate and systematise existing food controls, not to begin afresh.

In terms of its substantive elements, the Act[35] introduces few changes to the existing pattern of United Kingdom food law. The basis of modern food law has been established since 1938[36] and in relation to its underlying policy concerns, the 1990 Act follows similar patterns to the previous

---

[32] Cannon, *The Politics of Food* (1987), p 314. Of 370 people on government expert committees, 133 worked for the food industry, 65 were funded by, or were advisors to, the food industry and 156 had links to the British Nutritional Foundation which is funded by the industry. Only 100 advisors had no link with either the government or the food industry.

[33] Audit Commission, *Safer Food: Local Authorities and the Food Safety Act 1990*, (HMSO, Occasional Papers No. 15, 1990). The percentage of other types of food premises carrying a high risk were: open food retailers (12.8%); hotels (12.8%); pubs, clubs etc. (11.2%); supermarkets and grocers (9.1%); hospitals (7%); residential homes (6.2%); and educational establishments (4.9%).

[34] Cmnd. 732 (1989).

[35] The 1990 Act applies to England, Wales and Scotland.

[36] Most of the basic provisions within the 1990 Act have been in place since the Food Act 1938. The Food and Drugs Act 1955, the Food and Drugs (Scotland) Act 1956 and the Food Act 1984 were essentially amending and consolidating legislation. For a history of food law in the United Kingdom, see Paulus, *The Search for Pure Food* (1983); Yellowlees, "Food Safety: A Century of

law in emphasising its four, by now traditional, planks: fraud and adulteration; the use of additives and the prevention of contamination; composition; and labelling.[37] Much of the previous, more particularistic, food legislation is repealed in favour of a general framework which can apply to all types and stages of food production and distribution and the scope of the terms used in the Act are enlarged so as to include virtually any consumable substance, except animal feedstuffs[38] within its ambit.

But whilst the general concerns of Directive 89/397/EEC can be seen as a timely parallel to those of the legislation which the government in any case wished to enact, the Act (and therefore the control regime which the Directive fits into) must be understood within the context of the government's other, non-EC oriented, concern in relation to deregulation and the lifting of "burdens on business".[39] The government's deregulatory drive was undoubtedly crucial in determining the form in which the new legislation appeared. The general thrust of this thinking is, that in balancing social needs with the needs of enterprise, the scales in the United Kingdom are tipped too far against business because of too many complicated or obsolete regulations. The aim of the government was therefore to achieve quality in regulation (rather than quantity) by repealing legislation which no longer served its purpose, duplicated other legislation and imposed burdens disproportional to the benefits.

More recently, a series of DTI publications has specified more clearly what such an initiative is to consist of and a range of Deregulation Task Forces was set up to investigate implementation of the policy in a number of areas and to recommend the form that "cutting the red tape" should take.[40] "Burdens" on business can be translated as the costs of complying with requirements to conform with health and safety legislation, broadly defined and in its most general sense. New strategies to reduce these costs were to be devised in relation to enforcement, to overcome "overzealous" behaviour by enforcers, some of whom were seen to "lack discrimination and see their role as ideological crusaders . . . without regard

---

Progress" in *Food Safety and Quality: A Century of Progress* (Ministry of Agriculture, Fisheries and Food, 1976).

[37] For an account of general United Kingdom food policy, see Jupe "Food Policy Issue and Government regulations" in *Food Policy Issues and the Food Industries* (Burns and Swinbank eds 1986). For a critical evaluation of the 1990 Act, see Scott, "Continuity and Change in British Food Law" (1990) 53 Mod. L. Rev. 785.

[38] Animal feedstuffs are regulated by the Agriculture Act 1970, the Animal Health Act 1981 and various EC regulations.

[39] See *Lifting the Burdens*, Cmnd. 9571 (1985); *Building Business. . . Not Barriers*, Cmnd. 9794 (1986); *Releasing Enterprise*, Cmnd. 512 (1988).

[40] See Department of Trade and Industry (DTI), *Working with Business – A Code for Enforcement Agencies* (1993); DTI, *Deregulation – Cutting the Red Tape* (1994); DTI, *Deregulation Task Forces: Proposals for Reform* (1994). Task Forces, with the general remit of providing for the repeal of existing regulations and developing strategies for the introduction of new ones, bearing in mind the requirement of public health and safety, were set up in the areas of: retail, tourism and other services; food, drink and agriculture; construction; chemicals and pharmaceuticals; engineering; financial services; and transport and communications.

to real risks or costs."[41] A second focus of this study, therefore, is to examine whether implementation of the Directive and the 1990 Act have achieved this goal; alternatively, if the burden still exists, on whom it now falls. Two strategic methods of dealing both with maverick enforcers, and with the problem of achieving national consistency generally have been developed, the first centrally, the second by local co-operation: first, by the use of Codes of Practice issued under the Act by the Minister; and secondly, by co-ordinating food enforcement policy and practice through enlarging the role of the Local Authorities Co-ordinating Body on Trading Standards (LACOTS).

(ii) **The division of powers under the Act**

The Minister of Agriculture, Fisheries and Food is named as the lead Minister in relation to the Act and is given general and wide-ranging regulation-making power in order to create much of the content of the Act[42], and the transposition of Community obligations.[43] The power also extends to making regulations to deal with any new, or unforeseen, circumstances which may arise after the passing of the Act.[44] Ministers are also given the power to make emergency control orders in cases where it appears that the carrying out of commercial operations, in respect of food, food sources or contact materials, may involve an imminent risk of injury to health.[45] This provision is intended to supplement the voluntary co-operation of the food industry in situations where such co-operation is inappropriate or inadequate.

A second type of delegated power is the power to regulate by the issuing of Codes of Practice. Under Section 40, the Minister is empowered to issue codes of recommended practice as regards the execution and enforcement of the Act and regulations made under it. It should be stressed that these Codes of Practice do not directly apply to the industry itself but are addressed to enforcement authorities for execution and enforcement under the Act and regulations made under it. The Codes are considered as binding; Section 40(2)(a) provides that every food authority shall have regard to any relevant provision of the Code and section 40(2)(b) provides that the Minister shall have the power to compel an authority to take specified steps to comply with the Codes.[46] Sixteen Codes of Practice have been issued thus far under the Act, and provide comprehensive guidance to food authorities and enforcement

---

[41] DTI, *Review of the Implementation and Enforcement of EC Law in the United Kingdom*, (1993), p 13.
[42] For example, sampling and analysis procedures under ss. 76–86, sched. 7.
[43] Section 17.
[44] For example, issues such as food irradiation, the production and sale of modified foods and novel foods, where the debate was not concluded at the time of the passing of the Act.
[45] Section 13.
[46] Any such direction is also enforceable by mandamus in Scotland.

officers on all those aspects of food control considered to require specific direction from central government.[47]

Section 40(4) requires the Minister to consult with organisations representative of interests likely to be substantially affected by the Codes. The Codes were initially drawn up under the auspices of the Implementation Advisory Committee (IAC) which was jointly chaired by representatives from the Department of Health and the Ministry of Agriculture, Fisheries and Food (MAFF). Representatives at the Committee included local authority representatives, representatives from the Institute of Environmental Health Officers (IEHO) and other bodies. The consultation process took place at initial discussions which led to early drafts of the codes, and on the Codes themselves. Consultation would therefore appear to have been detailed and thorough and copies of replies received during the consultation process are publicly available for inspection.

The DTI Single Market Compliance Unit has noted that there are two main methods of enforcement: first, by licensing or certification; secondly, by creating an obligation to do something (such as under an improvement notice), failure as to which results in liability to prosecution. The DTI favours the second approach; the Act formally includes the first also. Section 19 provides that the Minister may issue regulations requiring the licensing of food premises, but only where this is necessary for the purposes of ensuring that food complies with food safety requirements, is in the interests of public health or for the protection of consumers. This aspect of the Act might have had greater significance than it, in fact, has. Directive 89/397/EEC does not require a system of licensing and the power has not been used in the United Kingdom Licensing is, at present, required only in the case of slaughterhouses, dairies, irradiated foods and novel foods. Industry is implacably opposed to it (as is MAFF) and the IEHO has no expectation of it being introduced. It is now accepted that a widespread system will not be introduced. The reasons given for this opposition to widening the system of licensing to other premises, was that it was unnecessarily draconian.[48]

Section 19 also permits Ministers to make provision for the registration of food premises and for prohibiting the use, for a food business, of

---

[47] These are: Code of Practice No.1: *Responsibility for Enforcement of the Food Safety Act 1990*; No. 2: *Legal Matters*; No.3: *Inspection Procedures: General*; No.4: *Inspection, Detention and Seizure of Suspect Food*; No. 5: *Serving of Improvement Notices*; No.6: *Prohibition Procedure*; No.7: *Sampling for Analysis*; No.8: *Food Standards Inspection*; No.9: *Food Hygiene Inspections*; No.10: *Enforcement of the Temperature Control Requirements of Food Hygiene regulations*; No.11: *Enforcement of the Food Premises (Registration) regulations*; No.12: *Division of Enforcement Responsibilities for the Quickfrozen Foodstuffs regulations 1990*; No.13: *Enforcement of the Food Safety Act 1990 in relation to Crown Premises*; No.14: *Enforcement of the Food Safety (Live Bivalve Molluscs & Other Shellfish) regulations 1992*; No.15: (not yet published); No.16: *Food Hazard Warning System* (13 Prac.Food Rev., January 1994).

The specific obligations created under Directive 89/397 are transposed as directions under the Codes, raising the interesting theoretical question of their precise legal status.

[48] See discussion in Burrows and Hiram, *Implementing European Community Law: Official Control of Foodstuffs* (London: IALS Working Paper, 1993).

150

premises not registered. There is no element of control in registration since every relevant business registers as of right. The only offence in relation to the registration requirements is an omission to register. Registration is not contingent upon any inspection taking place and the business concerned simply completes a registration form, submits it to the authority and is thereafter placed on the register. New food premises are required to have been registered for at least 28 days before they are used. Registration is, therefore, the accepted principle with licensing as a last resort.[49]

Ministers are also given the power to make emergency control orders in cases where it appears that the carrying out of commercial operations, in respect of food, food sources or contact materials, may involve an imminent risk of injury to health.[50] This provision is intended to supplement the voluntary co-operation of the food industry in situations where such co-operation is inappropriate or inadequate.

The established system of enforcement is left unchanged by the Act and falls squarely into the traditional model of delegating enforcement at the local level to local authorities. "Food authorities" and "authorised officers" are set out in Section 5; in England and Wales, food authorities are each London borough, district or non-metropolitan county, the Common Council of the City of London and the treasurers of the Inner and Middle Temples. In Scotland, they are the islands and district councils. An "authorised officer" in relation to food authorities is any person, whether an officer of the authority or not, who is authorised by them to act in relation to matters regulated by the Act.[51] Although the section does not prescribe that an authorised officer must be an officer of the authority, in practice all authorised officers are, to date, Environmental Health Officers (EHOs) or Trading Standards Officers (TSOs). The Act does not specify that authorised officers must be qualified; rather, it provides that no person may be authorised if they do not hold qualifications which the Minister may prescribe by regulations.[52]

The division of functions between EHOs and TSOs within the United Kingdom varies according to geographic location. In metropolitan authorities in England and Wales and in London, where there is a single tier authority, both EHOs and TSOs may be employed by the food authority. This is at the discretion of the authority but, if both are employed, EHOs deal with hygiene and safety and TSOs with the composition and labelling of food and trade description and consumer protection legislation, adver-

---

[49] The emphasis on registration as opposed to licensing has been opposed by consumers and the IEHO. See Willctt, "The Food Safety Act: Substance or Symbolism" [1991] Stat.L.Rev. pp.146–155. He argues that although there have been advances in training, self-regulation and enforcement, there is no effective control of the "rogues" under the current system.

[50] Section 13.

[51] Section 5.

[52] Qualifications have since been prescribed under The Food Safety (Sampling and Qualifications) Regulations 1990 (SI 1990/2463).

tising and quality. At the level of county councils, TSOs deal with labelling and composition regulations. At the district council level, EHOs are responsible for all functions. In Scotland and Northern Ireland, EHOs are responsible for all food functions at district level where the district has total responsibility for the food function and TSOs are employed only at regional level.

To counteract the effects of both national consistency between local authority enforcement generally and the existence of two separate enforcement agents with, accordingly, different types of expertise and priorities, the role of LACOTS has been enlarged. LACOTS is not a named body within the Act but was conceived by local authorities in 1978 to co-ordinate the enforcement of trading standards. LACOTS' role now includes the co-ordination of food safety and hygiene enforcement.[53] As well as being responsible for co-ordination within the United Kingdom, LACOTS has played a major role in the co-ordination of EC-wide enforcement practices.[54] Within the United Kingdom, LACOTS have developed the "home authority" principle as the main method of tackling the problem of inconsistency. Where a company has more than one locus of operations, it will have only one local authority with whom it deals. The "home" authority will liaise with the authority in another area when problems arise outside the "home" area, informing it of the advice, or other action, which has been taken by it, with the aim of achieving consistency in the advice given to the company.[55]

(iii) Official enforcement

(a) *Inspection policy*

Enforcement is, of course, fundamentally linked to detection; detection is, in turn, dependent on inspection. The frequency of inspection is determined by MAFF's policy on risk assessment, set out in Code of Practice No. 8. This recommends a points system for the assessment of risk in relation to food premises and the criteria used in the example model given in the Annex includes whether the business's own quality systems are effective, the type of business and the relative local, national and international importance of the business. Having thus determined the risk presented by the business, the frequency of inspection is set out. Code of Practice No. 8 stipulates that high risk premises should be

---

[53] See Brooke, "LACOTS and the Co-ordination of Food Enforcement" (1991) 93 Brit.Food J., No. 8, pp 8–11.

[54] LACOTS is the UK co-ordinator for the Forum of European Food Law Enforcement Practitioners and was asked by MAFF to co-ordinate the 4-year Commission Study Tour Programme for foodstuffs inspectors. The results of the latter activity have been published as *Food Inspection in the EEC* (1990).

[55] See Jukes, "Regulation and Enforcement of Food Safety in the UK" (1993) 18 Food Pol. 131–142.

inspected at least once a year, medium risk premises at least once every two years and low risk premises at least once every five years. The frequency of inspection is therefore dependent on a number of factors but official statistics show that businesses assessed as being most at risk in 1993, as measured by the frequency of inspection in relation to the type of premises, are manufacturers, followed by slaughterhouses, importers/exporters and retailers.[56] The official statistics appear to show that, since the passing of the 1990 Act, the recommended frequency of inspections, in relation to the "risk quotient" of each category of premises, is being adhered to in practice.

(b) *Official enforcement*

Powers of enforcement in relation to offences have been considerably strengthened. The Act brings together, and supplements, powers which already existed under the Food Act 1984 and the Food and Drugs (Scotland) Act 1956. Both criminal sanctions and administrative powers are available to deal with breaches, or suspected breaches, of the Act. The introduction of new offences, more serious criminal sanctions, wider administrative powers and a commitment to training in relation to food safety would appear to indicate the rigour with which the government is determined to enforce its own, and EC, policy. On closer examination, however, the reality appears very different since each of the apparently tough enforcement tactics with which this aim is backed up are mitigated (or, indeed, offset) by other, rather less demanding, features.

The power to inspect and seize any suspected food[57] is a prerequisite of all the other powers at the disposal of food officers and the courts and has been widened considerably. As with the previous law, the officer may inspect any food intended for human consumption at any reasonable time and seize or detain it, but it is no longer necessary for the officer to actually inspect the food in order to believe that it is likely to cause a communicable disease before such seizure or detention may take place or an improvement notice served. It is sufficient that it appears to the officer that it is likely to cause a disease. Food officers can now, therefore, act on suspicion rather than waiting for evidence before any further action can be taken. Where it does appear to the officer that the food is likely to cause a disease, a notice may be served that the food is not fit to be sold for human consumption and that it be removed from sale or not; or the officer can seize the food and apply a justice of the peace[58]

---

[56] The percentage of premises inspected as a proportion of the total number of premises of each category in 1993 were: Manufacturers (99%); slaughterhouses (80%); importers/exporters (78%); retailers (78%); producers (74%); materials and articles in contact with food (78%); restaurants and other catering premises (78%); distributors (46%) (MAFF *Official Control of Foodstuffs Inspection Statistics 1993*). There are, however, significant variations in each of the three years since the Act was passed.

[57] Section 9.

[58] In Scotland, the sheriff or magistrate.

to obtain a notice for its destruction.[59] Authorised officers are given powers of entry to premises at all reasonable times but before entering domestic premises, 24 hours' notice must be given unless a warrant has been obtained.[60]

Food officers may also serve Improvement Notices where there are reasonable grounds to believe that the proprietor of a food business is failing to comply with food safety requirements under the Act.[61] The proprietor is then obliged to take measures to comply within a specified period. This provision replaces the previous system of issuing informal notices with a statutory duty to comply.

Where a proprietor of a food business has been convicted of an offence under the Act and the court is satisfied that the food business presents a health risk, the court may issue Prohibition Orders.[62] This prohibits the use of a specified process or treatment, or of premises, or equipment, for the purposes of a food business. It also extends to prohibiting the individual, who has been convicted of an offence, from being involved in carrying on or management of any food business. The effects of such an order are potentially severe and a business may be closed down entirely but the main aim of the section is to prevent a person whose business has been closed down from simply opening up another one.

Where a food business presents an immediate risk to health, a food officer or the court may issue an emergency prohibition notice[63] in the same terms as a prohibition order, except that the proprietor need not have been convicted and cannot be prohibited as an individual. There is no need for the officer to prove that there is an imminent risk of injury to health but the notice ceases to have effect if application to the court for an emergency prohibition order is not made within three days. Under the previous provisions, enforcement officers had no mandate to issue a prohibition notice which would take effect immediately and the introduction of this provision undoubtedly makes available an extremely powerful weapon in the service of food safety enforcement. However, the notice lapses unless a speedy application is made to the court and if no such application is made, the proprietor may claim compensation, provided that the court is satisfied that there was no imminent risk to health when the notice was issued.[64]

Enforcement officers are required to submit statistical returns in respect of all action which they take. These, in turn, form the basis of

---

[59] Section 9(3). Compensation may be claimed by the owner of the food where the notice is withdrawn or the court refuses a destruction order, but only to the extent of any depreciation in the value of the food resulting from the action taken by the authorised officer. It is not available where the food has been seized but the officer decides subsequently that it does, after all, comply with food safety requirements: Section 9(7).
[60] Section 32 and Code of Practice No. 2.
[61] Section 10.
[62] Section 11.
[63] Section 12.
[64] Section 10(10).

154

the United Kingdom's return to the Commission, in accordance with the reporting requirement in Article 14 of the Directive. Statistics for 1993 show that in relation to the total number of premises inspected or visited, the most widely used of the powers available to enforcement officers were written warnings, improvement notices and seizures or surrenders of food.[65] Closures, prohibition orders, emergency prohibition orders and withdrawal of licences represented a tiny proportion of the total number of actions taken.[66]

Added to the other functions of enforcement officers is the power to provide training courses to proprietors and employees in the food industry.[67] Enforcement officers had already assumed that the giving of advice and training constituted part of their responsibilities but this voluntary aspect has now been put onto a statutory footing. The Audit Commission identified training as an essential factor in promoting and attaining high hygiene standards.[68] In order to pay for it, an additional sum of £30 m was made available to local authorities when the Act came into force. However, since this sum was not "ring-fenced", it is unknown whether all, or indeed any, of it has been used for this purpose.

(c) *Offences and defences*

There are four statutory crimes under the Act: rendering food injurious to health; selling food which does not comply with food safety requirements[69]; selling food to the purchaser's prejudice which is not of the nature, substance or quality demanded by the purchaser[70]; and falsely

---

[65] Out of a total of 438,288 premises inspected or visited, 38% received written warnings, 6% were subject to improvement notices and 1% involved seizure or surrender of food. The types of premises which received most written warnings as a proportion of inspections and visits made to them were: restaurants and other caterers 45%; slaughterhouses 37%; manufacturers and processors 36%; distributors 33%; retailers 32%; importers/exporters 29%; materials and articles in contact with food 26%; packers 16%; and producers 14%: MAFF, *Official Control of Foodstuffs: Inspection Statistics 1993*. However, some premises were subject to more than one visit or inspection and therefore the rate would decrease if calculated as a percentage of total inspections and visits.

[66] Each represents less than half of one percent of total premises inspected or visited: MAFF, *op. cit.*, n 66.

[67] Section 23.

[68] Audit Commission, *Environmental Health Survey of Food Premises* (HMSO, 1990). No information was obtained in the course of the study in relation to the extent of training; but the authors have observed a number of take-away outlets displaying Hygiene Training Certificates, in respect of individual members of their staff, awarded by the local authority!

[69] The s. 7 offence is essentially a re-statement of the offence under s. 1 of the 1984 and 1956 Acts except that it is no longer necessary that the person rendered the food injurious to health with the intention of selling it in that state; it is enough that it is intended that the food be sold. It is the rendering the food injurious that is an offence, not its sale. The offence requires a positive act rather than omission, includes acts of sabotage and may be committed where the effects are cumulative rather than immediate. See *Bridges* v *Griffin* [1925] 2 KB 233; *Cullen* v *McNair* (1908) 99 LT 358.

[70] Section 8.

describing or presenting food[71] by selling, offering, exposing for sale or possession.[72] Only the second offence, selling food which does not comply with safety requirements is a new offence[73] although it combines elements of offences under the previous law.[74] In addition, regulations made under the Act may introduce other offences, criminal or civil, in relation to the particular subject of that regulation.

All of these offences carry criminal penalties and, in the event of a successful prosecution, these may be severe. A maximum fine of £20,000 can now be imposed under Sections 7, 8 and 14 and the statutory maximum fine of £5,000 is applicable to other offences, including obstructing an enforcing officer. These maximum fines were increased ten-fold under the 1990 Act.[75] Courts can also impose prison sentences of up to six months. In order that an offender cannot escape prosecution by claiming that he acted as part of a corporation and therefore cannot be held personally liable for its actions, the Act allows prosecution of an individual where it can be shown that commission took place with the knowledge, or at the instigation, of that individual. The individual is generally accepted to be part of the corporation's central management.

In Scotland, the decision to prosecute any such offence, or not, is taken by the Procurator-Fiscal and in England and Wales by food authorities. This difference may have a significant impact; it seems unlikely that the Procurator Fiscal is bound by directions of the Code of Practice which are addressed to food authority officials. Indeed, in recognising this, the DTI has noted that the practical result of the decision to prosecute being taken by the Procurator Fiscal, and therefore externally to food officers, is that "only the most serious cases with strong supporting evidence come

---

[71] Section 14 is essentially a re-statement of s. 2 of the 1984 and 1956 Acts, which themselves re-enacted older offences, except that the defence that the presence of extraneous matter was unavoidable, because of the process of collection or preparation, has been removed. It was, in fact, incapable of being used (see *Smedleys* v *Breed* [1974] AC 839). Many cases under these sections define the ambit of the offence: see *Meah* v *Roberts* [1978] 1 All ER 97, *Barton* v *Unigate Dairies* (1987) 151 JP 113, *McDonald's Hamburgers* v *Windle* [1978] Crim LR 200. Obviously, the wording of s. 14 means that it applies only where there has been an actual sale.

[72] Section 15. The offence is essentially the same as that under s. 6 of the 1984 and 1956 Acts but now includes possession.

[73] Section 15.

[74] Under s. 8(2) this includes food which is injurious to health under s. 7, food which is unfit for human consumption and food which is contaminated, whether by extraneous matter or not. The introduction of the offence effectively plugged the gap left in the Consumer Protection Act 1987 which expressly excludes food from its ambit but the implementation of the Product Safety Directive introduces a general safety requirement in prohibiting the sale or supply of any unsafe product (Council Directive 92/59/EEC of 29 June 1992 on General Product Safety, OJ 1992 L228/24).

[75] It has been noted, however, that it is as yet unknown whether the courts, in practice, will be willing to impose the maximum fine: Bradgate and Howells, "Food Safety – An Appraisal of the New Law" [1991] J.Bus.L. 320–332.

to prosecution and a more constructive and advisory relationship exists between businesses and enforcers."[76]

Prosecutions in relation to food safety offences have, traditionally, been low and they have continued to be so since the passing of the 1990 Act. The official statistics show that prosecutions arise from about a quarter of one per cent of hygiene and food standards inspections in all categories of premises[77]; in 1993 there were a total of 1,526 prosecutions arising from a total of 600,918 official inspections[78] and, of these, 1,278 (83%) resulted in convictions. This low level of prosecution, but high conviction rate, can be attributed to the prescriptions set out in Code of Practice No. 2[79], which embodies not only the general approach to regulation in this field but which now also forms a distinct aspect of official regulatory policy.

Until the 1990 Act, prosecution rates varied enormously, depending on the local authority involved and the enforcement personnel within it. Some prosecutions tend to be used as an exemplary "enforcement resource."[80] As one enforcement officer in Cranston's study of trading standards put it, "one little prosecution saves a lot of hard work".[81] In addition, enforcement officers may be reluctant to prosecute where they are not certain of obtaining conviction. The general conclusion of enforcement studies is that the incidence of prosecution ultimately depends on whether a "deterrence" approach, based on a vigorous prosecution policy, or a "compliance" approach, based on training and the informal giving of advice and warnings, is taken. In general, a compliance approach is the more common.[82] Public – and judicial – perceptions tend not to see regulatory breaches as real crimes nor do regulators and enforcement agents see more punitive approaches as efficacious.[83]

The policy which the Act favours is thus one of compliance and the

---

[76] DTI, *Review of the Implementation and Enforcement of EC Law in the United Kingdom* (1993), 22, para 2.28. However, whilst it is difficult to draw any firm conclusions about this, the only reported case in relation to a substantive breach of food legislation is Scottish: see *Guild* v *Gateway Foods Ltd* [1991] SLT 578.

[77] MAFF, *Official Control of Foodstuffs Inspection Statistics 1993*. The highest ratio of prosecution to inspection relates to manufacturers but the highest numbers of total prosecutions overall relates to retailers and restaurants (representing 37.5% and 37% respectively of all prosecutions). Both the ratio of prosecutions to inspections and the total number of prosecutions has fallen since the statistics were first produced in 1991.

[78] MAFF, *ibid.*

[79] Food Safety Act 1990, Code of Practice No 2: *Legal Matters*, 1991. p 4.

[80] Richardson, Ogus and Burrows, *Policing Pollution: A Study of Regulation and Enforcement* (1982), 198.

[81] Cranston, *Regulating Business: Law and Consumer Agencies* (1979), 112, 170.

[82] Whether this is as a result of perceived gains in efficacy or whether it is as a result of "agency capture" or the relationship between regulator and regulated is a matter of debate: see, *e.g.* Hawkins and Thomas, *The Enforcement Process in Regulatory Bureaucracies* (1984).

[83] As Reiss has noted, compliance strategies tend to be favoured where the processes of detecting violations are so complex, protracted or costly that they are seen to be inadequate remedies against a continuing, as opposed to a one-off or infrequent harm. Reiss in Hawkins and Thomas, *op. cit.*, n 83, p 26.

Code of Practice aims to standardise the incidence of prosecution; consistency in enforcement is, of course, the principal aim of Directive 89/397. The Code sets out the factors which should be taken into account in deciding whether to commence proceedings; these include the seriousness of the offence, the previous history of the party concerned, ability of witnesses to co-operate, willingness of the party to prevent a recurrence, probable public benefit of a prosecution, whether other action might prove more effective, any explanation offered by the company and, of prime importance, whether there is a likelihood of the defendant being able to establish a due diligence defence.

Section 21 offers the statutory defence of due diligence in relation to offences under the Act. The introduction of the defence brings the Act into line with the Trade Descriptions Act 1968, the Weights and Measures Act 1985 and the Consumer Protection Act 1987; it is not, therefore, an entirely new device but may be seen as the latest contribution to a developing corpus of law in relation to statutory crime.[84] The new defence has been identified by several writers[85], and by actors in the food area, as one of the most important aspects of the 1990 Act in relation to enforcement. Section 21 of the Act provides that in any proceedings taken under the Act it shall be a defence to show that a producer or trader "took all reasonable precautions and exercised all due diligence to avoid the commission of an offence by himself or by a person under his control."[86] There is an irrebuttable presumption that the defence is made out where (a) the offence relates to charges under Sections 8, 14 and 15[87]; (b) the person charged with the offence neither prepared the food nor imported it into the United Kingdom; and (c) the offence was due to the act or omission of a person not under the control of the accused or reliance was placed on information supplied by that person. Where the person charged is an own-brander, it is an additional condition that (d) all checks which were reasonable in the circumstances were carried out or it was reasonable to rely on checks carried out by the person who supplied the food and (e) that the person did not know, and had no reason to suspect, that their act or omission would amount to an offence. However, the Act itself does not specify or define "reasonable precautions" or "due diligence"; this becomes a matter for judicial

---

[84] On these developments, see *anon.*, "The Evolution of Statutory Defences" (1982) 1 Trading L. 181–183; Howells, "An Evaluation of the Role of Defences in Consumer Protection Statutes" (1988) 6 Trading L. 244–259; Wasik, "Shifting the Burden of Strict Liability" [1982] *Crim. L. Rev.* 567–574. See also Chapter 9, Section 2(i) on consumer safety legislation in the United Kingdom.
[85] See Scott, *op. cit.*, n 38; Willett, *op. cit.*, n 50.
[86] Section 21(2) provides the defence to a person charged with an offence who did not prepare the food or import it into the United Kingdom.
[87] Selling food not complying with safety requirements, selling food not of the nature or substance or quality demanded and falsely describing or presenting food.

interpretation and will depend on the facts of each case.[88] Where the charges relate to offences under Section 7 and where the person charged did prepare the food, or import it, the general defence applies.

The White Paper *Food Safety – Protecting the Consumer* stated that the introduction of a new defence was intended to strike the right balance between the interests of consumers, manufacturers, retailers and importers. It further stated that the warranty defence allowed retailers "to escape too easily from responsibility for the food they sell to consumers."[89] In relation to retailers, however, the form in which it emerged in the Act appears not to increase the onus but, in general, to reduce it.[90] Only in the case of retailers, however, does the burden appear to have lightened to some extent and the presumptions that the defence is made out do not apply at all to offences charged under Section 7, rendering food injurious to health.

That the introduction of the defence will tend to produce a self-regulatory response from industry has been well argued by several writers. Colin Scott suggests not only that the defence provides positive encouragement to businesses to put systems in place and ensure that they are working, but that the effect of the defence is such that "only those who commit the offence with intention or gross negligence are intended to be prosecuted."[91] Its overall effect is that the food industry itself should become actively involved in the introduction of systems which ensure that risks are defined and action is taken to avoid such risks. One such system – Hazard Analysis Critical Control Points (HACCP) – is increasingly used in the food industry.[92] Others exist in industry Codes of Practice or in

---

[88] Since the commencement of the Act, there has been only one reported case on what the defence requires: in *Carrick District Council* v *Taunton Vale Meat Packers* (1994) 13 Tr. L. R. 258 (QBD), the court held that nothing in s. 21(1) of the Food Safety Act 1990 prevented a meat trader from relying on a meat trader's certificate, if it was otherwise reasonable to do so, to show that he had taken all reasonable precautions and exercised all due diligence to avoid the commission of the offence.

[89] *Food Safety – Protecting the Consumer*, Cmnd. 732, at para 6.10.

[90] Section 102 of the Food Act 1984 provided that the defendant could plead that he/she had a written warranty from his/her supplier that the article or substance could be lawfully sold or otherwise dealt with; an invoice could constitute a written warranty. But the defence was not always easy to make out and prior to the 1990 Act, there had been a trend towards firming it up: see *London Borough of Camden* v *Fine Fare Ltd* (2 February 1987, unreported). Further, the defence in relation to cases against retailers under other consumer legislation could prove difficult to make out: see *Sherratt* v *Gerrards the American Jewellers*, (1970) 114 Sol. Jo. 147.

[91] See Scott, "Criminalising the Trader to Protect the Consumer" in *Frontiers of Criminality* (Loveland ed, forthcoming) and "Continuity and Change in British Food Law" (1990) 53 Mod. L. Rev. 785–801; Bradgate and Howell, "Food Safety – An Appraisal of the New Law" [1991] J. B. L. 320–332; Willett, "The Food Safety Act 1990: Substance or Symbolism?" [1991] Stat.L.Rev. 146–155. See particularly *Tesco Supermarkets Ltd* v *Natrass* [1972] AC 153; *Garrett* v *Boots Chemists Ltd* (16 July 1980, unreported).

[92] See joint publication of the Institute of Environment Health Officers, the Food and Drink Federation, the Local Authorities Co-ordinating Body on Trading Standards, the National Consumer Council, the National Farmers Union and the Retail Consortium, *Food Safety Act 1990: Guidelines on the Statutory Defence of Due Diligence*.

quality assurance procedures.[93] Industry is familiar with the need to develop such systems elsewhere, such as in health and safety at work, in order to avoid possible legal action, although the differences in both scale of operation and in awareness of management systems will differ considerably from one producer or retailer to another.

As well as the effects of both the Code of Practice (in standardising prosecution policy) and the defence of due diligence (in encouraging the development of industry self-regulation) in relation to prosecutions, the effect of LACOTS' "home authority" principle is to reduce the volume of prosecutions. Bearing in mind that this principle applies only to large companies (since only they are likely to have more than one authority enforcing food law), co-ordination means that they will face only one prosecution, regardless of the number of local authority areas in which the breach occurs. In other words, they will not be liable to more than one prosecution if the same offence is committed in more than one food authority jurisdiction.

6 The reactions of actors in the implementation of Directive 89/397/EEC[94]

Actors in the implementation of Directive 89/397/EEC comprise central government, Environmental Health and Trading Standards Officers, consumers, and the food industry itself. The responses of the main representatives of these groups to the current food law, including the implementation of the Directive, were sought in the course of our research. The Ministry of Agriculture, Food and Fisheries (MAFF) and the Secretary of State for Scotland are specified in Section 4 of the 1990 Act as the lead Ministries. The Department of Health is also involved with some of its aspects in England. Enforcement officers include both members of the Institute of Environmental Health (IEHO) and Trading Standards Officers.[95] The food industry is organised into three main associations rep-

---

[93] For a list of those which already exist in relation to quality systems, hazard analysis, manufacturing, agriculture, hygiene, health and safety and training, see IEHO *et al, op. cit.,* n 94.

[94] The responses of the actors were obtained in the course of the research by means of questionnaires, face to face interviews and at a Workshop attended by representatives of MAFF, IEHO, LACOTS, the food industry, Consumers in the European Community Group, the National Consumer Council and academics working in the areas of food law and European Community law. For more detailed information as to the precise responses of each, see Burrows and Hiram, *op. cit.,* n 49.

[95] The IEHO is a professional body which represents all Environmental Health Officers. Members of the IEHO are not necessarily employed by local authorities; many work in industry. LACOTS (Local Authorities Coordinating Body on Food and Trading Standards), on the other hand, represents all relevant professional interests within its field and takes a multi-disciplinary view. Trading Standards Officers are therefore represented amongst those interests but carry out their day-to-day responsibilities on behalf of the local authorities with whom they are employed.

resenting food producers (The National Farmers Union) (NFU), manufacturers (The Food and Drink Federation) (FDF) and retailers (the British Retail Consortium) (BRC). Consumers are represented by two main groups, the Consumers Association and the Consumers in the European Community Group (CECG).

No problems in relation to the manner of transposition were encountered; the Directive had been transposed timeously and accurately and, moreover, appropriately, by including its terms within the 1990 Act and Codes of Practice emanating from it. In relation to the general obligation of the United Kingdom to implement the Directive, all parties were broadly in support of its aims; this, however, depended very much on the larger question of whether or not the right balance had been struck between the interests of industry and those of consumers. The food industry expressed this as a fear that the United Kingdom may, in comparison to other Member States, be over-scrupulous in its compliance. Both the British Retail Consortium and the Food and Drink Federation felt that, due to variation in standards throughout the EC, harmonisation would tend towards the lowest common denominator.[96] The NFU also objected that the aims of the "level playing field" were being defeated by a perceived unevenness of enforcement throughout the EC and also that some producers from other Member States were openly admitting that they receive "special allowances" from their governments in relation to enforcement.[97] Whilst consumer groups were generally in favour of the SEM and the horizontal approach, they felt that mutual recognition of standards remained a problem. Enforcement officers, however, expressed fears in relation to the question of differentials between Member States rather differently. In the view of the IEHO, the overall objective of eliminating barriers to trade would not be achieved unless proper standards were prescribed and enforced in all Member States and if such standards were at least as good as those in the United Kingdom.[98]

Since the Directive does not specify the actual mechanisms of control or methods of inspection required, the capacity for differential standards to be applied was infinite. Indeed, MAFF expressed the view that without any reference in the Directive to penalties available to inspectors, there was a real risk of the United Kingdom being more stringent in its enforcement practices than other Member States. The danger, clearly, was that the United Kingdom food industry would be disadvantaged. At the same

---

[96] See Burrows and Hiram *op. cit.*, n 49. This view echoes that of some commentators that mutual recognition of standards inevitably results in the so-called "race to the bottom" (see, Charney, "Competition Among Jurisdictions in Formulating Corporate Law Rules: An American Perspective on the 'Race to the Bottom' in the European Communities" (1991) 32 Harv.Int'l L.J. 423; Fischel, "The 'Race to the Bottom' Revisited: Reflections on Recent Developments in Delaware's Corporation Law" (1982) 76 Nw.U.L. Rev. 913), see also Chapter 12, text at n 70).

[97] *Ibid.* The NFU representative did not, however, specify what such "special allowances" consisted of, but did say that NFU members in the UK were being encouraged to seek similar treatment.

[98] Response to proposed Directive COM(86)747 final, from IEHO, 7 April 1987.

time, the additional duties imposed on local authority inspectors would require additional resources to be made available in order to comply with the Directive.[99] The system of targeting high risk premises in the United Kingdom is not duplicated in, for example, the Netherlands. There, enforcement officers inspect premises on the basis of a random sample within a geographic area. Problems of equivalence of implementation – to say nothing of identity of effect – are not, therefore, in the view of the food industry, being fully resolved at present. The question of the qualifications of inspectors had been another major doubt; however, for this reason, all parties were fully in support of the imminent implementation of the Additional Measures Directive.[100]

MAFF consulted with some 500 organisations at the time the Directive was proposed. These include all representatives of food producers, manufacturers and retailers, consumer bodies, and enforcement authorities. In addition, any other group or individual wishing to be included in discussions were sent the working document and was welcome to take part in consultations. The IEHO was, however, dissatisfied with the consultation afforded them. In particular, much of the focus of their dissatisfaction centred on the emphasis being place by MAFF on the views of LACOTS who, the IEHO pointed out, have no training on hygiene or bacteriology[101]; neither is the IEHO represented on LACOTS. In the view of the IEHO, this meant that the interests of consumers were unprotected. However, these comments were made at the consultation stage when there was some ambiguity between the roles of the EHOs and TSOs as a result of the meaning of the word "fraud" in the draft Directive. In the United Kingdom legal context, fraud has a more circumscribed meaning than in other Member States, connoting actual deception and criminal intention rather than, for example, breaches of labelling requirements. Clearly, fraud in the United Kingdom sense would come squarely within the remit of TSOs. Since the Act has come into force, however, the fears of EHOs in relation to TSOs appear to have been assuaged since they report that they see no real problem with enforcement.

The issue of the relative importance given to the interests of industry and consumers was, however, seen by all groups as the most contentious, and indeed, central, issue. On whether or not the right balance is being struck between industry and consumers there is, as might be expected, a strong divergence of opinion between representatives of industry, on

---

[99] Ministry of Agriculture, Fisheries and Food Memorandum: *Proposal for a Council Directive on the Official Inspection of Foodstuffs* (1987). Whilst MAFF's view was that compliance with the Directive should not inevitably carry resource implications, an additional amount of some £30 m was in fact made available to local authorities. See Section 5(iii)(b) above.
[100] OJ 1993 L290/14.
[101] The IEHO went so far as to state that LACOTS were "neither competent nor experienced in local authority hygiene enforcement" and that such duties were "at present, outside their terms of reference" (response from IEHO to proposed Directive (COM(86)747 final, 12 May 1987). This statement is indicative of the traditional rivalry between EHOs and TSOs; for discussion of differences in approach, prior to the 1990 Act, see Chapter 5, Section 5(iv)(a).

the one hand, and enforcement officers and consumers on the other. Where the perceptions of MAFF lie is rather more difficult to discern. Consumers have lobbied for a separate government department to deal with consumer interests, maintaining that it is impossible for MAFF to represent them and oversee the food industry. In requesting this, the implication that MAFF are, in fact, representatives of the industry is inescapable. In response to this particular point, MAFF have set up a Food Safety Directorate within the Department. They maintain that it ensures that consumers' views remain sufficiently independent from those of the food industry by the fact that they have a direct channel to the Minister. Further, it states that it is better able to deal with food policy in general and deal with emergencies if all aspects of foodstuffs are kept within the one Ministry and that it feels better placed to present the case for the United Kingdom at EC discussions if it is able to speak for all those with an interest.[102]

According to MAFF, the point of regulation in relation to consumers, from the point of view of industry, is to protect them insofar as they could not reasonably be expected to protect themselves. Whatever particular form regulation takes, the responsibility is ultimately on traders and handlers to ensure conformity with standards since total surveillance is impossible. The important point about regulation is that it should be at the right level in each particular set of circumstances. Knowledge of reasonable standards of food safety should also be taught in the education system; whatever regulatory measures are taken, only consumers can be responsible for food safety after the point of ultimate sale. Industry did, indeed, echo this view; the British Retail Consortium feels that the rise in food poisoning cases, despite the new legislation, can be accounted for by such varied reasons as a consumer-led demand for fewer preservatives and additives, decreasing resistance to bacteria because of decreased exposure to them and insufficient food safety at the point of consumption – usually, the consumer's home. Both MAFF and the industry agree that where responsibility lies with industry, the main problem lies with the "rogues" who, they estimate, make up about 5% of the total traders and handlers.

Notwithstanding the extent to which responsibility for food safety also lies with individual consumers, the IEHO firmly believes that the ultimate aim of the Directive is the facilitation of free trade within the EC, and not the protection of the consumer, since the Directive is led by Directorate General III whose interests lie with industry.[103] In its view, the raison d'etre of the SEM is based on the market economy, not social well being.

---

[102] See Burrows and Hiram, *op. cit.*, n 49, p 30.
[103] Burrows and Hiram *op. cit.*, n 49, p 32.

7 Conclusions

The general issues which arise from this particular case study will be taken up in Part Three of this book. There are some specific points which should be noted here.

The first issue relates to the need to transpose and the method of transposition of the Directive into United Kingdom legislation. The Directive itself is only part of the framework of legislation adopted at the European level and therefore must be seen in that context, and it has to be implemented into an existing, complex regulatory framework at the United Kingdom level. The Directive in this case study is being used to attempt something new; the development of a system of control which will be operated at the national level but which will be monitored, ultimately, at the European level. The Community is delegating powers of control to national authorities and the national authorities must adapt to the imposition of this additional level of control onto existing methods of regulation. One question which might be asked is whether adapting old forms to new circumstances is such a good idea or whether the introduction of new forms would have been better. In the past, the food industry has been controlled locally in the sense that Environmental Health Officers and persons responsible for inspection of premises have been appointed to, and operated under the constraints of, local authorities. MAFF has argued that control of foodstuffs is part of the national agenda, on the assumption that central government is responsible for implementing the Directive. In fact, this is not the case. The responsibility for implementation of directives rests on all levels of government, in all governmental institutions.[104] MAFF specifically rejects this approach.[105] Despite protestations by the United Kingdom that it is committed to the principle of subsidiarity, it appears that this is one area where administrative subsidiarity has been lost, supposedly in the interests of achieving consistency and, therefore, uniformity in national compliance.

Closely related to this is the question of whether a distinction between centralised and co-operative enforcement can be, or is being, maintained. On the evidence of this case study, the distinction is more apparent than real. MAFF seems to prefer co-operation as a method of enforcement, where co-operation means the achievement of a common understanding in relation to the aims and outcomes of regulating the food industry. This common understanding quite clearly exists between MAFF, LAC-

---

[104] See Chapter 12, Section 2(ii).

[105] See Burrows and Hiram, *op. cit.*, n 49 p 29. MAFF's rejection may derive from its interpretation of the Article 5 "fidelity clause" that Member States should "take all appropriate measures" to ensure the effective application and enforcement of Community rules within the national legal order. For the view that this involves an implicit conferral of Community executive powers on Member States see Lenaerts, "Regulating the Regulatory Process: 'Delegation of Powers' in the European Community" (1993) 18 E. L. Rev. 23–49.

OTS, representatives of the food industry and even, to a limited extent, consumers, with perhaps the IEHO taking a more sceptical view. Perhaps MAFF would like to be described as the "honest broker" in this process but this inevitably brings with it a centralisation of enforcement, thereby belying the distinction between centralisation and co-operation.

This raises the further question of whether increased centralisation can be reconciled with those aspects of the 1990 Act which some writers have identified as encouraging self-regulatory tendencies by industry.[106] From this case study, it is apparent that the industry is involved both in participating in standard-setting as well as in the implementation of those standards by the development, for example, of industry-wide Codes of Practice. Whether or not this can be described as self-regulation is open to question, given the degree of direction and control imposed by MAFF. The National Consumer Council take the view that self-regulation can be instrumental in raising standards and providing protection for consumers which goes beyond the law itself. In defining self-regulation, it notes that whilst it generally refers to the method by which rules which govern behaviour in the market are developed, administered, and enforced by those whose behaviour is to be governed, the extent to which the governed actually control the rules varies considerably.[107] This would seem to tie in with the weaker concept of "regulated autonomy"[108], where the state oversees self-regulatory systems, rather than full-blown self-regulation.[109] As far as the control of foodstuffs in concerned, it appears that the concept of regulated autonomy is more helpful, in understanding the relationship between the actors, than is that of self-regulation.

The case study raises further questions, in relation to "lifting the burden", which it is impossible, empirically, to resolve at this stage. For example, might it not be said that whilst the legal burden (for example, the liability to sanctions) may have been lifted, the economic burden (the "costs of compliance") remains firmly with business? Since there is no sign of increased expenditure by central or local government (who in any case may charge for the provision of training to business) in

---

[106] See n 94 *supra.*

[107] See National Consumer Council, *Self-Regulation* (NCC, 1986). However, the NCC set down clear criteria, the existence of which they view as being essential within any self-regulatory scheme. These include requirements that the scheme must command public confidence, that its operation and control should be separate from industry institutions, that consumers must be fully represented, there must be meaningful sanctions for nonobservance and there must be public accountability (NCC, 1986) p 15.

[108] On the concept of regulated autonomy as an aspect of the corporatist approach to institutional policy development and control, see Birkenshaw, Harden and Lewis, *Government by Moonlight* (1990) 240–246.

[109] There are many definitions of self-regulation, differing between various writers and depending on the particular object or emphasis of their concerns. See, *e.g.* Daintith, "Regulation" in Vol. XVII, *State and Economy: International Encyclopedia of Comparative Law* (forthcoming); Graham *et al.,* "Self-Regulation" in *Administrative Law and Government Action: the Courts and Alternative Mechanisms of Review* (Genn and Richardson eds, 1994). The latter defines it as "the delegation of public policy tasks to private actors in an institutionalised form".

implementing the Directive, or the Act, the burden does not seem to have shifted to them. And even if there is a trend to lowering of standards (as a result of industry standard-setting through expert committees, HACCP, etc., and interpretation of due diligence), is there not still an economic burden in relation to the administrative costs (even if not actual production costs) of keeping such systems going? If the burden has changed its form, can it be said to have been lifted? What does this mean in relation to consumers?

The study also tends to show that despite consultation processes, consumers can hardly be considered as full participants in the regulatory process. They must, ultimately, continue to rely on enforcing private law remedies within the official legal system.[110] Whilst it may be argued that greater consumer awareness, through the development of more sophisticated information systems, may constitute a form of regulatory participation by virtue of consumers exercising their preferences in the market, this is not the approach taken by the European Commission. On the basis of Article 129a[111] (introduced by the Maastricht Treaty), the Commission is aiming to realise consumer rights in the internal market, in order to combat the subordinate role of consumers in the operation of market processes. In other words, a reliance on marketisation of consumer protection is not only misplaced but undermines the principle of the rule of law upon which the Community claims to be based.[112]

NOREEN BURROWS AND
HILARY HIRAM

---

[110] See Chapter 10.
[111] Article 129a on Consumer Protection states:
  (1) The Community shall contribute to the attainment of a high level of consumer protection through:
  (a) measures adopted pursuant to Article 100a in the context of the completion of the internal market;
  (b) specific action which supports and supplements the policy pursued by the Member States to protect the health, safety and economic interests of consumers and to provide adequate information to consumers.
  (2) The Council, acting in accordance with the procedure referred to in Article 189b and after consulting the Economic and Social Committee, shall adopt the specific action referred to in paragraph 1(b).
  (3) Action adopted pursuant to paragraph 2 shall not prevent any Member State from maintaining or introducing more stringent protective measures. Such measures must be compatible with this Treaty. The Commission shall be notified of them.
[112] These points are developed in more general terms in Chapter 12 below.

Welcoming the Well and the Wealthy: Implementing Free Movement Rights in the United Kingdom

1 Introduction

The achievement of full free movement of persons is one of the central aims of the Single Market. Since its inception, the Community has recognized that its primary economic aim of the creation of a free market in goods and services could not be realised without the abolition of controls over the individuals who would deliver them. In the early days of the Common Market this was seen largely as a process in which a surplus of labour and skills in one Member State could meet a shortage in another. It was, however, soon recognised that free movement of persons has a social as well as an economic dimension. Secondary legislation and the decisions of the European Court of Justice have attempted not only to remove national barriers to employment and self-employment but to help to integrate the individuals engaged in those activities and their families fully into the life of the host State.

More recently, the European Commission and, to a lesser extent, the governments of the Member States, have shown an awareness that the Community is unlikely to be successful unless it attempts more consciously to engage the sympathy and support of the citizens of the Member States. During the early years of the Community, in a period of rapid economic growth, such support was more or less taken for granted. The recessions of the late seventies and the early years of this decade appears to have convinced substantial parts of the electorates in some of the States that Community membership no longer guaranteed a rising standard of living. Low turnout in the last European Parliament elections, the referenda in Denmark and France and the rejection of participation in the new European Economic Area by the Swiss have all been interpreted as indications of growing disillusion with the idea of European union.

The Commission has responded to this apparent alienation in a number of ways. It has sought to address the "democratic deficit" in the Community by consistently supporting reforms giving enlarged powers to the European Parliament and by showing a marked preference for using legislative bases requiring the use of the co-operation procedure. It has promoted the idea that the Community should concern itself more with the individual than it has in the past, and the concept of a "People's Europe", is intended to give expression to this policy.[1] Central to that programme is the new European Citizenship of the European Union and the essential attribute of citizenship, the right to move freely and to reside anywhere in the state of which one is a citizen. The free movement rights that attach to the new Citizenship remain substantially qualified, but the Citizenship nonetheless provides some real gains for the individual in the shape of an entitlement to participate in the political life of the host State in both local and European Parliamentary elections. In addition, the European Citizen can expect to receive help and protection from the diplomatic missions of all the Member States when he is outside the Community if those of his own State are not available.

Directive 90/364[2], the subject of this study, was originally intended to break the hitherto essential (but increasingly tenuous) link between free movement rights and the involvement by the individual concerned in some kind of economic activity. As originally conceived by the Commission in 1979, it was intended to confer general rights of residence on all Community nationals and their families, irrespective of any economic nexus. The Directive, as it was finally approved eleven years later, is subject to two major qualifications, one in relation to self-sufficiency in resources and the other with regard to comprehensive health insurance protection. Subject to these qualifications, it establishes a right of entry and residence of indefinite duration. The beneficiaries include anyone visiting another Member State in a social capacity, those who live there on their own resources but who are not sufficient users to constitute recipients of services, those who have been self-employed but whose businesses have ceased to operate, those who have sought work for more than six months and who have failed to find it and those who have had work but have given up employment voluntarily. It is in the nature of a residual category of this kind that it is impossible to make an exhaustive list of those who will qualify. All the three hundred, and more, million citizens of the Community, and the participating EFTA States who have either not yet qualified under existing Treaty free movement rights or currently qualify but may cease to do so, are potential beneficiaries.

The Directive, as it was finally approved, was accompanied by two others in the same field: Directive 90/365[3], which gives rights of entry

---

[1] Report of the Committee on People's Europe (Adonnino Committee) March/June 1985 COM(88)331 (7 July 1988); Hartley, Green and Usher, *The Legal Foundations of the Single Market* (1991), 92.

The EC Treaty (as amended by the Treaty on European Union) refers variously to 'Citizens of the Union', Citizens of Member States' and 'Nationals of Member States' to indicate individuals who hold the nationality of one of the Member States'. 'Community Nationals' and 'EC Nationals' are used synonymously.

[2] OJ 1990 L180/26.

[3] OJ 1990 L180/28.

and residence to people who wish to live in their retirement in another Member State and Directive 90/366[4], which confers rights of entry and residence on vocational students. Non-vocational students, and students who wish to enter to study in the state system in another Member State at secondary level would, therefore, also have to bring themselves within the terms of Directive 90/364 to qualify for entry and residence rights. The three Directives all incorporate, by reference, the specific rights of entry and residence of workers set out in Directive 68/360.[5] Family rights are, however, confined to the immediate family of the beneficiary. Exercise of the rights can only be limited by the sending and host States according to the criteria laid down in Directive 64/221[6] relating to public policy, public security and public health grounds. The procedural rights conferred by the same Directive are also applicable.

All three Directives were to have been implemented by 30 June 1992. At a late stage in this study the United Kingdom had not amended either the Immigration Acts or the Immigration Rules to give effect to the Directives. It did, however, claim to be implementing them 'administratively'. This approach was not accepted by the Commission, which commenced the first stages in Article 169 enforcement proceedings in April 1993. The three Directives were not formally incorporated into United Kingdom law until the Immigration (European Economic Area) Order 1994 came into effect on 20 July 1994.[7]

When the United Kingdom joined the Community in 1973 the main features of the present system to enable free movement rights to be exercised by individuals were in place, including almost all the current secondary legislation. All the original six Member States had contiguous land borders, and the United Kingdom has had to adjust to Community laws framed to accommodate national legislation designed to deal with the realities of daily 'tidal' movements of people across long, largely unpoliced, frontiers. The emphasis in such States, tends to be on post-entry controls. In contrast, Britain's geography has dictated a port-control orientated system. Much of the last twenty years of Britain's Community membership has seen a somewhat halting attempt to adjust to the Community system. The construction of the Channel Tunnel and the implementation of the common travel area demanded by Article 7A of the EC Treaty call for an acceleration of that process of adjustment.

The difficulties of the United Kingdom in this area have been compounded by two other factors. Firstly, although primary immigration from third states has now come to be perceived as a problem in all Member States over the last decade, with an alarming growth in racism and xeno-

---

[4] OJ 1990 L180/30; now replaced by the almost identical Directive 93/96 (OJ 1993 L317/59), following the decision of the ECJ in *Parliament* v *Council* (Case C-295/90) [1992] 3 CMLR 281.
[5] OJ 1968 L257/13.
[6] OJ 1964 L56/850.
[7] SI 1994/1895; Immigration Act 1988 Commencement Order 1994, SI 1994/1923.

phobia, in the United Kingdom it has been a major political issue since, at least, the early sixties. The Commonwealth Immigrants Act 1962 effectively terminated primary immigration from the Commonwealth. However, any kind of 'weakening' of immigration controls remains a matter of acute political sensitivity. The second factor is a consequence of the first. The Immigration Act 1971 was intended to create a comprehensive system of control that effectively excluded the possibility of any further primary immigration. It came into effect on the day Britain entered the Community. There is no recognition of British membership of the Community or of the free movement rights of Community nationals in the Act. Fundamental Community rights are substantially at odds with the philosophy of the 1971 Act.

As with free movement of goods, Community law on free movement of persons is de-regulatory in the sense that it is directed at the removal of regulatory controls over the free movement of Community citizens and their families, and regulatory in the sense that it imposes minimum standards on Member States in relation to the way in which they deal with the entry, residence and expulsion of those enjoying free movement rights. In this sense, free movers are the beneficiaries or 'consumers' of free movement rights, and the Member States are regulated in the process of their delivery. Unlike the free movement of goods, however, the regulation of the entry and residence of persons is seen as an integral function of national government in all Member States at all stages of the process of control. It is probable that nowhere is this view more strongly held than in the United Kingdom, where fierce resistance has been shown by successive British Governments to any attempt to create a common visa policy in relation to Third State nationals. In France, too, the Conseil Constitutionel ruled recently that the Common visa policy under Article 100C of the Treaty on European Union was contrary to the constitution in that it may affect "the exercise by the State of powers which form part of the essential condition of its sovereignty".[8]

A study of the implementation of legislation directed at securing free movement rights for Community at national level must, therefore, be primarily a study of the work of Government at both central and local level and of the way in which the law, policy and practice impact upon the intended beneficiaries. The Departments most closely involved in the process of the implementation of Community law in this area in the United Kingdom are the Home Office (Immigration and Nationality Department), and the Departments of Employment and Social Security.

(i) **Research methodology**

This study builds upon earlier work on the operation of immigration controls affecting Community workers and the self-employed in the per-

---

[8] *Re: Ratification of the European Union Treaty* [1993] 3 CMLR 45 at para 49.

iod 1984–1985[9], and a further study relating to the delivery of housing, education and welfare rights in 1987–1988.[10] Research in both studies examined the purpose and scope of the relevant Community rules and the extent to which they were reflected in national law and policy. The studies looked at the way port and post-entry controls were operated, how benefits to which Community nationals were entitled were delivered, and assessed the extent to which United Kingdom law and practice were compatible with the Community provisions. The study of the implementation of Directive 90/364 has broadly followed the same approach, although the United Kingdom's failure to transpose the Directive while purporting to implement it 'administratively' has created problems of the visibility of the implementing measures.

The study has relied on five major sources of data: (i) rules of practice of the Departments concerned (including the Immigration Rules (HC 251 as amended by HC 725 of July 1993), (ii) statements of policy and practice made to the researchers and others in response to letters, questionnaires and interviews, (iii) physical observation at ports of entry, (iv) responses to letters and inquiries by agencies assisting Community nationals and their families and (v) determinations of the Immigration Appeal Tribunal and reported cases. The breadth of the concept of "effectiveness", as defined by Francis Snyder in Chapter 3, in relation to the application of Community law would seem to require an evaluation not only of the extent to which the official actors have or have not implemented Community law, but also of the extent to which the motivation and behaviour of the intended beneficiaries have been affected by the conduct of the official actors. Lack of resources has prevented the identification and questioning of a representative sample of those affected. Very little work has been done in this area and it remains a potentially fruitful field for future research activity.

Valuable support for the study has come from AIRE (Advice on Individual Rights in Europe), the major advice agency in this area, and the European Committee of the Immigration Law Practitioners Association (ILPA). ILPA was set up more than ten years ago as a support organization for solicitors, barristers and advice workers engaged in advising and representing individuals affected by decisions relating to immigration and nationality law. The Association has more than three hundred members. Besides having undertaken discussions with individual members, the study has been able to draw upon the responses to a letter sent in September 1993 to all members by AIRE on current practice relating to Community law in a number of fields, including the implementation of Directive 90/364.

---

[9] Connor and Vincenzi, *EEC Nationals and Rights of Freedom of Movement in the United Kingdom* (1986).
[10] Turkas and Vincenzi, *Welfare, Housing and Education Rights of EEC Nationals and the United Kingdom* (1988).

All the embassies of the Member States and many of the consulates in the major conurbations have been approached for information on the extent of problems encountered by their nationals in relation to the exercise of free movement rights. The few embassies and consulates that responded referred to inquiries relating to the effect on residence rights of claims to benefits and the likely effect of a conviction by a criminal court. The poor response to these inquiries may indicate either a lack of difficulty in exercising free movement rights or, alternatively, an unwillingness to provide the sort of information that would present its nationals in an unfavourable light in an already hostile climate.[11] The embassies and consulates which replied to our inquiries all indicated that all inquiries identifying a problem relating to the exercise of legal rights were referred to advice agencies and law centres. All law centres in the major conurbations throughout the United Kingdom were approached with a request for information on the extent to which they have provided advice, or assistance to Community nationals on matters affecting their free movement rights, or both. Approaches were also made to the National Association of Citizens Advice Bureaux (NACAB), and to local Bureaux in areas where there were known to be settlements of Community nationals. Contacts have also been made with advice and cultural bodies in the Dutch, French, German and Italian communities.

Information on policy relating to benefits has come from the overseas section of the Department of Social Security and on practice from officials in local offices of the DSS and the Department of Employment.

Questionnaires on current policy and practice with regard to the provision of medical treatment were sent to eight Area Health Authorities (AHAs) and four Regional Health Authorities. Replies were received from four AHAs and one Regional Health Authority. Information on the response of the insurance industry to the provision of all-risks insurance has come from the British International Insurance Committee, the Association of British Insurers, British United Provident Association (BUPA), and Western Provident Association (WPA).

The study has received valuable help on policy and practice from B6 Division of the Immigration and Nationality Department (IND) of the Home Office and port offices of IND at Manchester, Leeds, and Bradford Airports, and the ports of Hull, Harwich, and Dover. Information on the current state of implementation of Directive 90/364 and current Commission policy and practice on non-implementation has been provided by officials in the Free Movement Taskforce in Directorate General V.

---

[11] There is evident concern not to provoke hostile political and press comment of the 'Spaghetti Scroungers' type in relation to claims for benefit, which have been current at least since 1985 (*Daily Mail*, 8 October 1985) and which were reflected in the speech of Peter Lilley, the Social Secretary Minister, at the 1993 Conservative Party Conference (*The Guardian*, 10 October 1993); and see Lipsedge, Dianin and Duckworth, *A Preliminary Survey of Italian Intravenous Heroin Users in London*, Addiction (1993) 88, 1565; *The Guardian*, 4 November 1993.

(ii) **Demographic data**

No records are kept of the numbers of Community nationals who enter or leave the United Kingdom annually. Since they are not required to obtain prior entry clearance, leave on entry or variation of leave, they are not included in the statistics published annually by the Home Office.[12] Non-Treaty Community nationals, although still required to obtain leave on entry, are not obliged formally to apply for it, and are deemed to have received it under paragraph 73 of the current Immigration Rules. Records are maintained of the number of residence permits issued, and the number of Community nationals given indefinite leave to remain, but since neither of these are required for Community nationals exercising free movement rights ("Treaty nationals") they are not helpful in making an estimate of the number of Community nationals resident in this country.

A very rough indication of the size of the different national groups resident in the United Kingdom can be gathered from the 1981 and 1991 census returns. The figures are, however, based on the country of birth and not nationality. The figures for the censuses for Great Britain are as follows:[13]

Table 1

Country of Birth	1981	1991
Belgium	14,834	16,410
Denmark	9,480	14,226
France	39,052	53,443
Germany	176,431	215,534
Greece	12,112	14,610
Ireland	607,428	804,935
Italy	97,848	91,010
Luxembourg	392	705
Netherlands	23,761	29,442
Portugal	16,510	19,775
Spain	40,041	38,729
Totals	1,037,897	1,298,825

Although the place of birth is widely accepted as a basis for nationality, the figures given have to be treated with considerable reserve for a number of reasons. At first sight, for example, it would seem that Germans are the largest resident group after the Irish. This is not the case, however. The German-born individuals include not only the remnants of the 50,000 or more Jewish refugees who lost their nationality under Nazi legislation, but also the far greater number of children born to British service personnel in Germany since the last war. Coleman and Salt have esti-

---

[12] *Control of Immigration Statistics*, Cm. 2368 (1992), p 120, para 6.
[13] Office of Population Censuses & Surveys, *Census 1981*, Table 2; *Census 1991*, Table 50.

mated that only 52,000 of the 176,431 individuals giving Germany as their country of birth actually hold German nationality.[14] All the other figures will also include British citizens born abroad. The Irish are by far the largest group, having enjoyed almost unqualified rights of entry and residence under the Immigration Act 1971.

The largest resident group to benefit from the new directives are the Italians. Italian immigration dates back at least to the nineteenth century, but it peaked in the two decades before the United Kingdom entered the Community. The resident population is ageing, but the Labour Force Survey shows a substantial group of young, mainly unskilled, workers entering to work for short periods, mainly in the hotel and catering trades.[15] There is evidence that some of this group, mainly in London, become or remain homeless and rely either upon their own resources or upon State benefits when they lose or fail to find employment.[16]

The number of resident Community nationals is, however, dwarfed by the number of visitors. According to the latest *International Passenger Survey*, more than 8.5 million European Community nationals (excluding Irish nationals) visited this country in 1992.[17] This figure will include tourists, students, business people and "social visitors", any of whom may benefit from the Directive according to whether or not the degree of their economic activity gives them Treaty status.

2 Free movement rights in the Union

Article 8A of the Treaty on European Union (TEU) establishes a new "Citizenship of the Union". Citizenship confers the "right to move freely within the territory of the Member States, *subject to the limitations and conditions laid down in [the] Treaty and by the measures to give it effect*". (emphasis added)

The new benefits which the TEU attaches to the new citizenship are modest, and it adds little, if anything, to the rights of free movement already conferred by the EEC Treaty. It has, however, considerable symbolic significance.[18] Most significantly, perhaps, it marks the final stage in a process under which free movement rights have moved from being simply the means by which labour shortages in different parts of the Common Market could readily be satisfied to one where such rights have come to be recognized, especially but not exclusively, in the jurisprudence of

---

[14] Coleman and Salt, *The British Population: Patterns, Trends and Processes* (1992), 447.
[15] 1987 Labour Force Survey: unpublished data in Coleman & Salt, *ibid.* Table 11.8, p 463; see Colpi, *The Italian Community in Great Britain* (1991).
[16] Lipsedge, Dianin and Duckworth, *op. cit.*, n 11, p 1568.
[17] *Control of Immigration Statistics*, Cm. 2368 (1992), p 121, para 7.
[18] See Wyatt and Dashwood, *European Community Law* (1993), pp 659, 660; O'Keefe, "The Free Movement of Persons in the Single Market" (1992) 17 E. L. Rev. 3.

the European Court of Justice as being part of the fundamental rights of those whom they benefit. It must, however, be conceded that this was not always a conscious or coherent policy of the Court or the Commission.[19]

(i) **The dynamic nature of free movement rights**

The primary free movement provisions of the Treaty all have an obvious economic dimension: the free movement of workers, the self-employed providers of services and those wishing to establish themselves in business. The secondary legislation on family rights and the jurisprudence of the European Court of Justice have, however, tended to stretch the economic nexus, and to broaden and deepen the political and social context. Work seekers benefit from the right to enter and remain conferred by Article 48, although the wording of the Article appears to militate against it.[20] The definition of "worker" has been expanded to encompass those who do only a small amount of paid work supplemented by state benefits[21] or even work that is done for no pay at all.[22] Recipients of services benefit, although they are not mentioned in Article 59 of the Treaty and derive their free movement rights from a Directive.[23] The Court has held that such recipients include tourists, those receiving private medical treatment and fee-paying students.[24] In *Cowan* the Court held that even those receiving only a small amount of services may be protected by the free movement provisions.[25] Commenting on *Cowan,* Judge Mancini noted that "the Court has, of course, been aware that certain progressive forces are trying to give rise to a form, albeit still imperfect, of European Citizenship. . . .and seizing the opportunity, legitimized their efforts with one of its shrewdest judgments."[26]

The Court has also recognised that freedom of movement is facilitated not only by the existence of legal rights to enter and reside, but by a receptive and accommodating legal and administrative environment in the host State. This has led it to a very broad interpretation of the provisions of Regulation 1612/68.[27] Although the Regulation is primarily directed at the elimination of all forms of discrimination in the working

---

[19] Mancini, "The Making of a Constitution for Europe" (1989) 26 *Comm. Mkt. L. Rev.* 595; Slynn, *Introducing a European Legal Order* (1992), 92–97; Coppel and O'Neill, "The European Court of Justice: Taking Rights Seriously?" (1992) 12 Legal Stud., No. 2, p 227.

[20] Case C-292/89 *R* v *Immigration Appeal Tribunal, ex p. Antonissen* [1991] ECR 1745.

[21] Case 139/84 *Kempf* [1986] ECR 1741; Case 53/82 *Levin* [1982] ECR 1035.

[22] Casc 196/87 *Steymann* [1988] ECR 6159.

[23] Council Directive 73/148, art. 1(1)(b) (OJ 1973 L014/10).

[24] Joined Cases 286/82 and 26/83 *Louise and Carbone* [1984] ECR 377.

[25] Case 186/87 *Cowan* v *Tresor Public* [1989] ECR 195; [1990] 2 CMLR 613, [1990] 2 CMLR 613, para 20 and see Lenz at p 623.

[26] Mancini, *op. cit.,* n 19, p 607.

[27] OJ 1968 L257/2.

environment, it has been applied by the Court in a much broader context. In particular, Article 7(2), which relates to equal treatment in connection with "social advantages", has been given a very wide interpretation. 'Social advantages' were "those which, whether or not limited to a contract of employment, are generally granted to national workers primarily because of their objective status of workers or by virtue of their residence on national territory and the extension of which to workers who are nationals of other Member States therefore seems suitable to facilitate their mobility".[28] The provision has been held to cover such diverse matters as the right of a Community worker to be joined by a cohabitee and the right to have criminal proceedings conducted in the worker's own language.[29] Article 7(2) of Regulation 1612/68, has also been used to supplement the provisions of Regulation 1408/71[30], where a benefit has fallen outside the ambit of Article 4. Minimum support ("social assistance") payments have been held payable to individuals who have attained worker status, even where they are no longer employed.[31] However, the general non-discriminatory rule of Article 7 of the EC Treaty did not enable work-seekers, who had not yet achieved worker status, to benefit from Article 7(2). Work-seekers of the host State and work-seekers of other Member States do not, therefore, under Community law, compete for employment on equal terms.[32]

An open and accessible administrative environment is one in which thought is given, in both the formulation of policy and the application of legal rules, to the needs of migrant workers. The obligation imposed by Article 5 of the EC Treaty to "take all appropriate measures. . .to ensure fulfilment of the obligations arising out of [the] Treaty or resulting from action taken by institutions of the Community", has been interpreted in the context of free movement rights to impose particular obligations on host Member States. In relation to the implementation of directives, the Court has said, in *Commission* v *Germany* (*Re Nursing Directives*) in 1985:

"The implementation of a Directive does not necessarily require legislative action in each Member State. In particular, the existence of general principles of constitutional and administrative law may render the implementation by specific legislation superfluous, *provided, however, that those principles guarantee that the national authorities will, in fact, apply the Directive fully, and where the Directive is intended to create rights for individuals, the legal position arising from those principles is sufficiently clear and precise, and the persons concerned are made fully aware of their rights, and where appropriate, are afforded the possibility of relying upon them before national courts"* (emphasis added).[33]

---

[28] Case 207/78 *Even* [1979] ECR 2019 at 2034.
[29] Case 59/85 *Reed* [1986] ECR 1283; Case 137/84 *Mutsch* [1985] ECR 2681.
[30] OJ 1971 L149/2.
[31] Case 122/84 *Scrivner* [1985] ECR 1027.
[32] Case 316/84 *Lebon* [1987] ECR 2811.
[33] Case 29/84 *Commission* v *Germany (Re Nursing Directives)* [1986] 2 CMLR 579 para 23.

Where Community law creates rights, inconsistencies between Community and national law cannot simply be overcome by a willingness on the part of State authorities to waive national rules. The exercise of Community rights should not depend on the exercise of administrative discretion, or the issue of administrative instructions or departmental circulars.[34] This is particularly the case with regard to the exercise of free movement rights by Union Citizens in other Member States. The guiding principles in these cases should be transparency and rights awareness.[35] The Council of Ministers has recently given some impetus to this principle by passing a resolution on the transparency of qualifications to facilitate the free movement of professionals.[36] In *EC Commission* v *Denmark*[37], the Court emphasised the link between transparency and legal enforcement: "the principles of legal certainty and the protection of individuals *require an unequivocal wording which would give the persons concerned a clear and precise understanding of their rights and obligations and would enable the courts to ensure that those obligations are observed*" (emphasis added). That principle of openness is carried through into the process by which decisions are made by Member States, and undertakings within them, affecting Community workers' rights:

> "Since free access to employment is a fundamental right which the Treaty confers individually on each worker in the Community, the existence of a remedy of a judicial nature against any decision of a national authority refusing the benefit of that right is essential in order to secure for the individual effective protection for his right. . .the latter must also be able to defend that right under the best possible conditions and have the possibility of deciding with a full knowledge of the relevant facts, whether there is any point in their applying to the court."[38]

The Court has frequently reiterated the fundamental nature of free movement rights, and rejected any national attempts to impose measures which limit their exercise. Significantly, in relation to conditions contained in the Immigration Rules (HC 251) prohibiting access to public funds during the first six months of residence, the Court has recently ruled that "the right of residence cannot be made conditional on compliance with national provisions on social security or on any other matter, nor can non-compliance with a social security scheme justify a deportation order".[39]

European Commission policy has, since the sixties at least, been to broaden the scope and application of free movement policy, and to give

---

[34] Case 167/73 *Commission* v *France (Re French Merchant Seamen)* [1974] ECR 349; Case 102/79 *Commission* v *Belgium* [1980] ECR 1473; Curtin, (1990) 27 *Comm. Mkt. L. Rev.* 709 at 716.
[35] [1986] 2 CMLR 579 at 585 (*per* Slynn Att-Gen).
[36] OJ 1992 C49/91.
[37] [1985] ECR 427.
[38] Case 222/86 *UNECTEF* v *Heylens and Others* [1987] ECR 4097, paras 14 and 15 of Judgment.
[39] Case C-363/89 *Roux* [1991] ECR 1–273, paras 10 and 11 of Judgment.

it a more human, social and less economic focus. That aim is reflected in the preamble to Regulation 1612/68, in which freedom of movement of workers is recognised as a "fundamental right" by which "the worker is guaranteed the possibility of improving his living and working conditions and promoting his social advancement". It is to be exercised "...by objective standards in freedom and dignity". The Commission has, for a number of years, continued to press for the expansion of the economically-orientated free movement rights into a full-blown general right of free movement for Community nationals.[40]

(ii) **The origins and aims of Directive 90/364 on the rights of residence**

Despite the liberal and creative interpretation of both the primary and secondary rules relating to freedom of movement by the Court, there remains a significant, though not readily definable, periphery of activities carried out by Community nationals in other Member States which fall outside the ambit of Community law. Their common characteristic is that they are quite unconnected to any form of economic activity, and are therefore beyond the original objectives of the Treaty. As competence under the Treaty has broadened so, too, has the move towards a general right of residence for all Community citizens developed. As early as December 1974 the Heads of States and Governments agreed at their Paris Summit to set up a working party to study "the conditions and timing under which citizens of the nine Member States could be given special rights as members of the Community".[41] The Commission was charged with developing ideas and elaborating proposals which, in aggregate, would constitute an European Citizenship.[42]

The original draft Directive defined the intended beneficiaries as "nationals of another Member State who reside or wish to reside in another Member State of the Community" and who were not already beneficiaries of such rights.[43] To propitiate widely held fears of "social tourism", the "general" right of residence was predicated upon the Community national having sufficient means to maintain himself and his family. The European Parliament received the draft favourably[44] and Council approval appeared imminent, but the Directive ultimately ran foul of a perception that there had been a sudden increase in immigration from Third States, primarily by asylum-seekers. Although this had nothing to

---

[40] Sandri, "Free Movement of Workers in the European Community" (1968) 11 Bull.EC 5, 9; Evans, "European Citizenship" [1982] *Mod. L. Rev.* 4979.

[41] Point 11 of the Final *Communique*, Citzens Europe, (1975) 7 Bull.EC Supp. 25.

[42] Taschner, "Free Movement of Students, Retired Persons and Other European Citizens" in *Free Movement of Persons in Europe* (Schermers *et al.* eds, 1993).

[43] OJ 1979 C207/14.

[44] Taschner, *op. cit.,* n 42, p 431.

do with the general Directive, political sensitivity made Council members back off. "The preponderant opinion was that a foreigner is a foreigner."[45] Ultimately, the general residence Directive became three directives, one for students, another for retired people who wished to live in a different Member State from which they had worked, and the general residual Directive. Member States are to "grant the right of residence" to the beneficiaries. The words are taken from Article 4 of Directive 68/360, which provides the means by which workers are able to exercise rights of entry and residence. They now have a somewhat dated quality and it is surprising that they were used, since the European Court has held that the primary law of the Treaty and the secondary legislation created fundamental rights and did not require any "grant of leave" to give it effect.[46] The relevant provisions of Directive 68/360 on entry and residence have, however, all been incorporated into the new directives.

The original single draft Directive had been based upon on Article 56(2) of the EC Treaty, which, by the time it came before the Council for approval in 1989, required only a qualified majority vote. The three new Directives, as drawn by the Commission, were based on Article 100 (for Directive 90/364), Articles 49 and 54 (for Directive 90/365 – retired persons) and Article 7(2) (for Directive 90/366 – vocational students). The Council of Ministers altered the legislative base of all three Directives to Article 235, which requires unanimity. Although this did not prevent approval, it indicated an unwillingness to allow free movement of persons provisions to pass beyond the possibility of a national veto. The change of base for the student Directive was subsequently challenged in the Court by the European Parliament and the Court, in effect, reinstated the original legal basis.[47]

All three categories of entrant must have sufficient means to avoid becoming a burden on the host State, but there are now different means of proof. Sufficiency of student means needs simply to be "glaubhaftmachung", which, apparently, means rather more than 'credible' in the German civil process from which it was drawn.[48] Under the general residence Directive 90/364, and the retired persons Directive 90/365, the beneficiaries are obliged to bring full proof of their resources or pensions, the sufficiency of which is to be determined by whether they will avoid becoming a burden on the social assistance system of the host Member State. The British Government appears to have supported an attempt to insert a requirement that proof of means should be established at the point of entry but this was abandoned after determined opposition by the Commission.[49] The Council of Ministers added the proviso that all benefici-

---

[45] *Ibid.* p 434.
[46] Case 157/79 *R. v Pieck* [1980] ECR 2179.
[47] Case C-295/90 *Re Students' Rights: European Parliament* v *EC Council* [1992] 3 CMLR 281.
[48] Taschner, *op. cit.,* n 42, p 434.
[49] *Ibid.* p 435.

aries should be covered by an all risks sickness insurance policy.[50] The Directives were due to be implemented by 30 June, 1992.

The Commission appears to be unsure what an "all risks" sickness insurance policy is.[51] Although the insurance industry in the United Kingdom were notified of this measure they do not appear to have been consulted before the Directives were unanimously approved by the Council in December 1989. It is unlikely that the British insurers would have approved such a condition, because an insurance policy of such a comprehensive kind is not currently available in the United Kingdom.[52] There is, however, a provision in German aliens law in relation to students, who are required to have "comprehensive" sickness insurance, and this may well be the source of the provision in Directive 90/364.[53]

(iii) Support for Directive

The three Directives were strongly supported in the European Parliament.[54] Support outside Parliament for the free movement rights of the retired came from the European Trade Union Council (ETUC), and within, for all three Directives by the Parliamentary Group for Free Movement, the Kangaroo Group. This latter group is primarily concerned with the removal of restrictions on the movement of businesses and goods, but it offers some support for liberalising measures relating to persons.[55]

(iv) Implementation in other Member States

The implementation of the Directive in other Member States must be seen in the broader context of the implementation of free movement rights. Before doing so, it is worth mentioning that much of what has been described in this study, except that related to the peculiar geography of this island, would seem to apply with equal, or more force, to the immigration control systems of other Member States. There appears to be no comprehensive study and to attempt one would go far beyond the bounds of this project. What evidence there is is impressionistic and anecdotal. Other Member States figure more frequently than the United Kingdom in free movement matters in Article 169 proceedings or references in Article 177. The Commission's solicitors in London, acting on

---

[50] Article 1, Directives 90/364, 90/365 and 90/366.
[51] Interview, Phelps with DG III, 21 April, 1993.
[52] British Assurance Association, April 1993.
[53] Hooghiemstra, *Visa Requirements for Visitors and Students to the Twelve Member Countries of the European Community* (1993), 41.
[54] Taschner, *op. cit.*, n 42, p 430; Opinion of 13 June 1990, OJ 1990 C175/100 (now replaced by Directive 93/96) and see *Re Students' Rights: European Parliament* v *EC Council* [1992] 3 CMLR 281.
[55] See *Kangaroo News*, February 1993.

a brief to advise Community nationals on the implementation of the professional qualification Directive 89/48 find that their time is devoted almost entirely to helping British nationals overcome the most basic obstacles to employment in other Member States.[56] In their 1993 Report on implementation, the professions report that implementation has been "relatively smooth" in the United Kingdom and that "the majority of the problems United Kingdom professions have experienced have been in dealing with problems which United Kingdom nationals have faced when attempting to get their qualifications recognised in other Member States".[57]

A report on the implementation of visa policies and procedures of the Member States in relation to Community and third state nationals was published early in 1993.[58] It indicates that only Belgium, the Netherlands, West Germany and the United Kingdom have effective and independent immigration appeal systems. Even those States which have them demonstrate a certain lack of transparency in their operation:

> "Both the Netherlands and Germany try, somewhat feebly, to conceal the availability of appeals to persons refused a visa by not informing anyone of the existence thereof, or by trying to confuse visa applicants by handing them written decisions only in Dutch or German. The theory is apparently that few aliens will be able to read these decisions, and they will resign themselves to the refusal without seeking to find out the grounds."[59]

In relation to Directive 90/364, the following States have either transposed the Directive into national law, or amended national provisions to give it effect: Belgium[60], Denmark[61], Greece[62], Italy[63], Spain[64], and Portugal.[65] France has sent copies of the Directive to all prefectures with instructions to implement, although this practice has been found by the Court on several occasions not to amount to effective implementation.[66] The Netherlands has also sent copies of the Directive to local aliens police with a legally enforceable circular.[67] It is also doubtful if this meets Community Law requirements. No information on implementation is available in relation to Germany, Ireland and Luxembourg.

---

[56] Conversation with Adkins, S.J. Berwin & Co., Solicitors, London, 4 April 1993.
[57] Directive 89/48, art. 11, Report by United Kingdom Authorities, July 1993.
[58] Hooghiemstra, *op. cit.*, n 53.
[59] *Ibid.* p 117.
[60] [1992] Arrete Royal, Source: EC Commission Doc. 790 L/0364, November 9, 1993.
[61] [1992] Lov.Nr. 482 AF , June 24, 1992.
[62] [1992] Decret Presdiential No. 278.
[63] [1992] Decreto Legge N. 470 DEL, January 26, 1992.
[64] [1992] Real Decreto N. 766, June 26, 1992.
[65] [1993] Decreto-Lei N. 60, March 3, 1993.
[66] Interview with Beaudu, DG V, EC Commission, April 1993.
[67] Interview, Phelps with Dutch Foreign Ministry, April 1993.

3 Immigration and free movement: the United Kingdom context

(i) Union Citizens as aliens

Central to the operation of immigration control is the issue of nationality and subject status. With the exception of citizens of the Republic of Ireland, Union Citizens are aliens at common law.[68] To understand their current position it is necessary to undertake a brief excursus into the historical status of aliens in Britain and how that status has been modified by statute.[69] Aliens were those born out of the allegiance of the King; that is, abroad. They were divided into alien friends and alien enemies. Alien friends, once in the country were "local subjects", not originally allowed to own land, but able to bring an action in tort to protect their goods and persons, at least since the seventeenth century.[70] Alien enemies had few legal rights, and could be killed and detained at will, at least if they were combatants, although once captured, they become entitled to the protection of the Crown and could even bring civil actions, except to obtain their release from captivity.[71]

Any controls exercised over aliens during the Middle Ages and subsequently until the late sixteenth century were exercised by the Crown. Aliens benefited, indirectly, in relation to their personal freedom at least, from statute and caselaw reducing the Crown's powers of arbitrary detention, starting with the Petition of Right in 1629, the Habeas Corpus Act 1689 and through to the three great cases establishing the limits of the Crown's powers over the property and person of the subject, *Entick* v *Carrington*, *Wilkes* v *Wood* and *Leach* v *Money*, decided in the middle of the eighteenth century.[72] The perceived decline in the Crown's powers over aliens was such that, by the end of the eighteenth century, legislation was introduced to authorise the detention and exclusion of non-combatant enemy aliens during the Napoleonic Wars, and throughout the nineteenth century, in relation to both alien friends and alien enemies, legislation was invariably used to legitimise detention (Aliens Act 1793, Aliens Act 1848, Foreign Deserters Act 1852, Extradition Act 1870). They remained, however, subject to severe disabilities in relation to the ownership of land and ships, employment in the army, Civil Service and participation in juries and the franchise.[73]

A bold statement by Earl Granville in 1852 that "By the existing laws

---

[68] British Nationality Act 1981, s. 50(1).
[69] For a full account, see Dummett and Nicol, *Citizens, Aliens and Others* (1990).
[70] *Calvin's Case* [1608] Coke Litt. 129b.
[71] *Sylvester's Case* [1701] 7 Mod. 150; *Porter* v *Freudenberg* [1915] 1 KB 857.
[72] (1865) 19 St.Tr. 1030, 19 St.Tr. 1153, and 3 Burr. 1092.
[73] Nicol, "Nationality and Citizenship Rights" in *Rights of Citizenship* (Blackburn ed 1993), 258–262.

of England, all foreigners have the unrestricted right of entry and resi-dence in this country" probably marked the high point of the laissez-faire aspirations of a Liberal government, rather than a definitive statement of the law.[74] At the other end of the political spectrum, the opinion of the Conservative Lord Halsbury forty years later in the Privy Council, that aliens could be excluded because they could not show that they had any "right" to enter the territory of the Crown, was equally misconceived.[75] The common law does not deal in "rights" in the sense understood by Continental jurisprudence. One does not have to demonstrate a right to do something in English common law. As Sir Robert Megarry said in *Malone* v *Commissioner of the Metropolitan Police* (No 2) in 1979, in relation to listening to other people's telephone conversations: "England is a country where everything is permitted except what is expressly forbid-den".[76] Police officers did not, therefore, any more than private individ-uals, have to demonstrate a right to listen. If no interest was protected at common law, or no right protected or duty imposed by statute, then it could be done. A statement similarly founded on such a false premise as that of Lord Halsbury in *Musgrove* is the declaration by Lord Diplock, in *DPP* v *Bhagwan* in 1971, that a British subject had ". . .the right at common law to enter the United Kingdom without let or hindrance".[77] He was, however, unable to cite a single authority for this apparently fundamental "principle" of the common law. The common law only offers protection to a limited set of interests. The "right" to enter is no more than an aspect of the protection afforded by the law to the security of the person. The Crown had not the power to detain British subjects (any more than aliens) without cause at ports of entry or anywhere else within the country. That is not a "right of entry" any more than the ability to do anything else which one can do as a result of the protection provided by the common law against arbitrary exercise of the Crown's power of detention could be said to be a "right".

This may seem a diversion in relation to an examination of the position of aliens in a European Community context, but it is crucial to under-standing the difficulty which our legal and administrative system has in coming to grips with the Community concept of freedom of movement as a "fundamental right". At English common law, both friendly aliens and subjects start at the same point in relation to free movement. The difference in their status is almost entirely the creation of statute, and the consequence of some ill-defined, and probably insignificant, powers of the Crown at common law which survive the statutory regime of immi-gration control.[78] There are no "fundamental rights" in immigration law,

---

[74] State Papers, (1852–1863), Vol. 42, p 421.
[75] *Musgrove* v *Chun Teeong Toy* [1891] AC 272 (PC).
[76] [1979] Ch. 344, 36.
[77] *DPP* v *Bhagwan* [1972] AC 60, 74.
[78] Section 33(5) Immigration Act 1971 and see Vincenzi, "Aliens and the Judicial Review of Immigration Law" [1985] *Pub. L.* 93.

as the history of immigration control this century has amply demonstrated. All that there could be said to be is a presumption in favour of the liberty of the person, which has frequently had to give way to statutory intervention.

(ii) **Statutory control of alien migration**

Immigration control of aliens pre-dates that of Commonwealth Citizens by almost sixty years. The Aliens Act 1905 was passed in response to an upsurge of anti-semitism that followed a large influx of Russian Jewish refugees in the last years of the nineteenth and the early years of this century. The Act, which only applied to "pauper aliens" travelling steerage class, did not apply to genuine asylum-seekers and provided a port system of appeals.[79] It was, however, swept away, by the Aliens Restriction Act 1914, passed for the duration of the war time emergency. It was renewed and amplified by the Aliens Restriction (Amendment) Act 1919 which created a comprehensive and draconian system of control of aliens that lasted until it was superseded by the Immigration Act 1971.

There was no system of appeals and only a minimal opportunity for judicial review under the Aliens Orders. The case of *R. v Inspector of Leman Street Police Station, ex p. Venicoff*[80] firmly established the principle that, since decisions concerning the deportation of aliens, were purely 'administrative', they did not attract the rules of natural justice. Aliens were given or refused leave to enter according to a series of Aliens Orders, which were highly unspecific as to who was a "desirable" and an "undesirable" alien. Controls were operated by visa and immigration officers working to instructions which were unpublished and, indeed, secret. Some visa officers in British legations abroad were, in fact, members of the secret service with a special brief to detect and exclude Bolsheviks.[81] Issues of exclusion and deportation were therefore regarded by the courts as almost beyond the bounds of justiciability.

For the space of more than fifty years there are no more than a handful of successful actions in the courts by aliens of immigration, detention or deportation decisions by aliens. *Küchenmeister v The Home Office*[82] was one of the few. The plaintiff, had, in 1946, unsuccessfully challenged his detention as a prisoner of war many months after the war was over because the court accepted a Foreign Office certificate that the war was continuing, and that Britain, as one of the Allied Powers governing Germany, was in effect, at war with itself. At his second attempt, he was success-

---

[79] Gainer, *The Alien Invasion* (1972).
[80] [1920] 3 KB 72.
[81] Minutes of the Interdepartmental Aliens Committee, 1919–1925, (unpublished) Home Office Library.
[82] [1958] 2 KB 496.

ful in obtaining damages for his unlawful detention in the transit lounge at Heathrow en route for Dublin. The majority of cases failed because the alien was said to have no right to enter and could therefore have no "legitimate expectation" that the rules of natural justice or fairness applied to him.[83] By contrast, Commonwealth Citizens, with a "right" of entry as British subjects at common law, were so entitled.[84]

For a brief period, following the report of the Wilson Committee in 1967[85] aliens were entitled to appeal against refusals of leave to enter, variations of such leave and deportations made under the Aliens Order 1953.[86] The Immigration Act 1971 largely assimilated the position of Commonwealth Citizens to aliens in immigration law, although preserving rights of residence for Commonwealth Citizens settled here.[87]

Other benefits enjoyed by Commonwealth nationals and Irish citizens, such as open access to the Civil Service and the franchise at both local and national level continued. Both remained denied to aliens.[88]

(iii) United Kingdom structure of immigration control

The new system adopted for the control of immigration under the 1971 Act laid down no detailed criteria for admission and exclusion, but conferred very wide powers on the Home Secretary to formulate immigration rules for the admission of foreign and Commonwealth nationals.[89] These rules are directions to immigration officers. They contain detailed provisions for the grant of leave to enter, the variation of leave and the removal and deportation of a wide range of passengers, including visitors, students, asylum-seekers, ministers of religion and people of independent means. The categories subject to control, and the degree of control in each case, have changed in response to political and economic pressure, and decisions of the courts and the Immigration Appeal Tribunal. They are not law[90] but are binding in the sense that a decision of an immigration officer or the Home Secretary which breaches a rule may be subject to appeal, which may, in turn, result in a decision adverse to the Secretary of State to which he is bound to give effect.[91]

---

[83] *Schmidt* v *Secretary of State for Home Affairs* [1969] 2 Ch. 149; *R.* v *Secretary of State for the Home Department, ex p. Hosenball* [1977] 1 WLR 766 (Lord Denning MR); but see *R.* v *Secretary of State for the Home Department, ex p. Khawaja* [1984] AC 74, 110–112 (Lord Scarman).
[84] *Re HK (An Infant)* [1967] 2 QB 607.
[85] Cmnd. 3387 (1967).
[86] Immigration Appeals Act 1969.
[87] Section 1(5) now repealed by Immigration Act 1988, s. 1.
[88] Aliens Employment Act 1955; Representation of the People Act 1983, s. 1; but see now European Communities (Employment in the Civil Service) Order 1991 (SI 1991/1221).
[89] Section 3(2), HC 251. A new statement of Changes in Immigration Rules came into effect on 1 October, 1994 (HC 395).
[90] *R.* v *Secretary of State for the Home Department, ex p. Hosenball*, see above, n 83.
[91] Section 19(3).

The rules are not exhaustive, but there is a general provision in the current rules that where a passenger does not satisfy any of the criteria for entry, he is to be refused.[92] In such cases, recourse is had to the grant of "exceptional leave" by the Home Secretary.[93] There is no power in the Act for the Home Secretary to grant leave, a function which appears to be the exclusive province of immigration officers.[94] Besides the published rules, there are internal Home Office departmental instructions, which are unpublished, and indeed secret, but which may reflect important policy changes by the Department.[95]

(iv) **Appeals and judicial review**

The 1971 Act largely incorporated and continued the new appeals system set up by the Immigration Appeals Act 1969. It provides a right of appeal against all decisions made under the Act and the rules, although it has been substantially modified by the Immigration Act 1988 in relation to deportation appeals and by Sections 10 and 11 of the Asylum and Immigration Appeals Act 1993 which abolish appeals against refusal of leave to enter, or variation of leave, by visitors, short-term students and those for whom a refusal is mandatory under the rules. The new appeals process was intended to bring decision-making in immigration into the open. Introducing the Bill, Mr J. Callaghan, the then Home Secretary said that it marked "an important extension of the rule of law in this country. . . it will require [the Home Office] to make manifest the grounds on which decisions are taken about immigration control".[96] Since that time, there has, unfortunately, been a considerable growth in extra-statutory and extra-Rules decisions made according to unpublished criteria not approved by Parliament and which are not subject to appeal.[97]

There are important limits to the right of appeal. A decision to make a deportation order cannot be appealed if the ground is that the deportation is conducive to the public good as being in the interests of national security or of the relations between the United Kingdom and any other country or for other reasons of a political nature. There is a right of

---

[92] Paragraph 320(1) HC 395.

[93] In 1990–1991 more than sixty per cent of asylum-seekers, who did not qualify under the 1951 Geneva Convention and the Immigration Rules, were granted "exceptional leave" outside the Act and the Rules: Earl Ferrers, *Hansard* HL Vol. 542, col. 546 (9 February 1993).

[94] Immigration Act 1991, s. 4; and see Vincenzi, "Extra-Statutory Discretion in Immigration Law" [1992] *Pub. L.* 300.

[95] See, *e.g.* the instructions relating to marriages of convenience by Community nationals following the decision of the European Court of Justice in Case C-370 *R.* v *Immigration Appeal Tribunal, ex p. Surinder Singh* 3 CMLR 358: "Home Office Instructions on Marriage and Children" (1993) 7 Imm.and Nat.L.& P. 101; on unpublished instructions, generally, see Macdonald and Blake, *Macdonald's Immigration Law and Practice* (1991), 21, 34–36.

[96] *Hansard*, HC Vol. 776, col. 490 (22 January 1969).

[97] Vincenzi, *op. cit.*, n 94, p 321.

appeal to three advisers but this is of limited utility.[98] Decisions to deport those who have been in this country for less than seven years are not now appealable on the merits only the *vires* of the decision.[99] Decisions taken outside the rules are not subject to appeal because appeals rights are only applicable to decisions made to "refuse leave. . .under [the] Act".[100] They may be subject to judicial review, but that will not enable the merits of such decisions to be tested.

4 Integration of free movement rights into United Kingdom immigration law and practice

(i) The British approach to integration: the 'island' problem

The maintenance of strict immigration controls at the ports of the United Kingdom has characterised British immigration policy since the First World War. The then Home Secretary, Kenneth Baker, emphasised the Government's continuing commitment to this policy in a Commons debate on immigration and asylum collaboration in the European Community in 1992:

> "Our island geography enables us to place the main weight of our immigration control at the ports of entry. For us, that is by far the most effective way of doing it. It also means that we can avoid the need for intrusive in-country controls. . .such as sanctions on employers who employ illegal immigrants or identity cards or random police checks, which other countries without effective means of controlling their borders find necessary."[101]

Even after the effective date for the creation of the internal market had passed, the Government continued to maintain the need for strict frontier controls and nationality checks on all passengers coming from within the Community. This has involved a rejection of the Commission's view of Article 7A of the Treaty and, indeed, a willingness to defend Article 169 proceedings in the European Court of Justice.[102] The Government's view is based on a narrow interpretation of 'persons' in Article 7A and on both practical and ideological grounds.[103] As Kenneth Baker

---

[98] *R. v Secretary of State for the Home Department, ex p. Chahal* [1988] *The Times*, 12 March; a similar process relating to those subject to exclusion orders under the Prevention of Terrorism Act 1989 is probably contrary to Community Law: *R. v Secretary of State ex p. Gallagher* [1994] 3 CMLR 295.

[99] Immigration Act 1988, s. 5(2).

[100] *R. v Immigration Appeal Tribunal, ex p. Bastiampillai* [1983] 2 All ER 844.

[101] *Hansard* HC No. 73, col. 31 (2 March 1992).

[102] Wardle, Parliamentary Under Secretary for the Home Department, *Hansard* HC Vol. 216, cols. 664, 665 (11 January 1993).

[103] Lewis, [1992] L.E. 2. The Government threatens to block EC legislation relaxing border controls, *The Times*, 14 February 1995.

implies, a port control system is, arguably, both more effective and less intrusive once the individual has secured admission. The Immigration and Nationality Department of the Home Office has shown some ambivalence over the issue of a "smart" computer-readable identity card to improve internal controls. That position may change, as the Government appears to be moving towards the issue of such a card to avoid benefit fraud. It does, however, remain extremely resistant to the imposition of a Community solution in this area, which it regards as exclusively a matter of internal State policy.[104]

As a consequence of this approach, successive British Governments have used the existing system of controls to give effect to Community law. In some areas, such as registration with the police under the Immigration (Registration with the Police) Regulations 1972, Community nationals are not required to register, and they benefit from a more relaxed internal regime. Community law permits the taking of steps to keep a check on the numbers of Community nationals in a Member State at any one time, although compliance should not be made a condition of the right of residence.[105] This more relaxed internal policy accords with the Government's current aim of implementing Community law in a way that is "least intrusive in the lives of British citizens", if that aim is also to be applied to Community nationals in the United Kingdom, as it should.[106]

(ii) Rights and discretion

The combination of alien status and a long history of largely unfettered statutory discretion does not make a propitious basis for the incorporation of Community rights into United Kingdom law. Until the Immigration (Europe Economic Area) Order 1994 (the "EEA Order")[107] came into effect, the Immigration Rules contained the criteria under which decisions concerning the grant of leave or variation of leave were be made. Some, but not all, categories of Treaty nationals with rights of entry were included in the Rules and referred to as being entitled to admission. Under the primary legislation all Community nationals required leave to enter. In fact, the Secretary of State's supposed discretion to admit individuals outside the Rules was used to justify the admission of those not included in them. The rights of Union Citizens to entry, to residence permits, to appeals in those cases were all enjoyed as a result of the exercise of discretion and concessions by the Secretary of State. The right of appeal under English law is intimately linked to the grant of leave. The

---

[104] *Hansard* HC Vol. 73, col. 29 (Baker); but see IND evidence to Home Affairs Committee on Passport Controls, HC 247 of May 1987, paras 42–44. of May 1987, paras, 42–44.
[105] Case 118/75 *Watson and Belmann* [1976] ECR 1185.
[106] See *Review of the Implementation and Enforcement of EC Law in the United Kingdom*, Department of Trade and Industry, July 1993.
[107] SI 1994/1895 (20 July 1994).

grant or refusal of that leave is the precondition for the exercise of that right. The prohibition of the grant of leave to Union Citizens under Community law meant that there was no access to an 'in-State' appeal, as of right, under English law until the EEA Order came into effect, and, even then, an 'in-State' appeal is only available to those threatened with deportation or refused a residence permit.[108]

Aspects of English immigration law relevant to the exercise of the rights conferred by the new Directive are considered below in connection with entry, residence, and appeals. The Immigration Appeal Tribunal, the final stage in the appeal process, regards itself as not bound to interpret the Acts and the Rules to enable unimplemented Community rights to be given effect through the appeal process. Delivering a determination of the Tribunal early in 1993, the Vice-President observed:

> "There is no principle of English law which requires that the rights based on European Law should be treated in accordance with the same scheme as those based on English law. In our view, the only way in English law a claim based directly on European law falls within the statutory scheme of the Immigration Acts is by express or implied incorporation by statute, rule or the exercise of the Secretary of State's discretion under the Acts or (possibly) the prerogative. *The only ground on which any argument for such incorporation by any of those methods can presently be based is the reflection of Community rights in the Rules*" (emphasis added).[109]

This determination by the Tribunal fails to take into account the judgments of the European Court of Justice in the *Von Colson* and the *Marleasing* decisions.[110] There can be little doubt that the Tribunal is a body bound to give effect, in its interpretation of national law, to the rights conferred by Article 52 of the EC Treaty (the rights in issue in the case at hand) and the unimplemented provisions of Directive 64/221 which provide the necessary procedural protection for those rights. There is no need for the national tribunal to await 'incorporation' of a Community right in the Immigration Rules. The Tribunal concluded that the appropriate remedy was judicial review rather than an appeal through the immigration appeals process. Judicial review is not, however, the "same legal remedy" to which Community nationals are entitled under Article 8 of Directive 64/221, where the comparison should be to the appeal right which is available to United Kingdom nationals whose nationality is disputed. Judicial review considers only the narrow *vires* of a decision, and not the full facts and the merits of an immigration decision which can be canvassed before an adjudicator in an immigration appeal.[111]

---

[108] EEA Order 1994, arts. 15(2), 18.

[109] *Pasha* v *Home Office* [1993] 2 CMLR 350, 355, para 18; See HC 251, paras 68–74, 146–153.

[110] Case 14/83 *Von Colson* v *Land Nordrhein-Westfalen* [1984] ECR 1891; Case C-106/89 *Marleasing SA* v *La Comercial Internacional de Alimentacion SA* [1990] ECR I-4135; see further Chapter 3, section 4(iii).

[111] *R.* v *Secretary of State for the Home Department, ex p. Khawaja* [1984] AC 74.

(iii) **The current extent of implementation**

There are three areas of implementation of Community law which have particular relevance to the new general Directive 90/364 which is the subject of this case study. The Directive incorporates by reference Articles 2, 3, 6 (1)(a) and (2) and 9 of Directive 68/360, and the whole of Directive 64/221. The effect of such incorporation means that the rules relating to departure of workers from the home State, entry, residence, and the issue and renewal of residence permits, and all the limits on public policy decisions and procedural protection imposed by Directive 64/221 are applicable to the beneficiaries of the new Directive. Before moving on to deal with the specific provisions of Directive 90/364, it will be necessary to outline briefly the current extent of implementation of those general facilitative measures in the United Kingdom because they are integral to the full implementation of the Directive itself.

Section 7 of the Immigration Act 1988 removes the requirement of the Immigration Act 1971 that Community nationals require leave to enter, and was intended to be part of a wider process of more effective implementation of Community free movement law. However, it was not brought into effect until 20 July 1994.[112] B6 Division of the Immigration and Nationality Department of the Home Office, which has the responsibility for Community free movement rights implementation, responded to the first stages of Article 169 proceedings in relation to Directives 90/364, 90/365 and 90/366, by giving an assurance that a comprehensive Order, incorporating provisions not only implementing the new Directives, but also bringing the whole of national immigration law into line with Community law, would "certainly" be laid by the Autumn of 1993.[113] In the meantime, the Immigration and Nationality Department frankly acknowledged that "the Immigration Rules, paragraphs 68–74 [dealing specifically with entry and residence of Community nationals] *no longer accurately reflect current interpretation of Community law, and are therefore not relied upon by immigration officers*" (emphasis added).[114]

(iv) **The Immigration (European Economic Area) Order 1994**

The draft Order in Council, made under Section 2(2) of the European Communities Act 1972, was finally laid before the House of Lords on 21 March 1994 and before the Commons on 28 March. This Order, which, for the first time in more than twenty-one years of European Community

---

[112] The implementation of the section and a related Order in Council were promised "soon" by the Government in 1988, *Hansard* St.Comm.D, col. 601, but the section and the EA Order did not come into effect until July 20, 1994. Immigration Act 1988, Commencement Order SI 1994/1923.

[113] Conversation between writer and B6 Division, 13 September 1993.

[114] Letter to Phelps from B6 Division, 17 August 1992.

membership, gave specific legal effect to free movement rights in the Community, was perfunctorily debated for a little over half an hour in the Commons before it was approved by resolution on 9 May 1994. The debate in the House of Lords was a little longer and explored some of the issues. The Order was approved there on 18 July 1994 and it came into effect on 20 July 1994.[115]

The Order creates, for the first time, a distinct body of legal rules applicable to rights of entry and residence of European Union and European Economic Area nationals.[116] The Order applies to all EEA nationals except British Citizens, but does not include any reference to European Citizenship or the general rights of entry and residence conferred by that Citizenship. It deals only with the specific rights of entry and residence laid down in the Treaty and the implementing legislation. The failure to deal with European Citizenship as such may not appear to create any problems, because the rights enjoyed under it are those conferred by the Community legislation, with the same qualifications.[117] However, European Citizenship raises a presumption of a free movement entitlement, where, for example, a worker has become voluntarily unemployed, or has ceased to be engaged in business.

In addition, the Order does not deal with the position of British Citizens, who enjoy rights of exit and to travel documents under Article 2 of the Directive 68/360, and rights of re-entry where they have worked in other Member States or the EEA.[118] Nor does it cover the position of Third State nationals, except those enjoying rights as family members. So, for example, those who are entitled to enter as part of the workforce of an undertaking in another Member State, or who enjoy extended employment rights and social security rights under association agreements with the Community once they have been given leave to enter, cannot, prima facie, rely on the order.[119] They may, however, ask a court to "interpret" national law in the light of the Community provisions.[120]

The specific effects of the Order will be examined in relation to the exercise of rights of entry and residence, and procedural and appeal rights in the appropriate following sections. Since, in some cases, those rights have been exercised for more than twenty-one years without the

---

[115] SI 1994/1895; *Hansard* HC vol. 243, No. 99, cols. 65–74 (9 May 1994), HL Vol. 554, No. 79, cols. 974–984 (29 April 1994), vol. 557, No. 120, cols. 114–124 (18 July 1994).

[116] The European Economic Area Agreement 1992 came into effect on 1 January 1994 and, *inter alia*, confers free movement rights in the States of European Community on nationals of Iceland, Norway, Sweden, Finland and Austria and the same rights on EU Citizens in those States; European Economic Area Act 1994. Citizens of Sweden, Finland and Austria have been EU citizens since enlargement on 1 January 1995. 95/1/EC OJ L1/1.

[117] Article 8A of the Treaty on European Union.

[118] Case C-370/90 *R. v IAT ex p. Singh* [1992] 3 CMLR 358.

[119] Case C-43 *Vander Elst v OMI* [1994] 9 August (unreported); Case C-18/90, *ONEM v Bahia Kziber* [1991] ECR I-119.

[120] Compare *Pasha v Home Office* [1993] 2 CMLR 350.

benefit of any legally enforceable national provisions, the position both before and after the implementation of the Order will be considered.

(v) Entry of Union Citizens under United Kingdom law and practice: the situation before the EEA Order 1994 came into effect

Until 1994, Union Citizens, as aliens, required leave to enter the United Kingdom: Section 3 (1)(a). That remained the case until Section 7 of the Immigration Act 1988 was brought into effect in July 1994. Until that time the situation of Union Citizens was governed by the Immigration Rules. These Rules, as noted above, were substantially at odds with Community law. The Rules are not law, but are directions to immigration officers but breach may form the basis for a successful appeal.[121] Immigration Officers were required to admit Community nationals who were coming to exercise Treaty rights. Part VI of the Rules for the Control on Entry (HC 251) did not reproduce the content of the relevant regulations and directives, nor set out an exhaustive list of the beneficiaries of Community free movement rights, but described Community nationals coming "to take or seek employment, to set up in business, to become self-employed or otherwise to exercise the right of establishment or the right relating to the provision or receipt of services" as being "entitled to admission".

Many of the other rules appeared to be applicable to all foreign nationals, irrespective of nationality. Paragraphs 68 (relating to Community nationals seeking entry) and paragraph 146 (relating to post entry controls) provided that the rules applied "only to the extent permitted by Community law". It is unlikely that such bald statements, without any qualification of the offending rules, met the transparency requirement of the *Nursing directives* Case discussed in section 2(i), above.

Although no attempt to incorporate Community law fully was made until July 1994, it would appear that, in practice, over the eight years during which the writer monitored the process of control, the vast majority of Community nationals experienced little difficulty at the point of entry. Several million such nationals enter annually, but no records are kept of the numbers. Only details of residence permits issued are maintained and only a very small proportion of the estimated 400,000 European Community nationals (excluding Irish citizens) living in the United Kingdom at the last census hold them.[122] This is, in part, because residence permits have, since January 1985, only been issued to workers and self-employed people. The failure by a large number of employed and self-employed people to obtain a permit probably reflects the fact that under neither national law or Community law are access to national

---

[121] Immigration Act 1991, s. 19.
[122] See *Control of Immigration Statistics 1992*, Cm. 2368, Table 31.

rights or welfare benefits made contingent on the possession of a permit. Since Community nationals have not, for many years, been interviewed on entry, they were very unlikely to be aware of the provisions in the Rules requiring them to obtain a residence permit if their stay exceeded six months.[123]

No records are now kept of the number of appeals brought by Community nationals, either against refusal of entry, the refusal of residence permits or against deportation, although these may commence shortly.[124] Statistics were, however, maintained in relation to EC nationals refused leave and who appealed in the early eighties. They indicate that, in 1982, 1983 and 1984, more than sixty per cent of the seven or eight hundred EEC nationals refused leave annually were refused on the ground that they had "insufficient means" or were "not *bona fide* visitors". Neither of these were justifiable grounds for refusal under Community law. Immigration officers who were interviewed indicated that they were able to assess, using an undefinable "sixth sense", whether or not a person was genuinely seeking work.[125] Such questioning, and the refusals based upon it have, on two occasions been upheld by the Immigration Appeal Tribunal.[126] Questioning an individual's means has long been rejected by the Commission.[127] This view has now, unequivocally, been upheld by the European Court of Justice.[128]

Recent observations of immigration control carried out at both Dover and Hull indicate that Community passports continue to be examined, not only as proof of Community nationality, but for endorsements on subsequent pages (indicating, for example, that the individual may have been deported at some stage from the United Kingdom or elsewhere). Questioning on means does appear to have been discontinued.[129]

Routine passport checks breach not only the United Kingdom's obligations under Article 7A of the EC Treaty, but the clear statement of the European Court of Justice, made before the implementation date for the Single Market, that, in the absence of grounds for suspicion that action would be justified on public policy grounds, such routine checks are unlawful.[130]

---

[123] HC 81 para 3 (1982) permitted admission without formality.

[124] Letter to the writer from Professor Jackson, Vice-President, Immigration Appeal Tribunal, dated 30 April 1993.

[125] See generally, Connor and Vincenzi *op. cit.*, n 9, pp 7–9 and Appendix I.

[126] *Nijssen* v *Immigration Office, London (Heathrow)* [1978] Imm.AR 226; *Tisseyre* (unreported), Case 6052 (1988).

[127] See answer to Written Question 1789/85 (OJ 1986 C314).

[128] Case C-68/89 *Commission* v *Netherlands* [1993] 2 CMLR 389.

[129] Observations carried out by Phelps at Manchester, Leeds, and Bradford Airports and at the ports of Hull, Harwich, and Dover in 1992/93.

[130] Case 321/87 *Commission* v *Belgium (Re Belgian Passport Controls)* [1989] ECR 1007; [1990] 2 CMLR 492.

(vi) **Entry under the EEA Order 1994**

The Order does not confer a right of entry on EEA nationals. Instead, EEA nationals have a right to admission on production of a valid passport or identity card.[131] A similar right to admission is conferred on family members on proof of their relationship. Non-EEA nationals are required to obtain a "family permit" from the British Embassy in the country of departure and will be refused entry if they do not produce one.[132]

The term "admission" does not accord well with the rights of entry conferred by Community law. Indeed, one definition attributed to the word is "leave to enter"![133] However, once admitted, the EEA national has, under the Order, a "right of residence . . . without the requirement for leave to remain under the 1971 Act, for as long as he remains a qualified person."[134] A "qualified person" is one of the specific beneficiaries of Community free movement rights, including, *inter alia*, individuals in the residual category enjoying rights under Directive 90/364, the subject of this study.[135]

Under Directive 68/360 and Directive 74/148, spouses are entitled to enter as family members.[136] "Spouse" is defined in the Order as excluding "a party to a marriage of convenience". Such a marriage is not defined in the Order, but, during the debate in the House of Lords, the Minister described it as a marriage which ". . . is entirely bogus, the purpose of which is simply to circumvent immigration controls".[137] There is no such qualification in Community law to the definition of "spouse". Indeed, proof of the existence of a subsisting marriage is all that is required to obtain a residence permit.[138] The Government justified inclusion of the qualifying provision on the basis of two recent decisions of the Immigration Appeal Tribunal, *Kwong* and *Lau*[139], in which the Tribunal had rejected claims to rights of residence based simply on the fact of marriage to European Union Citizens working in the United Kingdom. The Tribunal held that a marriage entered into for the purpose only of securing a right of residence was not a marriage such as to constitute a person a "spouse" for the purpose of Community residence rights.[140]

The decision is not without difficulty. It may or may not be desirable to place limits on the purposes for which marriages may be entered into, but Community law, as it stands, simply requires the existence of a sub-

---

[131] EEA Order, arts. 2, 3.
[132] EEA Order, arts 2(1), 19. Such a refusal will not attract a right of appeal: Asylum and Immigration Appeals Act 1994, s. 11(1).
[133] *Chambers Twentieth Century Dictionary* (4th ed, 1965).
[134] EEA Order, art. 4(1).
[135] EEA Order, art. 6(1) and (2)(f).
[136] Directive 68/360, art. 1(2) and Directive 73/148, art. 1(1)(c).
[137] *Hansard* HL Vol. 557, no. 120, col. 116 (18 July 1994) Earl Ferrers.
[138] Case 267/83 *Diatta* [1985] ECR 567. Directive 68/360, art. 4(1)(3)(d).
[139] Cases 10661 and 10859 (unreported) (1994).
[140] Page 10 of Determination in *Kwong*.

sisting marriage. The European Court of Justice has, on a number of occasions, warned Member States against adding qualifications to those required by Community law for the exercise of free movement rights.[141] In addition, if a person attempting to enter as a spouse has to prove to an immigration officer that the marriage was not entered into for the purpose of securing admission to the United Kingdom, then this would clearly constitute an "additional requirement" imposed on entry.[142] It is likely that *Kwong* will be challenged in judicial review proceedings, and may, ultimately, be sent to the European Court of Justice which will then rule on the validity of this qualifying provision.

More generally, the Order retains powers for immigration officers to examine all the beneficiaries of the Order. There is no qualification in Schedule 2 to the Immigration Act 1971, which is incorporated by the Order, confining examination to those whom, it is suspected, might be detained on public policy/public security or public health grounds. Under Article 20(2), any EEA nationals may be detained for questioning or for medical examination. The use of these powers in such an indiscriminate way would clearly be unlawful, and they have no place in legislation of this kind. Their retention would appear to indicate that the United Kingdom has not abandoned its claim to be able to continue to engage in routine immigration control, despite opposition to this policy by the European Commission.

(vii) Residence rights and residence permits: United Kingdom law and practice before the EEA Order 1994

As noted above, there is no provision in the Immigration Act 1971 for the recognition of Community rights of residence, or the issue of residence permits, although these are now dealt with in the EEA Order. Paragraph 147 of the Immigration Rules (HC 251 of March 1990), however, provided that nationals exercising Treaty rights "may normally remain in the United Kingdom for six months before applying for a residence permit".

The implication was that a residence permit is the basis of the right of residence, not merely proof of it. That is, of course, wrong.[143] In addition, the grant of a residence permit was made conditional upon (a) the applicant having established himself in employment or self-employment during the first six months after entry and (b) on not having claimed public funds during that period: Paragraphs 148, 149 and 150. "Public funds" include family credit (a family benefit under Article 4 of Regulation

---

[141] See, for example, Case 293/83 *Lair* v *Universität Hannover* [1988] ECR 3161; Case C-363/89 *Roux* ECR I-273.

[142] See above, section 4(v).

[143] Case 157/79 *R.* v *Pieck* [1981] ECR 2171; Cases 389/81 and 390/81 *Echternach* [1989] ECR 723.

1408/71), housing benefit and income support ("social advantages" under Article 7(2) of Regulation 1612/68). The attachment of such conditions to the grant of a permit breached Community law in the case of a Community national who had worked at any time in those first six months, since, as a worker, he had an absolute entitlement to them. In addition, the time at which a Community national becomes employed or self-employed was irrelevant, provided that he or she had that status when the application was made for the residence permit. Nor is any prior claim to social assistance significant in this context.[144] The Court held, quite specifically in *Roux* that lack of compliance with social security provisions was not, *per se*, a public policy ground justifying derogation from the free movement rights of employees and the self-employed.[145]

These conditions no longer apply under the EEA Order. Until 1994, when the Order came into force, the issue of residence permits provided for Directive 68/360, was dealt with 'administratively', in breach of *Commission* v *Germany* (above, section 2(i)). The other rules for the issue and renewal of residence permits reflected the provisions of Directive 68/360.

(viii) Residence rights and residence permits under the EEA Order 1994

"Qualified persons" are, under the Order, entitled to reside in the United Kingdom, without the requirement for leave to remain under the 1971 Act for as long as they remain "qualified persons". This falls short of a general right of residence for EU Citizens, but is a welcome recognition in United Kingdom law of Community residence rights.

The conditions for the issue of a residence permit contained in the two Directives[146] are fully reflected in the Order. The former conditions relating to public funds have gone. There is, however, no mention of the fact that a residence permit is not required, although neither is there any indication, as there was under the old Immigration Rules, that residents need to acquire one.

(ix) Deportation and removal of Community nationals: United Kingdom law and practice before the EEA Order 1994

The beneficiaries of Directive 90/364, like all Community nationals are subject to detention and removal under Schedule 2 to the 1971 Act, and

---

[144] Case C-363/89 *Roux* [1991] 1 ECR 273.

[145] The linking of residence rights to social assistance is based on a Declaration made by the Council of Ministers at the time of approval of Regulation 1612/68. The ECJ has confirmed that this Declaration is "without legal effect", Case C-292/88, *R.* v *Immigration Appeal Tribunal ex p. Antonissen* [1991] ECR I-745.

[146] Directive 68/360, arts. 4–9 and Directive 73/148, arts. 4–7.

198

deportation under Section 3. Where beneficiaries of free movement rights are involved, paragraph 152 of the Immigration Rules limited deportation or removal under Section 3(5), Immigration Act 1991 (deportation "conducive to the public good") to cases where this was justified on grounds of public policy, public security or public health. However, none of the limitations imposed by Articles 1–4 of Directive 64/221 were incorporated in any way into English law. There was no mention of them in the Immigration Acts or in the Immigration Rules. A person unfamiliar with the Directive would, on reading the Rules, have been excused for believing that individuals who had been reliant on public funds for long periods, or who had been convicted of a serious offences where there was no evidence of the likelihood of further offending, might be deported. Deportation of both is, however, prohibited by Articles 2 and 3 of the Directive. This failure, and its adverse affect on the position of appellants, was noted by the Immigration Appeal Tribunal in *Pasha*.[147]

Again, the provisions of the Directive were implemented "administratively". In any event, the writer was assured by an officer in B6 of the Immigration and Nationality Division, that since the Directive was vertically effective, (following *Van Duyn* v *Home Office (No.2)*)[148], there was no need to implement it. There can hardly be a more striking case of making a virtue out of necessity, nearly twenty years after the United Kingdom had been found in breach of Community law for not implementing that same Directive! Not only did non-implementation mean that individuals remained unaware of their rights under Community law, it also meant that courts have not taken Community law properly into account when making recommendations following a criminal conviction.

Most importantly, trial courts have not been able to make a full assessment of an individual's propensity to re-offend when a recommendation to deport was implemented because, despite the ruling of the European Court of Justice in *Santillo*, there was (and remains) no procedure enabling the court to do so.[149] Judicial review can be used to prevent deportation from being carried out in breach of Community law but it cannot provide an acceptable alternative to an appeal in which the merits of an individual's case can be fully explored.

In dealing with deportation cases the courts have had intermittent regard to the Directive, although the view of the Court of Appeal (Criminal Division) appears to be that, in relation to the criteria for a recommendation for deportation following the commission of a criminal offence at least, Community law "mirrors English law".[150] In fact, there is an increasing divergence between Community law and national law and

---

[147] *Pasha* v *Home Office* [1993] 2 CMLR 350.
[148] [1974] ECR 1337.
[149] Case 131/79 [1980] ECR 1585.
[150] *R.* v *Escauriaza* [1987] 87 Cr.App.Rep. 344, 349.

practice in relation to the deportation of Community nationals who have offended. The need to assess whether or not an individual has a continuing propensity to re-offend is often overlooked at the time when the decision is to be implemented, especially in the case of serious offenders. The commission of sufficiently serious offence appears now to be regarded by the Court of Appeal as, without more, a ground for deportation, despite the clear words of Article 3(2) of Directive 64/221.[151]

(x) Deportation and removal under the EEA Order 1994

EEA nationals and their families may, under the Order, be removed from the United Kingdom either on ceasing to be a qualified person, or the family member of such a person, or on grounds of public policy/public security.[152] The public policy limitations are, for the first time, set out, in extenso, in British legislation.[153]

These provisions raise a number of difficulties. Although removal on ceasing to qualify may be acceptable in relation to non-EU Citizens, the presumption in favour of a right of residence for EU Citizens should mean that a worker who leaves employment voluntarily, a self-employed person who ceases to trade, or a self-sufficient person who claims social assistance, should not, simply by virtue of the fact that they have apparently placed themselves outside the range of specific Community residence entitlements, render themselves automatically liable to removal. Nor should the fact that the principal family member ceases to qualify, or is to be removed on public policy grounds, mean that, as a matter of course, other family members may be removed also.

Under Article 3 of the Directive 64/221, individuals may only be removed as a result of "personal conduct". In other words, they can only be penalised for their own actions and not for someone else's. They may well qualify, if they are EU Citizens or EU nationals, under some category by virtue of their own circumstances or activities.

---

[151] *R* v *Secretary of State for the Home Department, ex p. Marchon* [1993] 2 CMLR 132; There seems to be a divergence on this point between the Civil and Criminal Divisions of the Court of Appeal: *R* v *Spura* (1988) 10 Cr.App.R. (S)376. Deportation cases come before both courts according to whether they result form a purely "administrative" decision by the Home Secretary or a recommendation of a trial court under Immigration Act 1971, s. 3(6). See Vincenzi, "Deportation in Disarray: The Case of EC Nationals" [1994] *Crim. L. Rev.* 163. The number of Community nationals deported annually following a criminal conviction (with or without a recommendation) for the years 1988, 1989, 1990, 1991 and 1992 were, respectively, 52, 46, 8, 12 and 63. (Unpublished Home Office figures, B6 Division, 30 November, 1993).
[152] Article 15(2)(a) and (b).
[153] Article 17.

(xi) **Appeals: law and practice before the EEA Order 1994**

Any passenger refused leave to enter has a right of appeal under Section 13 of the Immigration Act. This right is available to all Community nationals, irrespective of whether they enjoy free movement rights under the Treaty, including the beneficiaries of Directive 90/364. However, the right to remain to present such an appeal in person is only available to those with prior entry clearance or who claims a right of abode under the 1971 Act.[154] Others refused in the country of origin or at the port of entry have to conduct the appeal (which is held in the United Kingdom) from abroad. Community nationals cannot be required to obtain prior clearance, since this is expressly excluded by Article 3 of Directives 68/369 and 73/148. The combined effect of these provisions was that Community nationals had no "in-State" appeal right under United Kingdom law, contrary to Articles 5–9 of Directive 64/221.[155]

Since the *Van Duyn* case in 1974[156] it has, however, been the practice to allow Community nationals to remain, if they request it, when they give notice of appeal. There was nothing in the Immigration Rules to this effect. The form of notice of refusal used for Community nationals was the same as for other passengers. No information on the appeal concession was contained in the notice.[157]

It is far from clear how a non English-speaking Community national from, say, Southern Europe, who was refused admission, would have known about this concession if it had not been drawn to his or her attention by the immigration officer. No separate figures for appeals by Community nationals are now kept. However, during the period 1973–82, in which figures were maintained, of 367 port exclusions of Community nationals, not one exercised the right to appeal from within the United Kingdom. Of those 367 appeals, 22 lodged from abroad in *absentia*, were allowed by the adjudicator.[158] There appears here to be another instance where a concession lacked both the force of law and the transparency to ensure its effectiveness.

The other major deficiency in the appeals process, which affected all Community nationals in the United Kingdom until the EEA Order 1994 came into force, including the beneficiaries of Directive 90/364, was the absence of any right of appeal against refusal to issue or renew a residence permit. Although the issue of residence permits to Community nationals was dealt with in paragraphs 147 and 148 of the former Immi-

---

[154] Section 13(3).
[155] Arnull, *The General Principles of EEC Law and the Individual* (1990).
[156] Case 41/74, [1974] ECR 1337.
[157] Letter to Phelps from IND, August 1992. An attempt to provide advice 'port-side' to Community nationals (funded by the Commission) was ineffective because of lack of support by the Immigration Service: *UKIAS Annual Report 1988/89*. It is not yet clear whether separate refusal notices will be issued following the coming into force of the EEA Order 1994.
[158] *Immigration Control Procedures: Report of a Formal Investigation*, Commission for Racial Equality, 1985, Table 10.5.

201

gration Rules, there was no mention of them in the Immigration Acts, and consequently there are no appeal provisions. By another concession, Community nationals were, however, allowed to appeal to the Immigration Appeal Tribunal.[159] However, in relation to matters falling outside the 1971 Act the Tribunal can, under Section 19, only make a nonbinding recommendation if it finds against the Home Office. This remedy fell far short of the equal treatment in administrative remedies required by Article 8 of Directive 64/221, which should allow appellants in such cases, an appeal to an adjudicator as of right and a further appeal on a point of law to the Tribunal if the initial appeal is unsuccessful.

(xii) Appeals under the EEA Order 1994

For the first time since Britain joined the Community, those exercising free movement rights have specific rights of appeal in relation to refusal of entry on public policy/public security/public health grounds, and in relation to the issue and revocation of residence permits and deportation.

As we have seen, when a passenger is refused entry he has no right to be present at the subsequent appeal unless he holds an entry certificate. Since EU Citizens may not be issued with such certificates, they were bound to exercise any appeal rights from abroad. They were, as a concession, however, allowed to remain for the appeal. That concession has now gone, but so, too, has the chance for an in-State appeal. The Order requires that all those refused entry on public policy or public security grounds exercise that appeal from abroad.[160] That type of appeal cannot be the "effective remedy" required by Community law.[161] Nor does it meet the requirements of Directive 64/221, which prohibits expulsion for at least fifteen days after the decision. Ironically, non-EEA family members who have a "family permit" who are refused at the port of entry will be able to remain, because they would be in possession of the equivalent to entry clearance.[162]

In addition, there is no appeal at all where the Home Secretary has personally ordered exclusion or expulsion.[163] Such decisions may concern national security, or simply the political relations between Britain and another State. Although such a decision is open to judicial review, this is not the equivalent of an appeal, the merits of the case are not considered, only the bare legality of the decision.

Finally, there is still no right of appeal where a court has made a recommendation for expulsion, and that recommendation is acted upon by the Home Secretary following the conclusion of a prison sentence.

---

[159] *Rubruck* v *Home Secretary* [1984] 2 CMLR 499.
[160] Article 15(1).
[161] see, below, Chapter 12.
[162] Immigration Act 1994, s. 13(3).
[163] Article 20(2).

5 Implementation of Directive 90/364: the specific provisions

It will be recalled from the outline of the origins of the Directive, in section 2(ii) above, that the beneficiaries are the residual category of individuals not hitherto enjoying free movement rights under the Treaty or the secondary legislation. The beneficiaries are entitled to the rights of entry, residence and residence permit procedures which apply to workers by virtue of Directive 68/360, and the limitations on exclusion and expulsion and the procedural protection conferred by Directive 64/221 examined in section 3, above. Entitlement to the new "general" right of residence was, by Article 1 of the Directive, made conditional upon the beneficiary having: (1) sufficient resources to avoid becoming a burden on the social assistance scheme of the host Member State and (2) being covered by an all-risks sickness insurance policy in the host State. Although, as noted earlier, the first stages in Article 169 proceedings were taken, the Directive was, finally, formally incorporated into United Kingdom law by the Immigration (European Economic Area) Order 1994, more than two years after the date set for its implementation.[164]

(i) Preliminary steps: consultation

All of the agencies contacted, both public and private, were aware of the new Directives. None of the private agencies was aware of any consultation about the content of Directive 90/364 at draft stage, nor had they been consulted on the content of the draft Order in Council intended to give effect to the Directive. The principal agency specifically advising Community nationals in the United Kingdom asked to be consulted, but was told that, because of the urgency arising as a result of the Article 169 proceedings, this would not be possible.[165] It has not, in any event, been the practice of the Home Office to consult further than with affected Ministries before new draft Immigration Rules were laid before Parliament. In 1994, however, for the first time, the new consolidated Immigration Rules were sent in draft to the Immigration Law Practitioners Association.[166] The specific provisions relating to Community nationals have been omitted, since these are now all contained in the Order in Council.

---

[164] See above, Section 1.
[165] *Advice on Individual Rights in Europe* (AIRE), 13 September 1993.
[166] HC 395, laid before Parliament on 23 May 1994.

(ii) **Legal and administrative action taken in relation to the residual category of beneficiaries before the EEA Order 1994**

Under paragraph 73 of the former Immigration Rules, a Community national "who would be entitled to benefit from the Community law provisions relating to the free movement of labour . . . will normally be admitted for six months, if the purpose of his visit does not fall within the terms of [Community free movement rights], provided that he satisfies the immigration officer that he is not likely to become a charge on public funds or otherwise liable to refusal under Part IX of these rules". Part IX included grounds for refusal for medical reasons, a criminal record, deception in obtaining a previous leave and a number of other grounds, all of which are excluded for Treaty nationals by Directive 64/221.

This provision was intended to enable the residual category (not covered by Treaty rights when the former Rules were made in 1990) to enter and to qualify, if they so wished, for full free movement status by undertaking one of the recognised activities. It effectively granted six months leave, a process, following the decision of the European Court of Justice in *R.* v *Pieck*[167], that is not permissible in relation to Community Citizens exercising Treaty rights. Such entrants were subject to all the disabilities affecting other foreign nationals who require leave, except the prohibition on taking employment. As the Rules stood, they could, for example, have been required to produce evidence of sufficient means on entry, or an undertaking from a sponsor in the United Kingdom who would have been responsible for their maintenance here. The only other reference in the Rules to non-Treaty Community nationals were those to au pairs from the European Community. Under Paragraph 33 an au pair was "an unmarried girl aged 17 to 27 inclusive without dependents, who is a national of any Member State of the European Community. . . . A girl coming for full-time domestic employment requires a work permit." Women given leave to enter on this basis were allowed to remain for up to two years, "with a prohibition on taking employment". This part of the Rules received such sustained criticism because it manifestly breached a whole raft of Community and ILO rules, that it was revoked on 26 July 1993. The replacement provision in HC 725, paragraph 33, now contained no mention of Community nationals, and the current rule makes a similar omission.[168]

There were a number of other categories of passenger referred to in the former Rules who might, depending on the extent and nature of their activities, have been within Directive 90/364, such as persons of independent means (paragraph 44), writers and artists (paragraph 45), visitors (paragraph 22). If they were recipients of services for remuner-

---

[167] Case 157/79 [1980] ECR 2179.
[168] Paras. 88–94, HC 395 (23 May 1994).

ation, they fell within Article 59 of the EC Treaty and Directive 73/148[169] and could not be subject to the restrictions on employment and to the capital requirements which the rules contained. If they were self-employed or part-time employed as writers and artists, the rules were wholly at odds with Directive 73/148 or Directive 68/360. If they qualified under neither of these headings, they should have been able to benefit from Directive 90/364. In any event, the rules were quite inapposite for Community Citizens. It was presumably intended that they should be inapplicable to Community nationals by virtue of paragraphs 68 and 146[170], but this was in no way apparent in the rules themselves. Section 10 of the Asylum and Immigration Appeals Act 1993 abolishes rights of appeal for visitors. There is no saving for Community nationals, who may have a right of appeal under Directive 64/221, either as recipients of services or under Directive 90/364. It is tedious to repeat the point, but there is here, again, at the very least, both a lack of transparency and implementation of Community law (if there is to be implementation) by concession.

Until the EEA Order came into effect, beneficiaries of Directive 90/364 were dealt with "administratively".[171] In practice, this meant that all Community nationals were admitted unless they had defective documents or there was some public policy ground justifying their exclusion.[172] Difficulties, however, were encountered when individual resources were exhausted and recourse was had to public funds, and this situation will continue under the Order.

(iii) Sufficiency of means

As we have seen, the rights under the Directive are conditional upon possession by the individual concerned of sufficient resources:

> "The resources referred to. . .shall be deemed sufficient where they are higher than the level of resources below which the host Member State may grant social assistance to its nationals, taking into account the personal circumstances of the applicant and [the spouse and dependent children]."[173]

Under Article 2(1) of the Directive, the host Member State may, when

---

[169] OJ 1973 L172/14.
[170] See section 4(v) above.
[171] B6 Division, 13 September 1993.
[172] The United Kingdom Government maintains (and the ECJ appears to have accepted the UK Government's submission in Case C-68/89 *Commission* v *Netherlands* [1993] 2 CMLR 389, paras 14 and 15 of judgment) that passport examination to verify authenticity is permissible under Article 3 of Directive 68/360, although this should not be a matter of routine but only where there are grounds for doubting the genuineness of a traveller's document.
[173] Articles 1(1) and 2(2).

the beneficiary applies for a residence permit, require only the production of a valid identity card or passport and proof that the applicant meets the conditions as to resources and sickness insurance. Residence permits are, however, not the basis of the right of residence but proof of that right, despite the requirements of the former Immigration Rules paragraph 147.[174]

No proof of means may be demanded on entry and the British Government has now, implicitly, abandoned any claim to do so.[175] The position of the beneficiaries of the Directive is likely to be examined at any time after entry when a claim for income support is made or if an application is made for a residence permit. The current policy of the Department of Social Security Overseas Benefits Directorate is to treat all European Community applicants for benefits on the same basis, including the beneficiaries of the new Directive. European Community nationals can claim income support for up to six months, provided that they can, like other United Kingdom applicants, demonstrate that they are "available for work".[176] The Secretary of State for Social Security, Mr Peter Lilley, announced at the Conservative Party Conference, in October 1993, that this right was to be curtailed to discourage "social tourism".[177] As soon as EC nationals make a claim, the Home Office is notified on a standard form used for all overseas claimants. After six months the individual claim will be reassessed by the adjudication officer at the Overseas Benefits Directorate in Newcastle. At this assessment, the EC national will have to show that: (1) he is available for work and (2) he is actively seeking work and (3) has a genuine chance of securing employment. The adjudication officer may decide, at this stage, whether or not to discontinue income support. If income support is terminated, the individual will be told that he or she is no longer lawfully present, and will be told to leave the country by the Home Office. Since 12 April 1994, the category of persons ineligible for benefit has been extended to include someone who "is a national of a Member State and is required by the Secretary of State to leave the United Kingdom".[178]

This addition will enable the Home Office to ensure that a person's residence is terminated before completion of the six month review. If, for example, a person is incapable of working, but has sufficient funds

---

[174] Case 48/75 *Royer* [1976] ECR 497. In Cases 389 and 390/397 *Echternach* [1989] ECR 723 at p 762 the Court emphasised the point: "The issue of such a permit does not create the rights guaranteed by Community Law, and the loss of a permit cannot affect the exercise of those rights." (para 25 of judgment).

[175] In its submission in *Commission* v *Netherlands* (*op. cit.*, n 173) and see *Hansard* HC Vol. 216, cols. 464, 465 (11 January 1993).

[176] *DSS Adjudication Officers' Guide*, paras 25–28; DSS Overseas Benefits Directorate, Newcastle; DSS International Relations Division, London. The reference to a "genuine chance" seems to have been imported from the judgment in *Antonissen* (*op. cit.*, n 20).

[177] See, now, The Income-related Benefits Schemes (Miscellaneous Amendments) (No. 3) Regulations 1994 SI 1994/1807.

[178] By an amendment to Income Support (General) Regulations 1987, para 21(3).

to bring him within the Directive, his right of residence will be treated as subsisting until his funds are exhausted and he applies for income support. He could then be required by the Home Office to leave the country, having failed to provide the proof of having sufficient resources under Article 1 of the new Directive. This new provision illustrates the somewhat uneasy relationship between the new Directive, the right to seek work for a "reasonable period" as defined in *Antonissen*[179] and the prohibition against, *inter alia*, expulsion to "service economic ends" in Article 2 of Directive 64/221. It is clear that a breach of social security provisions is not a lawful ground for expulsion, following *Roux*[180], but, at the same time, the right to remain under the new Directive requires a sufficiency of means above the level of income support. Qualification for income support therefore demonstrates loss of entitlement to residence under the Directive.

Contact with a wide range of advice agencies and welfare organizations in 1992 indicated that the energies of both the Department of Social Security and the Home Office were directed at reducing benefit claims.[181] In 1993, the principal advice agency for Community nationals, reported a significant increase in attempts by the Home Office to secure the departure of Community nationals following benefit claims.[182] Whether or not this is a consequence of the means requirement contained in all three of the new Directives or part of a wider policy of discouraging benefit claims by Community nationals is not clear.

(iv) **All risks sickness insurance cover**

This condition is not defined in any of the three Directives in which it is used. It does not appear to have been intended to mean any more than that individuals should have a sickness insurance policy of the kind normally obtained by visitors and tourists. These policies are, typically, subject to numerous limitations in terms both of the ceiling of claims and the nature of illness/accidents to which they apply. A comprehensive all risks insurance policy is currently unavailable in the United Kingdom. If it were to be had, the premium level would be so high as to make it beyond the means of most travellers.

The British insurance industry was not, apparently, consulted in the formulation of this condition when the Directive was in draft, and the Commission acknowledged in April 1993 that it was not clear what an "all risks" insurance policy would have to cover.[183] Currently, both the

---

[179] See above, n 20.
[180] Case C-363/89, [1991] ECR I-273.
[181] B6 Division and DSS Newcastle, August 1992.
[182] AIRE, 13 September 1993. Unpublished figures of B6 Division indicate a rising trend in removals following income support claims over the last eighteen months.
[183] Phelps interview with Directorate General III, 21 April 1993.

Home Office and the Department are, in effect, ignoring this requirement. Community nationals who are resident or working in the United Kingdom have received free medical treatment under the National Health Service. Under reciprocal agreements, EC nationals who are contributors to their own national schemes are entitled to free treatment on production of form E111 for up to three months. Community workers would, of course, be entitled to free medical treatment under Article 7(2) of Regulation 1612/68, as a "social advantage".[184] Examination of practice by many Area Health Authorities and National Health Trust Hospitals indicates that the form is not always required. In some cases, a Community passport is accepted as evidence of entitlement and in others even this is waived. It was announced in October 1993 by the Secretary of State for Health that a more restrictive approach would be adopted with regard to treatment of foreign nationals but, it would seem that the proposed restrictions are not to be applied to Community nationals.[185]

(v) Incorporation of the Directive by the EEA Order 1994

Under Article 3(1) of the Order, beneficiaries of the Directive are entitled, as EEA Nationals, to "admission" to the United Kingdom. Once admitted, they have a right of residence without leave as "qualified persons" under the Order.[186] A "qualified person" includes someone (called a "self-sufficient person" in the Order) who does not enjoy a right of residence under any other provision of Community law, has sufficient resources to avoid becoming a burden on the social assistance scheme of the United Kingdom, and is covered by all-risks sickness insurance.

Self-sufficient persons are entitled to be issued with a residence permit, but only for an initial period of two years, and for three years on the second application.[187] This provision seems unduly restrictive. The Directive specifies that a residence permit shall be for five years, but Member States can limit the first residence permit to a period of two years "when they deem it to be necessary". Such a wording would seem to indicate a limitation to two years on the facts of specific cases, rather than a blanket limitation.

The more general problems relating to entry, residence, procedural protection and family all, of course, apply to the beneficiaries of the Directive 90/364. The problems of sufficiency of means remain and are not affected by anything in the Order.

---

[184] It is arguable that some types of medical treatment are 'benefits in kind' under Regulation 1408/71, art. 24, although Article 4 of the same Regulation expressly excludes 'medical assistance'; see Morris, Rehal and Storey, *Ethnic Minorities Benefits Handbook* (1993), pp 298, 299.
[185] *The Guardian*, 10 October 1993; Conversation, Phelps with Department of Health, 17 December 1993.
[186] Article 6(1).
[187] EEA Order, art. 12(6).

6 Conclusions

Free movement implementation in the United Kingdom well exemplifies what happens, even in a country proclaiming a high respect for compliance with EC law, when deeply rooted national practice encounters Community requirements based on other, incompatible, principles. By way of conclusion we may summarise some of the outstanding issues and difficulties:

(i) Alien status

The retention of alien status for Union Citizens, with the limitations on political rights, access to public employment, the franchise and lack of expectation of fairness in the administrative process that this implies in the United Kingdom, seems hardly compatible with the new Citizenship of the Union. The position of Irish nationals provides an acceptable and practical precedent of a status that confers full rights of free movement in a common travel area and full civic and political rights, and could easily be extended to all Union Citizens.[188]

(ii) A port control system

A port control system, predicated upon the grant of leave, and a vigorous, nationally-orientated system of immigration control seems increasingly at odds with the open area of free movement which is the aim of Article 7A of the Treaty. It is also at odds with the accelerated communication offered by the Channel Tunnel. It seems inevitable that the United Kingdom will have, in the long run, to move to a more open frontier policy, coupled with a closer form of internal monitoring of Community and Third State nationals, and, probably, the adoption of identity cards. However, the specific retention in the EEA Order of a power to examine all passengers, irrespective of objective grounds for suspicion, seems to indicate a continuing commitment to port controls.

(iii) Private rights and administrative discretion

Closely linked to a port control system is the essential incompatibility of a discretionary system of immigration control operated by the Immigration and Nationality Department of the Home Office, the post-entry monitoring by the Departments of Employment and Social Security on

---

[188] Irish nationals, as non-aliens, are entitled to all civic rights, and benefit from the Common Travel Area with the Republic of Ireland created by Immigration Act 1971, s. 9(2).

the one hand and the rights-based nature of Community freedom of movement on the other. The national system is primarily directed at exclusion and regulation, the Community system is intended to be empowering and facilitative, encouraging those who wish to migrate and assisting in the process of their social and political integration in the host State.

An important step has been taken in the EEA Order by the establishment of a separate body of legally enforceable rules for Citizens of the Union and the EEA States. The rules are, however, far from exhaustive. The Order does not recognise a general right of residence of the European Union Citizen qua Citizen. The Citizen is treated simply as any beneficiary of Community free movement rights. The Order has a grudging quality. Appeals are to be allowed for refusal of entry, but they are to be exercised from abroad. Ceasing to qualify for a specific Community right of residence is, in itself, a ground for removal. Full family rights are not included, and a spouse may be challenged on the purpose for which their marriage was entered into. The Community free movement rights of British Citizens are unrecognised.

It may well be that some of the unimplemented rights will be implemented in practice by the exercise of discretion, and that the full powers of detention and questioning will not be used. A wide area of discretion, however, remains, which is contrary to both the letter and spirit of the Community provisions.

(iv) **A tradition of secrecy**

The sensitive nature of immigration control, for both political and security reasons, has made British immigration service secretive and inward-looking. Where rights exist, there is little attempt to make those who benefit aware of them, or to facilitate their exercise. The abandonment of record-keeping on refusals of entry, deportations and appeals is unhelpful in making any useful assessment of the degree of compliance with Community law of those processes. The White Paper on Open Government, which recommends the exclusion of the decision-making process in immigration cases from public access, does not give much hope of any change in approach.[189] This country is still a long way from providing an open and accessible system for the facilitation of free movement rights.

(v) **Private Enforcement**

Linked to 6(iii) above is the problem of the need for individual initiative to activate enforcement. Although the Treaty imposes the obligation of

---

[189] White Paper on Open Government, Cm. 2290, para 5.16.

implementation on the State and its agencies, the enforcement of free movement rights is, essentially, left to individual initiative. Even in a country like the United Kingdom where there is an independent appeal system, such a system (for which there is no Legal Aid) is not effective to ensure that national administrative policy complies with Community law. Although Article 169 proceedings can be brought, that process is slow and it imposes heavy burdens on the small number of Commission staff in Directorate General (DG) III and V charged with implementing free movement law. In the United Kingdom individual case are settled by the Home Office when it is challenged, but the overall policy may continue. This is evident in the pursuit of income support claimants. It may be that a sufficient number of successful and well-reported *Francovich*[190] claims for damages against the Home Office will have a salutary effect. There can be no doubt that attempts by the Home Office to secure the departure of those who have attained worker status and who have claimed public funds breaches Article 2(2) of the Directive 64/221 (which prohibits expulsion "to service economic ends").

(vi) **Lack of collective representation**

Linked to 6(v) is the absence of any organized groups in the United Kingdom participating in the formulation of policy at Community level, in the drafting of directives and in the oversight of the implementing legislation in this country. This is, primarily, because the major organizations such as the Joint Council for the Welfare of Immigrants and the (now defunct) United Kingdom Immigrants Advisory Service saw, and see themselves, essentially as representatives of Third State nationals and use their limited resources for their assistance. Community nationals are seen as a fortunate and privileged group for whom there are few problems. Immigration policy and Community law on free movement rights are largely beyond the competence of the Commission for Racial Equality.[191] Other organisations, such as AIRE, Interights, and the European Committee of the Immigration Law Practitioners Association have made great efforts both collectively and individually to ensure that Community free movement rights are delivered, but they lack the resources and the ear of Government to make their involvement effective at the policy level in the way that large industrial and commercial organizations are used to doing.

---

[190] Case C-6 & 9/90 *Francovich* v *Italian State* [1991] ECR I-5357; [1993] CMLR 66; and see Chapter 3, text at n 31 and section 4(iv).
[191] See Race Relations Act 1976, s.41; and see *Home Office* v *Commission for Racial Equality* [1982] QB 385.

(vii) **Lack of procedural protection**

The retention in the EEA Order of detention and questioning powers for immigration officers at the point of entry, the failure to include any objective criteria for the exercise of these powers[192], the omission of the procedural protection requirements contained in Directive 64/221 on information and in-State challenges to decisions, are disturbing. Although such wide powers are routinely used by immigration officers in the process of control, the position of European Union Citizens is meant to be different. The retention of these powers, without qualification, demonstrates the fundamental incompatibility between a system of immigration control and a system for the implementation of fundamental free movement rights.

(viii) **Means-testing of residence rights**

The new provisions in the three Directives relating to sufficiency of means appear to be regarded by the Home Office as providing grounds for terminating the exercise of residence rights of those who may have lost the protection of other free movement rights. The new Directive, which was introduced to facilitate the entry and residence of those not hitherto benefiting from other provisions of Community law, has now provided the grounds, in the EEA Order, for their removal. The right of residence conferred by European Citizenship is in danger of becoming a means-tested benefit.[193]

CHRISTOPHER VINCENZI

---

[192] Compare ss. 1(3) and 24 of the Police and Criminal Evidence Act 1984.
[193] The writer acknowledges with thanks the assistance given by his colleague Ian Phelps in the collection and collation of data.

Chapter 8
Television Without Frontiers

> "...[I]f nobody's managed to implement it correctly it can't be much of a Directive"
> (Unnamed United Kingdom official quoted in *Financial Times*, 16 November 1992).

1 Introduction

This Chapter looks at transposition and implementation in the United Kingdom of the so-called Television without Frontiers Directive.[1] The Directive has been controversial, its implementation patchy and difficult across the Community, its future endangered by uncertainty and confusion about what Europe's policy for television should be in a period of rapid technological and commercial change, and about what instruments should be employed to advance it and by whom. We look first at the development of that policy (section 2), next at the content of the Directive itself (section 3), then at its implementation in the United Kingdom (section 4), and finally at two specific disputes to which that implementation has given rise (section 5).

2 The Community's policy in the audiovisual area

(i) Objectives

European Community policy is a response to the combination of highly dynamic technical, regulatory and market developments in Member States in the audiovisual area.

The Commission's 1993 White Paper *Growth, Competitiveness, Employment: the Challenges and the Ways Forward into the 21st Century*[2] discusses the need for Community enterprises to position themselves for a bigger role

---

[1] Directive 89/552/EEC, OJ 1989 L298/23, on the co-ordination of certain provisions laid down by law, regulations or administrative action in Member States concerning the pursuit of television broadcasting activities.
[2] 6 Bull. EC Supp. 1993.

in new growth areas – such as the audiovisual sector. Specifically, the Commission predicts that demand for audiovisual hardware and software will be ECU 45 billion by the end of century (up from ECU 23 billion); that up to 500 channels will be created; that the channels will produce three million broadcast hours every year; and that two million jobs may be created by the year 2000 – if there is not a financial transfer outside the European Community.[3]

The Commission's view, in sum, is that the audiovisual sector will become one of *the* major service sectors of the 21st century. In passing it may be noted that the underlying agenda for the Community's policy is the creation of a large domestic market to challenge that which exists in the United States.[4] However, the shape of that market is currently exercising the Commission, which wants to protect a multi-organisational media industry in the context of the internal market and restrict concentration in television (as well as in radio and the press).

In 1992, speculative discussions on issues of pluralism and media concentration were published[5], followed by public hearings and a questionnaire.[6] Subsequent criticism of the Commission, for its lack of coherent industrial policy targeting the audio-visual industry[7], led to the publication of a further Green Paper in April 1994.[8] This was supposed to contain concrete proposals, but is stronger on analysis of the European industry's problems, on requests for advice, than on solutions.[9] The United Kingdom's response to the Green Paper, initiated by the Secretary of State for National Heritage who invited the British Screen Advisory Council (BSAC) to prepare "a considered statement of opinion from the British [Audiovisual] Industry as a whole"[10], was published in October 1994.[11]

(ii) **Development**

The audiovisual policy of the Community was first comprehensively laid out in the Green Paper on the establishment of the common market for

---

[3] *Ibid.* p 104.
[4] See below, n 48, for the US reaction to this.
[5] Green Paper, *Pluralism and Media Concentration in the Internal Market : An assessment of the need for Community Action*, COM(92)480 final, 23 December 1992. For a discussion of the paper, see Hitchens, "Media Ownership and Control: A European Approach" (1994) 57 Mod. L. Rev. 585.
[6] European Commission, *Pluralism and Media Concentration in the Internal Market : Initial Reactions to the Green Paper*, Information Memo, 12 May 1993, IP(93)351.
[7] See Enser, "Audio-visual Policy: The European Commission's Green Paper – Much Ado About Nothing?" (1994) 4 Ent.L.Rev. 135.
[8] *Strategy Options to Strengthen the European Programme Industry in the Context of the Audiovisual Policy of the European Union*, April 1994. See below section 3(iii).
[9] See Kern, "EU Audiovisual Policy" (1994) 12 (No. 10) Int.Media L. 77.
[10] British Screen Advisory Council, *EC Audiovisual Policy Green Paper: UK Industry Response*, 3 October 1994, p *ii.*
[11] See below, section 3(iii).

broadcasting, especially by cable and satellite[12], commonly called Television without Frontiers. This followed a request to the Commission by the European Parliament that framework rules for radio and television broadcasting in the European Community should be formulated[13] to facilitate the "free flow of existing national programmes within the Community and the creation of a Community-wide broadcasting area."[14] This and other Resolutions[15] reflected a growing perception that the European Community was not, and should not be regarded as, merely an economic unit. As Ivo Schwartz puts it: "A process got under way in 1984 that can be described as the discovery by the general public of the European Community's cultural or civilising dimension."[16] The capacity to watch television programmes transmitted from one Member State to another, largely achieved through Belgian and Dutch cable networks, "...has helped increasingly to foster a gradually emerging awareness of cultural attributes shared in common by all Member States." The process would be speeded up by satellite television which would "...pave the way for a new process of cultural interpenetration."[17]

While the European Parliament saw action in the audiovisual area as closely connected with the development of a European identity, Member States' Ministers responsible for cultural affairs, meeting in June 1984 for the first time within the European Community Council of Ministers, had somewhat different concerns. Three strands of action were proposed, on the initiative of the French Minister Jack Lang: the establishment of a common system of support for the production of television programmes; a minimum European content for television programming; and the drawing up of a sequence for film distribution – basically that the showing of films should be restricted initially to the cinema, films might then be transmitted on television and, finally, released on cassette. A resolution on the last two points was adopted.[18] Subsequently, the Commission sent the Council a working paper advocating the creation of the common support fund.[19]

---

[12] Commission of the European Communities, *Green Paper on the Establishment of the Common Market for Broadcasting, Especially by Satellite and Cable* ("*Television without Frontiers*"), COM(84)300 final, 14 June 1984.

[13] Resolution on radio and television broadcasting in the European Community (*Hahn* Resolution), OJ 1982 C87/110.

[14] Schwartz "Broadcasting without frontiers in the European Community" (1985) 6 J.Media L.& P. 26 at p 30.

\[15] These include Resolution on a policy commensurate with new trends in European television (*Arfe* Resolution), OJ 1984 C117/201; Resolution on broadcast communication in the European Community (the threat to diversity of opinion posed by the commercialisation of new media) (*Hutton* Resolution), OJ 1984 C127/147; and Resolution on European media policy, OJ 1984 C172/212.

[16] Schwartz, *op. cit.*, n 14 at p 26.

[17] *Ibid.*

[18] Resolution on the rational distribution of films through all the audio-visual communication media, OJ 1984 C204/2.

[19] Promotion and development of a European programme industry: Study of an aid scheme for cinema and television co-production, document SEC(84)1798 final, 12 November 1984.

The Commission, in the Television without Frontiers Green Paper published a few days before this Council meeting, advocated, as a first step, that action should be taken to permit the free movement of television programmes and information across Member States' national borders particularly by satellite and cable systems. The Commission appears to have taken the view that the EEC Treaty should be read as fostering "ever closer union among the peoples of Europe"[20] which can only be achieved "...if Europeans want it. Europeans will only want it if there is such a thing as a European identity. A European identity will only develop if Europeans are adequately informed. At present, information via the mass media is controlled at national level."[21]

Varying national laws might however subsist under Article 36 of the Treaty on such matters as the regulation of advertising, the protection of children and young persons, and the definition of copyright and related rights. Community measures, obliging national legislators to bring their laws into line on the basis of binding directives, were accordingly proposed in the Green Paper.

By the time the Community managed to give a legislative response to the Commission's proposals, in the 1989 Directive examined here, major political and other changes had occurred. Member States had reached an agreement, but within the framework of the Council of Europe rather than the Community, in the form of the European Convention on Transfrontier Television[22], broadly endorsing freedom of television reception subject to the enforcement of minimum licensing standards. At the same time they decided to carry back this commitment into the Community framework and to adjust the Commission's original proposals accordingly, but were only able to pass the Directive by a qualified majority and after extensive argument on the wording of provisions relating to the European content of programming, reflecting tensions between *laissez faire* and *dirigiste* views of a single audiovisual market, tensions which persist in the implementation of the Directive itself.[23]

While the conclusion of the Convention was motivated by cultural and human rights arguments, its purpose is to provide a framework for the transfrontier circulation of television programmes while preserving the integrity of national media structures.[24] Unlike the Directive, the Convention does not seek to regulate the broadcasting activities, policies and

---

[20] Article A of the Treaty of European Union. See also Chapter 1, Section 2(ii).

[21] Commission of the European Communities, 1984, *op. cit.*, n 12 at p 28 cited in Collins, "The Single Market in Broadcasting and the Audiovisual, 1982–92" (1994) 32 J.Com.Mar.St. 89 at p 95.

[22] European Convention on Transfrontier Television, 5 May 1989, Eur.TS No.132; see also, Council of Europe, *Explanatory Report on the European Convention on Transfrontier Television* (1990); for commentary see Hondius, "Regulating Transfrontier Television – The Strasbourg Option" (1988) 8 Y. E. L. 141–169; Barendt, *Broadcasting Law. A Comparative Study* (1993), 222–229; Winn, *European Community and International Media Law* (1994), 334–352; Cassese & Clapham (eds), *Transfrontier Television in Europe: The Human Rights Dimension* (1990), esp. at pp 215 *et seq.*

[23] These tensions are discussed further by Collins, *op. cit.*, n 21.

[24] Barendt, *op. cit.*, n 22, p 236; See also Council of Europe, 1990, *op. cit.*, n 22, para 24.

structures of the Member States. It lacks juridical means to secure its enforcement, and is therefore only relevant to Community States when no applicable provision exists in the Directive.[25] It sets out a number of basic standards on such matters as the rights of viewers (following Article 10 of the European Convention of Human Rights on freedom of expression[26]), the duties of States, programming standards, advertising and sponsorship.

Copyright is not covered in the convention and has been considered "the missing chapter" from Television without Frontiers.[27] The Commission responded by seeking to fill this lacuna by the production of a further Green Paper in 1988: *Copyright and the challenge of technology*[28], with a third in 1990: *A common approach in the field of satellite communications in the European Community.*[29] Legislative instruments which have emerged from this process include, besides the Television without Frontiers Directive, the Directive on Rental Rights and Lending Rights, and on Certain Rights Related to Copyright in the Field of Intellectual Property[30]; the Cable and Satellite Copyright Directive[31]; and the Duration of Copyright Directive.[32]

3 The Directive

(i) Aims, structure and content

The principal aim which is to be facilitated by the Directive is the creation of a European market for programmes.[33] This is to be achieved by the primary purpose of the Directive:

---

[25] Hondius, *op. cit.*, n 22, p 159; and see Article 29(1) of European Convention on Transfrontier Television, *op. cit.*, n 22; Article 24 of the Directive provides that in fields which are not co-ordinated by the Directive, rights and obligations resulting from broadcasting conventions are unaffected by it. Barendt, *op. cit.*, n 22, p 229, n 57.

[26] For the debate on the compatibility of Article 10 of the ECHR (protecting the freedom to communicate ideas and information "regardless of frontiers") with quota provisions, see Cassese & Clapham (eds), *op. cit.*, n 22, Parts III & IV; Barendt, *op. cit.*, n 22, pp 222–29; Eeckhout, "Audiovisual and Telecommunications Services" in *The European Internal Market and International Trade: A Legal Analysis* (1994), 125.

[27] Collins, *Broadcasting and Audio-Visual Policy in the European Single Market* (1994), 73.

[28] Document COM(88)172 final.

[29] Document COM(90)490 final.

[30] OJ 1992 L346/61. The deadline for implementation of this Directive came and went on 1 July 1994. The Department of Trade and Industry (DTI) has not been able to meet the deadline and is still in the process of drafting implementing legislation: Frere Cholmeley Bischoff, *Audio and Audiovisual Industries in the European Union*, October 1994, p 9.

[31] OJ 1993 L248/15. The Directive must be implemented by 1 January 1995.

[32] OJ 1993 L290/9. The Directive must be implemented by 1 July 1995.

[33] A market which now includes Austria, Finland, Iceland, Norway and Sweden under the European Economic Area (EEA) Treaty which came into force on 1 January 1994: *The European Economic Agreement and its Adjusting Protocol*, OJ 1994 L1/1. See especially Annexes X & XI EEA. The Television without Frontiers Directive has already had implications for Sweden concerning regulatory jurisdiction, see further Frere Cholmeley Bischoff, *op. cit.*, n 30, pp 27–28.

> "...to permit television broadcasts which comply with the Directive's requirements to be received and retransmitted freely in all Member States. The consequential effect ...will be that any television broadcast, complying with the law of the Member State in which the broadcast originates, should be able to circulate freely throughout the Community unrestricted by divergent national requirements in the receiving State."[34]

This 'freedom of reception' entails the application of minimum standards in the particular areas of advertising and sponsorship; the protection of minors; the right of reply; and quotas of programming originating from 'European' and 'independent' producers.

A subsidiary reason for supporting the passage of the Directive (or, at least, the reason some Member States might have been favourable towards it), is the mechanism that it imports to restrict the possibility of otherwise unrestricted transfrontier pornographic satellite programmes flowing between Community countries. The point of Article 22 of the Directive[35] is to allay fears that transfrontier satellite broadcasts would only have to satisfy the law of obscenity of the most liberal State.

The Directive comprises twenty-seven Articles divided into seven Chapters. It begins by defining, in Article 2(1), the bases on which Member States are to exercise control over television broadcasting[36]; Article 2(2) lays down the basic freedom of transmission and the very limited exception to it under Article 22. Article 3(1) permits stricter national standards. Articles 4 to 6, which were highly controversial, are concerned with quotas, seeking to ensure, "where practicable and by appropriate means" a majority programme content for European works (Article 4), with provision within this for a quota of such works (10 per cent) by independent producers (Article 5). 'European works' are defined in Article 6. The remainder of Chapter III (Articles 7–9) is concerned with rebroadcasting of films (a French worry), language policy, and purely local television. The weightiest Chapter, Chapter IV, contains detailed provision for the regulation of television advertising, extending over twelve Articles (Articles 10–21), and containing both general principles, such as that television advertising shall not prejudice respect for human dignity (Article 12(a)) and specific quantitative rules on percentages of transmission time devoted to advertising, and the frequency of advertising

---

[34] Wallace & Goldberg, "The EEC Directive on Television Broadcasting" (1989) 9 Y. E. L. 175.
[35] Article 22 states: "Member States shall take appropriate measures to ensure that television broadcasts by broadcasters under their jurisdiction do not include programmes which might seriously impair the physical, mental or moral development of minors, in particular those that involve pornography or gratuitous violence. This provision shall extend to other programmes which are likely to impair the physical, mental or moral development of minors, except where it is ensured, by selecting the time of the broadcast or by any technical measure, that minors in the area of transmission will not normally hear or see such broadcasts.

Member States shall also ensure that broadcasts do not contain any incitement to hatred on grounds of race, sex, religion or nationality."
[36] For the dispute this has occasioned between the United Kingdom government and the Commission, see below, section 5.

spots (Articles 18, 11). Article 22, as noted, is for the general protection of minors, while Article 23 guarantees a right of reply, leaving a large discretion to Member States as to how to secure it. The usual "final provisions" (Articles 24–27) complete the Directive.

(ii) Feedback mechanisms internal to the Directive

Article 25 of the Directive gives Member States two years within which to comply with its provisions, *i.e.* until 3 October 1991. It further requires States to report to the Commission on the administrative and legislative steps they have taken to implement the provisions of the Directive. In the case of the United Kingdom, this was done on 22 August 1991.[37]

A general review of the Directive in the light of "developments in the field of television broadcasting" is to be undertaken by the Commission by the end of the fifth year following the Directive's adoption. The report – to be done every two years thereafter – is to be communicated to the European Parliament, the Council of Ministers and the Economic and Social Committee (Article 26).

Member States are, additionally, required to provide a report to the Commission on the application of Articles 4 and 5 for each of the television programme services falling within their jurisdiction.[38] The reasons for any failure must be stated and the measures adopted or envisaged to achieve the required proportions of European and independent programming identified. The Commission is to give an opinion on the report to other Member States and to the Parliament, accompanied, if appropriate, by an opinion. In forming its opinion, the Commission may take account of such factors as progress achieved in relation to previous years; the share of first broadcast works in the programming; the particular circumstances of new broadcasters; and the specific situation of countries with a low audiovisual production capacity or restricted language area.

The Council is to review the implementation of Articles 4 and 5 in the light of the report of the Commission, which should submit any proposals for amendment by the end of the fifth year from the adoption of the Directive.[39]

In order to assist Member States in their "duty to monitor the application of Articles 4 and 5 of the Council Directive. . .and to render transparent to all interested parties the manner in which this legislation will be implemented by the Commission's Services" the Commission sent guidelines to all Member States, "suggesting" definitions of such matters

---

[37] Letter from N.M. McMillan (Home Office) to Bruehann (DG III), 22 August 1991, with attached Schedule: *Implementation of Directive 89/552 on Television Broadcasting*, dated 25 July 1991.
[38] Article 4(3).
[39] Article 4(4); Wallace & Goldberg, "Television Broadcasting: the Community's Response" (1989) 26 *Comm. Mkt. L. Rev.* 717–728 at p 721.

as who is a broadcaster; the extent of Member States' jurisdiction over broadcasters; measurement of relevant programme transmission time on which the quotas are calculated; the nature of a European work; the concept of an independent broadcaster; reporting periods; and the collection of data.[40]

Detailed Commission monitoring arrangements have prompted queries as to whether Articles 4 and 5 constitute "political" rather than 'legal' obligations.[41] A distinction might well be drawn, for the purposes of implementing mechanisms, between a legal, binding process which includes a reference to the Court with a chance of a clear answer; and a political, supervisory process within which there is a role for the Commission in ensuring that the Member States' obligations are fulfilled. Kenneth Collins MEP, in a Written Question[42], asked the Commission to confirm press reports that "statements in the Council Minutes interpret the Directive." Entered at the insistence of the German Delegation[43], the statement that the quota is only "politically binding" has been backed by authoritative sources[44] claiming that the "minutes statements are essentially political glosses and . . .. have no legal force".[45]

However, Mr Bangemann, putting the Commission's point of view in a written answer dated 4 January 1990[46], noted that the *entirety* of the Directive is legally binding on Member States. This means that the Commission will monitor the States' fulfilment of their obligations. Such monitoring can, in principle, result in an action being brought before the European Court of Justice. The wording of Articles 4 and 5 is the result of a "difficult compromise" which departs from the Commission's initial proposal and Parliament's wishes. Member States are allowed a great deal of discretion in choosing the means to attain the desired result ("by appropriate means") and an element of flexibility is introduced ("where practicable"). This means that the attainment of the objectives can be overridden by "technical constraints or economic imperatives."

The Commissioner emphasised, however, that "flexibility" does not detract from the legal nature of what amounts to an obligation to behave in a certain manner. He conceded, though, that it would be difficult to

---

[40] Commission of the European Communities, *Communication from the Commission to the Council and the European Parliament on the application of Articles 4 and 5 of Directive 89/552/EEC Television without Frontiers*, Document COM(94)57 final, 3 March 1994, Annex 1 (*Suggested Guidelines for the Monitoring of the "TV Without Frontiers" Directive*).
[41] *Agence Europe*, 4 October 1989, p 7.
[42] No. 758/89, OJ 1990 C97/21.
[43] Filipek, "'Culture Quotas': The Trade Controversy over the European Community's Broadcasting Directive" (1992) 28 Stan.J.Int'l L. 323 at 353.
[44] The Head of the Broadcasting and Media Group at the Department of National Heritage (the Ministry responsible for broadcasting in the United Kingdom), quoted in Porter, "Transfrontier Television Services: Implementing the Rules of the Single European Market," paper presented to the ESRC Single European Market Programme/COST A7 Action Conference, University of Exeter, 8–11 September 1994, p 3.
[45] A gloss that Germany interprets to mean "not juridically binding". See Filipek, *op. cit.*, n 43.
[46] OJ 1990 C97/22.

imagine cases regarding the application of these Articles that could be the subject of a clear ruling by the European Court of Justice.[47] The weakness of the legal instrument is counter-balanced by the political force of the supervisory role assigned in Article 4(3) to the Commission. That role would be the principal mechanism for ensuring that the undertakings entered into by Member States would be effectively fulfilled. Finally, the written answer says that considerations are entered into the Council minutes which do underscore the political nature of the undertakings and the context in which they are to be fulfilled.

(iii) The present situation

Results of the first review of the Directive by Directorate General (DG) X were to be presented to the Council of Ministers and the European Parliament by October 1994. The Commissioner stated that the Commission would, in its review, strengthen the Directive in its aims of promoting the free circulation of channels and programmes and giving support to European film.[48] It is unlikely, however, to conduct an extensive review of Chapter III[49] as it has stated that this *acquis communautaire* "...provides a sound framework for the cross-border development of the European programme industry and that it should be retained for the time being".[50]

The review is going on against the background of the Commission's latest Green Paper on audiovisual policy, the stated aim of which was

---

[47] *Audiovisual Communications*, Euroscope, 5 March 1992, (*LEXIS*); Note also Bangemanns former defence of Article 4: "It is not a legal obligation, it's a political commitment" cited in Presburger & Tyler, "Television Without Frontiers: Opportunity and Debate Created by the New Community Directive" (1989) 13 Hastings Int'l & Comp.L.Rev. 495 at 502, n 49.

[48] This, and other incidents (see text accompanying n 86, *re* the refusal of Belgium and France to allow cable relays of channels with content approaching 100% US programmes), have angered US officials who decry Europe's "trade restrictive" practices as falling foul of the General Agreement on Tariffs and Trade (GATT) (even though it applies to goods and not services) and Section 301 of the United States Trade Act, as amended. See Eeckhout, *op. cit.*, n 26, pp 132–135; Presburger & Tyler, *op. cit.*, n 47, p 501 *et seq.*; Williams, "Television without Frontiers: An EEC Broadcasting Premiere" (1991) 14 Boston Coll.Int'l & Comp.L.Rev. 195 at pp 205–211. However, the audiovisual sector was effectively removed from the final agreement of the GATT Uruguay Round, resulting in stalemate – the EU is not obliged to apply Most Favoured Nation status nor to increase market access and the US is free to retaliate: Frere Cholmeley Bischoff, *Audio and Audiovisual Industries in the European Union*, January 1994, pp 36–37.

US reaction to Article 4 may have a deleterious effect on the development of East European broadcasting: East Europe wants American investors to lend both money and expertise but the effect of Article 4, on a potentially profitable market place, may threaten that. See further, Lewengrub, "European Unification, Broadcasting Law, Eastern Europe and the 'Television without Frontiers' Directive: Radio Freed Europe – Can Television Unify it?" (1992) 22 Ga.J.Int'l & Comp.L. 547.

[49] Chapter III covers the Promotion of distribution and production of television programmes, see above section 3(i).

[50] European Commission, *Strategy Options to Strengthen the European Programme Industry in the Context of the Audiovisual Policy of the European Union*, Document COM(94)96 final, 1994, p 36; Kern, *op. cit.*, n 9, p 78.

to launch a debate on "how can the European Union *contribute* to the development of a European film and television programme industry which is competitive on the world market, forward-looking and capable of radiating the influence of European culture and of creating jobs in Europe."[51] (emphasis added). The pragmatic emphasis on *contribution* was off-set by the input from a Commission Think Tank[52], who considered themselves as being "a kind of Maginot line [to contain] the advance of the Hollywood machine of war".[53] Their report, containing strategic proposals for the industry, was delivered in February 1993.[54]

The Commission concluded, as foreshadowed by the White paper on Growth, Competitiveness and Employment, that the European Union should devise an ambitious industrial policy to implement four main objectives, *i.e.* to put an end to the partitioning of national markets; to guarantee real choice to the European public; to optimise opportunities in an industry with a future; and to secure the long-term profitability of a loss-making industry.[55] Exactly how all this was to be done, it did not say.

In relation to Television without Frontiers, the response of the United Kingdom industry to the Green paper, published in October 1994[56], focused on the future of European-wide programme quotas, with a split between those who seek a tighter quota system (BBC, ITV and Channel 4) and those who say it should be abolished (cable television operators and BSkyB).[57] However, despite these differences, it was agreed that, in the longer term, technological advances may make the current programme quotas unworkable.[58]

4 National transposition measures

(i) General remarks

What the Commission calls the transposal process is discussed in the Communication on the application of Articles 4 and 5.[59] "Transposal" is

---

[51] European Commission, 1994, *ibid.* p 2.
[52] Composed of five eminent European audiovisual figures: Antonio-Pedro Vasconcelos (former Co-ordinator of the National Secretariat for the Audiovisual Sector in Lisbon), David Puttnam (film producer, Director of Anglia TV), Michlèle Cotta (journalist, TV producer with France 2, former Chairwoman of the Audiovisual High Authority), Peter Fleischmann (film director, founder of the European Federation of Audiovisual Film Makers) and Enrique Balmaseda Arais-Davila (lawyer, former legal advisor to Spanish television): European Commission, 1994, *op. cit.*, n 50 at p 3, n 7. Two other sources to the Green paper include trade organisations and Member States.
[53] Direct quotation from the Think Tank report (unpublished) cited in Enser, *op. cit.*, n 7, p 137.
[54] 1/94 *Eurofocus*, p 8.
[55] European Commission, 1994, *op. cit.*, n 50, p 56.
[56] British Screen Advisory Council, 1994, *op. cit.*, n 10.
[57] *Ibid.* at p 5, paras 3 & 4; "TV firms clash over European quotas", *The Independent*, 4 October 1994, p 9; and section 4(iii) below.
[58] British Screen Advisory Council, op. cit. n. 10.
[59] Commission of the European Communities, *Communication from the Commission to the Council and the European Parliament on the application of Articles 4 and 5 of Directive 89/552/EEC Television without Frontiers, op. cit.*, n 40.

understood as meaning that Member States are required to transform the Directive into their own legal order in the form of laws, regulations or administrative provisions. As is well known, Article 189 of the EC Treaty leaves to the national authority the choice of form and method whereas the Directive is binding as to the result to be achieved. When the Commission finds that the transposal process has failed to take place, it may take infringement proceedings or enter into negotiations with the State concerned.

In the particular context of Articles 4 and 5, the Commission also regards itself as under a duty to "monitor the reality of the various national systems. . .".[60] It therefore sought the active assistance of States in order to obtain the detailed figures and explanations to make them comprehensible. "Regular meetings" have been held with their representatives to discuss "questions of interpretation in the transposal of the two Articles". The main point of these meetings was to formulate and produce a common methodological approach. The outcome was that States – who have the responsibility for compiling the national reports – could work with ". . .common definitions and information categories based on concepts underlying the Directive itself and on the Commission's review obligation, especially where the language used in the Directive is liable to give rise to differing interpretations."[61]

Thus, the definition of a "broadcasting company" includes the channels it operates; the jurisdiction to which a broadcaster is subject is dependent on its place of establishment[62]; "broadcasting time" does not include test-card display time for the purpose of calculating proportions of time; "European works" can be defined so as to include factors concerning the place of establishment of the production company or staff involved; and there are two cumulative criteria used to define a producer as being independent of a broadcaster: the broadcaster's capital holding (a maximum of 25%) and proportion of business done with the same broadcasting company (maximum of 90% over a three year period).[63]

(ii) **The Broadcasting Act 1990 and the structure of United Kingdom broadcasting**

The United Kingdom's technique of transposition has been different from that of other Member States. In many other jurisdictions, specific laws or other instruments have been enacted to pass the measures required by the Directive into local law. Transposition has not always satisfied the Commission which, for example, initiated an infringement pro-

---

[60] *Ibid.* p 5.
[61] *Ibid.*
[62] A matter, as mentioned later, that has brought the Commission and the United Kingdom into formal dispute, see section 5(i).
[63] Commission of the European Communities, 1994, *op. cit.*, n 40, pp 5–6.

cedure, under Article 169, against Italy during 1993. In the United Kingdom, the passage of the Directive coincided with the drafting of a general Broadcasting Act which aimed at changing the structure of broadcasting. The Home Office (then responsible for broadcasting)[64] took cognizance of the Directive's requirements, which were perceived to be largely required domestically in any event, and introduced the measures by way of particular sections of the general Act. With the passing of the 1990 Act, and the promulgation of certain statutory instruments under the Act[65], the government regards the task of transposition as discharged, and has advised broadcasters of their obligation to comply with the requirements of the Directive.[66]

The Broadcasting Act 1990 came into force on 1 January 1991. The Act, as noted above, was not passed specifically to transpose the Directive into United Kingdom law, but as a major piece of reforming legislation which affects the structure of broadcasting in the United Kingdom. It is largely concerned with independent television, but there are references and obligations imposed on the British Broadcasting Corporation as well. Its preparation, and the drafting and finalising of the Directive proceeded, to some extent, in tandem.

Analysis of the accuracy of implementation is complicated both by the fact that there is no specific legal instrument explicitly transposing the Directive, and by the need to read the Broadcasting Act itself against earlier subsisting legislation which establishes the basis for the transmission of radio signals in general within the jurisdiction of the United Kingdom. As Thomas Gibbons points out:

"Although broadcasting owed its beginnings to private enterprise, its public dimension was identified at a very early stage and had a profound influence in shaping the industry's organisation and financial base."[67]

This 'public' characteristic was underpinned by the passage of the Wireless Telegraphy Act 1904, which made the reception and transmission of radio signals unlawful unless authorised by a licence issued by the Post Office. The present law is contained in the Wireless Telegraphy Acts 1949–1967. Section 1(1) of the 1949 Act provides that:

---

[64] The broadcasting functions of the Home Secretary have since been transferred to the Secretary of State for National Heritage: SI 1992/1311.

[65] See e.g. the Broadcasting (Independent Productions) Order 1991 (SI 1991/1408); The Broadcasting (Prescribed Countries) (Amendment) Order 1993 (SI 1993/3046); The Broadcasting (Foreign Satellite Programmes) (Specified Countries) (Amendment) Order 1993 (SI 1993/3047); The Broadcasting (Foreign Satellite Programmes) (Specified Countries) Order 1994 (SI 1994/453); The Broadcasting (Prescribed Countries) Order 1994 (SI 1994/454).

[66] Below, section 4(iii).

[67] Gibbons, *Regulating the Media* (1991), p 50.

"No person shall establish or use any station for wireless telegraphy or install or use any apparatus for wireless telegraphy except under the authority of a licence in that behalf. . ."

The Directive's implementation also reflects the institutional structure of British television broadcasting, which is controlled by three public corporations: the British Broadcasting Corporation (BBC); the Independent Television Commission (ITC); and Sianel Pedwar Cymru (the Welsh TV Authority).

(a) *The BBC*

The British Broadcasting Corporation, a ". . .body corporate with perpetual succession and a common seal"[68], operates under a Royal Charter, first granted in 1927, which details the constitution, objectives, powers and responsibilities of the Corporation in providing domestic and overseas broadcasting services.[69] The current Charter, granted in 1981 (as amended by a supplemental Charter in 1983), lasts for fifteen years.[70] The BBC's principal object is the provision of sound and television broadcasting as public services. Under the Wireless Telegraphy Act 1949 it has to obtain, from the Secretary of State, the necessary licence. The current licence is contained in the Licence and Agreement between Her Majesty's Secretary of State for the Home Department and the British Broadcasting Corporation, 2 April 1981, and primarily contains the conditions under which it may broadcast, as well as provisions as to the contents of broadcasts.

The Licence and Agreement have been the traditional means whereby governmental control has been exercised over the BBC, and the primary vehicle for translating the requirements of the Directive into domestic legal obligations for the BBC.[71] Changes to the Licence and Agreement would appear to be sufficiently transparent to meet Community requirements for transparent and binding implementation of directives, but the Commission has raised the question as to whether administrative changes of interpretation of the existing Licence can be adequate for this purpose. Thus the provision of the Licence requiring the BBC to favour "British" programming is now to be read as if "British" meant "European".[72] This device, though convenient pending the award of a new Licence to the BBC in 1996, might be a little too Humpty-Dumptyish to appeal to the Court.

---

[68] *Halsbury's Laws of England*, Vol. 45, "Telecommunications and Broadcasting", pp 301–302, para 517; The Royal Charter is published in Cmnd 9013; the Licence and Agreement in Cmnd 8233; See also, 1993 Cumulative Supplement, Part 2, para 522.

[69] Mac Donald, *Broadcasting in the United Kingdom: a Guide to Information Sources*, 2nd ed (1993), 77.

[70] Thirteen Royal Charters (including supplemental Charters) have been published by HMSO since 1927. A list of these can be found in MacDonald, *ibid.*

[71] See Home Office, Schedule, *op. cit.*, n 37, Article 2.1.

[72] *Ibid.* Article 4.

So far as the Directive (and for that matter the Council of Europe Convention) are concerned, licence discipline is backed up by additional statutory powers under the Broadcasting Act 1990. Under Section 188, the BBC, along with the other broadcasting corporations, must carry out any functions which the Secretary of State may by order direct it to carry out for the purpose of enabling Her Majesty's government to give effect to any international obligations of the United Kingdom. This is a cumbersome procedure, involving the possibility of Parliamentary debate and disapproval, and one would expect to see it used only to fill unexpected gaps or as a last resort. All the obligations of the Directive are capable of being supported in this way, including the transmission of the required proportion of programmes of European origin (Articles 4 and 6) and from independent producers (Article 5). In relation to commercial television, these issues are dealt with primarily through the licensing procedure.[73] In relation to the BBC alone, further provision on independent productions is made by Section 186(1) of the Act. This requires the BBC

"...to secure that, in each relevant period, not less than the prescribed percentage of the total amount of time allocated to the broadcasting of qualifying programmes in the television broadcasting services provided by them is allocated to the broadcasting of a range and diversity of independent productions."

The Director-General of Fair Trading is required to report to the Secretary of State on the extent the BBC has performed this duty during each of the qualifying periods (Section 186(3)).

(b) *Commercial television*

The present legal basis of the other two bodies is the Broadcasting Act 1990. In replacing the Independent Broadcasting Authority (IBA) with the ITC, the Act significantly changed the mode of regulation of non-BBC broadcasting in the United Kingdom.[74] The principal functions of the IBA, laid down by the Broadcasting Act 1981, together with provisions laid down in the Cable and Broadcasting Act 1984 and the Broadcasting Act 1987, were selection and appointment of the programme companies; supervision of programme planning; control of advertising; the transmission of programme services through transmitting stations built, owned and operated by the Authority; and the provision of satellite television (DBS) services. The IBA was both the broadcaster/publisher, and the regulator, of the independent broadcasting services. ITC, by contrast, is charged under Section 2 only to regulate the provision of, *inter alia*, television programme services other than those provided by the British

---

[73] Below, text accompanying n 77.
[74] See Redley, "Quality of Service as a Focus for Regulation: The Regulators' Role" (1993) 4 (No. 1) Utilities L.Rev. 38; Reville, "The New Regulatory Regime for Programmes Broadcast in the UK" (1991) 12 (No. 1) J.Media L.& P. 78.

Broadcasting Corporation and the Welsh Authority.[75] The Commission is to provide for a variety of services – television programme services, additional services and local delivery services – by licensing them on frequencies assigned by notice to it by the Secretary of State. The Commission's duty to discharge its functions as respects the licensing of the various services has to be done in a manner best calculated to achieve several statutorily prescribed objectives, including good taste and decency, accuracy and impartiality, and the avoidance of incitement to violence, and of subliminal advertising.[76]

Like the BBC, the Commission, under Section 188, may be directed by the Secretary of State to carry out any functions to give effect to the United Kingdom's international obligations. In addition, the Act creates a range of statutory obligations for ITC, designed to put more flesh on the general statutory objectives relating to acceptable programme content. The licensing of programme companies may serve as a vehicle not only for securing respect for these explicit statutory policies, but also for transmitting Directive obligations reflected (but not explicitly) in the Act. Thus applicants for terrestrial television licences and domestic service licences must undertake to provide a "proper" proportion of European programming and at least 25 per cent of independently produced programming[77]; while Channel 4's Licence from the ITC provides that:

> "references to programming, programmes or matter of *'European origin'* shall be interpreted in accordance with the definition of 'European Works' in Article 6 of the EC Directive on Television of October 3, 1989."[78]

The policies of the Act are to be further developed by the Commission through the device of Codes of Practice, which are explicitly contemplated in respect of requirements of impartiality (Section 6(3)–(7)), standards in relation to violence (Section 7), and advertisements (section 9).[79] Thus Section 9(1) provides:

> "It shall be the duty of the Commission –
> (a) after the appropriate consultation, to draw up, and from time to time review, a code
> (i) governing standards and practice in advertising and in sponsoring of programmes, and
> (ii) prescribing the advertisements and methods of advertising or spon-

---

[75] ITC did however continue the dual broadcaster/regulator role (which involved prior approval of programme schedules) until the end of 1992 (the end of the 1982–92 ITV contract period).
[76] Broadcasting Act 1990, s 6(1).
[77] Sections 16(2), 25(2), 29(2), 44(3). These provisions, with s. 186 (above), are the only (indirect) references in this Act to the Directive's quota provisions. They do not apply to the non-domestic satellite services, such as BSkyB: see further below, section 4(iii).
[78] Part I(i): Definitions and Interpretation.
[79] For the use of this device in another context (food safety) as a instrument of *intra-governmental* control, see Chapter 5, section 5(iv), and Chapter 6, section 5(ii).

> sorship to be prohibited, or to be prohibited in particular circumstances; and
>
> (b) to do all they can to secure that the provisions of the code are observed in the provision of the licensed services;..."

Significantly, under Section 9(9), the Commission is under a duty, when drawing up or revising a code or giving directions thereunder, to "take account of such of the international obligations of the United Kingdom as the Secretary of State may notify to them. . ." The United Kingdom Government takes the view that this provision applies the Directive.

There are three relevant Codes on advertising and sponsorship: the Code on Advertising Standards and Practice; the Rules on Advertising Breaks; and the Code of Programme Sponsorship. In the view of the United Kingdom Government, all the relevant provisions of the Directive are incorporated in the various Codes.

Outside the advertising and sponsorship area, the ITC has also drawn up a Code which implements the Directive's provision for the protection of minors: Article 22. As noted above, Section 7 of the Act directs the Commission to draw up a general code for programmes which gives guidance, *inter alia*,

> "...as to the rules to be observed with respect to the showing of violence, or the inclusion of sounds suggestive of violence, in programmes included in licensed services, particularly when large numbers of children and young persons may be expected to be watching the programmes."

The Commission argues that the Codes not only cover the matter required by the Directive but more besides. Article 3(1) of the Directive permits Member States to ". . .require television broadcasters under their jurisdiction to lay down more detailed or stricter rules in the areas covered by this Directive" and the ITC is of the opinion that this may be, and has been, done through the Codes.

The foregoing provisions are directed to ensuring compliance with the Directive by broadcasters within United Kingdom jurisdiction. The limiting control which the Directive permits over material transmitted from other European countries, 'import control', as it were, is provided for under two sections of the 1990 Act. Section 177 enables the Secretary of State to proscribe a foreign satellite service if the Independent Television Commission has notified him that they believe the service is unacceptable by reason of repeated breaches of requirements of good taste, decency, or of the prohibition of incitement to crime or disorder, or of matter offensive to public feeling, and he believes that proscription is compatible with the United Kingdom's international obligations, and would be in the public interest. Section 79 relates to the retransmission of foreign satellite services by cable, and enables ITC, in granting the cable licence, to impose conditions requiring respect for domestic standards relating to morality (the same tests as for Section 177), religion, and subliminal advertising. As we shall see, the operation of the first of these provisions has already led to allegations of breach of the Directive by the United Kingdom, while the second, incorporating criteria which are not referred to in the Directive, might also cause trouble in the future.

(iii) **Quotas**

In August 1991, the United Kingdom responded to the requirement of Article 25 of the Directive which prescribes that Member States shall "inform" the Commission "forthwith" of the measures taken to comply with the Directive whether by laws, regulations or administrative provisions. It furnished the Commission with copies of the Broadcasting Act, information about what action the relevant broadcasting bodies were taking and copies of the Codes, and expressed confidence that all the required measures would be taken by the time the Directive came into force, 2 October 1991. It then proceeded to have further consultations with the broadcasting bodies on the implementation of measures which required confirmation. Such confirmation was made to the Commission at the end of September.

Special steps have to be taken as regards the Directive's Articles 4 and 5.[80] Article 4(3), it will be recalled, requires Member States to provide the Commission every two years with a report on the application of the Articles. The report is to include a statistical statement on the achievement of the proportion referred to for each of the television programmes falling within the jurisdiction of the Member State; the reasons in each case for failure to attain the proper proportion; and the measures adopted or envisaged to achieve it.

The United Kingdom filed the first of the required reports with the Commission, announcing the fact on 4 November 1993 in the form of a written answer to a Parliamentary Question.[81] The statistics were gathered and presented to the Commission in accordance with Commission document: *Suggested guide-lines for the monitoring of "TV Without Frontiers" Directive.*[82] The Government was pleased to note that the channels which accounted for over 90 per cent of viewing as assessed by television ratings broadcast around 70 per cent of European material and met in full the requirement to broadcast a proportion of programming independently produce within the Community.

The Government admitted, however, that it was concerned that a number of broadcasters had not yet met the levels of prescribed European

---

[80] *Supra*, section 3(ii).
[81] See Department of Heritage News Release: DNH 157/93, Peter Brooke: "Satellite television should provide more European programming"; *Hansard* HC, Vol. 231, col 310, 4 November 1993.
[82] Published as Annex 1: Commission of the European Communities, 1994, *op. cit.*, n 40, p 26.

or independent programming. Some broadcasters, indeed, had fallen well short of those levels. Article 4's performance assessment largely turns, however, on the phrase "where practicable and by appropriate means".[83] The Government initially took the view, in seeking compliance from satellite broadcasters, that it might never be 'practicable' for certain broadcasters, transmitting material to ethnic or expatriate audiences[84], or even to specialised audiences (as for film channels) to reach the levels of the quotas. This suggested readiness to tolerate low levels of compliance not only by channels like TV Asia – for which any European quota is clearly inappropriate – but also by channels such as those of British Sky Broadcasting (BSkyB): Sky One shows only 8.3 per cent of European programmes; and the BSkyB's three film channels show between 13.7 per cent and 19.1 per cent of European proportion.[85] The almost complete absence of European material in two foreign satellite channels licensed by ITC under Section 45 of the Broadcasting Act (the Cartoon Network and TNT channels) has caused French and Belgian authorities to refuse licences there for cable relay of these transmissions, on the ground that they breach the Directive's quota rules.[86] This restriction of retransmission is itself a breach of the Directive[87], notwithstanding its basis in an alleged breach by another Member State.

Under pressure from the Commission, the Government has since written again to all the errant broadcasters and those who had not yet been transmitting long enough to appear in the tables, asking them to confirm that the hours broadcast during the reporting period did in fact fail to reach the Directive level; to offer reasons why it was not practicable to reach the level; to confirm that what date in the future it would be so practicable to transmit the prescribed level; to say what levels of European and independent produced material it would be practicable to transmit and the period of time over which these levels could be progressively achieved; and to give projections for 1994 and 1995 (or longer). However, this is not necessarily to be reflected in rigid legislation and regulatory

---

[83] This disputable phrase was adopted largely as a result of pressure from the United States who threatened to challenge the implementation of any television quota legislation. See further, Lupinacci, "The Pursuit of Television Broadcasting Activities in the European Community: Cultural Preservation or Economic Protectionism" (1991) 24 Vand.J.Transnat'l.L. 113–154 and above text at n 48.

[84] Frere Cholmeley Bischoff, *op. cit.*, n 48, p 6.

[85] Date of statistics: 4 November 1993. Commission of the European Communities, 1994, *op cit.*, n 40, Annex 2, p 45. Note that compliance has been sought from non-domestic satellite services despite the fact that provisions in the Broadcasting Act 1990 regarding the quota requirements do not apply to them: above n 77.

[86] Porter, *op. cit.*, n 44, p 17; Enser, *op. cit.* n 7, p 135. France, unlike most Member States, have been staunch supporters of the quota provisions, imposing a strict sixty per cent quota for its domestic programming. French legislation provides for fines of ten thousand dollars for each hour of non-European programming shown beyond the sixty per cent quota: Lupinacci, *op. cit.* n 83 at p 123. In the words of one Hollywood executive, "We have seen the future and it is France": Frank, President, Walt Disney Studios, cited in Filipek, *op. cit.*, n 43 at p 362, n 216.

[87] Article 2(2) permits such restriction only on grounds of breach of Article 22 (protection of minors).

action: consequently, satellite broadcasters who up-link from outside the United Kingdom, as does BSkyB[88] which qualifies as a non-domestic satellite service under Section 43(2) of the Broadcasting Act, licensed and regulated by the Independent Television Commission[89], do not appear to be bound by legal means to the quota provisions of the Broadcasting Act even though they should be in order to meet the requirements of the Directive and the Council of Europe Convention.[90]

Finally, although the Government took the view that it would only be fair to allow the broadcasters concerned an opportunity to present their case, it was for it to determine what was practicable or over how long a period of time a reasonable implementation should be achieved. It would decide on the next steps to be taken to secure continued compliance with the Directive after receiving the relevant information from the broadcasters concerned. While this approach is arguably within the spirit of Articles 4 and 5, and is certainly no less co-operative than that of most other Member States in this area[91], the reactions of the French and Belgian authorities show the dangerous consequences of divergent national practice in this area.

5 Two areas of dispute

It may be useful to focus, by way of conclusion, on two further issues on which the United Kingdom's implementation of or compliance with the Directive has been called into question.

(i) Jurisdiction

The first of these relates to the fundamental question of jurisdiction. It will be appreciated from the previous discussion that the Directive's open

---

[88] BSkyB is transmitted from a privately owned ASTRA satellite operating from Luxembourg. For discussion of international satellite service providers, see White, Bate & Johnson, *Satellite Communication in Europe: Law and Regulation* (1994), Chapter 4; Pichler, "Private satellite television in the EC – broadcasters' perspectives" (1993) 14 J.Media L.& P. 101.

[89] Section 45. See Letters from Gallagher, Director of Public Affairs, BSkyB, "BSkyB is regulated by ITC", *The Independent*, 23 January 1994, "Regulating the skies", *The Independent*, 2 February 1994.

[90] White, Bate & Johnson, *op. cit.*, n 88, p 261; Barendt, *op. cit.*, n 22, p 221, n 28. This has prompted the Independent Television Association (ITV) to demand that the Government remove such inconsistencies of regulation and frame new legislation to provide a "level playing field" for all commercial services in terms of regulation. ITV believe that this may be achieved by the amendment of Section 43, *i.e.* to reclassify BSkyB as a *domestic* satellite broadcaster, in order to make it more accountable: ITV, *ITV Comments on EC Green Paper on Media Ownership*, March 1993, p 14.

[91] General levels of compliance with the provisions have clearly been low: see Commission of the European Communities, 1994, *op. cit.*, n 40, sections 4 and 5; Porter, *op. cit.* n 44, pp 6–9.

door to retransmission from other EC countries makes the assertion of jurisdiction over broadcasting by each Member State a matter of common concern. The Directive accordingly defines common tests for the assertion of jurisdiction.[92] The Commission has notified the United Kingdom of its intention to bring proceedings in the European Court of Justice on the basis that the United Kingdom has not properly transposed Article 2 of the Directive.[93] The difficulties arise in connection with satellite broadcasting, in relation to which the Broadcasting Act grounds jurisdiction on the fact of transmission by satellite "from a place in the United Kingdom" (referred to as "up-link"); or as a subsidiary test applicable where there is reception in the EC but no up-link there, on the fact of control by a person in the United Kingdom on the content of programmes transmitted.[94] The Commission's view is that if a channel is established in a Member State for taxation purposes, that country should be responsible for licensing it and regulating it throughout the Union. Only if there is no such country should the authorities should move on to the other tests of jurisdiction. The United Kingdom argues that the country where the up-link is situated should have jurisdiction, since this is where the signal leaves the ground and is, thus, the last "point of control". Further, the United Kingdom argues that the criteria of Article 2(1) are to be interpreted as alternatives rather than in a hierarchy; though the Directive appears to envisage up-link as a basis for control only where general bases for jurisdiction (such as establishment) are absent.

The United Kingdom's approach may lead to conflicts of jurisdiction where broadcasters up-link from the United Kingdom but are established elsewhere in the Community as with CNN, up-linked from the United Kingdom but established in Luxembourg.[95] This, according to the Commission, is precisely what the Directive was designed to avoid.

---

[92] Article 2(1): "Each Member State shall ensure that all television broadcasts transmitted by broadcasters under its jurisdiction, or by broadcasters who, while not being under the jurisdiction of any Member State, make use of a frequency or a satellite capacity granted by, or a satellite up-link situated in, that Member State, comply with the law applicable to broadcasts intended for the public in that Member State".

[93] *Hansard* HC, Vol 241, col 190, 13 April 1994.

[94] Section 43(1) and (2): the up-link test applies both to "domestic satellite services" broadcasting on satellite frequencies allocated to the United Kingdom, which are subject to controls and procedures broadly similar to those for terrestrial stations (s. 44), and to "non-domestic satellite services" broadcasting on other frequencies, to which the "content of programmes" test also applies; for these services a more relaxed regime (though still one which must respect the basic programme principles of s. 6(1)) is stipulated (s. 45). This test meets the requirements of the European Convention on Transfrontier Television.

[95] See Commission of the European Communities, 1994, *op. cit.*, n 40, p 13. In addition, the United Kingdom regulatory authorities are now responsible for certain services which uplink from the United Kingdom, but are not received at all within the United Kingdom, *e.g.* Scandinavian services, TV3 Denmark and TV1000: Davey, "Implementation of the Broadcasting Directive in the United Kingdom", paper presented to the *Broadcasting in Europe* Conference, Café Royal, London, 3 December 1993, p 2.

(ii) **Proscribing pornography**

A second dispute before the European Court of Justice stems not from action by the Commission, but by a broadcaster seeking to rely on the Directive's abolition of national barriers to television transmissions. It arises out of the making of a Foreign Satellite Service Proscription Order[96], under Section 177 of the Broadcasting Act 1990, in respect of *Red Hot Television* (formerly *Red Hot Dutch*), a channel put out by a Dutch company, broadcasting encrypted signals from Denmark.[97] Under Section 177(4)(b)[98], the Secretary of State has to ensure that the making of the Order is compatible with, *inter alia*, the Television without Frontiers Directive.

The legal basis for making the Order was the ITC's[99] and the government's view that the channel had repeatedly infringed Article 22 of the Directive[100], which, subject to certain procedural requirements, justifies a Member State, under Article 2(2)[101], in provisionally suspending retransmissions of television broadcasts. The effect of the Order was to make it a criminal offence for persons in the United Kingdom to do such things as publish details of *Red Hot Television's* programmes, supply equipment in connection with the running of the service, or supply decoding equipment for its reception.[102] The company sought judicial review of the Secretary of State's decision to make the Order, on the ground that the programmes were received directly in the United Kingdom, not "retransmitted" as required by Article 2(2), and that there was no such risk as was contemplated by Article 22 of impairment of the development of minors, because the programmes were broadcast in encrypted form after midnight. Proscription was, in consequence, not justified by the Directive.

Before the Divisional Court, the Secretary of State argued that one of the main purposes of the Directive was to prevent harm to minors from pornography; this need to protect, furthermore, was the same whether the programmes were received directly or rebroadcast; and that power to take action cannot have been intended to be at the mercy of the technical means of reception. A supporting letter from the European Com-

---

[96] SI 1993/1024, coming into force on 1 May 1993.
[97] See Coleman & McMurtrie, "Too hot to handle" (1993) 14 (No. 6582) N. L. J. 10.
[98] Section 177(4) states: "Where the Secretary of State has been notified under subsection (2), he shall not make an order under this section unless he is satisfied that the making of the order (a) is in the public interest; and (b) is compatible with any international obligations of the United Kingdom." See above, section 4(ii)(b).
[99] Under Section 6(a) of the Broadcasting Act 1990, the ITC must do all they can to secure that every licensed service complies with the requirement "that nothing is included in its programmes which offends against good taste or decency or is likely to encourage or incite to crime or to lead to disorder or to be offensive to public feeling."
[100] For the content of Article 22, see above n 35.
[101] Under Article 2(2)(a), the receiving State is allowed to intervene if "a television broadcast coming from another Member State manifestly, seriously and gravely infringes Article 22."
[102] Broadcasting Act 1990, s. 178.

mission argued that the word "retransmission" was used as the only suitable word to describe "transfrontier transmission". The Court expressed its own agreement with these propositions, but referred these questions of interpretation of Articles 2(2) and 22 to the European Court of Justice[103], the Court of Appeal subsequently confirming that despite the reference to the European Court, the proscription Order should come into effect.[104] This decision demonstrates the critical concern that if the United Kingdom were to have no authority with which to regulate broadcasts from other Member States, the pace of permissiveness in the Community, as noted in section 3(i) above, would be decided by the most liberal State – which some would suggest is the price to be paid for a Europe without "frontiers".[105]

6 Conclusion

The Television without Frontiers Directive has posed difficult issues for the United Kingdom, in common with other Member States, because of the way in which its provisions cut across both the policy preferences and the policy style established at national level in this area.

The Government's general belief in freedom of markets is reflected in the overall purpose of the Directive, yet its quota provisions are clearly unattractive: they heavily qualify the overall effect, and in addition involve new administrative and regulatory tasks which the Government clearly does not relish. It is noteworthy that the European quota provisions of the Directive appear in the Act only in general terms, without attribution of their Community origin, and as part of a licensing procedure which leaves unclear the question of how (if at all) they will be enforced as legal obligations. Explicit arrangements for such legal enforcement are to be found only in the new control over the use by the BBC of independently produced programmes (Section 186). Compliance by commercial licensees with both the European content provisions and the independent production provisions has, as already noted, been sought through administrative means, by way of Departmental notifications and letters to licensees. Given that the BBC is in public ownership, whereas commercial broadcasters are, especially since 1992, subject to an "arm's-length" licensing regime, this is exactly the opposite of the legislative articulation of the Directive's provisions that might ordinarily have been

---

[103] For a discussion on the use of interim relief in Article 177 cases, see Lindsay, "Red hot issue" (1994) 138 (No. 11) Sol.J. 280. See also Chapter 11, section 2.
[104] R. v Secretary of State for the National Heritage, ex parte Continental TV BV and others [1993] 2 CMLR 333, DC; [1993] 3 CMLR 387 (CA).
[105] See also, Coulthard, "Dutch television – too Red Hot for UK!" (1993) 14 J.Media L.& P. 116; Dann, "The Red Hot Channel: Pornography without Frontiers" (1993) 6 Ent.L.R. 191; "Satellite porn ban to be challenged in Europe", The Independent, 14 April 1994, p 3.

expected. The question whether such administrative implementation satisfies general principles of Community law is difficult, in light of the arguably 'political' character of the Articles[106], but seems unlikely to be tested
in view of the Community's fundamental problems with the whole quota
policy.[107] Substantively, as well, official foot-dragging here is in striking
contrast to the loyal and efficient attitudes displayed in areas investigated
in other Chapters, such as food labelling and safety systems, and toy
safety. This may serve to strengthen the view that the United Kingdom's
good record in implementation reflects a broad convergence between
the general trend of Single Market legislation and the United Kingdom's
own market and deregulatory goals, falling away rapidly where that convergence weakens.

In broadcasting, the United Kingdom's problems are further compounded by the fact that despite its general preferences, its regulation
of programme content is probably broader and stricter than that of other
Member States. Even if the *Red Hot Television* case goes in its favour in
the European Court, the disparity between the very narrow scope of Article 22 of the Directive, and the broad terms of Section 6(1) of the Broadcasting Act, which permeate the United Kingdom licensing system, seems
likely to cause difficulties in the future. This provides an additional
motive for the United Kingdom to persist in defending its view of its
jurisdiction under Article 2(1) of the Directive, as failure here would not
only complicate its relations with satellite broadcasters like BSkyB, but
would also significantly limit its scope to protect its island morality.

CECILIA O'LEARY AND
DAVID GOLDBERG

---

[106] See above, section 3(ii), and in general below Chapter 10, section 4.
[107] See, *e.g.* "Caution on broadcast quotas", *Financial Times*, 15 July 1994, p 2; "Threat of Brussels
split on TV quotas", *Financial Times*, 23 November 1994, p 3.

Chapter 9

Playing Safe: The United Kingdom's Implementation of the Toy Safety Directive

1 The Toy Safety Directive

The Toy Safety Directive is, more formally, Directive 88/378 of 3 May 1988 on the approximation of the laws of the Member States concerning the safety of toys.[1] It is a harmonisation measure based on Article 100a of the EEC Treaty (now EC Treaty).[2] According to its Preamble, it is designed to remove obstacles to the attainment of an internal market in which only sufficiently safe products would be sold. This is achieved by setting uniform rules for the marketing and free movement of toys.[3]

The Toy Safety Directive follows the "New Approach" model.[4] In accordance with the New Approach formula, harmonisation consists of establishing the "essential safety requirements" to be satisfied by all toys to be placed on the market. These requirements are elaborated in Annex II to the Directive. Annex II comprises two parts. First, it contains a short statement of General Principles, which begins by declaring that "the users of toys as well as third parties must be protected against health hazards and risk of physical injury when toys are used as intended or in a forseeable [sic] way, bearing in mind the normal behaviour of children". This is followed by treatment of six Particular Risks; physical and mechanical properties; flammability; chemical properties; electrical properties; hygiene; radioactivity.

The Directive envisages that all toys placed on the market shall conform to the "essential safety requirements". This is to be secured by the Member States. The Directive provides that "Member States shall take all steps necessary to ensure that toys cannot be placed on the market unless they meet the essential safety requirements set out in Annex II".[5] Toys

---

[1] OJ 1988 L187/1.
[2] Chapter 2 examines the EC constitutional framework in more depth.
[3] As defined in Article 1 of the Directive.
[4] Council Resolution of 7 May 1985 on a new approach to technical harmonisation and standards OJ 1985 C139/1. See further Chapter 2.
[5] Article 3 of the Directive.

that conform to this standard are entitled to market access; "Member States shall not impede the placing on the market on their territory of toys which satisfy the provisions of this Directive".[6]

Pursuant to the New Approach strategy of permitting flexibility in production techniques, there are two routes to showing conformity with the essential safety requirements. First, toys may be presumed to comply with the essential requirements where they are in conformity with harmonised standards.[7] The relevant European standard is EN 71, The Safety of Toys. Second, toys that conform to a model approved by an approved body may also be regarded as complying with the requirements. This is the "type examination" procedure. The approved bodies are appointed by national authorities in accordance with criteria found in Annex III. Approved bodies shall be notified by national authorities to the Commission which shall then publish a list in the Official Journal.[8] A number of such lists have been published in the Official Journal in accordance with this procedure.[9] The Directive also establishes relevant procedures for application and grant of type approval.[10]

The existence of the second route, type examination leading to type approval, prevents harmonised standards being mandatory for manufacturers and permits them flexibility in methods of achieving the required level of safety, albeit through a managed procedure involving prior acquisition of the type-examination certificate. This opportunity for innovation, unconfined by existing standards and specifications, represents a major motivation for the development of the New Approach.

Under the Directive as originally adopted, a manufacturer declared conformity with the essential safety requirements (by either route) by affixing the "EC Mark" to the item.[11] Information must be retained by the manufacturer relevant to the affixing of the mark.[12] This may involve a technical file or a test report showing how the manufacturer has made its own checks of conformity to standards or to the model granted type approval. The "EC mark" is now properly referred to as the "CE Marking" as a result of the amendments of Directive 93/68 of 22 July 1993.[13] This Directive amends several New Approach directives in order to introduce a common approach to the CE marking process. Apart from the transformation of the "EC mark" into the "CE marking", some other relatively

---

[6] Article 4 of the Directive.
[7] Article 5 of the Directive.
[8] Article 9 of the Directive, amended by Article 3(4) of Directive 93/68.
[9] OJ 1990 C154/3, 162/25, 278/3, 320/3; OJ 1991 C13/3, 32/6, 68/3, 264/4, 272/3, 279/4, 282/12, 307/3; OJ 1992 C25/3, 73/2, 97/3, 264/7; OJ 1993 C87/3. The most recent version is, helpfully, a complete list covering all bodies notified up until 15 April 1994 by the Member States and the EFTA countries for all New Approach directives: OJ 1994 C203.
[10] Article 10 of the Directive.
[11] Articles 5, 11 of the Directive.
[12] Article 8 of the Directive.
[13] OJ 1993 L220/1.

insubstantial amendments to the Toy Safety Directive are effected by the Directive.

The Directive envisages monitoring of the market by national authorities. The "Safeguard Procedure" provides for the management of situations where toys are imperilling health and/or safety despite bearing the CE marking. Management and information communication involving the Commission is envisaged. The Directive also envisages checks on the safety of toys already on the market being undertaken by national authorities.[14] Moreover, it includes an amendment procedure to be invoked where harmonised standards are suspected to fall below the essential safety requirements.[15]

Every three years Member States shall send to the Commission a report on the application of this Directive.[16] Less specifically, the Directive also declares that the Member States "shall regularly inform" the Commission of activities carried out under this Directive by the approved bodies.[17] Such transparency is explicitly designed to assist Commission monitoring.

Directive 92/59 on General Product Safety[18] now introduces a broader control in the field of product safety. The General Directive is inapplicable in areas already subject to Community rules.[19] So where the Toy Directive deals with the aspect of safety in question, it applies. Otherwise, the General Directive applies.

The Commission reports that the Toy Safety Directive has now been implemented by all the Member States. It has commented that "[g]enerally speaking, the New Approach has proved successful and the approved certification bodies are now working effectively."[20]

2 United Kingdom implementation: The Statutory Instrument

(i) Consumer safety legislation in the United Kingdom

The first general statute in the field of consumer safety in the United Kingdom was the Consumer Protection Act 1961. It was enabling legislation. The statute provided the power for delegated legislation to be made to govern particular product areas seen from time to time to require specific regulation. This structure was carried over into the Con-

---

[14] Article 12 of the Directive.
[15] Article 6 of the Directive.
[16] Article 12(2) of the Directive.
[17] Article 13 of the Directive.
[18] OJ 1992 L228/24.
[19] Article 1(2) of Directive 92/59.
[20] Document COM(93)320, Tenth Report on the Monitoring of the Application of Community Law. *Cf.* Lewis, member of the Commission Legal Service writing in a personal capacity: "It would appear that, so far, [the Toy Safety Directive] has worked well", "The Protection of Consumers in European Community Law" (1992) 12 Y. E. L. 139 at p 168.

sumer Safety Act 1978. Under this rather more sophisticated statute, four specific types of measure were made available – the safety regulation, the prohibition order, the prohibition notice and the notice to warn. The safety regulation was the most commonly used measure. Such measures were directed at particular products seen to require specific detailed control. However, the supply of an unsafe product was not of itself an offence in the absence of pre-existing rules governing that product.

The statute which now governs the field is the Consumer Protection Act 1987. The relevant provisions are contained in Part II of the Act. The principal innovation introduced by this Act is the General Safety Requirement under Section 10. This imposes a duty to supply only safe goods. It is accordingly a criminal offence to supply unsafe goods even in the absence of pre-existing specific regulations applicable to the product category in question. Supply is widely construed.[21] Traders at all stages in the supply chain are subject to these obligations, although retailers benefit from a special defence.[22] The 1987 Act retains the structure of delegated legislation to amplify requirements in particular product categories, including the safety regulation, but shifts the emphasis of control towards the new flexible general duty.

Toys were the subject of regulations made under the 1961 Act. They are now subject to regulations made, *inter alia*, under the 1987 Act, considered below, which are designed to implement the EC Directive 88/378. Accordingly, there is an existing structure of law and policy in the United Kingdom applicable to product safety in general and toy safety in particular. EC intervention does not occur against a blank domestic backdrop.

(ii) **The implementing Regulations**[23]

The United Kingdom's implementation of Directive 88/378 is found in the Toys (Safety) Regulations 1989.[24] The Statutory Instrument is made in exercise of powers conferred on the Secretary of State by the Consumer Protection Act 1987 (described above) and the European Communities Act 1972. These Regulations are assimilated to the "normal" safety regulations made as Statutory Instruments under that Act. The Toy Safety Regulations "shall be treated for all purposes as if they were safety regulations within the meaning of the 1987 Act", subject only to a minor qualification relating to a penalty.[25]

The basic requirement is simple and brief: "Toys to which these regulations apply shall satisfy the essential safety requirements".[26] The Regu-

---

[21] Section 46.
[22] Section 10(4)(b).
[23] Chapter 4 examines the general framework in the United Kingdom.
[24] SI 1989/1275.
[25] Regulation 15.
[26] Regulation 4.

lations also include appropriate provision requiring the use of the CE marking.[27] Toys shall not be supplied which fail to conform to either of these requirements.[28] It is an offence to supply toys which do not satisfy the essential safety requirements or which do not bear the CE marking.

In accordance with the characteristic New Approach structure reflected in the Directive, the Regulations offer "two routes" to satisfying the basic requirement of conformity with essential safety requirements. Toys may bear the CE marking where this denotes conformity with the relevant national standards where those standards relate to all matters covered by the essential safety requirements.[29] The relevant national standards in the United Kingdom are those which correspond to the European standard EN 71, which are published in the United Kingdom as BS (British Standard) 5665. EN71 and BS 5665 are one and the same standard. Alternatively toys may bear the CE marking where this denotes conformity with a model for which an EC type-examination certificate is in force.[30] Whichever route is chosen by the trader, toys bearing the CE marking are to be presumed to satisfy the essential safety requirements ". . . unless there are reasonable grounds for suspecting that the toy does not satisfy that requirement".[31]

For the purposes of the second route, type examination, the Regulations provide that bodies are approved by the Secretary of State.[32] Procedures are put in place for application for an EC type-examination certificate.[33] Procedures for the affixing of the CE marking are included in the Regulations, whichever route is chosen to show conformity with the essential safety requirements.[34] Pursuant to the Directive, provision is made for the requirement that traders retain relevant information.[35]

The amending Directive 93/68 has not yet been implemented in the United Kingdom. Its provisions must be applied from the start of 1995. A period of consultation was initiated by a Department of Trade and Industry letter of 22 August 1994, which included draft regulations. The proposal is that the existing Regulations should be consolidated with the amendments required to implement Directive 93/68 in a new set of regulations made under the Consumer Protection Act 1987 and the European Communities Act 1972.

---

[27] Regulation 9.
[28] Regulation 12.
[29] Regulation 5.
[30] Regulation 6.
[31] Regulations 5, 6.
[32] Regulation 7.
[33] Regulation 8, reflecting Article 10 of the Directive.
[34] Regulation 9, reflecting Articles 5 and 11 of the Directive.
[35] Regulation 10 reflecting Article 8 of the Directive.

(iii) **Enforcement**

Although much policy co-ordination in the United Kingdom is the preserve of the Department of Trade and Industry (DTI), through its Consumer Safety Unit, whence emanate, for example, safety regulations under the 1987 Act, the DTI does not dictate enforcement policy. It does not unify enforcement practice, nor does it determine how particular problems will be dealt with, except in so far as it may choose to exercise its regulatory powers at the general level. Enforcement is a local responsibility in the United Kingdom.

The provision that the Toy (Safety) Regulations "shall be treated for all purposes as if they were safety regulations within the meaning of the 1987 [Consumer Protection] Act" [36] means that the Regulations are enforced by Trading Standards Officers in Trading Standards Departments of local authorities in Great Britain (district councils in Northern Ireland).[37] Trading standards officers operate as part of the structure of local government. There are 126 trading standards departments and some 1,500 officers in Britain.

The Toy Safety Regulations form part of the officers' normal diet of enforcement activities, which range across a wide field of consumer and general trading law. In the field of consumer safety, which is at the general level governed by Part II of the Consumer Protection Act 1987, these Regulations take their place alongside other regulations made under that Act, covering products as diverse as babies' dummies and upholstered furniture.

The powers which are available to enforcement authorities under the 1987 Act are found in Part IV and the schedules to the Act. Criminal penalties may be imposed for offences committed by traders. The penalties for infringement of any Regulation are, on summary conviction, a fine not exceeding £5,000 or up to six months in prison or both. The statute includes a "due diligence" defence which is common to many consumer protection statutes in the United Kingdom.[38] This provides that a person charged with, *inter alia*, an offence against a safety regulation has a defence where that person can "show that he took all reasonable steps and exercised all due diligence to avoid committing the offence".[39] This might commonly involve a claim by a trader that he or she was relying on information about the item provided by his or her own supplier, although, to forestall abuse of the defence, the statute specifically provides that the defendant must in such circumstances show "that it was reasonable in all the circumstances for him to have relied on the information". [40] The application in practice of the defence depends on

---

[36] Regulation 15(1).
[37] Customer Protection Act (CPA) 1987, s 27.
[38] *Cf.* Chapter 6.
[39] CPA 1987, s 39.
[40] CPA 1987, s 39(4).

246

the facts of individual cases and is rather unpredictable. As a general observation, the smaller the trader, the less is expected by the courts in carrying out checks on goods and information received.[41]

Action may also be taken against goods themselves. These powers include a suspension notice prohibiting disposal of the goods in question, where there is reasonable suspicion of contravention of the general safety requirement or a specific measure (including a safety regulation); powers to enter business premises and seize and detain goods; and application to a magistrates's court for a forfeiture order against goods. These powers are exercisable at all levels in the supply chain. It is recognised that it will often be efficient to take action at point of first supply, rather than subsequently, once goods are dispersed to retail outlets across a wide geographical area.[42] In fact, the Consumer Safety (Amendment) Act 1986, the provisions of which were consolidated in the Consumer Protection Act 1987, was enacted in part in order to provide for this switch in the focus of enforcement activity.[43]

Traders in safe goods affected by the exercise of these powers may be able to claim compensation for seizure and detention.[44] Where an officer seizes and detains goods under the statutory powers there arises a liability to pay compensation "if there has been no contravention in relation to the goods of any safety provisions or of any provisions made by or under Part III of this Act; and [if] the exercise of the power is not attributable to any neglect or default by [the trader]".

In furtherance of the policy of catching goods prior to their widespread distribution, special provision is made for detention of goods by customs officers. Imported goods may be seized and detained "for not more than two working days".[45] Typically this will occur with the involvement of local trading standards officers, who after a (necessarily brief) investigation may choose to exercise their own more extensive powers, subject to the risk of incurring an obligation to pay compensation. There was fierce debate in Parliament about the proper length of detention. Pressure for a longer period was resisted by the Minister, Michael Howard, in part with reference to the suggestion that a longer period might violate EC law, specifically Article 30.[46]

---

[41] *E.g. Rotherham MBC* v *Raysun* [1989] CCLR 1.

[42] See especially s 29(4).

[43] Discussed by Weatherill, "Consumer Safety Legislation in the United Kingdom" (1987) 2 Euro.Consumer L. J. 81.

[44] CPA 1987, s 34.

[45] Section 31.

[46] Discussed by Weatherill, "Consumer Safety Legislation in the United Kingdom and Article 30 EEC" (1988) 13 E. L. Rev. 87 at p 94.

(iv) **Formal compliance with European Community law**

The assimilation of the Toy Safety Regulations to the normal structure of CPA 1987 Safety regulations suggests that these EC-derived legal provisions are accorded a priority in the United Kingdom which is neither higher nor lower than that accorded to provisions deriving from a purely domestic source. There are no significant inconsistencies between the Directive and the United Kingdom's implementing regulations. In practice too there seems no evidence that there is any reluctance to enforce these rules as conscientiously as "normal" domestic law simply because they have an EC background. The toy safety rules, in common with other consumer safety provisions, are enforced by trading standards officers using a mix of formal action and informal persuasion and guidance. It seems that the United Kingdom has met its obligations under Articles 5 and 189 of the EC Treaty.

However, although equality in enforcement between EC-derived law and similar domestic law is a *necessary* element of implementation of EC law obligations[47], it may not be *sufficient*. EC-derived rules must be effectively implemented. In the absence of such effective implementation, it will be no defence to point to equally ineffective implementation of national law. This point runs parallel to that which underpins the European Court's ruling in *Factortame*.[48] The fact that under English law the interim remedy in question was unavailable to *any* litigant did not preclude the ruling that it had to be made available in an EC law context where this was essential to secure effective protection. Following this line of reasoning, the fact that the Toy Safety Regulations have been implemented by the United Kingdom in a fashion commonly used domestically in the field of consumer safety law does not automatically mean that the implementation is in conformity with EC law.

A point of implementation which might be challenged relates to the combination of the due diligence defence and the compensation provisions.[49] Neither is required under the Directive. Both serve to protect traders. Both may inhibit effective enforcement action because of the financial risks which confront the trading standards authority. Authorities are subject to tight budgetary constraints and do not pursue formal prosecutions readily. They may be dissuaded from pursuing cases should costs be awarded against them, as is probable where a "due diligence" defence is successfully advanced; and *a fortiori* they will be dissuaded by the risk of having to pay compensation. Indeed, at the time of the passage through Parliament of the Bill which became the 1987 Act, strenuous but ultimately fruitless efforts were made to amend the compensation provisions to favour protection of the careful enforcement officer rather than the

---

[47] Case 68/88 *Commission* v *Greece* [1989] ECR 2965.
[48] Case C-213/89 [1990] ECR I-2433.
[49] My thanks are due to Christopher Vincenzi for raising this point.

careful trader.[50] It was feared that the provisions which were finally adopted would deter enforcement authorities from taking action in any but the clearest cases.

It may accordingly be submitted that the pattern of the CPA 1987 is unduly weighted in favour of the trader; that this inhibits the effective enforcement of the rules requiring toys to conform to the essential safety requirements; and that this renders the United Kingdom's implementation of the Directive via the CPA 1987 inadequate as a matter of EC law.

The European Court has declared that Article 5 of the EC Treaty requires Member States to take all measures necessary to guarantee the application and effectiveness of Community law and that penalties, where left to national law, must be effective and dissuasive.[51] It has ruled that Community law did not preclude Denmark from imposing strict criminal liability for infringement of a Regulation dealing with driving time[52], a ruling which is towards the other end of the spectrum from the present concern with an allegedly lax control. The problem rests with the vague nature of "effectiveness". The submission that the United Kingdom has tied the hands of its enforcement agencies to the point where control of the market is ineffective could be vigorously met by the submission that the structure of the CPA 1987 provides adequate powers to control suspect traders and suspect goods, especially at point of first supply, in combination with proper safeguards for fair traders. The matter turns on the need more fully to elaborate the notion of effectiveness. This is a pressing concern for the European Court in several areas. It is difficult to conclude with conviction that the United Kingdom's implementation is inadequate when it falls to be measured against such an imprecisely calibrated Community standard.

The issue here is the obligations of national administrative authorities under Article 5; most of the Court's attention in recent years has been focused on the obligations of national judiciaries under Article 5.[53] The Court has converted the notion of effectiveness under Article 5 into a pivot on which turns the relationship between Community policy making and Member State administration, yet the stability of that pivot may yet need closer attention.

(v) **Deregulation and toy safety**

In the United Kingdom governmental policy on deregulation touches obligations arising as a result of EC membership. In 1993 the DTI pub-

---

[50] *E.g. Hansard* HC Vol. 116, col. 347–349, 364–365 (13 May 1987); *Hansard* HL Vol. 483, col. 915–918 (20 January 1987); *Hansard,* HL Vol. 485, col. 919–922 (9 March 1987).
[51] Case 68/88 n 47 above; *cf.* Cases C-382/92 and 383/93 *Commission* v *UK,* Judgments of 8 June 1994, albeit not arising in the criminal sphere.
[52] Case 326/88, *Hansen* [1990] ECR 2911.
[53] *E.g. Factortame* above; and *cf.* Case C-48/93 *Factortame* OJ 1993 C94/13 as a follow up to Cases C-6, C-9/90 *Francovich* [1991] ECR I-5357. See further Chapter 11, section 4.

lished its *Review of the Implementation and Enforcement of EC Law in the United Kingdom*, which is designed to deepen the deregulation initiative. In the area of toy safety, the 1989 Regulations were amended in July 1993 by the Toys (Safety) (Amendment) Regulations.[54] These Regulations relieve suppliers of secondhand toys of the need to ensure that toys bear the CE marking and the name and address of the first supplier. Such toys remain subject to the requirement of compliance with the essential safety requirements.

As part of the Deregulation Initiative the DTI has also initiated a review of the impact of Part II of the Consumer Protection Act 1987. A questionnaire of 29 June 1993 was circulated to interested trade associations and other organizations. More specifically, consultation has been initiated in respect of individual regulations made under the Act. This process includes consultation on the impact of regulations applicable to "Toys and Related Products", initiated by the Consumer Safety Unit of the DTI.[55] This covered the Toys (Safety) Regulations 1989 and four other more specific instruments.[56] The deadline for consultation was 29 October 1993. The matter remains under review. In this area as in others, it is not clear how profound the consequences of the review are likely to be.

The implementation of the General Product Safety Directive was required by 29 June 1994. A discussion paper on United Kingdom proposals was published by the DTI in January 1994. However, the United Kingdom did not implement the Directive on time. The implementing Regulations were scheduled to come into force on 3 October 1994. The Regulations amend the CPA 1987 in some, albeit relatively insignificant, respects. A policy of reducing compliance costs and legal uncertainty would seem to dictate the desirability of consolidating changes to existing measures in a new instrument, rather than simply making a bolt-on set of new regulations. The DTI's 1993 *Review of the Implementation and Enforcement of EC Law in the United Kingdom* expressed firm support for such consolidation. This is planned for the rules governing Toy Safety.[57] However, pressures on Parliamentary time may make this a vain hope where existing rules are contained in primary legislation. Consolidation has not occurred in relation to the General Product Safety Directive, nor is it likely in relation to the Directive on Unfair Terms in Consumer Contracts.[58]

---

[54] SI 1993/1547.
[55] Letter of 28 June 1993.
[56] The Food Imitations (Safety) regulations 1989; The Benzene in Toys (Safety) regulations 1987; The Novelties (Safety) regulations 1980 amended 1985; The Pencil and Graphic Instruments (Safety) regulations 1974.
[57] Section 2(ii) above.
[58] A DTI Consultation Document of October 1993 proposed a rather messy implementation by SI of Directive 93/13 alongside the Unfair Contract Terms Act 1977. For criticism, see (1994) 110 L. Q. R. 1. It seems probable that the plans will be rethought, although primary legislation remains highly unlikely. See now SI 1994/3159.

3 Aspects of implementation in practice

(i) The function of the CE marking

It is fundamental to the structure of the Toy Safety Directive that the attachment of the CE marking is performed by the trader without the scrutiny of a third party. This is faithfully reflected in the United Kingdom's implementing regulations.

The attachment of the CE marking represents a statement by the trader that the item meets the essential safety requirements by conforming either to the relevant standards or to a type-examination certificate issued by an approved body. The CE marking is *not* a proof that the conformity of the product bearing the CE marking has been checked by a third party. At the time of the adoption of the Directive there was some pressure from consumer organisations to have third party testing incorporated into the system.[59] This was unsuccessful. In view of the cost of putting in place such a system for toys, which are for many models plentiful and cheap, this was perhaps understandable.

The point that the CE marking is neither proof of conformity nor consumer guarantee is repeatedly made in documentation concerning the toy market issued by a variety of interested parties, including consumers' organisations, trading standards authorities and the DTI. For example, the DTI's August 1993 *Toy Safety* brochure, part of its "Business in Europe" series, insists that the "CE marking is not a European safety mark or quality symbol intended for consumers." This point is reinforced by printing this comment in a separate box, highlighted against a blue background on the white page.[60]

Nonetheless it remains the widespread perception that consumers may not appreciate the true position; that they may mistakenly view the CE marking as a guarantee rather than as the manufacturer's statement that he or she believes that the item complies with the essential safety requirements. This concern is reflected in comments from all sides; trading standards officers, the DTI, trade associations with interests in the toy sector and consumers' organisations.

Moreover, marks may appear on toys other than the CE marking. The British Toy and Hobby Association sponsor the "Lion Mark" which is an assertion of both safety and quality and is designed expressly to reassure the consumer about the product.[61] Supporting documentation provided by the Association points out the differences between its Lion Mark and the CE marking and asserts firmly that the CE marking is solely intended as a passport for free movement, not a guarantee to the consumer. Although the Directive contains provisions controlling the affixing of

---

[59] *E.g.* by BEUC – Bureau Européen des Unions de Consommateurs.
[60] Page 5.
[61] The mark is triangular and carries a stylised rather amiable lion.

marks to toys other than the CE marking, it seems that the Lion Mark does not contravene those provisions.[62]

(ii) Unsafe CE marked goods

There is evidence of the supply in the United Kingdom of goods which do not conform to the essential safety requirements. Some are not marked with the CE marking; others are.

It is clear under the structure of the Directive that national authorities are entitled and indeed obliged to take action against goods which are unsafe even where a CE marking is affixed.[63] This applies whatever the source of the toys may be – British, non-British EC or non-EC. The CE marking simply represents the trader's claim. The law requires conformity with the essential safety requirements. The Directive requires that where action is taken against a CE marked toy the safeguard procedure must be invoked (below).

One Midlands trading standards authority has experience of a CE marked toy which it considered did not comply with the essential safety requirements (and in respect of which it is presently pursuing legal proceedings), but would not consider there is evidence of "abuse" by traders. A neighbouring authority commented that in the majority of cases unsafe CE marked goods are, on inquiry, supported by traders by a test certificate. These come in varied forms and are often difficult to understand, yet, the authority commented, sometimes the "due diligence" defence is successfully invoked. A third authority found "a number" of items carrying the CE marking which failed to comply with the essential safety requirements. It considered that "there is some evidence that the self-certification system is being abused", but that "this may well be because of confusion", principally over what should be classified as a toy for these purposes.[64]

Given the structure of local enforcement in the United Kingdom, practice and perceptions vary. Among trading standards officers there seems to be some concern about the operation of the system in practice, especially in relation to non-British EC goods where the climate of market integration affects their perception. Strictly, they are entitled to seize unsafe, CE marked goods. However a typical response by a trader, often an importer, may be to produce a certificate from another State which is claimed to show that the toys are in fact safe. Such certificates are not conclusive. The test remains conformity with the essential safety requirements. However, the existence of such a certificate, which may or may

---

[62] Article 11(3), amended by Directive 93/68, art. 3(6).
[63] Article 7 of the Directive.
[64] Art.1, Annex I Directive, Regulation 3, Sched. 3, United Kingdom Regs. cover this definitional issue, but cannot shed light on every grey area.

not be easily decipherable, will affect the approach of the trading standards officer, because of the possibility, mentioned above, of a "due diligence" defence. Moreover if goods seized turn out to be safe, there is a lurking risk of a compensation award against the authority. In practice, the matter is commonly resolved by informal negotiation between trader and officer, which is normal in enforcement of most aspects of domestic consumer safety law. However, there is at least some evidence that an item with an EC, rather than a non-EC origin, derives some benefit from the climate of market integration and the influence this exerts on enforcement practice. Very few notifications by the United Kingdom under the Safeguard Procedure (below) concern non-British, EC goods, which may also point in the direction of a certain wariness on the part of trading standards officers.

Consumer organizations, national and European, have performed checks on the market and have had little difficulty in discovering infringing items. There is accordingly no shortage of reports of unsafe CE-marked toys. For example, the January 1994 issue of *Which?*, the Consumers' Association magazine, contains an item about a CE-marked box of 64 crayons. The crayons were bought at a "car boot sale" in Bedfordshire and five were sent for testing at a laboratory. One contained almost five times the permitted level of lead. The importers are reported as having checked the items before and after this discovery and found no infringement. They suggested the crayons could be fakes. The report concludes that this episode "is further evidence that the CE mark can't be relied on as a guarantee of safety".[65] It may be observed again that under English law the due diligence defence means that it is by no means inevitable that a trader who supplies such unsafe goods would be convicted of a criminal offence under the Consumer Protection Act 1987.

In November 1992 the Consumers' Association undertook a small project to test the market.[66] Eighteen toys were purchased from several different retailers in Boulogne, France. Twelve were then submitted to a British test house.[67] Ten were found to fail the European standard for toy safety, EN 71, for reasons ranging from capacity to poison, wound, or choke a child. Eight of the ten carried the CE mark. The places of manufacture were France (two), Spain (one), Germany (one), Italy (one), Taiwan (one) and Hong Kong (one). Three were not known. Three of the items not sent for testing were not CE marked. The Consumers' Association wrote to the manufacturer (or the retailer, where the manufacturer was unknown) of the ten products failing EN 71 and the three lacking the CE marking. By early 1994 four replies had been received in respect of

---

[65] "Toxic Crayons", p 6.
[66] Consumers' Association Press Release of 18 December 1992.
[67] Name withheld at the request of the Consumers' Association; it was an approved body for the purposes of the Directive, n 71 below.

toys failing EN 71. All enclosed certificates which stated that the products complied with EN 71.

Such reports of CE-marked unsafe goods could be replicated many times over.[68] The Consumers in the European Community Group concludes:

> "There is clearly some way to go before the welcome standards set by the Directive are properly enforced in all Member States, both in relation to products made in their own countries and to products admitted from non-EC countries."[69]

(iii) The consequences

Explanations for these infringements vary, as do assessments of the frequency with which this occurs. No one denies that CE-marked unsafe goods have been found on the market. However no interested party seems to hold the view that the phenomenon is overwhelming the whole market. There seems to be no common view on the depth of the problem. How significant is this for the implementation of the Directive (and perhaps for the whole New Approach)?

Were it the case that systematic abuse of the CE marking procedure were occurring, then the whole structure of "self-certification" would seem hard to defend. There is anecdotal evidence that abuse may be occurring on occasion – "in Member State X they just slap the CE marking on as if it's part of the packaging" – but it does not seem to be perceived as an overriding problem.

It seems more probable that difficulties are arising because of differing applications of the relevant standard, EN 71; and, perhaps, differing interpretations of the essential safety requirements which are the cornerstone of the Directive. The Consumers' Association project mentioned above has uncovered the fact that certificates of compliance with EN 71 may exist for products which a British test house would not so certificate. Trading standards officers come across similar problems. This arises where a manufacturer has opted for the first route to show compliance with the essential safety requirements, conformity with harmonised standards, in this case EN 71. A manufacturer may choose to check this for itself by having the goods tested and may thereby obtain a certificate of compliance with EN 71. It will then attach the CE marking. An enforcement officer may subsequently decide that the goods in fact fail to meet the essential safety requirements. If the goods are indeed unsafe on this test, the certificate of conformity with EN 71 offers for these purposes

---

[68] The monthly *Consumer Safety Bulletin* of the Institute of Trading Standards Administration provides a regular supply.
[69] *Product safety and 1992*, p 6.

no protection to the trader. Leaving aside occasional cases of deception by traders, at work here are divergent approaches to any or all of several elements; methods of testing to EN 71; interpretation of EN 71; interpretation of the essential safety requirements.[70]

From a different perspective, no doubt, the British Retail Consortium expresses concern that approved bodies have taken different approaches and that generally there are different approaches to enforcement throughout the EC. Evidence exists (below) that the approved bodies for type approval themselves identify lack of consistency in the application of the rules.

If the problem lies in divergent interpretation of standards, or of essential safety requirements, or of both, then increased co-operation and co-ordination between agencies in different Member States is essential in order to establish a structure within which common approaches may be developed. The processes of co-operation are discussed in section 5 below.

(iv) **Type examination/approval**

In the United Kingdom there were 16 approved bodies duly notified to the Commission by 15 April 1994.[71] Information has been received from six of the bodies on their experiences, providing a reasonably representative country-wide sample.[72]

It seems that relatively few applications for type-approval, the second route to showing conformity with the essential safety requirements, have been received. By early 1994, the six bodies reported: four applications (all approved); 0 applications; 12 applications (all approved); approximately 20 applications (all approved); "few" applications (no information on approval); "probably no more than 20 applications" (all approved).

The perception of trading standards authorities is similarly that relatively little use is being made of the type approval route. The DTI too has no expectation that type approval will be widely used.

The European toy market is characterised by a high level of import penetration from outside the EC, especially from the Far East. Two approved bodies commented that most toys sold in the United Kingdom

---

[70] If the problem lies in the standard itself, not in its application, the Directive envisages a procedure for management; Article 6, note 15 above.

[71] List of notified bodies designated under the New Approach directives OJ 1994 C203. The 16 are; Lyne Martin and Radford, Reading; Trading Standards Laboratory, Nottingham; British Textile Technology Group, Leeds; Amtac Laboratories, Altrincham; SGS UK, Wembley, Middlesex; SGS UK, Bradford; Hereford and Worcester County Council, Worcester; BSI Testing, Hemel Hempstead; Central Scientific Laboratories, London; Inchcape Testing Services (ETL Albury), Cranleigh, Surrey; South Yorkshire Trading Standards Unit, Sheffield; Inchcape Testing Services (Labtest UK), Leicester; J & HS Pattinson Ltd, Newcastle; Birmingham City Council, Birmingham; SGS UK, Warley West Midlands; AH Allen and Partners, Bradford.

[72] The others were approached; some explicitly declined to comment, others failed to respond.

are imported from outside the EC and that type-approval would not in practical terms be readily accessible to such traders. Moreover most United Kingdom toy producers prefer to produce in accordance with recognised standards rather than pursue the alternative type-approval route. One body commented that it actively advised firms to conform to EN 71 wherever possible. The body which has carried out 12 type approvals observed that these largely arose because standards in the particular area were unavailable or inadequate. There was accordingly no alternative to type approval.

Three of the six bodies observed that companies do not submit samples "cold". A type of informal inquiry to the testing body is normal and submission of a model for testing occurs only once a degree of confidence in success has been engendered. This practice is substantiated by a failure to uncover any instance of refusal to approve. The practice of informal "negotiation" between trader and testing house minimises the administrative burden of the procedure. Failure would require notification to the DTI; a successful application is not notified. No such notifications of failure have been received by the DTI.

One body observed that there is a lack of precise rules on how testing laboratories should operate under the type approval procedure. It perceived a problem in different interpretations between different laboratories and, especially, between different countries. This may damage consistency of enforcement of the Directive. This seems to be an important point. B.III.1 of the Model for the New Approach declares that the essential safety requirements "shall be worded precisely enough in order to create, on transposition into national law, legally binding obligations which can be enforced. They should be so formulated as to enable the certification bodies straight away to certify products as being in conformity. . ." One can readily accept the vital need for predictability in the application of the New Approach, yet the perceived variation in approach to type approval casts doubt on its realisation.

4 The Safeguard Procedure

(i) The Safeguard Procedure

It is fundamental that the Directive envisages that action is legitimately taken against CE marked goods where national authorities consider them to be out of line with the essential safety requirements. The action taken is then subjected to management through Community channels – the "Safeguard Procedure". The Member State shall notify the Commission of action taken and the reasons for that action.[73] The Commission "shall

---

[73] Article 7 of the Directive.

256

enter into consultation with the parties concerned as soon as possible".[74] Where the Commission finds the action justified, it shall notify all the Member States. It should be noted that action against items which are *not* CE marked is not covered by the Safeguard Procedure (although it may be covered by RAPEX, Section 4(ii) below.)

One might speculate that the operation of Commission/Member State links under the Safeguard Procedure has the potential to create a fruitful exchange of information and practice which might lead to certain common approaches to the application of the Directive. However, it seems that the procedure is working very erratically as yet. The Sutherland Report of 1992 makes explicit reference to the "very uneven way in which certain 'safeguard' powers . . . have been used in practice by Member State authorities".[75] The evidence of the Toy Safety Directive supports such comments.

In response to an MEP's question the Commission revealed that by June 1993 it had received 67 notifications where Member States had withdrawn toys from the market invoking the safeguard clause.[76] The United Kingdom, specifically through the DTI, had by early 1994 made some 70–80 notifications of CE marked goods against which formal action had been taken. It is aware of only a very few notifications made by other Member States – fewer than ten in total.

It is plain that different approaches are being taken in different Member States in part because of different legal backgrounds. The United Kingdom regards its obligation to notify as triggered if formal legal action such as the issue of a suspension notice under the CPA 1987 occurs. To this end each local authority is obliged to inform the DTI of formal action taken.[77] This is a new requirement imposed on local authorities specifically in order to ensure that the United Kingdom is able to meet its obligations under the Directive. There would be no notification were informal action taken leading to, for example, a voluntary product withdrawal. This is significant because in practice much enforcement activity in the UK is informal, involving co-operation and "negotiation" between trader and trading standards officer.

The DTI perceives a reluctance on the part of Germany to participate in the notification system.[78] In Denmark a low level of notification may be attributable to a very different administrative structure. It is plain that different views are taken in different States of the triggering event for notification.

---

[74] Article 7(2) of the Directive.
[75] *The Internal Market after 1992: Meeting the Challenge*, the report to the EEC Commission by the High Level Group on the Operation of Internal Market.
[76] WQ 188/93 (Bangemann), OJ 1993 C264/18.
[77] SI 1989/1275, reg 13.
[78] This may be a manifestation of a reluctance which finds more formal legal expression in the unsuccessful challenge to the validity of Article 9 of the General Product Safety Directive, Case C-359/92, judgment of 9 August 1994.

The DTI feels that it is developing a *modus vivendi* with the Commission. A meeting in 1989 was followed by the first United Kingdom notification in March 1990, the Directive having come into force at the start of 1990. The Commission at that stage was relatively underprepared and did not have a complete system in place. The DTI has drawn up a form which it uses to provide information to the Commission. This form was developed by 1991 and is structured to provide a list of points about the product in respect of which a notification is being made. The DTI and the Commission have been able to establish a negotiating relationship of sorts. Some notifications have led to queries by the Commission about tests used. The DTI then refers these back to local level. On some occasions the matter has been resolved between local authority and trader and the notification has accordingly been withdrawn by the DTI.

The Commission had originally planned to respond to notifications by approaching firms concerned directly for their views. This was fiercely opposed by the DTI as a potential disruption of the enforcement and policy making chain. The compromise has been to permit affected firms to submit comments and to send these with the notification to the Commission. The Commission has not as yet taken up its "threat" to approach firms directly.

There is here the potential for the system to generate a method for dealing with Community-wide problems. This could be seen as a forum for learning about different approaches to the implementation of the Toy Safety Directive in different States. It is a very slow process. As yet it would be naively optimistic to see the emergence of a developed management structure for the control of CE marked but unsafe goods.

It might be added that although the Directive requires Member States to submit reports to the Commission on the progress under the Directive[79], no such report has yet been submitted. The Commission has announced a plan for bilateral talks with Member States about the operation of the Directive. The United Kingdom plans to await that process before submitting its report. These bilateral discussions are part of the liaison inspired by the Sutherland Report and are directed at the management of the internal market.

(ii) RAPEX and the Safeguard Procedure

The Rapid Exchange System (RAPEX) provides for the transmission of information about urgent measures taken at national level because of "the serious and immediate risk which that product or product batch presents for the health or safety of consumers when used in normal and foreseeable conditions". The State must inform the Commission, which

---

[79] Notes 16, 17 above.

then forwards information to other Member States. Those States then alert the Commission to any measures they have taken, which is then communicated on to the other States.

The System was first set up in 1984 for a four-year trial period.[80] It underwent short term renewal on two occasions[81] before securing a more permanent footing in the General Directive on Product Safety, which was due to be implemented by all Member States by 29 June 1994.[82] Detailed procedures in an Annex to the Directive govern the practical operation of the scheme.

In the United Kingdom the Consumer Safety Unit in the DTI receives the information from the Commission and communicates it to local level, where enforcement is undertaken. What happens thereafter depends on local enforcement priorities. The matter has no formal special status simply because of its source in the Rapid Exchange System.

RAPEX's function can be distinguished from that of the Safeguard Procedure under the Toy Safety (and other) Directives. The use of RAPEX is not related to whether the item is CE marked. The trigger to RAPEX is the "serious and immediate risk". The Safeguard Procedure must be invoked when action is taken against a CE-marked item which is considered unsafe, but there is no requirement that the item pose a serious and immediate risk. However, although the systems are distinct, there are analogies between them. Both involve the establishment of State – Commission – State networks. Both are constructed on the basis that the distribution of information is in practice essential to effective enforcement and to the operation of the internal market, in line with the Sutherland Report. So experience with RAPEX may shed light on the Safeguard Procedure.

In 1988, at the end of the initial, four-year trial period, the Commission submitted a report on the operation of RAPEX which was broadly favourable, although it admitted that use of the notification procedure had been at first erratic.[83] It conceded that different views were taken in different States of the nature a "serious and immediate risk". It also commented that notifications were not always sufficiently complete to allow identification of the product on the market. It claimed positively that:

"Although there is still much room for improvement it seems quite clear that the system is moving in the right direction and will continue to improve."

The most recent relevant Commission report is contained in a communication on the handling of urgent situations in the context of

---

[80] Directive 84/133, OJ 1984 L70/16.
[81] Directive 89/45, OJ 1989 L17/51, 90/352 OJ 1990 L173/49.
[82] Directive 92/59, OJ 1992 L228/24. See Section 2(v) above on the United Kingdom's (late) implementation of this Directive.
[83] OJ 1988 C146/8.

implementation of Community rules.[84] This discusses both RAPEX and the Safeguard Procedure. The link between the effective operation of these systems and the operation of the internal market generally is illuminated by the fact that this Communication is presented as a follow up to the Sutherland Report. The Communication reveals that under the non-food RAPEX system 90 notifications were received in the period 1984–1990, but that 96 notifications were received in 1991 alone.[85] The Commission suggests that this rise may in part be attributable to the establishment of more effective monitoring at national level but concedes that it may also derive from a wide variation in approaches to serious and immediate risks. Some States, it is suggested, may be notifying risks which would be more appropriately dealt with under the safeguard procedure. The Commission comments:

"In order to harmonise notification criteria the Commission asked Member States for a description of criteria used so that it could establish guidelines, a process which will be assisted by a study in progress at present."

The Communication also reveals that the follow up to notifications is patchy. The experience of notification relating to non-food products is that on average only seven out of twelve Member States reply. Eighty-nine days is the average time for a reply.

The Communication observes that the Safeguard Procedure contains no particular procedure for communication. However it notes that practice has developed in relation to Directive 73/23, the "Low Voltage" Directive, where a form has been drawn up in nine languages. This specifies the relevant information which should be provided, such as identification of product, the nature of the risk, etc.

A glimpse of the limitations of RAPEX is provided by a case arising in early 1993 of dangerous Chinese-made halogen lamps. The responsible Commissioner, Christiane Scrivener, was told by MEP Jan Bertens that the lamps had been banned in Germany, but had subsequently been removed from the Dutch market only after "appropriate action" by Konsumenten Kontact (KK), a Dutch consumer organization. Why, asked the MEP, had RAPEX not been invoked?[86] The Commissioner admitted that KK had informed the Commission of the dangerous lamps. The Commission had referred KK to the Dutch contact point in RAPEX. The Dutch authorities decided there was no serious and immediate risk and chose not to notify the Commission under RAPEX. No other State notified the product. Mme. Scrivener stated that RAPEX "may be triggered only by the Member States, at their responsibility". She added that efforts

---

[84] Document COM(93)430.
[85] There were 63 in 1992; WQ to Bangemann n 76 above.
[86] WQ E-1815/93, OJ 1993 C327/34.

were being devoted to drawing up common guidelines on the interpretation of a serious and immediate risk.

The system is evolving, but very slowly, perhaps painfully slowly. RAPEX has been in existence for 10 years, yet its capacity to breed common approaches is transparently limited. This perception seems, perhaps regrettably, readily transferrable to the likelihood of developing an effective, common approach to the Toy Safety Directive's safeguard procedure.

The provision of complete information seems vitally important to the construction of an effective cross-border enforcement pattern. The trail can quickly go cold if inadequate information is provided. The impression gained from trading standards officers is that there is a readiness to respond to information which has its source outside the United Kingdom, but that there is a sense of frustration and bewilderment if it is not possible to lay their hands on sufficiently clear detailed information about the suspected products. The DTI too stresses that the system is dependent on complete information and it has worked to supply this through its development of a standard form for Toy Safety notifications. The Commission accepts that the supply of inadequate information is a problem and in its Communication appeals for "clearer and more systematic presentation of information on the reasons for invoking the safeguard clause."

One can see arguments that these systems should be extended. One might suggest that the input of private bodies such as consumer organisations, which have their own cross-border networks, should be placed on a formal footing. One might propose that the Commission should be empowered beyond its present role which is essentially as a conduit; that, more generally, there could emerge a European structure of enforcement to complement the European structure of marketing. As yet practical experience suggests that this is a long road.

5 Cross-border communication

The development of any kind of effective common Community approach to enforcement depends on cooperation at EC level. This points in the direction of a need to develop a cross-border administrative and enforcement culture or, at least, cross-border information links on dangerous products. This raises important constitutional questions about how the integration of the product market has affected and should affect the capacity of public authorities, whether national or Community, to regulate that market. The previous section suggests that the State – Commission – State structure has major limitations to its capacity to generate a comprehensive system for dealing with dangerous products in the internal market. What of developments which "by-pass" the central State/Community nexus?

In the product safety field, existing research has revealed significant levels of "bottom-up" Europeanisation of enforcement. Enforcement authorities co-operate across borders because that is simply the only way effectively to discharge their functions in the wake of product market integration.[87] This is clearly of great importance in assessing the implementation in practice of the Toy Safety Directive.

(i) Information sharing – computerisation

Information sharing and, increasingly, use of computers has been pioneered by the Institute of Trading Standards Administration (ITSA), the professional body of trading standards officers. The ITSA established the National Information Service in 1983 as a means of circulating to members information about enforcement practice. In 1986 the Service was transferred to computer, and is known as TS-Link.

The project was initially undertaken in the United Kingdom in response to the need for some national co-ordination of information in the context of the local approach to enforcement which characterises United Kingdom practice. It was accordingly an attempt to bridge the gap between local enforcement and the prevalence of national patterns of marketing. The process of European market integration places further demands on the system of co-ordination. The gulf between local enforcement and marketing practice has grown as European marketing becomes more common. Accordingly effort has been devoted to "Europeanisation" of networks of information sharing.

TS-Link is a computerised database of information about activity in respect of trading standards issues generally. HAZPROD was part of TS-Link which covered product safety specifically. Through HAZPROD information about **haz**ardous **prod**ucts was communicated between different authorities in the United Kingdom. This did not disturb the rule of local enforcement but established mechanisms for pooling awareness about problems and a basis for pursuing common solutions to common problems. It proved possible to extend HAZPROD beyond the United Kingdom. This provides an example of *international* co-ordination which

---

[87] Findings of three Commission-funded projects into the law and policy of Product Safety directed through ZERP (Centre for European Law and Policy), University of Bremen, and each involving national reports and sociological and legal investigation of the "Europeanisation" of enforcement practice:

    (*i*) "General" law and policy: Joerges, Falke, Micklitz, Bruggemeier (eds), *Die Sicherheit von Konsumgutern und die Entwicklung der Europaischen Gemeinschaft*, (1988).

    (*ii*) "Post-market" law and policy: Micklitz (ed), *Post Market Control of Consumer Goods*, (1990).

    (*iii*) "Emergency" law and policy: Micklitz, Roethe and Weatherill (eds), *Federalism and Responsibility: A Study of Product Safety Law and Practice in the European Community*, (1994).

developed in response to need, just as *national* co-ordination was developed because it too was needed.

HAZPROD itself no longer exists. It has been replaced by a system of electronic mail operated by the ITSA through its Telecom Gold network. This is PRODLINK. There are some 100 subscribers. These are predominantly the trading standards authorities in the United Kingdom, but there are also subscribers in Sweden, Norway, the Netherlands and the Republic of Ireland. There are continuing discussions with other countries. The EC has provided some funding for PRODLINK.

(ii) "PROSAFE" – the product safety enforcement forum of Europe

PROSAFE is an institution which was established to improve communication between enforcement authorities across borders. It is designed as a forum for solving problems which might crop up. It acts as an aid to developing common solutions. PROSAFE does not act as a formal decision making body. It will not eliminate differences between States by legislating a common approach into existence. It is part of the process of developing institutional links within which a common framework may evolve.[88]

PROSAFE draws its membership from all the EC and EFTA countries with the sole exception of Greece. It is therefore properly seen as a body of the European Economic Area, not simply as a European Community or Union body. It provides the structure for regular meetings of enforcement professionals. It has also hosted two international conferences, in Edinburgh and in Rome.

PROSAFE concerns enforcement of legislation regarding non-food product safety. The Forum of Food Law Enforcement Practice provides a complementary body in the food sector.

PROSAFE has received Commission-funding until 1995. This seems to reflect the importance attached to its potential for creating a forum within which there may evolve through co-operation an even approach to enforcement.

(iii) "LACOTS" – local authorities co-ordinating body on food and trading standards

LACOTS is a co-ordinating body set up by United Kingdom trading standards authorities. It has a small full-time secretariat of approximately 12 people. Its function was initially to promote national co-operation within

---

[88] PROSAFE is referred to in para 2.22 of the 1993 DTI Review: *Review of the Implementation and Enforcement of EC Law in the United Kingdom.*

the United Kingdom's structure of local enforcement. LACOTS is not itself capable of taking decisions binding individual authorities.

LACOTS has pursued internationalisation. This has been at the level of information gathering and building contacts. It is quite fundamental in developing "Europeanised" enforcement structures that the first obstacle is even to identify counterparts in other Member States. To this end, LACOTS has published two "European Directories" – *Consumer Product Safety* and *Consumer Protection Control Bodies* which contain names, addresses, telephone and fax numbers of relevant authorities throughout the Community. The publications were part funded by the Commission's Consumer Policy Service. These publications are explicitly designed to "contribute towards the solution of European trans-border consumer problems and complaints".

LACOTS is responsible for the development of the Home Authority Principle in the United Kingdom. Thereunder, a trader is entitled to expect that the trading standards authority for the area where it is based will provide authoritative guidance on the application of the law. This expectation arises even though the firm may supply throughout the United Kingdom and thus find itself subject in theory to many different authorities who may take different approaches to law enforcement. The Home Authority principle does not equalise enforcement practice in all areas of the country, but it serves to expose the trader to the practice of only one authority. It does not bind local trading standards authorities, because local enforcement remains the formal rule. However, its advantages are such that in practice it is largely, though not uniformly, adhered to.[89] The Home Authority principle is designed to reconcile the structure of "hands-on", well-informed local enforcement with the reality of national marketing. This raises the obvious question of whether a Home Authority principle would be suitable for development EC-wide. There too, precisely the same general policy question arises in the sense that the market is wider than the jurisdiction of individual enforcement agencies, which leads to the risk of fragmentation and commercial uncertainty.

At a still more local level, some individual authorities in the United Kingdom are establishing links with counterparts in other Member States. For example, officers in Kent meet with their equivalents in the Pas de Calais. This may be a special case. The perception of the ease with which international links may be forged seems to diminish as one moves North.

(iv) The International Marketing Supervision Network

The development of "Europeanisation" proceeds apace. Naturally it is not limited to safety matters. The *International Marketing Supervision Net-*

---

[89] Para 2.7 of the 1993 DTI Review: *Review of the Implementation and Enforcement of EC Law in the United Kingdom* observes that business welcomes the Home Authority principle.

work was set up in October 1992 to provide a cross-border structure for coping with trading malpractice causing prejudice to the economic interests of consumers. The Network's activities roughly reflect those of the Office of Fair Trading in the United Kingdom, which was instrumental in its establishment and which serves as one of the United Kingdom links in the network (the DTI also serves). Complaints about the practices of United Kingdom traders may be relayed through the Network to OFT/DTI, who will commonly pass them on to the appropriate trading standards authority. Equally complaints about practices which have their origins outside the United Kingdom can be relayed "up" from local level to OFT/DTI and on to the appropriate State through the Network. Although the Network has no specific standing in safety matters, it provides further evidence of the growth of internationalised administrative structures in the wake of economic integration. In fact it is viewed as much as an emanation of the OECD as of the EC. The inaugural meeting in London in 1992 included organizations from Australia, Canada, Japan and New Zealand the USA and, of the EC "Twelve", lacked Greece, Italy and Luxembourg. Nonetheless the EC Commission Consumer Policy Service sits as an observer on the Network and EC money part funded the 1992 London launch Conference. The Network does not explicitly envisage harmonisation of laws, merely effective application of existing laws. Co-operation is its focus, which may, of course, generate convergence of law and practice in consequence of exposure to and awareness of different systems.

(v) **Overview of progress**

It is not difficult to identify an evolving process of European co-operation between enforcement authorities, which is occurring to a significant extent independently of the State/Community axis. However, it is hard to determine the extent to which this may be taken as the basis for an effective regulatory structure for the integrating market. In no way has a cross-border network been constructed that is adequate to count as a European enforcement structure. Equally the initiatives taken have not been fruitless.

It should be observed that there are differing views on how user-friendly the apparently promising computerised links are. HAZPROD was regarded by some trading standards officers as "cumbersome" to use, and the information difficult to extract. The system has gaps. Certainly there remains a great deal of work to be done to create a fast, effective and reliable means of information sharing. This is in part a problem of computer hardware. It is also a problem of finding the correct interlocutors. It is a question of setting some common ground rules, which may be unfeasible, at least Community-wide. There remain significant geographical variations. The North/South divide is not to be overlooked. This is recognised by those involved in PROSAFE itself, which now has members in all the EEA States except Greece, but there is undoubted variation in the quality of membership State by State.[90]

The Safeguard Procedure has been shown to work slowly and at present highlights the divergence in practice much more than it serves to generate resolution of the problems which flow from such divergence.

The Home Authority principle has attractions and it is easy to recognise that there may be advantages to the development of a Europe-wide Home Authority principle. It could provide a means of creating mutual trust and confidence. However, a precondition for its coming into effect is an existing level of such trust. For all the co-operative links which are being forged, such confidence is not firmly in place and certainly varies State by State. Moreover, possible changes within the United Kingdom may in any event disrupt the pattern. In January 1994 Michael Heseltine, the President of the Board of Trade (DTI), announced a review into the organisation of enforcement functions of local authorities. There is an interest in reducing inconsistencies in enforcement to avoid duplication and to improve co-ordination. It seems possible that the Home Authority principle will be thought too weak to provide security for traders with national and international marketing activities. It is probable that this review will involve a close scrutiny of the "tradition" of local enforcement. It remains to be seen what specific proposals will emerge, but reduction in local autonomy is plainly capable of disrupting the patterns of incipient horizontal Europeanisation.

There are different opinions on the scope of the achievements thus far. There are those who emphasise progress, others who emphasise what remains to be done. To some extent, this is the glass which is either half-full or half-empty depending on the predilection of the observer (although in fact it is probably as yet more a case of partly filled or mostly empty). It is difficult to form an objective view of whether the evolving processes of Europeanisation of enforcement practice represent a valiant and promising attempt to bridge major cultural divides or a vain attempt to achieve regulation of a market in the wake of an integrative process which has brought about a profound effective deregulation of product safety law.[91]

(vi) **The Sutherland Report: an impetus to Europeanisation of enforcement?**

Regular invocation of the Safeguard Procedure by Member States will fragment the internal market. Regular appearance on the market of

---

[90] A commonly-told anecdote concerns the PROSAFE conference held in Rome at which no Italian delegate appeared.
[91] See further section 6 of this Chapter and, more generally, the concluding Chapter to this book.

unsafe, CE marked toys will destroy consumer confidence. In either event, the operation of the internal market will be seriously jeopardised. This perception underlies the Sutherland Report of 1992[92] which elaborated proposals relating to administrative co-operation and information transmission as key elements in ensuring confidence about the viability of the internal market.

Section IV of the Report is entitled "Enforcing the Rules through Partnership". It is based on the notion that Member States bear responsibility for enforcing the law within their jurisdiction and that the Commission supervises the Member States. The Sutherland Report strongly supports the need for construction of open, transparent crossborder enforcement networks and it remains to be seen whether the initiatives mentioned above, such as PROSAFE, will be or can be lent impetus by the Commission's follow up to Sutherland. The Sutherland Report seems prepared to push beyond the basic notion that States are responsible for law enforcement on their own territories. It suggests that:

> "Each authority responsible for applying and enforcing Community legislation at national and local level should accept a duty to cooperate with other such bodies, both through direct contact and via central contact points. This requires them to recognise and respond to their Community-wide responsibilities which arise from the fact that their official functions directly affect citizens of all other Member States. Their officials have Community-wide responsibilities. . ."

This reference to both "direct contact and via central contact points" embraces both the horizontal and vertical aspects of cross-border communication discussed above. The horizontal approach may subvert the State/Community axis. National authorities are presented as Community authorities, via the pivotal Article 5. This may represent an effective means of securing meaningful protection for the rights of the Citizen of the Union.[93] Such discussion falls beyond the scope of this Chapter which is limited to the United Kingdom. However, these observations suggest tensions for the United Kingdom which are appropriate for consideration in the Conclusion to this Chapter.

6 Conclusion

There are tensions in the development of "bottom-up" or "horizontal" cross-border links. It is regarded as effective by the officers on the ground

---

[92] *The Internal Market after 1992: Meeting the Challenge*, the report to the EEC Commission by the High Level Group on the Operation of Internal Market.
[93] Article 8 of EC Treaty.

to participate in the construction of networks of co-operation. Risk managers typically prefer a bottom up approach and are sceptical about non-expert intervention.[94] However, the Community is built on certain expectations about the Community/State axis. It is well known that Community law, including directives, is capable of binding organs of the State below central government, but nevertheless the obligation to implement directives rests on the State and it is the State which would be obliged to defend Article 169 infringement proceedings in the event of failure to implement. The suggestion of subversion of the central State through developing local level cross-border links fits uncomfortably with some of the assumptions of the EC legal order. These resonances grow louder when the unitary tradition of the United Kingdom is taken into account and, moreover, the Heseltine Review gives the impression of working against the grain of local initiatives in the Community which by-pass the central State.[95]

The DTI is concerned to conserve its place. It is actively aware of the obligations of the United Kingdom as a Member State. Notification under the safeguard procedure comes from the DTI not the local level (although the form which the DTI has devised makes clear which authority is involved). There is wariness about the appropriateness of Commission links below the level of the central State, whether with local authorities or with the firms themselves. It is intriguing to observe that on the side of the Commission there is a publicly expressed concern, at least, to insist on State responsibility to notify under RAPEX and to decline to take action prompted by private notification, in this instance by consumer organizations.[96] At the very least, this bears witness to the sensitivity of the constitutional issues which are at stake here.

The tension between the Community law assumption of a Community/State axis and the development of horizontal patterns, seemingly approved by the Sutherland Report, offers potential for persisting challenge to the pattern of distribution of public functions in the Community. The process of integration through law has disabled Member States from regulating their markets without reference to the demands of an integrated market. The New Approach has contributed to an alteration in the style of regulation to which traders are subject in the Community by raising the profile of private standards and, in the case of toy safety, employing self-certification. The Sutherland Report insists that market integration cannot survive without effective administration of market regulatory laws. On one level this is a practical matter of managing the

---

[94] Roethe, Chapter 3, in Micklitz, Roethe and Weatherill (eds.), *Federalism and Responsibility, op. cit.*, n 87.
[95] Section 5(v) above.
[96] Halogen lamps: n 86 above.

internal market. On another level it engages the responsibility of national governments to their citizens and, as Sutherland explains, to those of other Member States and also the responsibility of the Community institutions to the citizens of the European Union.[97]

STEPHEN WEATHERILL

---

[97] See further the first and last Chapters in this book.

Part Three

Effects of Implementation

Chapter 10
Private Initiative and Public Control in the Regulatory Process

1 Introduction

It is a fundamental principle of the EC Treaty that the implementation of Community law in general, and of directives in particular, in Member States is primarily the duty of the Governments of the Member States.[1] However, the scope given by Article 189 of the EC Treaty to the States to determine the "manner and form" of implementation allows a considerable measure of discretion to each State. That discretion could be said to be even wider, following the insertion of Article 3b by the Treaty on European Union. Article 3b affirms the limits of Community powers and emphasises the role of the Member States in achieving the objectives of the Treaty.

The discretion in manner and form of implementation will extend not only to decisions about transposition or non-transposition of the text of a directive but to the type (if any) of regulatory structure and its relationship with any system devised for the implementation of *national rules,* including the system of enforcement through either the civil or criminal process. The European Court of Justice has, however, made it clear in a number of cases that where a directive creates rights these must be "transparent" to those who are intended to benefit from them, and also that an effective enforcement system is integral to effective implementation.[2] The system adopted for implementation will be almost as important where the directive is intended to confer benefits not on identifiable individuals but the community at large, or a section of it, such as in directives relating to the environment or for the protection of consumers. In such cases, Community law may be much more willing to

---

[1] EC Treaty, art. 5.
[2] Case 29/74 *Commission* v *Germany (Re Nursing Directives)* [1986] 2 CMLR 579; Case 222/86 *UNEC-TEF* v *Heylens* [1987] ECR 4097; Case 271/92 *Marshall (No. 2)* [1993] 3 CMLR 2931; and see above Chapter 7.

recognise the creation of rights for individual beneficiaries than the national law which is intended to implement it.[3]

The object of this Chapter is to consider how the choice of regulatory structure affects the protection and delivery of those interests, rights, and benefits which a directive may be intended to create, and particularly, how implementation may be affected by the choice of enforcement through direct governmental action, self-regulatory structures, by dependence on local authority or other agency initiatives, and by the use of courts and tribunals by those on whom rights are conferred by a directive or by those who are intended to benefit from it.

As we have seen in Chapter 4, the implementation of directives may take place at a number of different levels within the State, according to the method chosen for implementation by that State, and such choice may be determined by the nature and content of the directive and the number and nature of actors or beneficiaries. Implementation may be achieved simply by each State adopting certain policy objectives at national level and by promulgating those objectives downwards through the executive hierarchy. Usually, however, especially where autonomous agencies are involved or rights are intended to be created by the directive, implementation will require the transposition of the content of the directive into some internal Ministerial directive or circular, backed by a change in the national law. Alternatively, the Government may confine itself to the creation or adaptation of rules of national law, and delegate the process of implementation to existing national/local government or other statutory bodies. In the United Kingdom the choice of implementing methods will be influenced by a number of factors. These will include the objectives of the directive and the extent to which the Government is politically committed to them, the availability of existing national legislation and regulatory systems and bodies, and the extent to which both may be used or adapted for the purposes of implementation. The trend in this country in recent years has been towards "self-regulation" and "de-regulation".[4] Deregulation has been accompanied by a considerable degree of delegation of powers and functions to autonomous and semi-autonomous agencies. This has been particularly marked in the transfer of functions of central government to executive agencies.[5] Paradoxically, the reduction in local government involvement and the move to de-regulation and self-regulation may actually increase the role

---

[3] Caranta, "Governmental Liability after Francovich" (1993) 52 Camb.L.J. 272, 284.

[4] See, DTI, *Review of the Implementation and Enforcement of EC Law in the United Kingdom*, July 1993; *Deregulation: Cutting the Red Tape*, DTI, January 1994 and Deregulation and Contracting Out Act 1994. See also Chapter 1, section 2(i).

[5] See, Goldsworthy, *Setting up Next Steps: a Short Account of the Origins, Launch and Implementation of the Next Steps Project in the British Civil Service*, HMSO, 1992; Daintith, "Regulating by Contract: the New Prerogative" [1979] Curr.L.P. 41; Freeland, "Government by Contract and Public Law" [1992] *Publ. L.* 80; Bogdanor, "Ministers, Civil Servants and the Constitution: Revolution in Whitehall" *IALS Bulletin*, 15 October 1993.

of central government in the monitoring of the self-regulatory process and of the standards to be attained.

The trend over the last decade has not been wholly towards self-regulation[6], and recent events in the financial services sector may slow the process or even reverse it, after the current examination of the whole field of financial regulation has been completed by the Treasury Select Committee.[7] However, it remains a main plank of governmental policy and is likely to be a significant factor in both the implementation and enforcement of Community law. If self-regulation is chosen, policy objectives may be attained through agreed Codes of Practice with the industry concerned or simply by negotiation with the largest actors in that industry.[8] The adoption of this self-regulatory approach may have important consequences for attempted challenges by individuals and interested organizations.

2 Some peculiarly English obstacles to implementation

Before considering the effect on enforcement resulting from the choice of regulatory structure, it is useful to touch on some general points about the nature of English public and private law which might constitute barriers to the effective implementation of Community law in some areas.

Such an examination is necessary because the legal status, powers and immunities of the bodies and individuals chosen to secure implementation may vary significantly, and have a substantial effect on the extent of enforcement options. The problems that have been created by the somewhat uneven development of English remedies in public law, and their relationship to private interests were addressed by the Law Commission, who recommend a number of changes intended to facilitate the enforcement of Community provisions.[9] Changes have already resulted from the unwillingness of some senior judges to allow too great a divergence to develop between remedies for the enforcement of Community rights and those originating wholly in national law.[10]

Some of the difficulties that do arise are matters of substance, and not

---

[6] See, Police Complaints Procedures, s 84, Police and Criminal Evidence Act (PACE) 1984.
[7] See, Rodgers, "Patching up the City Protectors", *The Independent*, 15 February 1994.
[8] See, Ramsay, "The Office of Fair Trading: Policing the Consumer Market Place" in *Regulation and Public Law* (Baldwin and McCrudden eds, 1987), and see the recent agreement between the Government and the water industry on the achievement of water quality goals set by Directive 80/778, considered by the court in *R. v Secretary of State for the Environment ex p. Friends of the Earth*, *The Independent*, 12 April 1994.
[9] See, Law Commission, *Administrative Law: Judicial Review and Statutory Appeals*, Consultation Paper No. 126 (1993), paras 2.10, 2.11, Report (Oct. 1994) Law Comm. No 226 H. C. 669, paras. 2.9, 2.10, and see Chapter 12 below.
[10] *M. v Home Office* [1992] QB 270, 36OG-307A (Lord Donaldson) and *Woolwich Equitable Building Society v IRC* [1992] 3 WLR 366, 395–396 (Lord Goff).

mere procedure, and make the protection of certain rights and interests more difficult. The limitations of the common law are especially relevant to those Community measures which have as their object the creation of a benefit for society as a whole, or a section of it, such as employees or consumers or for livestock or the environment, and those problems will be primarily addressed. Difficulties are likely to arise because, under Community law, the fact that the provisions infringed were enacted in the general interest will be irrelevant, because this does not mean that they were not also intended to protect the interests of particular individuals. Such an inference is much less likely to be drawn by an English court.[11] Some of the more general problems of enforcing rights and securing benefits conferred on individuals by Community law in the United Kingdom are addressed by Imelda Maher in Chapter 11.[12]

(i) Judicial review and private law remedies

(a) *Choosing the right process*

The first decision that has to be made in relation to a legal challenge to a public body following the denial of a right or damage or injury to an interest is in relation to the process to be used. In the case of certain statutory benefits, or employment rights, the law may provide an appeal, and this process must generally be exhausted before any alternative legal challenge can be considered.[13] Many decisions affecting individuals made by public bodies, however, are not subject to a special appeal process, and the alternatives are most often a challenge by way of judicial review or an ordinary action in damages where a private right is infringed.

The value of judicial review in the enforcement of Community directives for a large group of potential beneficiaries was recently demonstrated in the field of equal opportunity in employment. In *R* v *Secretary of State for Employment ex p. EOC*[14], the Equal Opportunities Commission argued that the Employment Protection (Consolidation) Act 1978 was contrary to Community law. The Act provided that full-time workers (who are largely male) qualified for unfair dismissal and redundancy rights after a period of two years, while part-time workers (who are largely female) qualified for such rights after a period of five years. The case of the EOC was, briefly, that these provisions clearly discriminated, indirectly, against the part-time, female work-force. The application for

---

[11] Caranta, *op cit.*, n 3, p 296.

[12] See also, D'Sa, *European Community Law and Civil Remedies in England and Wales* (1994).

[13] *Ellis & Sons Fourth Amalgamated Properties* v *Southern Rent Assessment Panel* (1984) 270 EG 39; *Bone* v *Mental Health Panel* [1985] 3 All ER 330; *R.* v *Secretary of State for the Home Department ex p. Swati* [1986] 1 WLR 477.

[14] [1994] 2 WLR 409. See also Chapter 11 below, text accompanying n. 95.

judicial review followed a refusal by the Secretary State for Employment to amend the legislation.

The Minister contested the application on both substantive and procedural grounds. He did not accept that the differences in qualifying times infringed Article 119 of the EC Treaty and Directive 75/117 on equal pay, or Directive 76/207 on equal employment rights. His counsel also took the procedural point that there was no "decision" to be judicially reviewed and that if there was, the EOC did not have the legal status[15] to challenge it. The House of Lords, by a majority (Lords Keith, Lowry, Slynn and Browne-Wilkinson, Lord Jauncey dissenting) found that the provisions of the Act did conflict with both the Community equal pay and equal opportunity directives, and, although the refusal to legislate was not a "decision" which could be judicially reviewed, the alleged incompatibility between English and Community employment law was a proper subject for review, and the EOC was the proper body to bring the proceedings. Interestingly, a parallel application by a private individual was dismissed, on the ground that it was, essentially, a private law claim against her employer, and should have been commenced in an industrial tribunal rather than by way of judicial review.

The requirement to distinguish at the commencement of proceedings stage between a private and a public law matter is not peculiar to English law.[16] But it is a recent development and motivated more by expediency than by clearly discernible principles of what is a public and what is a private matter. It originates in the House of Lords decision of *O'Reilly* v *Mackman* in 1982[17] and was intended to create a separate category of cases for which judicial review was the only appropriate remedy. As we have seen, an application for judicial review is the normal means by which a legal challenge of a public body believed to have exceeded its powers is made. The commencement of proceedings by writ is the usual method for the initiation of a claim in private proceedings for damages for a tort or breach of contract. The choice of proceeding by writ, rather than by application for judicial review may, in some cases be fatal to a claim. The time limit of three months under Order 53 of the Rules of the Supreme Court for an application for judicial review may well mean that a litigant who has chosen to proceed by writ (for which the time limit is, in most cases, six years or more) will be out of time if the court decides that the case concerns a matter of public law for which judicial review is the appropriate remedy. Although there have been signs in recent years that the courts have become more flexible in entertaining claims by ordinary action where there is a public law element, it still constitutes a significant

---

[15] *Locus standi*, see below.
[16] See, Caranta, *op. cit.*, n 3.
[17] [1983] AC 237.

barrier to an action against the administration for failing to deliver a Community-originated benefit or for asserting a Community right.[18]

In English law, public law remedies in judicial review proceedings are discretionary. Most successful review proceedings result in the setting aside of an administrative decision, so that it can be taken again, according to the proper principles. Damages are not, generally, available against public bodies for the failure to discharge a duty unless the individual can establish a breach of a duty to an individual in respect of an interest which the common law has accepted is worthy of protection[19], or where a public officer has been guilty of misfeasance in office.[20]

(b) *Narrow common law concepts of legitimate interests attracting legal protection*

Closely linked to the type of process and availability of remedies is the limited nature of the interests or claims which the common law will protect. The conservatism of the common law has meant that the protection of property, albeit narrowly construed, has been given primacy over more general considerations of public benefit, even in preference to individual personal liberty. Only in times of national crisis are proprietorial interests sacrificed to the national good, and even then powers of private property appropriation are interpreted much more narrowly than powers under which individuals may be detained.[21]

The primary aim of the common law as the protector of private property interests originates in the Lockean concepts of the nature of government that dominated 18th century political thinking and permeated the law. They are adopted as self-evident precepts by Lord Camden in *Entick* v *Carrington* (1765).[22] Even apparent public law duties were re-cast into private rights.[23] When local authorities were established in the late 19th century, private law concepts continued to permeate judicial thinking. The local authority was seen as a trustee of the ratepayer's money accountable not to the community or the electorate at large but to the ratepayers. There could be no obligation to the elderly to provide subsidised public transport, or to the electorate who had voted for such a

---

[18] Jacob, in *The Fabric of English Civil Justice* (1987), condemns the introduction of the concept of public law into judicial review as "an unnecessary complication" and recommends its abolition (p 164). For signs of flexibility, see *Roy* v *Kensington and Chelsea and Westminster Family Practitioner Committee* [1992] AC 624; and see Bamforth, "The Scope of Judicial Review Still Uncertain" [1993] *Public Law* 231 and see Chapter 11.

[19] Order 53 Rules of the Supreme Court: damages only available where they would have been available in action commenced by writ.

[20] *Burgoin* v *MAFF* [1986] QB 716, and see now *Racz* v *Home Office* [1994] 1 All ER 97 (HL), or a recognised tort of breach of statutory duty.

[21] Compare *R.* v *Halliday ex p. Zadig* [1916] KB 738 and *Chester* v *Sateson* [1920] 1 KB 928, *Newcastle Breweries* v *The King* [1920] 1 KB 854, *R.* v *Bottril ex p. Küchenmeister* [1947] 1 KB 47 and *Burmah Oil* v *Lord Advocate* [1965] AC 75.

[22] 19 St. Tr. 1030 and see J.Locke *A Second Treatise on Government* (1671).

[23] See *Ashby* v *White* (1703) 1 ER 417, in which a right to vote was vindicated in the same way as an invasion of a property right, see Harlow, *Compensation and Government Torts* (1982), p 42.

policy, if that conflicted with the obligation to apply the ratepayer's money in the most business-like way with the best return.[24] Employees were to be engaged at the lowest wages at which they could be had on the open market.[25] Likewise, private companies were under an obligation to provide the best return to their owners, the shareholders, and on dissolution, owed no obligation in law to their former employees.[26]

Although the common law emphasised individualism, the protection of individuals was narrowly confined to protection of the physical person and proprietary rights. Unlike the United States, England developed no law of privacy.[27] As Birkinshaw has said, "in terms of civil liberties, this is a striking example of the common law's inability to protect those civil liberties which are not in proprietary form."[28]

"Natural rights" were dismissed as fanciful and positively harmful.[29] As we have seen in Chapter 7, there is no recognition of any right of subjects to free movement until 1972[30] and even now citizens have no right to a travel document; this is issued at discretion under the royal prerogative, subject only to a duty to act fairly when a decision to withhold it is made.[31] The Immigration (European Economic Area) Order 1994, (EEA Order), confers no entitlement to a passport, although it purports to implement the Directive. The law of the Republic of Ireland, the only other Member State with a common law system, but having also a written constitution makes a striking contrast. There the right to travel is "an unenumerated constitutional right . . . a fundamental right . . . in a free society".[32]

The narrowness of the common law can also be seen in an unwillingness to recognise new benefits conferred by statute as conferring new property-type rights on the beneficiaries, or creating new torts for a breach of such statutory duty. The general principle is that consumers are too wide a class of people to be protected by an action for breach of statutory duty.[33] Only where the legislation would be unenforceable without such liability, or where an official would otherwise escape liability for

---

[24] *Prescott* v *Birmingham Corporation* [1955] Ch. 210; *R.* v *GLC ex p. Bromley* [1983] AL 768 ('fares fair' policy).

[25] *Roberts* v *Hopwood* [1925] AC 578.

[26] *Hutton* v *West Cork Railway Company* (1883); *Parke* v *Daily News* [1962] Ch. 927; but see now Companies Act 1985, s 719.

[27] Warren and Brandeis, (1890) 4 Harv.L.Rev. 193; Wacks, *Personal Information: Privacy and the Law* (1989).

[28] Birkinshaw, "Citizenship and Privacy" in *Rights and Citizenship* (Blackburn, ed 1993).

[29] See, *The Works of Jeremy Bentham*, Bowring (ed), vol. 11, p 497: for a more modern positivist, Griffith, *Public Rights and Private Interests*, (1981); "The Political Constitution" (1979) 42 Mod. L. Rev. 1 and for a more sympathetic view of rights, see Dworkin, *Taking Rights Seriously* (1977).

[30] *DPP* v *Bhagwan* [1972] AC 60 and see Chapter 7, text accompanying n 77.

[31] *R.* v *Secretary of State ex p. Everett* [1989] QB 891; subject also to the right to a document for free movement purposes under Community law: Directive 68/360, art. 2.

[32] Finlay CJ in *Attorney-General* v *X*: [1992] 2 CMLR 277, 303; *The State (M)* v *Attorney-General* [1979] IR 73.

[33] See Cooke and Oughton, *The Common Law of Obligations* (1993), p 438; *Buckley* v *La Reserve* [1959] Crim. L. Rev. 451.

the most flagrant disregard of his legal obligations[34], are the courts prepared to contemplate a right to compensation.[35] As a general rule, however, where there is a duty imposed on an official or public body, there is a reluctance to recognise an obligation to compensate individuals for economic loss, even when that duty has not been properly discharged. Public financial regulatory bodies will not, for example, be held liable in negligence to private investors on the ground that the powers and duties owed by the regulators were conferred in the interest of the public at large.[36]

(c) Locus standi *and the right to commence proceedings*

The consequence of the narrowness of the interests recognised by the common law can be seen in the rules relating to *locus standi*. These rules determine whether or not an individual, a group of individuals or a company or organization can apply to the High Court for judicial review of a decision made by a public officer, or a body exercising public functions.[37] The rules are designed to exclude applications made by "busybodies" who have no personal or material interest in the decision made by the public body. "Personal" in this context refers to challenges to decisions which affect an individual's physical liberty and "material", broadly, means a decision affecting a person's property, livelihood or business reputation.[38] In the absence of such an interest it is open to individuals to seek the help of the Attorney-General in relator proceedings. If he agrees, he will commence the proceedings on behalf of the individual concerned. He is, however, free to decline to do so for whatever reason, and his decision is not open to control or review by the courts.[39]

The recent trend seems to fluctuate between an even tighter definition of standing, so that unincorporated bodies now no longer have status to make an application for judicial review, even on behalf of their members who will be very directly, and materially, affected by the decision[40], and a more relaxed one in relation to recognised bodies without the necessary

---

[34] See recent cases on the resuscitated tort of misfeasance in office: *Racz* v *Home Office, op. cit.*, n 20, and see *Weldon* v *Home Office* [1992] 1 AC 58.

[35] Housing (Homeless Persons) Act 1977, Housing Act 1985, Part III; *R.* v *Tower Hamlets, London Borough Council ex p. Khalique, The Independent*, 7 April 1994.

[36] *Yuen Kun-yeu* v *A-G*, [1988] AC 175, 191 f (Lord Keith), Caranta, *op. cit.*, n 3, p 276; *Murphy* v *Brentwood District Council* [1990] AC 278.

[37] *R.* v *Secretary of State for the Environment ex p. Rose Theatre Trust* [1990] 2 WLR 186.

[38] *Re Pergamon* [1970] Ch. 388.

[39] *Gouriet* v *Union of Postal Workers* [1978] AC 435 (HL).

[40] *R.* v *Darlington Borough Council ex p. The Association of Darlington Taxi Owners, The Times*, 13 January 1994; compare *R.* v *Liverpool Corporation ex p. Liverpool Taxi Fleet Operators' Association* [1972] 2 QB 299.

direct interest[41] or even to unincorporated organizations with such an interest.[42]

The consequence of a lack of recognition by the law of a community interest in relation to *locus standi*, and the predominance of private proprietary interests, is highlighted in the law relating to planning and the environment:

> "There is an underlying judicial bias in favour of financial interests. This was formed in the *laissez-faire* era of the nineteenth century upon the foundations of property rights and freedom of contract and was incorporated by judicial interpretation into the post World War II planning system.[43] Within this framework, environmental interests are not recognized as 'rights' and must be protected, if at all, by specific legislation."[44]

It is not possible to overcome the difficulty of a lack of a personal or proprietorial interest by a combination of concerned individuals, because a multiplication of a lack of *locus standi* in a number of individuals is still seen as productive of a total lack of standing.[45]

There is no *actio popularis* recognised by the common law. Representative actions are limited to a very narrow class of directly interested parties.[46] The Law Commission, in its consultation document on judicial review and statutory appeal rights, has suggested that there should be special rules designed to encourage "public interest" challenges to the exercise of public powers, but these proposals are a long way from adoption.[47] Classic liberal theory, which continues to permeate the common law, and to be echoed in Government, tends to regard litigation to protect individual material interests as legitimate, and attempts to represent public or ideological concerns as problematical.[48]

(d) *The Duty To Give Reasons*

As part of the Community requirement of transparency and to facilitate individual legal challenges to the denial of rights, it is a fundamental principle of Community law that sufficient reasons are to be given for an

---

[41] See *R. v Secretary of State for the Environment ex p. Friends of the Earth*, The Independent, 12 April 1994; *R. v Secretary of State for Foreign Affairs, ex p. World Development Movement* [1995] 1 All ER 611.
[42] See *R. v Somerset CC ex p. Fewings* [1995] 1 All ER 513.
[43] *Mixnams Properties v Chertsey UDC* [1965] AC 735; *Hall v Shoreham UDC* [1964] 1 WLR 240; *Buxton v Ministry of Housing* [1961] 1 QB 278.
[44] Alder, "Environmental Impact Assessment – The Inadequacies of English Law" (1993) 5 J.Env.L. 203, at p. 215, and see also Geddes, "*Locus Standi* and EEC Environmental Measures" (1992) 4 J.Env.L. 29.
[45] See the *Rose Theatre Trust* Case, *op. cit.*, n 37.
[46] Order 6, r 3; Order 15, r 12 RSC.
[47] See Cane, "The Law Commission on Judicial Review" (1993) 56 Mod. L. Rev. 887; Law Com. No 226 paras. 5.22, 5.39.
[48] See Feldman, "Public Interest Litigation and Constitutional Theory in Comparative Perspective" (1992) 55 Mod. L. Rev. 44.

administrative decision in which Community rights are involved.[49] The position on the giving of reasons in English administrative law is less clear. There is "no authority for the proposition that there is a general duty to give reasons for an administrative decision, and there is. . . high authority . . . to the contrary."[50] Cases where individual liberty is involved will almost certainly attract such a duty. Academic decisions may, however, not do so, and decisions by professional bodies on an examinee's expertise would, as a general rule, not involve a requirement to give full reasons for a candidate's failure.[51] Only where important issues, such as the liberty of the individual, or where Community law specifies in a directive that reasons are given, can they be expected in an English administrative decision.[52] In other cases, where a right may originate from a Community directive but where there are no specific rules in the directive as to the giving of reasons, the right to reasons may not be acknowledged and the ordinary common law principles may be applied.

(e) *"Effective" remedies*

In the absence of major reform, the administration will continue to be judged in the same courts but according to the peculiar rules of English administrative law and subject to the limits of the available procedure. Community law requires that the remedies be "effective" but does not determine the nature of those remedies. Even the fact that a Community law provision can be considered as directly effective does not, of itself, determine whether the right created in the individual is to be categorised by national law as a private right to be protected by such remedies as the national legal system provides, or as a right to have the public law enforced, to which are attached the remedies appropriate to such enforcement.[53] The concept of "an effective remedy" as a Community concept is, as yet, undeveloped although some attempts have been made both by the European Court of Justice and the Commission to address the issue.[54] As Francis Snyder has observed[55] "achieving harmonisation

---

[49] Case 222/84, *Johnston v Chief Constable of the Royal Ulster Constabulary*: [1986] ECR 1651; *UNEC-TEF v Heylons*: [1987] ECR 2605; Directive 64/221, art 6; European Convention on Human Rights, art 6; Article F(3) of the TEU.

[50] Rose LJ in *R. v Secretary of State ex p. Duggan* [1994] 3 All ER 277, 287, citing Lord Mustill [1993] 3 WLR 154, 173.

[51] *R. v Higher Education Funding Council ex p. Institute of Dental Surgery* [1994] 1 All ER 651.

[52] See below, in relation to expulsion under Directive 64/221, arts 6, 7 *R. v Secretary of State ex p. Dannenberg* [1984] QB 766, [1984] 2 CMLR 456, and in relation to the 'aptitude test' under Directive 89/48 and see *Vlassopoulo v Ministerium für Justiz* [1991] ECR 1–2357, in which the Court stated that an unsuccessful candidate had to be given the reasons for the failure of an examination.

[53] See Curtin, "Directives: The Effectiveness of Judicial Protection of Individual Rights" (1990) 27 *Comm. Mkt. L. Rev.* 709, 730.

[54] See Case 158/80 *Rewe v Hauptzollamt Kiel* [1981] ECR 1839; Case 68/88 *EC Commission v Greece* [1989] ECR 2964, and see Fitzpatrick, "The Effectiveness of Equality Law Remedies: A European Community Law Perspective" in *Discrimination: The Limits of Law* (Hepple and Szyszczak eds, 1993).

[55] See Chapter 3, section 5.

of national remedies *sufficient to ensure effective enforcement of Community rights, while simultaneously respecting the legitimate differences among Member States,* is a difficult task." (emphasis added). This is likely to become more, rather than less, difficult in a European Union committed to subsidiarity and a recognition of the "national way of doing things".

(ii) Criminal law

Since the nineteenth century minimum standards in public health and safety at work have been enforced by inspection and criminal sanctions.[56] In some cases, the criminal law has been bolstered by incorporation into the civil law by the recognition of new torts of breach of statutory duty.[57] In these cases, statutes intended to create criminal liability, with prosecutions instituted by the old Factories Inspectorate, have been held to create civil, tortious liability in suits brought by those injured when the statute has been breached, for example where a person sues who has been injured by an unfenced machine.

In others, criminal sanctions have proved ineffective, and a civil remedy in the form of injunctive relief has been sought to enforce, among other things, the Sunday trading provisions of the Shops Act 1950. This is the case also in planning legislation where persistent failure to observe enforcement notices, dealt with for many years by stop notices and prosecutions brought by local authorities, have now been reinforced by the power of local authorities to obtain injunctions against persistent defaulters.[58] Breach of an injunction is normally itself a criminal offence.[59]

The criminal process may also be an effective resource for individuals where the public body having the duty to enforce the legislation fails to do so, or is itself an offender. The legislation creating the modern prosecution structure specifically retains the individual right to bring criminal proceedings, although the Director of Public Prosecutions retains the right to take over the proceedings and, if he chooses, terminate them.[60] The higher standard of proof required in criminal proceedings and (for individuals) the lack of legal aid, may also be a deterrent to prosecution and is a factor in the choice of the civil or criminal process as a means of enforcement.

There is a lack, in English law, of a system of enforcement through

---

[56] See, *e.g.* Chapter 6, section 5(iii).
[57] Factories Acts; *Groves* v *Lord Wimbourne* [1989] 2 QB 402.
[58] Section 3 of the Planning and Compensation Act 1991, amending, Town and Country Planning Act 1990, s 187.
[59] Contempt of Court Act 1981, s 4(2).
[60] Section 6 of the Prosecution of Offences Act 1985; "*Whitehouse* v *Bogdanov*" in *Freedom, the Individual and the Law* (Robertson ed, 1989), p 203; *Salford City Council* v *McNally* [1976] AC 379 (private prosecution for failing to abate a statutory nuisance under Public Health Act 1936, s 99).

the use of administrative penalties, that is, by the imposition of a penalty by a body other than a court. This is common in Continental systems, and appears in Community law in the form of the penalties imposed by the Commission for breach of Community competition law under Articles 85 and 86 of the EC Treaty. Since the process does not carry the same stigma as conviction in ordinary criminal proceedings, there is a danger that it may be treated by large undertakings as simply an administrative expense. Such proceedings have, however, recently been held by the European Court of Human Rights to be protected against the rule against non self-incrimination, although an earlier decision of the European Court of Justice held that investigations in which companies were alleged to have broken economic and competition law attracted no such protection.[61]

3 Choice of regulatory structure: the consequences for enforcement

The actors in the process of implementing Community and national law will, self-evidently, differ according to the type of legislation and the activities and the individuals and organizations to be affected. But they will also differ according to the method and structure chosen for implementation, whether regulation is to be by central or local government, by the industry or individuals affected, or a combination of all three.

It is proposed in this section to look at the regulation of a number of activities, some of which have been considered in the case studies, and others which seem useful because they raise other important issues, and to consider, in each case, the questions: First, to whom are the obligations in the Directive addressed? Secondly, by whom and how are those obligations to be enforced if they are not duly performed? Thirdly, if enforcement fails, who may enforce enforcement or act as an alternative enforcer and by what means?

(i) **Food safety**

(a) *The objects of regulation*

Directive 89/397, the subject of the study reported in Chapter 6, was intended to harmonise the implementation of Community policy on food safety and inspection. The obligations of the Directive were imposed on the food producing, distributing and retailing industries. The nominal

---

[61] *Funke* v *France* (1993) 16 EHRR 297; Compare the judgment of ECJ in Case 374/87 *Orkem* v *Commission* [1989] ECR 3283, 3350.

beneficiaries of the Directive were to be consumers, but, arguably, the ultimate beneficiaries are the food producers for whom the harmonisation of food safety standards opens new markets in other Member States and the European Economic Area (EEA). The aims of the Directive appear to have had the support of the many actors having an economic or an administrative interest in the regulatory process.

(b) *The manner of regulation*

In common with other New Approach Directives, the food safety Directive laid down broad food health safety goals, monitored by inspection. The method chosen at national level to achieve those goals was a series of more specific food handling rules, monitored by inspection by Environmental Health Inspectors, with criminal prosecution as an ultimate sanction against offenders. The monitoring and enforcement structure is exactly the same as that used for domestically-originated food-health legislation.

(c) *Enforcement*

The first stage in the enforcement process is the periodic inspection by the environmental inspector. The adoption of a horizontal, or less prescriptive approach, in the Directive, to the manner of implementation, was broadly welcomed. Paradoxically, however, most of the actors in the implementation process expressed some regret, at the workshop convened to discuss the study, the failure of the Directive to define more clearly the nature of an "inspection". They knew what an inspection was. They were afraid that their Community partners did not. It is clear, from the study, that inspections of large producers is infrequent and of small producers rarer still, perhaps taking place only at five year intervals. One may, perhaps, doubt the deterrent effect of such inspections.

In the event of a breach, prosecutions are brought before the Magistrates' Court by the Environmental Health Inspectors. There was broad support by the food producers for the approach adopted by the by the Government in the Food Safety Act 1990 and a general welcome both for the availability of a "due diligence" defence to criminal proceedings and the abandonment of any attempt to introduce a food licensing system for food handlers. There appears to be a widely held view that, within the United Kingdom at least, there is a concurrence of interest between the regulators and the food industry. What is in the interest of General Foods Inc. is in the interest of the nation. There may be a few "rogues" in the industry, but they can be taken care of by the industry itself or by the local authority.

Doubts about this approach to implementation were largely articulated by the Institute of Environmental Health Officers (IEHO). On the content of the Directive, they expressed the view that "the ultimate aim of the Directive is the facilitation of free trade and not the protection of the consumer."[62] The doubts they expressed about effective inspections were largely based upon the constraints imposed on local authority budgets by central government restrictions on spending. The effect of these, even where additional monies had been provided by Central Government to implement the 1990 Act (usually not "earmarked" and often directed by local authorities into other budgets), was to limit the number of inspections for smaller food handlers to once every few years and to make the possibility of prosecution, in the event of breach of the Act and the Directive, remote indeed.

(d) *Alternative enforcement*

The effectiveness of a regulatory system can probably be best tested by examining some hypothetical examples. If one imagines a consumer concerned about the way in which certain local food processors are handling meat products, what should he or she do? They may draw the matter to the attention of the local authority (LA). The LA may send an Environmental Health Officer (EHO) to inspect, may ask for assurances from the businesses concerned or may simply respond by saying that it is satisfied that the processing methods of the operators meet the requirements of the Food Safety Act 1990. A complaint to the Ministry of Agriculture, Fisheries and Food, of inaction by the LA, is likely to be met with the response that the discretion in these cases is entirely a matter for the LA under the Codes of Practice. Constitutionally, one could say that this was entirely proper. A local authority which neglected its public health duties would have to account to its electors at the next local election. Realistically, one would have to recognise that this is unlikely to deter errant authorities. In the absence of a major food scare, local elections are not won and lost on food safety issues.

It is, in theory at least, possible for the Minister to use the default powers conferred on him by Section 42(1) of the Act and to order another food authority to discharge the functions of the failing authority. The default must affect "the general interests of consumers"[63] and the Act anticipates the holding of a public inquiry before action is taken. It is likely that in view of the upheaval and expense involved, action could, and would, only be taken in the case of an almost total failure by the food authority. In twenty-five years since this power first appeared in the Food and Drugs (Scotland) Act 1956 (Section 55), and then in the Food Act 1984 (Sections 113, 114), there appears to be no recorded cases of the use of the default power.[64]

If our concerned consumer has the resources or can obtain legal aid for a legal challenge, on what basis could this be done? The obvious avenue for a challenge to a LA exercising (or failing to exercise) statutory

---

[62] See Chapter 6, section 6.
[63] Section 42(1)(a).
[64] 16 *Current Law Statutes Annotated* 42–43.

powers is an application for judicial review. Assuming that our consumer is a council taxpayer he or she should have the necessary standing to mount such a challenge.[65] If the consumer is not a council taxpayer it is likely to fail at the outset. Although the consumer may be a beneficiary of Directive 89/397 that will not, apparently, give him or her the necessary standing. It was recently held in *Twyford Parish Council and Others* v *Secretary of State for Transport*[66] that beneficiaries of a directive (in that case Directive 85/337) which was sufficiently clear and precise (which it was) could not rely upon it to give them the necessary *locus standi* to complain of its non-implementation, where they had not themselves suffered damage from the decision of the Department. Even if the hurdle of standing can be overcome, only a total failure to take the Code into account reflected in, say, a policy decision by the appropriate LA Committee to initiate prosecutions or a complete refusal by the Minister to consider the exercise of his default powers under Section 42 is likely to prompt the grant of relief by the Court. The exercise of the discretion on whether or not to prosecute is generally unreviewable.[67]

The position would be somewhat different if an individual can point to a failure by a food processor as the cause of his or her own loss or injury. If the processor is prosecuted they may benefit from a compensation order under the Powers of Criminal Courts Act 1971. If the food authority declines to prosecute, even if there is evidence of a breach of the Directive and an offence under the Act, or the regulations, or both, made under it, the consumer may even, it would seem, initiate criminal proceedings him or herself. "The Act does not contain any limitation whatever on the common law right of any person to take proceedings if an offence has been committed, whether he is a person who is aggrieved or not."[68] That dictum, although delivered in relation to a precursor of the Food Safety Act 1990 (the Food and Drugs Act 1938) seems equally applicable to the 1990 Act. Since legal aid is unavailable for criminal prosecutions, the chances of one being launched by an aggrieved consumer, let alone a "concerned" individual, are remote indeed.

In the unlikely event of there being a contractual relationship between processor and consumer, the consumer may sue for breach of contract under Section 14 of the Sale of Goods Act 1979.[69] If there is no such relationship, there will be the difficult task of establishing negligence, unless the food can be categorised as a product to which strict liability may be applicable, or unless the presumption of negligence is raised by the circumstances under *res ipsa loquitur*.[70] The consumer is unlikely to

---

[65] *Prescott* v *Birmingham Corporation* [1955] Ch. 210.
[66] [1992] 1 CMLR 276, 288 (per McCullough J) and see Geddes "*Locus Standi* and EEC Environmental Measures" (1992) 4 J.Env.L., p 29.
[67] *R.* v *Metropolitan Police Commissioner ex p. Blackburn* [1968] 2 QB 118.
[68] Lord Goddard CJ in *Snodgrass* v *Topping* [1952] 116 JP 332.
[69] *Frost* v *Aylsbury Dairy Co.* [1905] 1 KB 608.
[70] *Colvilles Ltd* *Devices* [1969] 1 WLR 475, 479 (HL).

succeed on a claim based on breach of statutory duty, given the marked reluctance of English courts to recognise such a tort where a criminal prosecution is available.[71]

It is clear, therefore, that enforcement is likely to depend very much on the local food authority. Defaulting food processors who breach the Act and the Directive are likely to have little to fear from legal action by individual consumers.

(ii) **Health and safety at work**

(a) *Objects of regulation*

Some parallels to the development and enforcement of food safety law can be seen in the implementation of the Health and Safety Framework Directive 89/391 and the "daughter directives". The objects of regulation, in this case, are employers and the intended beneficiaries are their employees.

(b) *Manner of regulation*

Here there was also a well-established regulatory structure under the overall supervision of the Health and Safety Executive (HSE).[72] The Directives have been put into effect by regulations made under the Act, using the existing mechanisms of inspection, reinforced by criminal sanctions in proceedings brought in local magistrates' courts by the inspectorate.

(c) *Enforcement*

Failure to meet the appropriate safety standards laid down in the Directives gives rise to criminal liability. The HSE pressed the European Commission to take into account the traditional limitation qualifying United Kingdom statutory duties by an obligation of performance "so far as is reasonably practicable". In this case, however, they have had less success than food handlers in relation to their "due diligence defence".[73] Despite this, the United Kingdom Government has inserted "reasonably practicable" limitations into many of the implementing regulations, which are almost certainly unlawful in the light of the strict liability imposed by Community law.[74] The HSE apparently recognise that the United Kingdom Regulations do not go as far as the Directives require in relation to

---

[71] *Square* v *Model Dairy Co.* [1939] 2 KB 365; contra cases under Factories Acts and see Harlow, *Compensation and Government Torts* (1982), p 68.
[72] Health and Safety at Work Act 1974, s 18; see generally, Redgrave, Fife and Machine, *Health and Safety* (1993); Baldwin and Daintith, *Harmonization and Hazard* (1992).
[73] See DTI Report, *op. cit.*, n 4, para 18 and see above Chapter 6.
[74] See Redgrave, *op. cit.*, n 72, p lxii.

liability.[75] A consequence could be that the choice of criminal sanctions could make the implementation of the Directives less effective. Although a British court would be under a general obligation to construe implementing legislation (or even common law obligations in the same area) according to the terms of the Directive[76], this will not be the case in a criminal process.[77] Given that the consequences of a breach of an injunction are criminal liability[78], the difficulty could not be avoided by proceeding in a civil court.

(d) *Alternative enforcement*

Where the inspectorate has failed to prosecute, it would be open to an individual to attempt to challenge the decision in judicial review proceedings, but, failing a decision not even to consider prosecution, the court, in such proceedings, is likely to refuse to review the decision not to prosecute, even if that decision is based on shortage of resources.[79]

A private, civil action, based on breach of statutory duty could, however, succeed, because the *Kolpinghuis* exception (above, n 77) appears to be confined to criminal liability. Such an action, could, of course, only be brought by a person who had been, for example, injured by a failure to protect employees adequately from dangerous machinery.

(iii) **Toy safety**

(a) *The objects of regulation*

The Toy Safety Directive has been exhaustively considered in Chapter 9 by Stephen Weatherill. The objects of regulation in this case are the manufacturers, distributors, importers and retailers of toys. The direct beneficiaries of the Directive are, of course, toy purchasers but, as with food products, the toy industry benefits indirectly by acquiring access for its products to other markets in the European Economic Area through a system of harmonised standards.

(b) *The manner of regulation*

Primary responsibility for the safety of products rests with the Consumer Safety Unit of the Department of Trade and Industry. The Directive has been implemented by a statutory instrument made by the President of

---

[75] See Goddard, "European Law, New Origins for Health and Safety regulations" (1994) 11 J.P.I.L. 5, but compare scope, see DTI Report, *op. cit.*, n 4, which believes that the United Kingdom's 'add on' approach in relation to existing health and safety provisions has resulted in over-implementation.

[76] Case C-106/89 *Marleasing SA* [1990] ECR 1–4135; Case C-91/92 *Dori* v *Recreb, The Times*, 4 August 1994. See also Chapter 3, section 4(iii) (*Marleasing*) and Chapter 12, text at n 68 (*Dori*).

[77] *Office van Justitie* v *Kolpinghuis Nijmegen BV* [1989] 2 CMLR 18.

[78] Contempt of Court Act 1981, s 14(1).

[79] *R.* v *Commissioner of Police of the Metropolis ex p. Blackburn, op. cit.*, n 67.

the Board of Trade under powers conferred on him by the Consumer Protection Act 1987 and the European Communities Act 1972. The Department is responsible for the making of Safety Regulations, but it does not dictate enforcement policy.

(c) *Enforcement*

Decisions on general and specific enforcement of the Toy Safety Regulations are made by Trading Standards Officers, operating within the framework of local government. It is an offence to supply toys which do not satisfy the essential requirements or which do not bear the CE mark. Problems about the "effectiveness" of the criminal process in Community terms have been discussed by Weatherill, but it is clear that, as with food safety and safety at work, the availability of a "due diligence" defence, and the cost to local authorities of bringing proceedings, may actually deter effective action by them. As an alternative to the criminal process, individuals who have suffered injury or loss can take civil action on the basis of the breach of statutory duty created by the Consumer Protection Act 1987 in relation to a specific infringement of the Safety Regulation.[80] Such actions appear to be rare.[81]

(d) *Alternative means of enforcement*

The same problems that arise in relation to food safety and the role of the Environment Health Officer are almost exactly replicated in the area of toy safety.[82] Local Trading Standards Departments may have to make difficult decisions about relying on visits and warnings, or going for a magistrates' court prosecution, a risky and time-consuming process which may be met by a successful "due diligence" defence. The fact that the Regulations have a Community origin will not affect such decisions. It would certainly not seem to make a prosecution any more likely, even though prosecution may, in the last analysis be the only "effective" means of enforcement.[83] A group of, say, concerned parents, worried about the continuing sale of what they believe to be a dangerous toy, will be unlikely to be regarded as possessing the standing to apply for judicial review of the Trading Standards Department's failure to initiate seizure or prosecution. Nor would they be likely to succeed if they crossed that initial hurdle, given the generally unreviewable nature of such decisions. A private criminal prosecution would be a theoretical alternative, but such a group would be most unlikely to have the resources, or the expertise, to mount such a prosecution.

---

[80] But not in relation to the general safety requirement: Consumer Protection Act 1987, s 41.
[81] See Jones, *Textbook on Torts* (1993); Stapleton, *Product Liability* (1994).
[82] See above, section 3(i)(d).
[83] See Butt Philip *et al* in *Making European Policies Work* (Siedentopf and Ziller eds, 1988).

(iv) **Free movement rights**

(a) *Object of regulation*

Directive 90/364, the subject of the study in Chapter 7, is intended to confer free movement rights on all EU Citizens and their families not already enjoying free movement rights under the EC Treaty or under Community legislation. The objects of regulation in this case are not, as it might at first seem, the individuals affected by immigration control, but the governments and officials operating the immigration control process. It is the national barriers to free movement that the Community provisions seek to remove. Thus it is here the regulators at national level who are the objects of regulation. Paradoxically, they are also the primary actors in the process of regulation. The EU Citizens are the subjects of national immigration control, but they are also the beneficiaries of the Community legislation.

(b) *Manner of regulation*

Immigration control is seen by the United Kingdom government as part of the "irreducible minimum" of the governmental process. The detention of illegal immigrants may be undertaken, under contract, by private security firms, but the process of immigration control is, by statute, placed firmly in the hands of immigration officers and the Secretary of State.[84] All directives do, of course, bind governments and require them to take steps towards their implementation. But the free movement provisions require the United Kingdom government to legislate to create rights enforceable against the government itself, to administer immigration control in such a way as to ensure the delivery of those rights on a daily basis to the eight million or so beneficiaries who visit this country annually, and to provide an effective remedy against the administration if those rights are not delivered. The difficulty of using existing administrative structures under the Immigration Acts, which are intended to facilitate the wide discretion to allow or refuse entry and residence, and their inappropriateness to the implementation of directives which are intended to confer rights, as well as benefits, has been examined at some length in Chapter 7. Problems continue to exist even under the Order in Council adopted in July 1994 for the purpose of implementing all the current free movement directives (the EEA Order). It is sufficient to say here that all those who are subject to immigration control under the Immigration Acts (including all EU Citizens) continue to enter the United Kingdom at the discretion of an immigration officer. The only individuals who cannot be refused entry are British Citizens with a right of abode. Most significantly, there is no recognition in the EEA Order of the new European Union Citizenship, and the free movement rights of EU Citi-

---

[84] Section 4 of the Immigration Act 1971.

zens are not distinguished from those of Norway and Iceland under the EEA Agreement.

Under the new provisions there is no presumption of an entitlement to enter as an EU Citizen. Those refused entry have now an entitlement to appeal, but that must be exercised from abroad.[85] Forms used by the immigration service were designed for those without rights of entry and made no reference to any rights enjoyed by Community nationals. Such information is in English only. Attempts by the (now defunct) United Kingdom Immigrants' Advisory Service to provide such information "port side" to Community nationals and their families were not supported by the Immigration Service.[86] The story of free movement rights in the United Kingdom since our accession illustrates the dangers of using existing but inappropriate regulatory structures.

(c) *Enforcement*

In this system, the initiative for a challenge must come from the individual who may well not speak the language of the country and who will not be eligible to legal aid.[87] The first step in any challenge to either a refusal of admission or expulsion is an appeal to an adjudicator. Completion of this step will be impossible for the vast majority of beneficiaries of Community free movement rights without the help of a solicitor or advice worker. Expulsions are not infrequently effected by the Home Office in breach of Community rules giving workers and other categories of beneficiaries rights to public funds. Individuals simply received a letter telling them that they had claimed benefits to which they were not entitled and should immediately leave the country. They were not given any notification of the right of appeal which they enjoyed under Community law. Although this process has been publicly repudiated from time to time by the Immigration Service, it was still in use at the end of 1993. On each occasion that these instructions were drawn to the attention of the EC Group at the Home Office by the Joint Council for the Welfare of Immigrants, they were at once withdrawn. How many individuals have complied with such instructions and wrongly been deprived of their right of residence is unknown.[88] The EEA Order makes the *fact* of failing to qualify for one of the specific bases for residence (for example, by claiming Income Support) a ground, in itself, for removal.[89]

In these circumstances, enforcement at the suit of the individual affected is a far from satisfactory method of implementation. Even if individuals are made fully aware of their rights in a language which they readily

---

[85] Article 15(1).
[86] See above, Chapter 7.
[87] *Cf.* Widgery criteria relating to legal aid in the criminal process for those with an inadequate knowledge of English; Legal Aid Act 1988, s 22.
[88] See letter by D.Flynn, JCWI, to AIRE, 17 November 1993.
[89] Article 15(2)(a).

understood, they are unlikely to have the resources to mount an effective challenge themselves. The advice agencies are few enough in number and very poorly resourced, and immigration decisions are outside the jurisdiction of the Commission for Racial Equality, the only agency which might have a concern for their position. Success or failure in the realisation of a free movement right will, therefore, very much depend on fortuitous contact with an advice agency or a law centre and their willingness to support an appeal.

(d) *Alternative means of enforcement*

It is, theoretically, possible for an individual or an organization to challenge, by an application for judicial review, the way in which the immigration process is operated in relation to Community nationals. This might be desirable for an individual who has, for example, been excluded and does not wish to exercise the difficult and unsatisfactory process of challenging an appeal from abroad. That option is, unfortunately, excluded as a general rule of administrative law, until any existing appeal process is exhausted.[90] This means an appeal to an adjudicator, and thence to the Immigration Appeal Tribunal, a process that may take as long as two years.

In the case of individuals who are recommended for deportation by a court, there is no appeal within the immigration appeal process, but there is an appeal through the criminal appeal process, since the recommendation is considered as part of the sentence. The decision to implement the court's recommendation is taken by the Home Secretary, sometimes years after the court has considered the circumstances of the individual. There is no appeal against this subsequent decision, and the lack of an appeal at this stage has been held to breach Community law. This is a particular cause for concern, because there is evidence that English courts are at variance with each other and with Community law in the application of deportation criteria.[91] The EEA Order 1994 does nothing to remedy this deficiency.

United Kingdom agencies which might be thought to have a particular concern for proper enforcement, like the Commission for Racial Equality, or even the Equal Opportunities Commission, are by their originating statutes, prohibited from investigating or challenging immigration decisions.

---

[90] *R. v Secretary of State for the Home Department ex p. Swati* [1986] 1 WLR 4772.
[91] Case 137/79 *Santillo* [1980] ECR 1585; *Marchon* [1993] 1 CMLR 207; see Vincenzi, "Deportation in Disarray" [1994] *Crim. L. Rev.* 163.

(v) **The recognition of foreign qualifications**

(a) *Objects of regulation*

As part of the process of facilitating the free movement of those with professional qualifications in the Single Market, Directive 89/48 was approved to require host States to recognise qualifications obtained elsewhere in the Community. Only those who had a degree, obtained after a minimum period of three years study in higher education, and who had an additional period of practical experience to their credit were to be entitled to recognition. Individuals who wish to practice in another Member State could be subjected to either an aptitude test or to a period of supervised work experience in the host State. The objects of regulation are, in this case, the professional bodies and the beneficiaries are those enjoying Community rights who wish to practise the professions in the United Kingdom.

(b) *Manner of regulation*

In all except two of the Member States, this process is carried out by the Department of Education or by the relevant Government department. In the United Kingdom and the Republic of Ireland, however, the process of regulation of the recognised professions has been delegated to the professional bodies of those professions. The status of the professional bodies is a curious amalgam of public and private law. Members pay a fee and have a contractual relationship with them. At the same time, each enjoys official recognition as the sole body for regulating the entry, education, training and discipline of its members. Qualified members of the body enjoy an effective monopoly of professional practice. Powers are conferred by Parliament (or in some cases by Royal Charter) giving the professional bodies such powers as they need to exclude or expel, and to take disciplinary action against those who breach the rules of the profession. The absence of direct legal controls by Government reflects the somewhat uneasy relationship between the professions and the State, and is most acute between the Government and the professional associations of doctors and lawyers, where the professional bodies operate regulatory systems on a tightrope stretched between the market and the State, simultaneously seeking to protect themselves from competitive forces and, having allied themselves with the State in order to acquire some protection, in turn seek to keep the State at a distance.[92] Implementation of the Directive has been left to these bodies, under the general supervision of the Department of Trade and Industry. Professional bodies in the United Kingdom are obliged to recognise the qualifications of other Community

---

[92] *Cf.* Matthews, *The Evolution of Rules*, paper presented to the ESRC Single European Market Programme/COST A7 Action Conference, University of Exeter, 8–11 September 1994, and see Brazier *et al*, "Falling from a Tightrope: Doctors and Lawyers between the Market and the State" (1993) XLI Pol.Stud. 197.

professionals, to provide full reasons where this is not done, and to enable such decisions to be challenged before an independent appeal tribunal.[93] The initial stages appear to have gone well.[94]

(c) *Enforcement*

A failure to accept the qualifications of another Community professional could presumably be subject in the first instance to an appeal to the independent review body[95] and, subsequently, to judicial review, even though the body may be wholly private. Even a wholly private body regulating its members, but performing a public duty affecting the rights of citizens may be open to judicial review.[96] The negligent granting of approval causing loss or damage to an individual would, however, not be actionable[97] even though the regulation of professional practice is, at least in part, intended to protect the public from incompetent, dishonest or inadequately-trained professionals. This decision reflects the broader view of the lack of duty by regulatory bodies to the general beneficiaries of regulation, namely the consumers of the regulated service.[98]

The process here, is again, largely in the hands of individuals and will depend on their willingness to challenge decisions and to commence proceedings if the need arises. The procedures adopted in the United Kingdom appear to meet the requirements of the European Court of Justice as to effectiveness.[99] Anyone challenging a decision refusing acceptance of professional qualifications gained elsewhere in the Community had to be given the reasons for non-acceptance and to be able to bring legal proceedings to challenge the legality of the refusal.

(d) *Alternative means of challenge*

If the appropriate professional regulations are not in place, or no steps have been taken to ensure that the relevant professional body enables Community or EEA professionals to have access to employment, it would seem that a person denied access will have the right to bring proceedings against either the Government or the professional body for damages on the basis of the European Court of Justice's decision in *Francovich*.[100] Although the House of Lords suggested in the *Kirklees* decision that the onus of implementing legislation was cast by Article 5 of the Treaty on the State, a number of decisions of the Court indicate that the term is

---

[93] European Communities (Recognition of Professional Qualifications) regulations 1991, SI 1991/824.
[94] See Directive 89/48: *Article 11 Report by the United Kingdom Authorities*, July 1993.
[95] See *Europe Open for Professions: Guidance for Competent Authorities* (1989) p 3, para 8 and *Article 11 Report by the United Kingdom Authorities, ibid.*, para 4.
[96] *R. v Panel on Take-overs and Mergers ex p. Datafin* [1987] QB 815.
[97] *Wood v Law Society, The Times*, 30 July 1993.
[98] *Article 11 Report by the United Kingdom Authorities, op. cit.*, n 94, para 2.2.
[99] See Case 222/86 *UNECTEF v Heylens* [1987] ECR 4097; Case C-104/92 *Colegio Oficialde la Proprie-dad Inmobilaria v Aguirre Borrell and Others* (1992), *The Times*, 23 July 1992.
[100] See Chapter 3 above, section 4(iv).

broad enough to include any public body, and possibly, even, a private agency operating on behalf of the State.[101]

4 Enforcement by autonomous and quasi-autonomous public and private agencies: an alternative approach?

As we have seen, agencies of various kinds have a substantial involvement in the implementation of directives at an administrative level. Many also enjoy civil and criminal enforcement powers.[102] All of them exercise those powers, in some capacity or other, on behalf of the Government.

Community law does, of course, bind both Government and agencies. But who, at national level, ensures that Government itself meets the requirements of Community law in the implementation process?

Individuals, groups of individuals and various private bodies play a substantial role in that process, often despite the limitations of lack of standing or lack of means.[103] Some of these could be overcome by procedural changes. Recent British experience, does, however, indicate that an important and effective way of ensuring compliance with a new law that affects the country at all levels in both the public and private sectors, is to set up an agency dedicated to implementation of that law. Neither of the two most independent agencies that operate in this way, the Equal Opportunities Commission (EOC) or the Commission for Racial Equality (CRE), can be said to have been an unqualified success, but both have provided an effective focus for promoting racial and sexual equality.[104]

Sacks[105] recounts that, at a conference on the implementation of sex discrimination law attended by lawyers from all Member States, the United Kingdom and the Republic of Ireland were regarded as being in the forefront of implementation because of the very existence of such agencies. Proof of the importance of the EOC was deduced from the far larger number of cases which are heard in the United Kingdom, and which go on reference to the European Court of Justice.[106] The support given by the EOC to *Marshall* and the other retirement cases is widely seen as being responsible for the (relatively) prompt amendment made to the Sex Discrimination Act 1975 by the Sex Discrimination Act 1986. One could contrast the twenty years that it has taken to bring into effect amendments to immigration law, purporting to comply with the ECJ

---

[101] *Kirklees MBC* v *Wickes Building Supplies* [1992] 3 All ER 717, see Chapter 11 below, n 94 and accompanying text.
[102] See, for example, DSS, Customs and Excise etc.
[103] See above section 2.
[104] See Sacks, "The Equal Opportunities Commission – Ten Years On" (1986) 49 Mod. L. Rev. 560.
[105] *Ibid.* n 104, p 564.
[106] See Landau, *The Rights of Working Women in the European Community* (1985).

decision in *Van Duyn* v *The Home Office* (1974) through the Immigration (European Economic Area) Order 1994.

Both the CRE and the EOC have powers to assist individual litigants, to conduct investigations and to initiate proceedings against individuals and public or private bodies which continue to operate discriminatory policies, although both bodies want these powers to be strengthened.[107] Not only has the EOC assisted individuals, and initiated proceedings to ensure compliance with national law, it has also successfully challenged the compatibility of national legislation with the Equal Treatment Directive (76/207) and the refusal of the Government to amend it, and it has secured the recognition of the House of Lords that this is part of its function.[108]

5 A need for more prescriptive measures on enforcement from the Community

As Stephen Weatherill has said (above, Chapter 9), there is a continuing problem with the vagueness of the concept of "effectiveness". The Court has focused on the obligations of national judiciaries, but the need now is for some clarification of the role of national administrations in providing means of enforcement that secure the objectives set by Community provisions.

The Court has moved from a position under which remedies for the enforcement of Community measures are to be no less effective than equivalent measures for the enforcement of national law[109] to one in which national remedies must be objectively "effective", even if existing national remedies do not meet this standard.[110] National remedies may now have to be "as effective and rapid as possible"[111], or they may have to include "sufficiently effective and deterrent sanctions".[112] As we have seen, the concept of "effectiveness" may also include the right for those on whom a benefit is conferred to take the initiative in obtaining that benefit in the national courts. The method adopted for the implementation of a directive, should not have the effect of excluding that possibility.[113] It has been the position of the European Court of Justice since

---

[107] *Re* Reviews 1985 and 1991; *Equal Treatment for Men and Women: Strengthening the Acts* (1988).
[108] *R.* v *Secretary of State for Employment ex p. EOC and Another* (HL), see above, section 2(i).
[109] *Rewe* v *Hauptzollamt Kiel* [1981] ECR 1805, 1835.
[110] Case C-213/89 *R.* v *Secretary of State for Transport ex p. Factortame* [1991] 1 All ER 70; Usher, above, Chapter 4.
[111] Case C-87/94 *Commission* v *Belgium*, ECJ, 22 April 1994, unreported.
[112] Case C-382/92 *Commission* v *UK*, Opinion of AG Van Gerven, 1994, unreported.
[113] Case 29/84 *Commission* v *Germany, Re Nursing Directives* [1986] 3 CMLR 579; Case 222/86 *UNECTEF v. Heylens* [1987] ECR 4097.

1963[114] that "the vigilance of individuals to protect their rights amounts to an effective supervision, in addition to the supervision entrusted by Articles 169 and 170 to the diligence of the Commission and the Member States."[115] However, as the Commission recently declared in its Green Paper on consumer rights, "It is not realistic to provide for a right to bring proceedings when the holder of the right lacks the resources to do so."[116] One important way in which the lack of means or motivation of individuals to challenge decisions affecting their rights is by collective action or by representative action on their behalf.[117]

At both Community level and internationally there has been some recognition of the important role in which such non-governmental agencies can play in taking the initiative to ensure that the law is observed. In the Lugano Convention on Civil Liability for Activities Dangerous to the Environment, for example, there is a requirement that the acceding states recognise the right of "any organisation or foundation which according to its statutes aims at the protection of the environment [to]...request...the prohibition of a dangerous activity which is unlawful... In all cases provision shall be made for a right of review."[118]

Over the last decade some attempt has been made by the European Commission to include in draft directives a requirement that implementing measures open the way for enforcement by individuals and concerned organizations, where no individual would have a sufficient interest to bring proceedings in his own right under national law. Directive 84/50 on misleading advertisements, and Directive 93/13 on unfair terms in contracts, both require Member States to allow "persons or organizations *regarded under national law as having a legitimate interest in prohibiting misleading advertisements...*"[119] and to ensure that "...*persons or organizations having a legitimate interest under national law in protecting consumers* may take action before the courts." (emphasis added).[120] The recognition of which individuals and organizations have such a legitimate interest and other rules of admissibility of such proceedings is specifically left in the Lugano Convention, and in the directives, to the States concerned.

However, there are indications that the Commission is prepared to adopt a more prescriptive approach to national remedies. The directives on opening competition in relation to public works contracts contain

---

[114] *Van Gend en Loos* [1963] ECR 1. See also Chapter 12, text accompanying n 61.

[115] See Mancini, "Democracy and the European Court of Justice" (1994) 57 Mod. L. Rev. 175, who has described the *Van Gend en Loos* decision as "the unique judicial contribution to the making of Europe ... [taking] Community law out of the hands of politicians and bureaucrats ... to give it to the people." The development of the doctrine of direct effect has clearly been an expression of that position.

[116] *Access of Consumers to Justice*, COM(93)576 final, p 71.

[117] Hadley, "Group Personal Injury Litigation and Public Opinion" (1994) 14 Legal Stud. 70, 73.

[118] Article 18, paras 1(a) and 3; 21 July 1993 (Council of Europe) European Treaty Series 150.

[119] Directive 84/450, art 4(2) (OJ 1984 L250/17).

[120] Directive 93/13, art 7(2), emphasis added (OJ 1993 L95).

specific measures enabling unsuccessful bidders to a review of contractual procedures and a right to damages.[121] Problems about the enforcement of environmental provisions has led the Commission to support a greater role in the process for environmental groups. In a proposal for a Council Directive, the principle of subsidiarity is used to devolve the enforcement of environmental measures to environmental groups. The proposal is intended to ensure practicable access to the courts and to administrative complaints facilities for public interest groups in environmental matters. Such groups are to be defined by Community criteria, so that national rules on standing do not exclude them. An environmental association which considers an administrative act to be in breach of a rule of environmental law would be able to bring an action in the courts for the annulment of that act without having to show an impairment of its own interest.[122]

There are, nonetheless, as yet, no objective criteria established supranationally to determine what kind of "concerned" organization or individual will be able to initiate action. The European Court has recently shown itself reluctant to recognise the status of such organizations in relation to specific directives where the interest of that organization is not clearly recognized in the Directive.[123]

6 Conclusion

The position in the United Kingdom is, therefore, that, although the choice of regulatory structure may be significant in terms of the type of remedy used to secure implementation, the crucial factors in relation to the enforcement aspect of implementation will be either the availability of an independent and committed agency with the power, the will and the resources to take the necessary enforcement measures, or the existence of individuals, or groups of individuals, who are sufficiently resourced and who possess the necessary legal standing to pursue enforcement action themselves. It may well be that significant changes in behaviour on the part of those whose compliance is required by directives can be achieved by negotiation, and without litigation, but the existence of an effective national judicial liability system is an essential concomitant to any negotiated solution.

In that process, private initiative provides an important back-up to any state-sponsored system of enforcement, whether the burden of implemen-

---

[121] Directives 93/37, 93/38 and see Arrowsmith, *Civil Liability and Public Authorities* (1992), p 105.
[122] Article 4(1), Draft Proposal for a Council Directive Concerning Access to Justice in Environmental Matters: OKO Institute, November 1992.
[123] See Case C-236/92 *Comitato di Coordinamento per la Difesa della Cava and Others* v *Regione Lombardia*, (23 February 1994) (unreported); Directive 75/442 (disposal of urban waste).

tation of directives is cast on Departments of State, local government, quasi-autonomous or independent private agencies vested with public powers. The right for individuals to take enforcement action on their own initiative is undoubtedly a necessary but not a sufficient condition for effective implementation. The Court of Justice has recognised the rights of individuals to secure benefits conferred on them before national courts, although it cannot, of course, provide them with the remedies in national courts, or the financial means to enable them to have access to them. The difficult question, which the Community as a whole has yet to address, is whether the Member States are to be required to enable individuals to exercise their rights effectively, or groups to ensure that public and community interests are protected, by spelling out objective criteria for determining who shall have the right to initiate proceedings, what remedies are to be available, and what financial and other support should be provided to make access to those remedies a reality.

CHRISTOPHER VINCENZI

303

Chapter 11

A Question of Conflict: the Higher English Courts and the Implementation of European Community Law[1]

1 Introduction

The EC Treaties[2] originally envisaged responsibility for implementation as falling on the Member State governments who could then be brought to task before the European Court if they failed to properly implement a Community measure.[3]

This framework of Member State accountability in a body set up by international treaty seemed to operate within international law only and to create no specific rights for the people of the European Community who, in any event, did not have any direct democratic role to play in the legislative process as the members of the then Assembly were appointed by the Member States.[4] This original conception of the European Community was changed dramatically by the landmark case of *Van Gend en Loos* where the European Court held that the European Community constituted a new legal order and that its laws were capable of conferring rights on individuals which they could enforce in their own courts.[5] As a result of this decision, not only did individuals assume rights under EC law, but the national courts acquired the power to enforce those rights. Once national courts could enforce EC law, there was the potential for conflicts between national and EC law, especially where the Member State

---

[1] This Chapter arose out of a seminar given at the Institute of Advanced Legal Studies on 10 May 1993. I am grateful to the Institute for the support it provided while I was a visiting Fellow there and to Terry Daintith, Colin Scott, Sharon Turner and Daniel Wincott for their comments.
[2] This Chapter arises in the context of the European Union but deals exclusively with those aspects of the Union now known as the European Community, hereafter referred to as the EC.
[3] Article 169.
[4] Direct elections to the Assembly were first held in 1979 and it was renamed the European Parliament in Article 3(1) of the Single European Act. See generally, Weatherill & Beaumont, *EC Law* (1993), Chapter 4.
[5] Case 26/62 *Van Gend en Loos* [1963] ECR 1. The ability of EC law to confer rights on individuals directly enforceable in their national courts is known as the doctrine of direct effects.

had failed to implement EC rules. Thus two years later in the *Costa* case the European Court held that where there was conflict, EC law was to be given priority over national law.[6] Thus EC law was to be applied uniformly in all Member States and there could not be individual derogations which would lead to multiple variations on the law undermining its effectiveness.

Even by the time of the decision in *Costa*, only six years after the establishment of the EEC, it was becoming apparent that the Member States were failing to take all appropriate measures to ensure that they carried out their obligations under EC law.[7] In particular, non-tariff barriers to trade remained rife; directives were not being implemented and the legislative process itself was starting to stagnate, culminating in a retrenchment to unanimous voting in the Council of Ministers so all Member States had to agree to any legislation.[8] Even then, non-implementation was commonplace and the original dates for the completion of the common market ceased to have any significance.[9] The political disputes of the mid-sixties and recession in the seventies resulted in Member States resorting to protectionism. The political will that is an essential driving force for the Community simply waned, and with it, the implementation of the EC rules.

These problems of legislative stagnation and incomplete implementation of EC rules had highlighted the potential for a legitimacy crisis within the European Community. It was a new legal entity, with little or no democratic accountability and no precedent: it was the first attempt in history to unite Europe without coercion. Its raison d'être was the establishment of a common market – a primarily economic objective – and the original treaties did not expressly include any ethical values such as human rights, democracy, and protection of minority and religious rights.[10] The introduction of greater democracy in the Community would depend on agreement of the Member States, something that is still a major problem for the Community despite some reforms.[11] Thus it seemed that the European Court, as sole authoritative interpreter of EC

---

[6] Case 6/64 *Costa* v *ENEL* [1964] ECR 585. This rule of primacy is known as the doctrine of supremacy.

[7] See Article 5: "Member States shall take all appropriate measures, whether general or particular, to ensure fulfilment of the obligations arising out of this Treaty or resulting from action taken by the institutions of the Community. They shall facilitate the achievement of the Community's tasks. They shall abstain from any measure which could jeopardise the attainment of the objectives of this Treaty."

[8] Weiler, "The Transformation of Europe" (1991) 100 Yale L.J. 2403.

[9] Only the customs union was in place by the end of the transitional period. See Shaw, *European Community Law* (1993), 239, 259.

[10] Ward, "In Search of a European Identity" (1994) 57 Mod. L. Rev. 315 at p. 322, where he discusses Derrida's observation that there is as yet nothing to give the jurisprudence of the EC an ethical rather than an analytical or normative base.

[11] The democratic deficit has been the subject of much academic debate see, *e.g.* P.Pescatore, "Some Critical Remarks on the Single European Act" (1987) 24 *Comm. Mkt. L. Rev.* 9.

law[12] and by virtue of its position as a court, had to enhance its own position and with it, that of EC law to ensure legitimacy and hence to strengthen the integration of the European Community. This was the political vacuum in which the Court elaborated on the nature of the rights enjoyed by individuals under EC law and the obligations of national courts to implement those rights. The political process of the European Community was moving slowly, thus the Court turned to its brethren in the national courts to assist it in the process of integration. The national courts were obvious allies in upholding the rule of law. They enjoyed respect and were well entrenched in their own legal systems so they could also lend legitimacy to EC law. People were more likely to invoke EC law, if they could do so in national courts without any particular procedure being required. By accepting the jurisdiction of national courts to hear EC law issues, litigants also accepted the legitimacy of EC law. Thus national courts would act as a bridge between the Community and nationals of the Member States and as a result become instrumental in the integration of EC law into the domestic legal orders.

The combination of the direct effect of EC law for individuals and the supremacy of EC law created a new and powerful role for national courts that was a double-edged sword. On the one hand, the courts now had the power to enforce EC law and, according to the European Court, to disapply conflicting national rules. The dilemma for the English courts, as for other national courts, was how were they to exercise these new powers within their own constitutional frameworks. The question this Chapter addresses is how have the English courts responded to their duty to implement EC law. How have they reconciled their position under the United Kingdom constitution with their powers under Community jurisprudence?

2 Implementation of individual rights in national courts

The only provision of the Treaties that expressly acknowledges the enforcement role of the national courts is Article 177. That Article allows national courts to refer questions of EC law to the European Court for interpretation. This preliminary reference procedure involves a division of jurisdiction with the European Court interpreting the law and the national court applying it. The European Court has always emphasised

---

[12] See Article 164 of the EC Treaty "The Court of Justice shall ensure that in the interpretation and application of this Treaty the law is observed".

the cooperative nature of this procedure.[13] It has been facilitative of national courts, considering all but a very small number of the many references made to it each year.[14]

The judicial co-operation which is the core of this mechanism marks the relationship between national courts and the European Court and its importance goes beyond the boundaries of the preliminary reference procedure itself. Even as the European Court created the system of individual and directly effective rights it did not comment on the national laws under which these rights were to be exercised and enforced. In fact, up until recent years, it even refused to lay down common procedures for enforcement of EC law and has only recently modified its position.[15] Thus where there were tensions or inconsistencies in national law, it was for national courts to accommodate EC law primarily through reliance on the supremacy doctrine. This co-operation could best be seen in the ongoing debate on the implementation of directives. With Member State governments remiss in their implementation of directives, the European Court turned to national courts to fill the gap in the effectiveness of EC law. Thus when an individual sought to rely on a directive, the European Court consistently sought to ensure that government failure to implement would be minimised. Relying on Article 5, the Court indicated the nature of national court responsibilities under EC law. Thus in *Von Colson* it required national courts to interpret domestic law in a manner consistent with relevant directives, whether or not their time limits for implementation had expired.[16] In fact, in the *Marleasing* case the Court confirmed that not only did national courts have to interpret national law in light of antecedent EC law but also in light of subsequent EC law.[17] More recently in the *Francovich* case the Court again relied on Article 5 to increase the powers of national courts in relation to their maverick governments by allowing damages to be awarded against national governments where an individual has suffered loss due to the non-implemen-

---

[13] See, *e.g.* Case 16/65 *Firma Schwarze* [1965] ECR 877 at 886, where the Court noted that the preliminary reference procedure constitutes "a special field of judicial cooperation which requires the national courts and the Court of Justice, both keeping within their respective jurisdiction, and with the aim of ensuring that Community law is applied in a unified manner, to make direct and complementary contributions to the working out of a decision."

[14] The Court receives nearly 200 references each year, see Shaw, *op. cit.*, n 9 at p 148. It has only refused a handful of cases because they raised hypothetical questions or lacked a genuine dispute, see Kennedy, "First Steps Towards a European Certiorari?" (1993) 18 E. L. Rev. 121.

[15] See, *e.g.* C-208/90 *Emmott* v *Minister for Social Welfare* [1991] 3 CMLR 894, where the European Court held that time does not begin to run against a litigant seeking to rely on a Directive until that Directive has been transposed into national law.

[16] Case 14/83 *Von Colson* v *Land Nordrhein-Westfalen* [1984] ECR 1891. Particular reliance was placed on Article 5 by the European Court in that decision. This interpretive principle is broad and is only constrained by the principles of legal certainty and legitimate expectation, see Case 80/86 *Officier van Justitie* v *Kolpinghuis Nijmegen* [1989] 2 CMLR 18.

[17] Case C-106/89 *Marleasing SA* v *La Comercial Internacional de Alimentacion SA* [1990] ECR I-4135. In fact, even if there is no national legislation, it seems that national law must be interpreted in light of the Directive. See Steiner, *Textbook on EEC Law* 3rd ed. (1992), p 36. See also Chapter 3, section 4(iii).

tation of a directive.[18] For these rules of interpretation to have any impact in the enforcement of EC law, national courts have to accept the European Court's interpretation of their responsibilities under Article 5 thus their cooperation is vital.

To win the support of the national courts, the Court relies on its reputation[19], the acceptance of membership of the Community by the Member States and its own rhetoric to persuade national courts to co-operate.[20] Thus its members frequently invite national judges to Luxembourg and visit the judiciary and administrations of the Member States to discuss with them on an informal level the co-operative nature of the European Community enterprise. Members of the Court also write in learned journals and present papers at conferences thus furthering the academic debate on the Community and enhancing the stature of EC law in the process.[21]

The European Court also provides assistance by example through the operation of the Article 169 mechanism. Under this Article, Member States who have failed in their responsibilities under EC law can be brought before the Court by the Commission and have a judgment entered against them. This shows that national governments are not above EC law; that they accept the authority of the Court and of the rules it is applying, in particular the supremacy of EC law. If Member States can be held accountable for their actions before the European Court, this provides a powerful example of judicial review which national courts can follow.[22] The Court has also held that all Member States institutions are liable to be prosecuted under Article 169.[23] This means that the actions or omissions of the national courts themselves could also be subject to such proceedings before the Court. However, the importance of co-operation between the Court and national courts makes such coercive action by the Commission unlikely.

The system created by the European Court is organic.[24] The aim is to ensure the effectiveness of EC law through the creation of rights for individuals. The national courts have become instruments through which the effectiveness of EC law can be advanced. The Court did not set out to create a new court system: enforcement of EC law by the courts is

---

[18] Case C-6 & 9/90 *Francovich* v *Italian State* [1993] CMLR 66. For further discussion of this case see Section 4 below. See also Chapter 3, text at n 31 and section 4(iv).

[19] Members of the Court are appointed from candidates of who are eligible to hold the highest judicial offices in the Member States, see Article 167.

[20] Goodrich, *Reading The Law* (1986), Chapter 6.

[21] For a recent example, see Mancini & Keeling, "Democracy and the European Court of Justice" (1994) 57 Mod. L. Rev. 175, written while the first author was a judge at the Court.

[22] The is especially the case with the amendment of Article 171 by the Treaty on European Union so Member States can now be fined for their failure to comply an Article 169 judgment.

[23] See Case 77/69 *Commission* v *Belgium* [1970] ECR 237 where the Court held that delay in the legislature was no defence for failure to implement a law required under EC rules: the obligation to comply with EC law fell on the whole State and not just the executive.

[24] For further discussion see Maher, "National Courts as European Community Courts" (1994) 14 Legal Stud. 226.

simply a means to an end. As a result, and because of the limited support for national courts in the treaties, the powers that have been created for them come with onerous responsibilities that often conflict with their position in national law. The next two sections examine how the English courts have reacted to their European powers. First we shall look at how the English legal system lends itself to the incorporation of these new judicial powers before turning to examine the caselaw surrounding the implementation of directives and the provision of remedies for breach of EC law.

3 The European Community law challenge for the English courts

Because the doctrines of direct effect and supremacy were well established by the time the United Kingdom joined the Community, the legal system had advance warning of their new powers. The European Communities Act 1972 incorporated EC law into national law[25]; it required the judges to take judicial notice of EC law and to decide in accordance with it as a question of law what was the meaning and effect of EC law[26]; and stated that any statute is to be interpreted in light of EC law.[27] By requiring the English courts to take judicial notice of EC law, the Act in effect allowed for the incorporation of judicially created principles such as the doctrine of supremacy, as well as Community legislation into the domestic legal order.

The Rules of the Superior Courts were amended to allow for preliminary references to the European Court.[28] Although Lord Denning issued guide-lines in *Bulmer* v *Bollinger*[29] that seemed to discourage the use of the preliminary reference procedure, his views did not receive universal support although they did have a lasting influence leading initially to something of an independent mentality in relation to EC law in the English higher courts.[30] A more *communautaire* approach can be found in the judgment of Bingham J. in the *Samex* case where he acknowledged the expertise of the European Court, its unique position within the Community; its ability to deal with all language texts and its familiarity with

---

[25] Section 2(1). The Act extends to all the United Kingdom, *i.e.* Scotland and Northern Ireland as well a England and Wales. See further Chapter 4, section 2.
[26] Section 3(1).
[27] Section 2(4). This section has provoked considerable debate and will be discussed in greater detail below.
[28] See Collins, *European Community Law in the United Kingdom* 4th ed (1990), pp 200–207.
[29] [1974] Ch. 401.
[30] See for example the decision of Hoffman J. on the meaning of proportionality in *Stoke-on-Trent CC* v *B&Q* [1991] Ch. 48.

the teleological interpretation of EC law itself.[31] With Lord Denning retired from his position as head of the Court of Appeal and Sir Thomas Bingham MR now holding that post, the difference in approach can be seen as symptomatic of the incremental change of approach by the English judiciary as they have become more familiar with the culture and law of the European Community.

Despite early reticence, the English courts have referred to the European Court some cases important in the development of EC law. Two litigation campaigns in particular have led to EC law being discussed in the English courts. The Equal Opportunities Commission has been attempting to enforce the more liberal EC law on equal treatment for working women for several years, leading to the two *Marshall* cases being referred to the European Court.[32] The *Marshall* cases are important in the development of EC law because they deal with the extent to which an individual can rely on rights contained in a directive which the state has failed to implement. Having held that a state employee could rely on such a directive, in the second *Marshall* case it was confirmed that remedies available to an individual for breach of their rights under such a directive must be adequate. A different litigation strategy but one also predicated on EC law was that arising out of attempts to change the Sunday trading rules.[33] There, several references were made to the European Court, the English courts showing a reticence to apply the *acte clair* doctrine.[34] As a result of that litigation, a statute became law in July 1994[35] and the European Court expressly changed its former position on the application of the free movement of goods rules in relation to national marketing rules.[36]

---

[31] *Commissioners of Custom & Excise* v *Samex* [1983] 3 CMLR 194.

[32] In Case 152/84 *Marshall* v *Southampton & SW Hampshire Area Health Authority* [1986] ECR 723, (*Marshall* I) the European Court held that directives would enjoy vertical direct effect only, *i.e.* individuals could only enforce them against the State which had failed to implement them. In *Marshall* II, Case C-271/91 [1993] 4 All ER 586, it was held that victims of unequal treatment at work had to be adequately compensated hence the House of Lords held that statutory limitations on damages were too low, see note in [1994] 1 All ER 736.

[33] See Rawlings, "The Eurolaw Game: Some Deductions for a Saga" (1993) 20 J.L.S. 309.

[34] The EC law argument of the traders that the existing constraints on Sunday trading were contrary to EC rules on free movement of goods was not particularly cogent. Still, they persuaded *inter alia* a magistrate and later the House of Lords to refer the question to the European Court. See Case 145/88 *Torfaen BC* v *B&Q* [1990] 1 CMLR 337 and Case C-169/91 *Stoke-on-Trent CC* v *B&Q* [1993] 2 WLR 170.

[35] Sunday Trading Act 1994, coming into force 26 August 1994. The Act provides, *inter alia*, new rights for shop workers, preventing them from being dismissed or penalised for refusing to work on Sundays. See *anon.*, "Sometimes on Sunday" (1994) 9429 E.G. 112; Maher, "The New Sunday: Reregulating Sunday Trading" (1995) 58 Mod. L. Rev. 72–86.

[36] In Case C 267/91 *Keck*, 24 November 1993, (not yet reported), the Court reversed its previous position and held that national rules on selling arrangements did not fall within Article 30 provided the rules applied to all affected traders within the national territory and they affected in the same manner domestic and imported goods. See Chalmers, "Repackaging the Internal Market – The Ramifications of the *Keck* Judgment" (1994) 19 E. L. Rev. 385; Reich, "The 'November Revolution' of the European Court of Justice: *Keck*, *Meng* and *Audi* Revisited" (1994) 31 *Comm. Mkt. L. Rev.* 459.

The preliminary reference procedure has also been used by the House of Lords to protect its neutrality and impartiality. Because there is no single constitutional document on which the judges can rely to protect their position within the English legal system, they are reliant instead on their reputation, in particular their reputation of neutrality to safeguard their authority.[37] With the European Community a subject of keen political debate ever since the United Kingdom became a member, the courts have to be careful not to be seen as overtly political in their decisions. The Article 177 procedure facilitates the courts in that politically contentious issues can be referred to the European Court, thus deflecting criticism away from the English courts. This can be seen in both the *Factortame* litigation[38] and the Sunday trading cases[39], where "Europe" was blamed for the legal changes and confusion, with a lot of media attention on the decisions of the European Court.[40] The hands of the English courts thus appear tied because they are obliged to apply the authoritative ruling of the European Court. This also allows them to place themselves at one remove from contentious or problematic decisions.

One of the unique features of the English legal system is that it has no single written constitutional document. The absence of a written document, especially the absence of a Bill of Rights, means that the English courts have not had to grapple with the human rights questions that have dogged several other Member States.[41] The English courts have not queried the level of human rights protection at the Community level because there is no Bill of Rights that can be seen to conflict with any Community rule. The absence of a Bill of Rights and written constitution also means that the courts cannot point to a clear base for judicial review. As a result, judicial review has been of a limited nature in English law.[42] Although this is a rapidly developing area of the law, the traditional principle of supremacy of Parliament did not allow for much review of the legitimacy of statutes or executive decisions. Thus the courts had considerable difficulty initially in applying the doctrine of supremacy of EC law which necessarily involved holding a statute invalid. In addition to apply a direc-

---

[37] Cotterrell, *The Sociology of Law* 2nd ed (1992), p 229.
[38] *Factortame* v *Secretary of State for Transport* (No 1) [1990] 2 AC 85; (No 2) [1991] 1 AC 603. See Szyszczak, "European Community Law: New Remedies: New Directions?" (1992) 55 Mod. L. Rev. 690; Gravells, "Effective Protection of Community Law Rights: Temporary Disapplication of an Act of Parliament" [1991] *Publ. L.* 180. There is further discussion of this case in the next section.
[39] For a discussion of this litigation see Rawlings, *op. cit.*, n 33.
[40] See, *e.g.* the headline in *The Independent*, 20 June 1990: "EC Rewrites British Constitution".
[41] See, for example the German experience and the case of *Solange II* of 22 October 1986, 73 BVerfGE 339 discussed in Lanier, "*Solange*, Farewell: The Federal German Constitutional Court and the Recognition of the Court of Justice of the European Communities as Lawful Judge" (1988) 11 B.C.Int'l & Comp.L.Rev. 1. The Irish courts have also had difficulties reconciling their Bill of Rights with the supremacy of EC law see, generally, de Burca, "Fundamental Human Rights and the Reach of EC Law" (1993) 13 Oxford J.Legal Stud. 283.
[42] See generally, The Law Commission, *Administrative Law: Judicial Review and Statutory Appeals* (1994), Report No. 226.

tive which Parliament had failed to implement would blur the boundaries between the branches of government and undermine the supremacy of Parliament and its statutes. The courts had to develop a new attitude to undertake a review of legislation in order to give full effect to EC law. This has occurred only gradually, culminating in the *Equal Opportunities Commission (EOC)* case where the House of Lords held that a statute was inconsistent with EC law.[43]

Because the English courts do not have to negotiate between a written constitutional document constituting the national *grundnorm* and EC law, they have the advantage of a greater margin of flexibility than other national courts who are the guardians of their written constitutions and the rights contained therein.[44] As there can be no direct clash with a written constitution, the potential for a smooth acceptance of the hierarchy of EC law into the domestic legal order through the courts, exists. This potential is only being realised recently, especially and most importantly by the House of Lords. Thus the courts' acceptance of the supremacy of EC law has been incremental. This gradual development of the courts' position can be explained in part through the common law reliance on precedent which facilitates a gradual development of the law.[45] The law is developed through caselaw, with judges looking to earlier decisions for guidance and for the rules to be applied in the case before them. This sort of approach does not favour the adoption of radical change with its focus on former decisions but instead favours gradual incorporation of new rules, such as those of EC law.[46]

The requirement that national courts interpret national law in a manner consistent with EC law assumes a knowledge of Community rules on the part of the lawyers and judges in a case. If EC law is relevant in a case but is not raised by either party, then an individual is denied Community rights simply by virtue of omission and the effectiveness of EC law is undermined.[47] This situation can arise because many English judges do not have EC law as part of their intellectual heritage and have come to it rather late in their careers so its relevance would not necessarily be apparent to them. However, in the common law tradition it is for the judge to adjudicate and for counsel to present all relevant arguments. English judges do not have the support of *referendaires* therefore they are reliant on counsel to raise all relevant issues in a case, including EC law questions. Thus counsel have a vital role to play in discovering EC law

---

[43] *Equal Opportunities Commission* v *Secretary of State for Employment* [1994] 1 All ER 910. See Chapter 10, section 2(i)(a) and section 4 below.
[44] See Hoffman, "A Dog's Breakfast? The Supremacy of EC Law" (1991) 41 S.J. 1130.
[45] See the discussion of cases on the direct effect of directives in the next section.
[46] See generally, Goodrich, *Reading the Law* (1986), Chapter 5, for a discussion of the operation of precedent in the English courts.
[47] See Shaw, "United Kingdom Report" in *EEC Competition Rules in National Courts* (Behrens ed, 1992), p 79 *et seq.*

arguments and bringing them before the court.[48] At the moment, barristers, unlike judges, do not have any continuing education, and hence if EC law has not been part of their legal education they have little opportunity to engage with it. The culture in the legal professions is gradually changing with recommendations from the Council of Legal Education and the Bar Council to include EC law as part of the core training of both branches of the profession. The Lord Chancellor's Advisory Committee on Legal Education and Conduct has also proposed that law students should have an understanding of the fundamental principles of EC law; one of the central themes underlying their approach is that full recognition has to be given to the profound influence of European law on the English legal system.[49] Whatever approach to legal education is eventually adopted, it is clear that greater emphasis will be placed on EC law in the future leading to a necessary change in culture in the professions by increasing awareness of an EC Dimension to the law.

Links between the European Court and the English judicial and academic communities are also facilitated by the return of personnel from the Court to England. Lord Slynn, who was a former judge and Advocate General of the European Court, has moved to the House of Lords. Thus an eminent judge steeped in the jurisprudence of EC law is now a member of the highest English court. There is no doubt this will affect the development of EC law in the English courts by improving awareness of EC law.[50] Another recent phenomenon has been the return of *referendaires* from the Court to academic posts in England. The experience of these academics who are imbued with the culture of the Court is another factor which facilitates the embedding of EC law and culture into English law. All these developments indicate that familiarity with EC law will increase for practitioners and judges in future years, helping to integrate it further and making its appearance more commonplace in the courts.

4 The challenge of supremacy in the English courts

One of the key tenets of the English constitution is the sovereignty of Parliament[51] which means that Parliament has power to enact any meas-

---

[48] Of course, counsel may make a tactical decision not to raise EC law, because they do not want the delay and expense of an Article 177 reference.
[49] The Lord Chancellor's Advisory Committee on Legal Education and Conduct, Review of Legal Education Consultation Paper, June 1994 at pp 6, 12.
[50] The *EOC* case has been handed down since his move to the House. Lord Slynn is also a frequent speaker at conferences on EC law.
[51] Ridley, "Defining Constitutional Law in Britain" (1991) 20 Anglo-Am.L.R. 101. "The principle of Parliamentary sovereignty means neither more nor less than this, namely, that Parliament . . . has, under the English constitution, the right to make or unmake any law whatever, and, further, that no person or body is recognised by the law of England as having a right to override or set aside the legislation of Parliament." Dicey, *Introduction to the Study of the Law of the Constitution*, 10th ed (1959), pp 39–40. See also, Jennings, *The Law and the Constitution* 5th ed (1959), p 144.

ure it wishes and no Parliament can bind successive Parliaments.[52] Thus there is no real hierarchy of laws because no statute is beyond repeal. These principles apply just as much to the European Communities Act as they do to any other legislation. Theoretically, Parliament retains the power to repeal the statute.[53] On a pragmatic level, the political belief is that Britain cannot afford economically to be outside of the European Community therefore political and economic circumstances would have to be very different before Parliament would exercise its power to repeal the European Communities Act and with it its membership of the Communities.[54]

The question of the repeal of the statute may seem remote from the practicalities of the application of EC law by the English courts but the principles that surround the question of repeal are influential in the approach of the courts to EC law. They have developed their approach within the confines of the 1972 Act. Statutes are to be construed and have effect subject to EC law. This rule of construction originally was only invoked where there was ambiguity in the domestic law. This is essentially the standard rule of construction for international treaties – if the domestic law is ambiguous it is assumed that Parliament intended it to be in accordance with its obligations under international law.[55] In this sense, the rule applied to EC law seems entirely consistent with existing common law and constitutional principles and the sovereignty of Parliament remains intact. Thus in the *Garland* case the Sex Discrimination Act 1975 was construed in accordance with Article 119 so that the principles of equal pay for both sexes was held to extend to benefits that were given on retirement, in this case free travel for families of former British Rail employees.[56] The interpretation, although purposive did not require any undue straining of the ordinary meaning of the statute. In *Duke*, Mrs

---

[52] From the Scottish perspective, the position is not so clear-cut with differing views as to whether the principle applies there or not, see on the one hand *MacCormick* v *Lord Advocate* [1953] SC 261, where Lord President Cooper said "[t]he principle of the unlimited sovereignty of Parliament is a distinctly English principle which has no counterpart in Scottish constitutional law." This argument, based on the Act of Union 1707 which created the Parliament of Great Britain from the Scottish and English parliaments, is disputed elsewhere see, *e.g.* Wade & Bradley, *Constitutional and Administrative Law*, 10th ed (1986), p 84 *et seq.*; Mitchell, "British Law and British Membership" (1971) EurR. 97 at pp 100, 102, 108.

[53] The same power to repeal exists for the Italian parliament see the *Costa – ENEL* Judgment, 7 March 1964, Corte cost., Italy, 9 Giur.Cost. 129. However, in a later Judgment the Constitutional Court asserted the power to block acts of parliament so inconsistent with the EC system as to amount to an implied withdrawal from it. This clearly conflicts with its earlier view in *Costa*. See Cartabia, "The Italian Constitutional Court and the Relationship Between the Italian Legal System and the EC" (1990) 12 Mich.J.Int'l L. 173.

[54] MacCormick, "Beyond the Sovereign State" (1993) 56 Mod. L. Rev. 1 at p 3.

[55] See Diplock in *Salomon* v *Commissioners of Customs and Excise* [1967] 2 QB 116, 143–144.

[56] *Garland* v *British Rail Engineering Ltd* [1983] 2 AC 751. Retired male employees had the benefit of free travel for their families but retired female employees did not. The 1975 Act expressly excluded "provision in relation to death or retirement" from the equal pay rules. The House of Lords held that the benefit in issue was not a provision relating to retirement after the European Court had indicated that the equal pay principles extended to benefits.

Duke had to retire at 60 years while her male counterparts did not have to retire until 65 years. A Community Directive removed discrimination as to different retirement ages and was given effect in the Sex Discrimination Act 1986, which was not retrospective and hence did not apply to Mrs Duke who retired before the Act came into effect. She sought a purposive interpretation of the 1975 Act asking the courts to interpret it in light of the subsequent EC Directive.[57] The House of Lords refused, stating that Parliamentary intention had been to retain the discrimination the Directive sought to remove.[58] Lord Templeman went so far as to say that s. 2(4) of the European Communities Act only applied to directly applicable measures *i.e.* measures that did not require further incorporation into national law.[59] *Duke* was followed in the *Finnegan* case where the dispute concerned the same issue of discriminatory retirement ages.[60] Because the case arose in Northern Ireland the domestic provision in question was an order which had been passed after the European Court decision in *Marshall* which held discriminatory retirement ages to be contrary to EC law, but the House held that it was modelled on the 1975 Act and was to be interpreted in the same way as in *Duke*.[61]

A more dynamic approach to the implementation of directives is to be found in the *Pickstone* and *Lister* cases.[62] In the former, the House of Lords read certain words into regulations under the Equal Pay Act 1970 in order to achieve a result compatible with EC law. This departure from the usual approach of the courts still remains within the confines of the 1972 Act and the premise of Parliamentary sovereignty as it was clear from the history of the Act that Parliament intended to meet its obligations under Article 119 but the manifest words of the statute did not give effect to that intention. Therefore Parliamentary intention was preserved while compatibility with Community obligations was also achieved. This case was applied in *Lister* where regulations were again interpreted in a manner consistent with EC law. In fact, the *Von Colson* principle requiring

[57] Directive 76/207, (OJ 1976 L39/40).
[58] *Duke* v *GEC Reliance Ltd* [1988] AC 618. Noted by Foster, "The Effect of the European Communities Act 1972, s 2(4)" (1988) 51 Mod. L. Rev. 775. The Act had been amended to incorporate the European Court decision in Case 152/84, *Marshall* v *Southampton & South West Hampshire Area Health Authority (Teaching)* [1986] ECR 723, which held that sex discrimination at retirement age was contrary to Directive 76/207. The amendments were not retrospective and therefore did not extend to Mrs Duke.
[59] "Section 2(4) of the European Communities Act 1972 does not in my opinion enable a British court to distort the meaning of a British statute in order to enforce against an individual a Community Directive which has no direct effect between individuals. Section 2(4) applies and only applies where Community provisions are directly applicable." *Ibid.* at 639.
[60] *Finnegan* v *Clowney Youth Training Programme Ltd.* [1990] 2 AC 407.
[61] The private employers were acting in accordance with domestic legislation and it has been suggested that the House was concerned with the fairness of expecting them to comply with the oblique terms of a directive. See Steiner, *op. cit.*, n 17, p 35.
[62] *Pickstone* v *Freeman plc* [1989] AC 67; *Lister* v *Forth Dry Dock and Engineering Co Ltd* [1990] 1 AC 546.

national courts to interpret national law in a manner consistent with relevant EC directives was also cited while *Duke* was not mentioned.

These cases all preserve Parliamentary intention and thus are prepared to give effect to the words and objectives of directives only to the extent that a statute is ambiguous either on its face or in light of its legislative history. Although *Lister* and *Pickstone* do mark a development in judicial reasoning it still seems to fall short of the general obligations imposed by the European Court in the *Von Colson* line of cases.[63] The approach taken in *Doughty* also reflects a narrow perception of obligations under EC law.[64] There, the Court of Appeal in deciding that the privatised company, Rolls Royce was not a part of the State under the *Foster* test[65], did not mention *Marleasing* and therefore did not address the scope of the obligation to interpret national law wherever possible in accordance with EC law.[66] The limitation laid down in *Duke* to only construe legislation in light of directly effective EC law was cited with approval by the Court of Appeal in the *Webb* case.[67] In the House of Lords Lord Keith repeated the rule and then cited *Marleasing* immediately afterwards.[68] This would imply that he did not see any inconsistency between the position in *Duke* and the requirements on the House under *Marleasing* even though it seems clear that the *Marleasing* principle will require the English courts to move away from *Duke* and its adherence to parliamentary intention in relation to legislation adopted prior to a directive.[69] The courts will now have to construe domestic law as far as possible to comply with the relevant EC directive. The boundaries of possibility are not limited by the requirements of national law, as had been the case prior to *Marleasing*. Where the boundaries are is not clear though it seems unlikely that the European Court would require national courts to do violence to the language of a national statute.[70]

---

[63] See the earlier discussion of *Von Colson*, above text at n 16 and following.

[64] *Doughty* v *Rolls Royce plc* [1992] IRLR 126.

[65] *Foster* v *British Gas plc* [1991] 2 All ER 705 HL; [1990] 3 All ER 897 European Court, where the ECJ held that an entity was a public body if it was made responsible, pursuant to a measure adopted by the State for providing a public service; the service provided was at the material time under the control of the State; and it possessed or claimed to exercise any special powers.

[66] The public/private distinction is problematic but *Marleasing* is a key decision and even if a discussion of it would not have led to different outcome it still warranted the attention of the court. See Chapter 3, section 4(iii).

[67] *Webb* v *Emo Air Cargo Ltd* [1992] 2 All ER 33.

[68] [1992] 4 All ER 929 at 939, "The UK courts construe domestic legislation in any field covered by a Community Directive so as to accord with the interpretation of a directive as laid down by the European Court of Justice, if that can be done without distorting the meaning of the domestic legislation: [*Duke* cited]. This is so whether the domestic legislation came after or, as in this case, preceded the Directive [cites *Marleasing*]."

[69] See Mead, "The Obligation to Apply European Law: Is Duke Dead?" (1991) 16 E. L. Rev. 490 and McCaffrey, "Parliamentary Sovereignty and the Primacy of European Law: A Matter of Construction." (1991) 42 N.Ire.Legal Q. 109 at p 122.

[70] Curtin, "The Decentralised Enforcement of Community Law Rights: Judicial Snakes and Ladders" in *Constitutional Adjudication in European Community and National Law*, (Curtin & O'Keeffe eds., 1992), p 40.

The limitation of a purposive interpretation by the English courts to cases of ambiguity seems inconsistent with the *Marleasing* decision and the effectiveness of EC law.[71] The English courts have extended the scope of their purposive interpretation to ambiguity either on the face of the statute or in its Parliamentary history, but in order to interpret national law in light of a directive even where there is no ambiguity, a clear indication that this is intended seems to be required by the courts – hence the reference made to the European Court in Webb.[72] This cautious approach by the courts – where they look for specific guidance from the European Court that indeed their obligations under the Treaties do require them to give effect to EC rights at the expense of Parliamentary sovereignty, is reflected in the area of remedies also.[73]

In order for Community law to be effective, not only must it be applied in the face of inconsistent national law, but individual litigants must be given adequate remedies if their Community rights are infringed.[74] Damages are an important remedy and the English courts have held that they can be awarded for breach of EC law. However, in the two main cases to discuss the question of damages the courts operated under considerable procedural and jurisdictional constraints which undermined the effectiveness of the remedy available. In *Garden Cottage Foods*[75] the plaintiff no longer received butter as a result of rationalisation of the bulk butter distribution system by the Milk Marketing Board, the major producer of bulk butter in the UK. The plaintiff argued there was an abuse of a dominant position in breach of EC competition rules and sought an injunction. An injunction would only be awarded if damages were not an adequate remedy so the court first had to decide if damages could be

---

[71] For a discussion of the implications of *Marleasing* for the English courts see G. de Burca, "Giving Effect to European Community Directives" (1992) 55 Mod. L. Rev. 215, 227–233. The decisions of the House of Lords on the operation of the European Communities Act 1972 are probably binding in the Scottish courts because the statute is common to both jurisdictions. See *Inland Revenue* v *Glasgow Police Athletic Association* 1953 SC(HL) 13.

[72] Case C-32/93 *Webb* v *EMO Air Cargo Ltd.* [1994] 4 All ER 115 where the ECJ held that it would be unlawful discrimination to dismiss a woman who realised she was pregnant shortly after she was appointed to cover the maternity leave of another employee.

[73] This cautious approach can be compared with the enthusiastic reception of EC law by the Irish higher courts which reached its zenith in *Campus Oil* v *Minister for Industry & Energy* [1984] 1 CMLR 465 where the Supreme Court held that the decision to refer to the European Court by a lower court could not be subject to appeal. This enthusiasm has been dampened in recent years by the perceived threat of EC law to fundamental rights or national identity, see *Crotty* v *An Taoiseach* [1987] IR 713; G. Hogan, "The Supreme Court and the Single European Act", (1987) IJ 55; M. Reid, *The Impact of Community Law on the Irish Constitution*, Irish Centre for European Law, Dublin 1990 at 70–79; J. Temple Lang, "The Irish Court Case Which Delayed the Single European Act: *Crotty* v *An Taoiseach*", (1987) CMLRev 709.

[74] The European Court provided general principles on the provision of remedies: (1) the remedy provided cannot be less favourable than that available for a similar domestic action, nor can it be discriminatory; (2) the remedy cannot make it impossible in practice to exercise the right to relief see Case 45/76 *Comet* v *Produktschap voor Siergewassen* [1976] ECR 2034.

[75] *Garden Cottage Foods* v *Milk Marketing Board* [1984] AC 130. See, generally, Ward, "Government Liability in the United Kingdom for Breach of Individual Rights in European Community Law." (1990) 19 Anglo-Am.L.Rev. 1.

awarded for breach of the directly effective EC competition rules. The House of Lords held that damages could be awarded. Because directly effective EC rules were incorporated into English law via the 1972 Act, a breach of those rules was a breach of that Act. Thus any person suffering loss as a result of such a breach could claim damages under the tort of breach of statutory duty. The remedy was a common law one based on the 1972 Act.[76] The reliance on the 1972 Act and the tort of breach of statutory duty raised problems in the *Bourgoin* case where damages were also sought and technical problems of how to categorise the action brought arose again.[77] There, French turkey producers were seeking damages from the Ministry of Agriculture, Fisheries and Food for loss suffered as a result of an illegal government ban on importation.[78] The majority of the court held that the right in issue was the right to have the law administered and enforced fairly. This was a public right enforceable by judicial review only.[79] The tort of breach of statutory duty was not relevant. However, all the judges agreed that a private action for damages would be available under the tort of misfeasance in public office where there was an abuse of power.[80] To succeed, the plaintiffs would have to show the Minister knew he was acting contrary to his Treaty obligations and that his actions could affect the plaintiffs. It was not necessary to prove malice.[81] This decision does undermine the effectiveness of EC law for a party who only enjoys a public law right and must proceed by judicial review. There may be a time lag between breach of the right and issue of an injunction or declaration by the court. These factors coupled with absence of a remedy in damages may render EC law less effective.[82]

Subsequent decisions of the House of Lords indicate a major change in the application of EC law by the English higher courts both in relation to the availability of remedies for breach of EC law and the review of statutes in light of EC directives. In *Factortame*, the House of Lords

---

[76] For a discussion of this tort see, generally, Arrowsmith, *Civil Liability and Public Authorities* (1992), Chapter 7.

[77] *Bourgoin SA* v *Ministry of Agriculture, Fisheries and Food* [1986] 1 QB 716. Damages have never actually been awarded by an English court. *Bourgoin* was settled out of court and in *Garden Cottage Foods* the issue was whether damages was an adequate remedy so that an injunction would not be granted. For a discussion of the question of remedies see, generally, Steiner, "How to Make the Action Suit the Case" (1987) 12 E. L. Rev. 102.

[78] Case 40/82 *Commission* v *United Kingdom* [1982] ECR 2793.

[79] Where damages are rarely available, see Wade & Bradley, *op. cit.*, n 52, p 666 & Chapter 36.

[80] For a discussion of this tort see Arrowsmith, *op. cit.*, n 76, pp 226–234.

[81] It is not clear whether or not the same outcome would have been reached if the case had arisen in Scotland. The supervisory jurisdiction of the Scottish courts in matters of judicial review has traditionally been wider than in the English courts. See Lord Clyde, "The Nature of the Supervisory Jurisdiction and the Public/Private Distinction in Scots Administrative Law" in *Edinburgh Essays in Public Law* (Finnie, Himsworth & Walker, eds., 1991). The point is moot now in light of the decision in *Francovich*, see *Kirklees MBC* v *Wickes Building Supplies* [1992] 3 All ER 717, 734–735.

[82] For a discussion of an alternative basis for damages in light of the need for efficacy of EC law see Hoskins, "*Garden Cottage* Revisited: The Availability of Damages in the National Courts for Breaches of the EEC Competition Rules" (1992) 6 E.C.L.R. 257.

awarded an interim injunction against the Crown thus providing a remedy for breach of a Community right that did not exist previously in domestic law. The applicants were Spanish fishermen who did not comply with the conditions for obtaining fishing licences contained in the Merchant Shipping Act 1988. They sought an interim injunction to suspend the operation of the Act on the basis that it was contrary to EC law.[83] Without interim relief, the applicants would not have been able to fish and would be very quickly forced out of businesses. An Article 177 reference was made at first instance and an interim injunction was granted.[84] On appeal, the injunction was lifted because the Court of Appeal held it did not have jurisdiction to temporarily suspend the operation of any statute. The House of Lords, whilst agreeing jurisdiction did not exist, referred to the European Court the question whether it should uphold EC law against the statute even though it had yet to be established categorically that there was a conflict between them. The European Court held that on the basis of the supremacy doctrine, EC law had to be upheld and the interim injunction should be granted.[85]

The European Court had previously indicated that national courts were not required to devise new remedies to give effect to EC law.[86] However, this is exactly what the House had to do in *Factortame* as it was clear that there was no jurisdiction under English law to temporarily suspend the operation of an Act. Deference to the rules of the national courts had to give way to the needs of uniformity and supremacy. The fact the House had sent the reference shows that it was, in the spirit of co-operation under Article 177, looking for the guidance of the European Court in a clear case of conflict between a constitutional rule and an EC law.[87] By referring to the European Court, the House also received a categorical direction as to its duties under the Treaty which made it straightforward for it to modify the constitutional rules that they had previously being operating under, *i.e.* that no Act of Parliament could be suspended because Parliament is sovereign. The issue generated a lot of controversy at the time with the bulk of criticism directed at the European Court rather than the House of Lords – indicating the usefulness of the preliminary reference procedure in deflecting criticism from the courts when they move away from their traditional constitutional position to a new perspective required by their Community role.

In the *Francovich* decision, the European Court changed its previous

---

[83] The Act has since been found to be in breach of EC law see Case C-279/89, *Commission* v *UK* [1993] CMLR 564.

[84] [1989] 2 CMLR 353.

[85] See the judgment of the European Court in Case C-213/89 *R.* v *Secretary of State for Transport, ex parte Factortame* [1990] WLR 819 at paras 20–22.

[86] Case 158/80 *Rewe* v *Hauptzollamt Kiel* [1981] ECR 1805.

[87] It has been argued that the House did not need to make a reference as *acte clair* could have applied, see McCaffrey, "Parliamentary Sovereignty and the Primacy of European Law: A Matter of Construction." (1991) 42 N.Ire.Legal Q. 109.

position of providing general guide-lines only in relation to remedies.[88] There the Court held that an individual could claim damages from the State for its failure to implement a Directive provided three conditions were met: the result laid down by the Directive must involve rights conferred on individuals; the content of those rights must be identifiable by reference to the provisions of the Directive itself; a causal link must be shown between the failure of the Member State to carry out its obligations and the damage suffered by the individual.[89]

The combined impact of these two cases on the enforcement of EC law in the English courts is considerable. Not only has the decision in *Factortame* been extended to purely domestic law cases[90] but the parties in the *Factortame* litigation are now claiming damages from the state.[91] *Francovich* may also have made the *Bourgoin* case redundant with Lord Goff in the *Kirklees* case casting doubt on its continued validity.[92] There, the House of Lords decided that local authorities did not have to give undertakings in damages when seeking an injunction under the Shops Act 1950. The plaintiff argued that the Act was contrary to EC law. Lord Goff indicated that if the rules were held to be contrary then the plaintiff could seek relief directly from central government under *Francovich*.

Most importantly, the House of Lords recently decided in the *Equal Opportunities Commission* case to overcome considerable procedural difficulties and to disapply an English statute because it was in conflict with EC law.[93] There, the EOC sought to challenge a letter of the Secretary of State for Employment where he declined to accept that the English law on part time workers was in breach of EC law even though most part time workers are women and English law treats part-time workers less favourably than full time workers.[94] The House of Lords held that the EOC had sufficient *locus standi* to bring the action and that even though

---

[88] Case C-6 & 9/90 *Francovich* v *Italian State* [1993] CMLR 66. Maitland-Walker, "A Step Closer to a Definitive Ruling on a Right in Damages for Breach of the EC Competition Rules" (1992) 1 E.C.L.R. 3. In Case C-143/88 & C-92/89 *Zuckerfabrik Suderdithmaschen* [1991] ECR I-415 the European Court provided further specific directions as to the nature of remedies for breach of EC law by holding that a national administrative measure based on an EC Regulation could be suspended by a national court where it had serious doubts as to the validity of the Regulation. See the discussion in Chapter 3, section 4(v) (*Zuckerfabrik*), section 4(iv) (*Francovich*), and Chapter 4, text accompanying n 13.

[89] The right does not have to be directly effective.

[90] See *M.* v *Home Office* [1993] 3 All ER 537.

[91] See *R.* v *Secretary of State for Transport, ex parte Factortame*, QB CO/1735/88, Transcript M.Walsh Cherer (*Lexis*). At the moment there seems to be no satisfactory procedure in place for the award of damages under *Francovich*. The Law Commission in its *Report on Administrative Law* was of the view that differences between judicial review procedure in domestic English and EC cases need to be justified. See 1994 Law Comm. 226 at 9.

[92] *Kirklees MBC* v *Wickes Building Supplies* [1992] 3 All ER 717, 734–735. The fact that the plaintiff's argument on Article 30 was unlikely to succeed following the Article 177 reference pending at the time in *Stoke-on-Trent* v *B&Q* [1993] 2 All ER 297 had some impact on the outcome of the case see Lord Goff at 732.

[93] *Equal Opportunities Commission* v *Secretary of State for Employment* [1994] 1 All ER 910.

[94] The statute in question was the Employment Protection (Consolidation) Act 1978.

the letter in issue did not constitute a decision, the EOC could bring judicial review of the statute itself.[95] Lord Keith pointed to *Factortame* where it had never been suggested that the fishermen could not bring judicial review of the statute in light of EC law. The procedural argument that the House did not have jurisdiction to declare that the United Kingdom was in breach of its obligations under EC law was also rejected on the basis that the House did have jurisdiction to declare that the Act in question was incompatible with EC law. Only the European Court could declare the United Kingdom to be in breach of its Community obligations but that did not preclude an action for judicial review to have a statute declared incompatible with EC law.

In this case we see the House of Lords building on its experience in the *Factortame* litigation and openly engaging in the review of a statute in light of EC law. It was willing to hold English law incompatible with EC law without recourse to the Article 177 reference procedure and without looking to see if the statutory language was ambiguous either on its face or in light of its Parliamentary history. Thus the House seems to have departed from the earlier practice of seeking to reconcile Parliamentary sovereignty with the supremacy of EC law. It overcame potential procedural and jurisdictional problems to hold national law incompatible with EC law, thus opting for the supremacy of EC law. This augurs well for the future implementation of EC law in the English higher courts and opens the way for the interpretation of English law in a manner consistent with EC law.

5 Conclusion

On accession to the European Community, the English courts acquired the power to apply EC law and to give effect to the rights conferred on individuals by EC law. Coupled with this power was the authority to disapply national law which conflicted with EC law. It was this authority which created particular difficulties for the English courts as they sought to resolve conflicts between the two systems of law while at the same time retaining the fundamental principle of Parliamentary sovereignty which denied them all but the most limited powers of judicial review and required them to give effect to Parliamentary intention.

Initially, the courts only disapplied national law which conflicted with EC law where there was an ambiguity in the statute. In short, EC law was not seen as supreme as the courts continued to give priority to Parliamentary intention. This was due in part to the characteristics of the court system: EC law was not part of the intellectual heritage of the judges or

---

[95] Lord Jauncey disagreed on the question of *locus standi*.

lawyers; used to using precedent, the courts were unaccustomed to applying a new system of rules for which there were few English precedents; there was little experience of judicial review of statutes. In addition, the absence of a written constitutional base for the role of the courts within the legal system and the highly politicised nature of EC law, meant that the courts were careful to preserve their neutrality and slow to acknowledge the controversial doctrine of the supremacy of EC law.

At the same time as these characteristics seemed to restrain the English courts in their implementation of EC law, other features of the legal system seemed to facilitate the gradual acceptance of its supremacy. The absence of a written constitution did leave the courts with greater flexibility; in particular, the lack of a Bill of Rights removed a controversial area of conflict from the English arena. The use of precedent, while a limiting factor in the early stages of membership, also allows for gradual change which firmly embeds EC law into the English legal system. The House of Lords was willing to use the preliminary reference procedure in order to ensure constitutional changes were necessary under EC law. This is best illustrated by the *Factortame* litigation which marks a watershed in the implementation of EC law in the English courts with the House of Lords suspending a statute for the first time and in practical terms, giving full effect to the supremacy doctrine. In the subsequent *EOC* case the House went further by declaring a statute to be incompatible with EC law, thus removing EC law from the shadow of Parliamentary sovereignty and acknowledging its supremacy within the legal system.

The consequences of these two cases is likely to be far reaching with implementation of EC law in the higher courts being less constrained by constitutional conflicts in the future. Procedural difficulties remain, similar to those seen in the *Bourgoin* and *Garden Cottage Foods* cases, particularly if the courts continue to see EC law through the filter of the 1972 Act. The responsibilities that come with the power to implement EC law continue to require national courts to develop creative responses within the confines of their constitutional traditions in order to give effect to EC law. This is what the English higher courts have been doing, albeit gradually. The traditional constitutional principle of Parliamentary sovereignty has been seriously dented and as a result, the supremacy of EC law within the English system seems closer to becoming an accepted doctrine of both the English and Community legal systems.

IMELDA MAHER

Chapter 12
Implementation as a Constitutional Issue

1 Market and constitution in the European Union

(i) Negative and positive law – a framework for analysis

The process of integration through law is rapidly creating a European market, although the speed of the process and the shape of the market varies sector by sector. The anticipated basic pattern for a European market offers to traders the opportunity to build marketing campaigns for the most economically rational territory, irrespective of the constraint of national frontiers. This restructuring may involve increased production combined with enlarged distribution networks. It may involve a policy of merger and acquisition. Whichever method, or methods, for gearing up to a border-free market are preferred, the expectation is that the wider market will be more competitive and will permit the realisation of beneficial economies of scale. Consumers should become passive beneficiaries of this process of developing market integration, as their home market for available products and services becomes more competitive. In a more active sense, consumers are enabled themselves to cross borders to shop wherever most suits them and to return home uninhibited by import restrictions.

The basic legal framework for the replacement of the pre-existing European pattern of market fragmentation along national lines by an integrated market is the set of rules contained in the EC Treaty. The ground rules for economic integration are the law governing the four freedoms, the free movement of goods, persons, services and capital, combined with rules which establish common Community policies in the areas of, for example, competition and agriculture. The pattern of EC trade law is built on both "negative law", whereby national rules which obstruct cross-border trade are subjected to the demands of Community market integration, and "positive law", whereby the regulation of the market is conducted through common Community rules.

The application of negative law provisions such as Articles 30, 48 and 59 of the EC Treaty, governing the free movement of goods, persons and services respectively, undermines the pursuit of traditional functions performed at national level. The result is the deregulation of the national market as part of its absorption into the wider integrated European market. In this sense both market deregulation and market integration flow from the elimination of national measures which obstruct cross-border trade.

For example, national product safety laws require justification in so far as they impede cross-border trade. Likewise, national laws protecting the economic interests of consumers require justification where they act as an impediment to the construction of a Community-wide marketing strategy. A string of well-known cases reflect the role of the European Court in making a choice when the consumer interest in the wider availability of products and services in an integrated market is pitted against the consumer interest in maintaining legal protection at national level. On the one hand there are cases where integration is found to prevail over national protection and where national measures are accordingly incompatible with Community law. This yields a market that is both deregulated and integrated. For goods, the "classic" application of Article 30 to eliminate national technical standards which impede cross-border trade is found in the European Court's pathbreaking ruling in *Rewe Zentrale* v *Bundesmonopolverwaltung – 'Cassis de Dijon'*.[1] The application of Article 30 in this case reshaped the German market for the relevant liqueurs towards openness to import penetration by goods conforming to regulatory traditions different from those required under German law. Consumer choice was thereby enhanced.[2]

On the other hand, there are the cases (fewer in the Court's jurisprudence) where the consumer interest is deemed to be served more by national protection than by market integration and where national measures are ruled lawful. For example, in *Aragonesa de Publicidad Exterior SA (APESA)* v *Departamento de Sanidad y Seguridad Social de la Generalitat de Cataluna* (DSSC)[3] the Court accepted that restrictions on advertising of strong alcoholic beverages were capable of being held compatible with Article 30 where they formed part of a public health strategy. Such a ruling leaves the market regulated by national law and, in European terms, fragmented.

The application of negative Community trade law achieves integration and deregulation in some circumstances, but in others negative law alone does not suffice. Where the national measure survives the application of negative Community trade law, the restrictive effect of the national rule can be removed only through Community legislative activity, which puts in place common Community rules dealing with the interest in question that justified national measures. The development of positive Community

---

[1] Case 120/78 [1979] ECR 649. For a discussion of the *Cassis de Dijon* case, see Chapter 2, section 5(i).

[2] *Cf.* in the services sector, Case C-76/90 *Säger* v *Dennemeyer* [1991] ECR I-4221.

[3] Cases C-1, C-176/90 [1991] ECR I-4151.

rules serves to integrate the market through (re)regulation at European level.

Harmonisation of laws is based upon the creation of a Community-wide body of law. In some areas Community legislative activity has set up regulatory institutions at the European level. The Commission has had conferred upon it a range of functions in connection with the management of common policies. In budgetary terms the most notable example lies in the field of agriculture. Competition policy in the Community has been handled for over thirty years by the Commission, although national competence to apply competition laws is not excluded in so far as it does not frustrate the realisation of the objectives of Community policy.[4] Harmonisation of laws frequently involves Commission management, for example through the operation of safeguard clauses. Latterly there has been an increase in the creation of separate sector-specific European agencies, for example in the fields of trade marks and medicine evaluation. However, in the main, the implementation of Community rules at national level lies within the province of national bodies. Community law is digested into the national system and must be applied through national methods. This serves partially to conceal the fact that the origin of such laws lies outside the individual Member State, an intransparency that has both strengths and weaknesses.[5] On this model, a national body becomes an arm of the Community. This is the core of the notion of "indirect rule" to which reference is made in the title of this book.

In this sense, the creation of the European Market is to be achieved both by removing Member State restrictions on integrated cross-border economic activity (negative law), but also by establishing certain regulatory measures at transnational level (positive law). This does not by any means imply the necessary creation of a "European State". The construction of a European Market founded on a combination of negative and positive law is not dependent on, nor even necessarily particularly closely connected with, sophisticated notions of European State-building. However, the growth of such a market out of the pre-existing European patchwork, supported by legal rules, implies a necessary diminution in the independent regulatory capacity of national authorities, a necessary increase in rule-making at transnational level and, in consequence, a central role for national authorities in the implementation of the rules that are designed to establish a market unshackled from the constraints of political borders.

(ii) **Deregulation and Re-regulation**

Some sectors where (some) Member States chose in the past to regulate their markets have undergone transformation into sectors with a deregu-

---

[4] On the practical application of this principle, see Whish, *Competition Law* (1993) pp 37–43.
[5] *Cf.* Chapter 1.

lated, integrated European market. Other sectors have become integrated only because of the establishment of European regulation (of some kind). Under the influence of negative and positive law, markets are altering and so too are patterns of regulation.

Community law of integration causes an abolition of some public functions, not simply their redistribution. Customs controls and customs duties are the most visible example of this disappearing trick. In those instances, abolition is the logical consequence of economic integration. The shift from national to European market is marked by the development of common controls at the external frontiers of the Community and an abandonment of internal frontiers. Internally, that has been achieved relatively painlessly in relation to goods, but remains highly problematic in relation to persons. States remain more concerned to maintain control over persons crossing borders than goods. In relation to internal frontiers, there is therefore some ambiguity about precisely what is meant here by the European Market. With regard to external frontiers, the complex nature of the process that is underway in Europe is reflected in the post-Maastricht lack of clarity in the respective roles of the Member States acting alone, the EC and the Member States acting through the new 'intergovernmental' pillars of the Treaty on European Union.[6] It is instructive to appreciate the complexity that continues to surround the issue of abolishing border controls, which one would suppose to be fundamental to the process of creating an internal market. If there are still ambiguities on that basic point, how much more problematic might one expect more hidden consequences of integration to prove?

Environmental policy, social policy, product safety and fundamental rights are all fertile fields for examination from the perspective of the rise of the cross-border Market, the consequent decline of national regulatory competence and the ill-shaped development of a State at European level. Where national initiatives are conclusively invalidated under Community law or, at least, inhibited by that risk of invalidation, it may prove controversial whether Community rules should be devised as replacement regulation. There are many differing visions of precisely how the Community should respond to the process of market integration and the incursion of Community law into ever wider fields of activity. For States with deregulatory preferences, the removal of national measures may be seen as entirely desirable and sufficient. Negative law will be welcomed; positive law depicted as undue meddling with the market mechanism. Other States may prefer the Community to adopt a more interventionist approach and will push for reregulation. This perspective depicts negative

---

[6] Justice and Home Affairs: see Müller-Graff, "The Legal Bases of the Third Pillar and its Position in the Framework of the Union Treaty" (1994) 31 *Comm. Mkt. L. Rev.* 493; D'Oliveira, "Expanding External and Shrinking Internal Borders" in *Legal Issues of the Maastricht Treaty* (O'Keeffe and Twomey eds, 1994). On Common Foreign and Security Policy, see Cremona, "The Common Foreign and Security Policy of the European Union and the External Relations Powers of the European Community" in O'Keeffe and Twomey, *ibid.*

law as part of a process which can be complete only with a commitment to positive law. Some would go yet further and argue that the creation of a European Market brings with it a need for even more regulation than is required within a single State. For example, one might need laws which deal with the social implications of creating a larger area within which wealth may be maximised but within which distributional inequality is deepened. Such perceptions underlie the Treaty provisions on Economic and Social Cohesion which are strengthened by the Treaty on European Union.[7] One might argue that there is a need for European Industrial Policy to cope with the challenge of the global market. Industrial Policy now occupies a separate title in the post-Maastricht Treaty on European Union[8], although it has attracted criticism for an alleged risk that it will lead to restrictions imposed on the competitive market.[9]

The identification of the proper scope of Community common policy raises the core question of the extent to which the Market, adjusting through the loosening of State impediments to trade, should be managed by transnational regulation which affects private market freedoms. These are problems which were largely hidden in 1958 when the Treaty of Rome came into force, but they expand in scope as the Community assumes an ever broader, multi-dimensional role in the reshaping of not just the Community and the Union, but also the wider Europe through its influence in the European Economic Area and in the establishment of Association Agreements with countries in Eastern Europe.

The debate has been intensified by pressure from the United Kingdom, in particular, in the direction of downplaying the extent to which disparities between national regulations require the development of common Community rules emphasising, instead, the maintenance of "competition" between national regulatory regimes unconfined by Community rules.[10] It is argued that firms should be able to choose between national regulators and locate wherever best suits them as a base for supplying the wider market. Common Community rules, it is argued, damage such competition, reduce the choice of firms, consumers of regulation, and render the Community market inflexible. The counter-argument insists on the need for a common framework of law within a common market. The equalisation of competitive conditions on which the construction of an economically integrated territory is perceived to depend is shattered by such market-led competition between regulators. On this view, a common European market requires a bedrock of common legal rules which

---

[7] Articles 130a–130e of the EC Treaty.
[8] Article 130 of the EC Treaty.
[9] See especially Steindorff, "Quo Vadis Europa?" in Forschungsinstitut für Wirtschaftsverfassung und Wettbewerb (ed), *Weiterentwicklung der Europäischen Gemeinschaften und der Marktwirtschaft* (1992). Steindorff's essay scrutinises the new and expanded competences conferred on the EC by the Maastricht Treaty.
[10] For a powerful analysis of this issue, see Reich, "Competition Between Legal Orders: A New Paradigm of EC Law?" (1992) 29 *Comm. Mkt. L. Rev.* 861.

is broader and deeper than the United Kingdom would regard as appropriate.[11]

(iii) Resolution under the Community's constitutional charter

There is an uneven pattern to the process of deregulation at national level and reregulation at Community level. What is notably lacking in the modern Community is a consensus on when and how these choices shall be made. The European Court plays its part in determining how deeply it will intrude on national competence through its interpretation of the scope of negative law.[12] However, in determining the scope of Community common policy making, one engages in arguments of an economic and political flavour that lie at the very heart of the current debate about the future of the Union. A wealth of economic analysis is devoted to the costs and benefits of regulating markets. Political perceptions of the role of the State in the Market, and in society more generally, are at stake. The search for an Economic Constitution for the Community, popular in Germany especially, arouses a fierce debate about what regulatory activity should be permissible beyond the free (in the sense of opened to cross-border competition) market.[13] From the legal perspective, the question of how and where the Community will act then becomes a constitutional question. At present, the question has to be addressed on several levels. It is a disturbingly opaque enquiry.

In the celebrated words of Eric Stein, the Court has construed the Treaties "in a constitutional mode rather than employing the traditional international law methodology".[14] In *Les Verts* v *Parliament*[15] the Court described the Treaty as a "basic constitutional charter". The European Court proclaimed in Opinion 1/91 that the Treaty was "the constitutional charter of a Community based on the rule of law".[16]

This was far from empty rhetoric. In *Les Verts* the Court held admissible an application for annulment contrary to the apparently more limited wording of the Treaty. In Opinion 1/91, the Court decided that the draft

---

[11] Social policy has been an especially high-profile focus for this debate. See section 1(iv) below.
[12] Section 1(i) above.
[13] For a valuable recent overview of the issues, see Joerges, "European Economic Law, the Nation-State and the Maastricht Treaty" in *Europe after Maastricht* (Dehousse ed 1994).
[14] Stein, "Lawyers, Judges and the Making of a Transnational Constitution" (1981) 75 Amer.J.Int'l.L. 1. *Cf.* on the Court's activism Weiler, "The Community System: the Dual Character of Supranationalism" (1981) 1 Y.E.L. 267 and "The Transformation of Europe" (1991) 100 Yale L.J. 2403; Lenaerts, "Constitutionalism and the Many Faces of Federalism" (1990) 38 A.J.C.L. 205 and "Some Thoughts about the Interaction between Judges and Politicians in the European Community" (1992) 12 Y.E.L. 1; Mancini, "The Making of a Constitution for Europe" (1989) 26 *Comm. Mkt. L. Rev.* 595. Attempting to marry legal and political science traditions, Burley and Mattli, "Europe before the Court: A Political Theory of Legal Integration" (1993) 47 Int'l Organiz. 41.
[15] Case 294/83 [1986] ECR 1339.
[16] [1991] ECR I-6084, [1992] 1 CMLR 245.

Agreement on a European Economic Area was liable to violate the integrity of the EC legal order. This forced renegotiation of the Agreement. A revised Draft was approved by the European Court in April 1992.[17] The Court acts to extend and to defend the EC Constitution. The Treaty on European Union claims that the Union "shall be founded on the European Communities".[18] Therefore one might assume that the constitutional charter now extends throughout the scope of action of the European Union and that the Court will be able to paint on a bigger canvas.

However, the constitutional charter supplies a severely limited basis for resolving the key issues of integration, deregulation and reregulation. It is fair to conclude that many such problems commonly arise in any entity based on a divided power structure, but it is far from common to find a framework for their resolution that is as imprecise as that prevailing in the European Community. The next sub-section picks out four elements that contribute to the obscurity.

(iv) Community constitutional conundrums

(a) *Is the Community competent to act?*

The European Community enjoys no general competence, but rather the specific competences or enumerated powers conferred on it by its constitutive Treaties. Its scope for achieving regulation of the market is confined by the need to identify an appropriate provision in the Treaty. Much of the history of the Community is characterised by a gradual expansion in competence.[19] Provisions such as Article 100[20], and especially Article 235[21], are in practical terms sufficiently broad to provide the Community with competence to act in a broad range of fields. Both provisions require an unanimous vote in Council, which in political terms meant that the Community's competence was confined only by the need to secure agreement among Member States that an act was desirable. As a consequence of the broad view taken of the Community's law-making powers, Community legislative activity has bitten into wide areas of activity.

In combination with legislative practice that took a broad view of Com-

---

[17] Opinion 1/92 [1992] ECR I-282, [1992] 2 CMLR 217.
[18] Article A.
[19] For an extended account, see Weiler, "The Transformation of Europe", *op. cit.*, n 14, p 2403.
[20] Article 100 states: "The Council shall, acting unanimously on a proposal from the Commission and after consulting the European Parliament and the Economic and Social Committee, issue directives for the approximation of such laws, regulations or administrative provisions of the Member States as directly affect the establishment or functioning of the common market."
[21] Article 235 states: "If action by the Community should prove necessary to attain, in the course of the operation of the common market, one of the objectives of the Community and this Treaty has not provided the necessary powers, the Council shall, acting unanimously on a proposal from the Commission and after consulting the European Parliament, take appropriate measures."

munity competence, the European Court too was responsible for confirming and supporting an extended approach. For example, whereas Environmental Policy formed an explicit part of the Treaty only from 1987, on the entry into force of the Single European Act, the European Court in *ADBHU*[22] had already declared that environmental protection is "one of the Community's essential objectives". This was in many respects merely a confirmation of existing legislative practice based on Articles 100 and 235.[23]

In Opinion 1/91 on the draft Agreement on the European Economic Area, the Court continued in terms which plainly updated observations made thirty years previously. In Opinion 1/91, it referred to the States having "limited their sovereign rights, in ever wider fields".[24] In 1963 the Court referred in *Van Gend en Loos*[25] to States joining the Community having limited their powers "albeit in limited fields".

Questions of Community competence to act are increasingly sensitive. It seems likely that much more debate will, in future, centre on competence. This sharper awareness may be traced to 1987 and the increased opportunity for qualified majority voting in Council introduced by the Single European Act, especially in Article 100a. It is also plain in the structure of the Maastricht Treaty that the concern to confine Community competence has shaped parts of the Treaty and left it, for some observers, a "Europe of bits and pieces"[26] and, at the very least a hybrid structure which is very probably unstable and will require a thorough review at the intergovernmental conference planned for 1996.[27] The three-pillar structure of the Treaty may be taken as evidence of the Member States' concern to keep the Community at bay. The Treaty on European Union adds two new "pillars" of European Co-operation. These are in the areas of a Common Foreign and Security Policy and Co-operation in the Fields of Justice and Home Affairs. The Treaty envisages that the Member States shall co-operate in these areas and seek solutions in common. However, in these two new areas the developed pattern of the EC does not apply. For example, the Commission does not hold the sole right of initiative. According to the Treaty on European Union, the Court is an EC Court, not an EU Court.[28] This limited status jeopardises the capacity of the Court to stride beyond the EC pillar and to "constitutionalise" the whole Union Treaty.[29] The two new intergovernmental pillars

---

[22] Case 240/83 [1985] ECR 531.

[23] Usher in *Current Issues in European and International Law* (Smythe and White eds, 1990), Chapter 1.

[24] Note 17 above.

[25] Case 26/62 [1963] ECR 1.

[26] A very astute account is provided by Curtin, "The Constitutional Structure of the Union: a Europe of Bits and Pieces" (1993) 30 *Comm. Mkt. L. Rev.* 17.

[27] Looking forward, Harmsen, "A European Union of Variable Geometry: Problems and Perspectives" (1994) 45 North.Ireland L.Q. 109.

[28] Article L.

[29] *Cf.* Section 1(iii) above.

seem to be carefully designed to generate traditional international law, not EC law.

Problems lie ahead in defining the demarcation between these pillars.[30] For example, internal movement of people has connections to the EC pillar and the Justice and Home Affairs pillar. More fundamentally, the three-pillar structure adds a further layer to the discussion of the uneven development of Market and State in Europe. Negative EC law has implications for State competence to control the movement of persons. Positive action at transnational level may follow, but such action may occur within the EC or within the non-EC part of the EU. Questions of competence differ; so too the form of any positive action; and so too the prospects for transparency of decision-making. How can the Citizens of the European Union, a status that exists under the EC pillar[31], effectively exercise rights in the environment of intergovernmental co-operation in Justice and Home Affairs? Both the European Court and Parliament lack formal jurisdiction outside the EC pillar. National systems offer limited protection, because control has been shifted to the European level.[32]

The Maastricht Treaty also testifies to the determination of individual Member States to keep the Community at bay. The United Kingdom's stance on Social Policy provides the most vivid example. The United Kingdom was, and remains, vehemently opposed to enhanced Community policy making in the social policy field. It views such laws as unjustifiable interference with the operation of the market. It knew itself to be in a minority among the Member States and was therefore aware that, to yield to an extension in Community competence would lead in practice to further legislation, at least under bases permitting qualified majority voting in Council. In the Maastricht negotiations, it was unable to win the political argument against enhanced Community competence and therefore it chose to negotiate a settlement which allowed it, in effect, to "opt-out" of any deeper policy making in that field. The United Kingdom was not able to achieve a Community-wide "competition between regulators", but it was able to obtain a pattern allowing future competition between it and the bloc of eleven in the areas in which laws will be made under the Treaty's Social Policy Protocol-plus-Agreement.[33] For some, a "highly corrosive dynamic" is at work here[34]; it speaks of a Community too heterogenous to support a common framework and points towards a future of variable geometry. The unanswered questions revolve around the question whether such developments in the Community can be regarded as

---

[30] *Cf.* note 6 above.
[31] Articles 8–8e of the EC Treaty.
[32] Chapter 7 offers detailed material on the free movement of persons.
[33] Laws on Works Councils and on Paternity Leave seem likely to form the first two instances.
[34] Harmsen, *op. cit.*, n 27, p 129.

creative evolution or destructive fragmentation.[35] Such issues become ever more acute as the Community pursues the path of enlargement.

Here is not the place to explore in depth the extent to which these grey areas of competence may become the subject of judicial scrutiny. It seems probable that the European Court will find itself forced to identify the limits of its own jurisdiction in cases at the margins of the EC "pillar".[36] Within the pillar it may find itself asked to decide on the scope of and validity of the "1 v 11" Social Policy structure, which hardly seems compatible with a common legal order and the undistorted competition in the internal market to which reference is made in Article 3(f) of the EC Treaty.[37] More broadly, it remains to be seen whether the Court will accept confinement of its jurisdiction to the EC pillar alone.[38] A meek acceptance that the two new intergovernmental pillars spawn traditional international law, not EC law, would not accord with the Court's past expansionist tendencies.

The present climate of regular intergovernmental conferences may provide a reason for judicial caution. The Court's past activism was in part inspired by the perception that if it did not breathe life into the Community's legal order, no other body would. This is no longer the case. The Treaty revision effected by the Single European Act was followed by the Treaty on European Union, and 1996 is established as the next date for an intergovernmental conference at which Treaty revision will be at stake.[39] Another factor in the Court's attitude may prove to be the response of national courts. It has received warning that the German *Bundesverfassungsgericht*, at least, has a heightened sensitivity towards the outer margins of Community competence. In its October 1993 ruling that German ratification of the Maastricht Treaty was permitted[40], that country's highest constitutional court warned that future Treaty revision in the guise of interpretation would not bind Germany.[41] It is far from clear how readily revision may be separated from the technique of

---

[35] *Cf.* Weatherill, "Beyond Preemption? Shared Competence and Constitutional Change in the European Community" in *Legal Issues of the Maastricht Treaty* (O'Keeffe & Twomey eds, Wiley Chancery 1994).

[36] *Cf.* Case C-120/94R *Commission v Greece*, Judgment of 29 June 1994 (Macedonia).

[37] *Cf.* Shaw, "Twin Track Social Europe – the Inside Track" and Szyszczak, "Social Policy: a Happy Ending or a Reworking of the Fairy Tale?" in O'Keeffe and Twomey *op. cit.*, n 35; Whiteford, "Social Policy after Maastricht" (1993) 18 E. L. Rev. 202.

[38] Strongly of the view that the Court is so confined, Eaton (Deputy Legal Adviser in the Foreign and Commonwealth Office), "Common Foreign and Security Policy" in O'Keeffe & Twomey eds. *op. cit.*, n 35. Contrast the critical account of the "the charade of constitutional obscurity which is EU." and speculation, *inter alia*, about whether the Court will/should acquiesce in its jurisdictional confinement, by Allott, Written Evidence to the *House of Lords Scrutiny of the Intergovernmental Pillars of the European Union* (1992–93) HL 124.

[39] Article N(2) of the Treaty of European Union.

[40] English translation at [1994] 1 CMLR 57.

[41] The pattern of United Kingdom law, especially European Communities Act 1972, s 3(1), explained in Chapter 4, seems to preclude explicit adoption of such an approach by the United Kingdom Judiciary.

interpretation.[42] However, the Community legal order, and the pattern of "indirect rule" generally, is dependent on active and willing co-operation between Community and national bodies. It is therefore probable that the European Court, which has long been astute to the need to carry national courts with it[43], will take account of the flavour of such reservations about its activism when faced with controversial cases at the margin of the EC constitutional order.[44]

These are murky waters. If the Court perceives that the Member States are bent on damaging the constitutional order nurtured in Luxembourg for over thirty years, then tendencies towards judicial caution may be rapidly jettisoned. This is certainly the strong message delivered by the Court in its rejection of the first draft of the Agreement on a European Economic Area.[45] It goes to the very heart of the nature of the Community whether the Treaty is simply Treaty (and therefore the malleable creature of the States party to it) or now Constitution (and therefore subject to protection by its Court against unconstitutional intervention by, *inter alia*, States, perhaps even at the suit of private individuals as holders of constitutional rights).[46] Such issues could make the 1996 intergovernmental conference, and its aftermath, extremely lively.[47]

(b) *The legal base for Community legislation*

A further problematic constitutional feature of the Community lies in its legislative procedure. There is no single procedure. There are several, involving different inputs from the Parliament and different voting rules in Council.[48] Different procedures attach to different areas of competence. It is often difficult to identify rational reasons for the variety. However the Court has been forced to make choices between, for example, the internal market base, Article 100a, which allows the Council to adopt measures for the approximation of laws by a qualified majority for the purpose of establishing the internal market, and the environmental policy base, Article 130s, where legislation establishing Community-wide environmental standards has been made. Such laws may equalise competitive conditions while simultaneously developing an environmental policy

---

[42] *Cf.* the suggestion of Judge Joliet that where the Court refines its own jurisprudence in respect of matters not "laid down" in the Treaty it cannot be taken to be engaged in a process of revision: (1994) 19 E. L. Rev. 243, 254. This seems rather disingenuous.

[43] *Cf.* Weiler, "Journey to an Unknown Destination: a Retrospective and Prospective of the European Court of Justice in the Arena of Political Integration" (1993) 31 J.C.M.S. 417.

[44] *Cf.* Micklitz, Roethe and Weatherill, *Federalism and Responsibility: a Study on Product Safety Law and Practice in the EC* (1994), pp 25–28. The ruling in Case C-91/92 *Dori* v *Recreb* (below, Section 1(iv)(f), n 68) may provide an early manifestation of caution. Beyond specifically legal issues, *cf* Chapter 3 on the much more general phenomenon of non-compliance with EC law at national level as a strategy for dissatisfied States.

[45] Note 16 above.

[46] For brief discussion in this direction, see Bieber, "Les limites matérielles et formelles à la révision des traités établissant la communauté européenne" (1993) Rev.Marché Com.343.

[47] "Interesting days ahead" – the concluding sentence of Weiler, *op. cit.*, n 43.

[48] Weatherill and Beaumont, *EC Law* (1993), Chapter 5.

for the Community, but disparity between legal procedures has forced a choice between the two different bases.[49]

For the present purposes it is important to realise that where there is disagreement over the desirability of Community regulatory activity in a field in which it is competent, the question of whether the Community acts may be critically dependent on choice of legal base. If the dissenting States are too few to prevent adoption by qualified majority, they can forestall regulation only by showing that the measure is properly adopted under a base requiring a unanimous vote. Litigation has been pursued before the European Court on this very point.[50] The shape of the Market is dictated by the constitutional question of voting rules under competing legal bases.

Awareness of the precariousness of the single State in a minority was analysed above as stimulating sharper concern about the outer margins of Community competence. Within the sphere of Community competence the same concern manifested itself in the fierce negotiations at Ioannina, Greece, in March 1994, about the number of votes that will be required for a blocking minority under the qualified majority voting rules once the Community is enlarged. Plainly, any increase in the numbers required for a blocking minority would weaken a State's capacity to forestall action with which it disagreed. The United Kingdom sought to hold the blocking minority at 23 votes. The United Kingdom failed. 27 votes will be required to block.[51]

(c) *Does the subsidiarity principle have a role to play?*

The subsidiarity debate is obviously a reflection of sharper concern about the scope of Community action and, as a corollary, the permitted scope of State action.[52] The search is on for viable criteria. Article 3b, inserted into the EC Treaty by the Treaty on European Union, provides that;

> "The Community shall act within the limits of the powers conferred upon it by this Treaty and of the objectives assigned to it therein.
>
> In areas which do not fall within its exclusive competence, the Community shall take action, in accordance with the principle of subsidiarity, only if and in so far as the objectives of the proposed action cannot be sufficiently achieved by the Member States and can therefore, by reason of

---

[49] Article 100a was favoured in Case C-300/89 *Commission* v *Council* [1991] ECR I-2867, Art.130s in Case C-155/91 *Commission* v *Council*, Judgment of 17 March 1993 and Case C-187/93 *Parliament* v *Council*, Judgment of 28 June 1994.

[50] Case 68/86 *United Kingdom* v *Council* [1988] ECR 855. The significance of the precise details of this and other such cases alters as Treaty amendment alters procedures under specific bases, but the persisting lack of coherence establishes this as a fertile field for future litigation.

[51] As part of the agreement on the figure of 27, it was accepted that where there is a disagreement a reasonable period will be allowed for debate; there will not be immediate recourse to a formal vote. (27 became 26 after Norway chose not to join.)

[52] *Cf.* discussion in Chapter 1, section 2(ii).

> the scale or effects of the proposed action, be better achieved by the Community.
>
> Any action by the Community shall not go beyond what is necessary to achieve the objectives of this Treaty."

In fact, the core meaning of Article 3b is elusive. This is primarily because this formulation *reflects* the problem of dividing competences between Community and Member States instead of attempting directly to address it. One phrase, in particular, in Article 3b offers a vivid illustration of this evasiveness. The first clause in the second paragraph begs a hotly contested question – just what competences *are* exclusive to the Community? The Treaty provides no answer, case law is patchy, academic comment varies.[53] Such obscurity forms the reason why subsidiarity represents a continuation, even an intensification, of the competence debate, not its resolution.

(d) *Where the Community has acted, do Member States retain any residual competence in the field?*

The Treaty offers no statement of the consequences for national competence of Community competence in a particular field. Familiarity with federal systems immediately identifies this as the issue of "pre-emption" of sub-federal activity by federal norms. The Community has had to confront this issue, largely in litigation before the European Court. There are cases where Community action is deemed to rule out the possibility of national action in the relevant field, but this is not uniformly the outcome. A developed and predictable pattern of pre-emption law cannot readily be constructed from past practice.[54] Elements of Community policymaking such as the technique of minimum harmonisation and Treaty devices such as Article 100a(4)[55], do much to deprive the Community system of pre-emption of a clean-cut character.[56] In consequence, the patterns of permissible regulation at Community and at national level may remain obscure even after the Community has legislated. Doubts about the scope of national action following harmonisation are not conducive to commercial confidence in an integrated market where the

---

[53] See, *e.g.* the contrasting contributions of Emiliou, Toth and Steiner in O'Keeffe and Twomey, *op. cit.*, n 35. For an extended investigation see Lenaerts & van Ypersele, "Le principe de subsidiarité et son contexte: Etude de l'article 3b du Traité CE" (1994) CDE 3–83.

[54] For a careful survey, see Cross, (1992) 29 *Comm. Mkt. L. Rev.* 447.

[55] Article 100a(4) states: "If, after the adoption of a harmonisation measure by the Council acting by a qualified majority, a Member State deems it necessary to apply national provisions on grounds of major needs referred to in Article 36, or relating to protection of the environment or the working environment, it shall notify the Commission of these provisions.

The Commission shall confirm the provisions involved after having verified that they are not a means of arbitrary discrimination or a disguised restriction on trade between Member States.

By way of derogation from the procedure laid down in Articles 169 and 170, the Commission or any Member State may bring the matter directly before the Court of Justice if it considers that another Member State is making improper use of the powers provided for in this Article."

[56] *Cf.* Weatherill, *op. cit.*, n 35; Harmsen *op. cit.*, n 27.

source and consequence of regulatory action should be readily identifiable.[57]

In this book, it was seen in Chapter 5, dealing with Beer Labelling, that the application of stricter rules to domestic production alone was blocked. This contrasts peculiarly with the European Court's ruling in *R. v Secretary of State, ex parte Gallaher*[58], where the Court upheld the view of the Commission and United Kingdom that stricter rules on size of warning on tobacco products could be imposed on domestic producers alone, so that a challenge to the United Kingdom implementation of the relevant Directive by British producers failed. The example of regulation of minibus safety cited in Chapter 1[59], shows how doubts about the preemptive aspect of EC rules can engender evasion of responsibilities and public bewilderment.

Such problems can be traced back to the absence in the Community Treaty of clear principles for the allocation of regulatory powers between States and Community.

(e) *The Community as a process of dynamic development*

There is no necessary linkage between the scope of a market and the scope of a State. Many States the world over are characterised by a distribution of regulatory powers which in no way corresponds to the pattern of the market. The nature of a market is affected by the pattern of State intervention, illustrated by the growth of a European market in the wake of the withdrawal of State barriers to trade in Europe, but the existence of a market is not necessarily dependent on the existence of an accompanying State. However, because the nature of the Market *is* affected by regulatory activity, it is important to develop a framework for determining what are the respective roles of different public authorities. That is a dynamic constitutional process which is no doubt one characteristic of most emergent federations. However, in the Community the redistribution of public functions in the wake of the process of market integration is happening in the absence of any elaborated constitutional blueprint. This absence, in part, explains the unfocused ferocity of much of the debate.

However, it is an absence that is not accidental. The internal market project illustrates the need for the Community to advance by carefully *avoiding* planning the full implications. The objective of completing the internal market by the end of 1992 is ambiguously expressed in Article 7a of the EC Treaty, which was previously Article 8a of the EEC Treaty

---

[57] The House of Lords decision in *FTA* v *LBTC* [1992] 1 CMLR 5, [1991] 3 All ER 915 deserves consideration from this perspective, *cf.* Weatherill (1992) 17 E. L. Rev. 299. This decision reflects a concern about the implications of wider Community competence which has something in common with that of the BVerfG, *op. cit.*, n 40, albeit at a "micro" level.

[58] Case C-11/92, Judgment of 22 June 1993. Comment by Weatherill (1994) 19 E. L. Rev. 55, Stapleton (1994) 110 LQR 213. Chapter 5, n 55.

[59] Chapter 1, section 3(iii).

prior to the amendments effected by the Treaty on European Union. It is there provided that:

> "The internal market shall comprise an area without internal frontiers in which the free movement of goods, persons, services and capital is ensured in accordance with the provisions of this Treaty."

The absence of any explicit reference to common policy making in Article 8a of the EEC Treaty/7a of the EC Treaty suggested that the internal market was a rather less ambitious project than the common market referred to in Article 2 of the EC Treaty. For some this meant that the internal market was a mere staging post, after which further work would be directed at deepening other aspects of the Community's tasks and activities found in Articles 2 and 3. For others the internal market was an end in itself, and a happy rejection of some of the more ambitious plans for re-regulating the European market and for developing political institutions at European level. In agreeing to Article 8a/7a, it suited all concerned to bury the basic disagreement in textual ambiguity in order to ensure the political reinvigoration of the Community through the adoption of the 1992 agenda. Unsurprisingly, the lack of consensus on the status of the internal market has returned to haunt the policymakers. It is exemplified by the ferocious differences of opinion on the appropriateness of deeper spheres of competence for the Community after the end of 1992 and the consolidation of the internal market. The process of completing the internal market has overshadowed the development of regulatory laws and institutions at European level, but has not removed the desire for such developments among some Member States, at least.

In the Treaty on European Union, one of the best examples of how fundamental disagreement has been concealed behind textual ambiguity lies in the use of the subsidiarity formula. The United Kingdom doggedly stuck to its view that federalism is no part of the Community's mission and succeeded in deleting the f-word from the final text of the Treaty on European Union. Yet the United Kingdom welcomed the inclusion of the subsidiarity principle in Article 3b of the EC Treaty, even though it has been convincingly demonstrated that subsidiarity, built on an assumption that power is allocated to different levels within the structure, "can only be fully understood and defined within the context of federalism".[60]

This is not to criticise such compromise formulae. No Treaty could ever be finalised were it necessary to agree in advance how every point of controversy should be resolved. A Treaty serves a useful purpose by creating the framework within which such resolution can be achieved. So it is in the EC. However, the purpose of this discussion is to identify the

---

[60] Emiliou, "Subsidiarity: An Effective Barrier against the Enterprises of Ambition" (1992) 17 E. L. Rev. 383, 386.

areas in which future problems are likely to occur. Because economic change draws public structures into a rolling process of adjustment, one cannot simply view market integration as a phenomenon divorced from the position and power of the State. It is critical to the process of building the internal market to determine how the shifting patterns of market and state affect effective democratic accountability for decisions taken on behalf of the Citizens of the individual Member States, who are simultaneously Citizens of the European Union. The discussion above exposes the limitation of the current pattern of the Community's constitution in achieving a clear attribution of function.

The process of integration and its effects on a range of interested parties are charted in this book. In the absence of a developed constitutional blueprint for Europe, the practical processes of implementation which form the subject matter of this book assume considerable significance. In this sense, issues of implementation of EC law, examined in this book, are as important for the future of the Union as the grander schemes already being aired in the approach to the intergovernmental conference of 1996.

(f) *Private rights under EC law*

An important aspect to the process of market integration and regulation is that the law is driven by private litigants. Although the Commission has powers under Article 169 to bring State violations of the Treaty before the Court, many of the key decisions in the development of Community law have emerged as a result of private litigation before national courts. The combination of the principles of direct effect and supremacy and the Article 177 preliminary reference procedure serve to empower the private individual in the construction of the European Market. Private enforcement is a major cause of the inability of States to treat EC obligations lightly.

The Court explained in the *Van Gend en Loos* case[61] that:

> "The objective of the EEC Treaty, which is to establish a common market, the functioning of which is of direct concern to interested parties in the Community, implies that this Treaty is more than an agreement which merely creates mutual obligations between the contracting states... the Community constitutes a new legal order of international law for the benefit of which the states have limited their sovereign rights, albeit within limited fields, and the subjects of which comprise not only Member States but also their nationals. Independently of the legislation of the Member States, Community law therefore not only imposes obligations on individuals but is also intended to confer on them rights which become part of their legal heritage."

---

[61] Case 26/62 [1963] ECR 1.

Direct effect is also an avenue for establishing a form of democratic accountability of State to individual within the EC legal and political structure. Mancini and Keeling declare that:

> "As a result of *Van Gend en Loos*, the unique feature of Community law is its ability to impinge directly on the lives of individuals, who are declared to be the 'subjects' of the new legal order, entitled as such to invoke rights 'which become part of their legal heritage'. The effect of *Van Gend en Loos* was to take Community law out of the hands of politicians and bureaucrats and to give it to the people. Of all the Court's democratising achievements none can rank so highly in practical terms."[62]

This is a process carefully nurtured by the European Court. Examination in this book is found in Chapters 3 and 11. EC law rights become rights to open markets, to secure regulation of markets, to enjoy non-discriminatory treatment and to challenge State and in some cases private impediments to trade. Direct effect has long been the key to the empowerment of individuals, but strikingly the Court, in its landmark ruling in *Francovich* v *Italian State*[63], has paved the way for a wider notion of individual rights.

Private litigation based on the Court's conception of the scope of the economic constitution has become a major accelerator in developing the market. In fact such litigation has stimulated the Court to develop such a conception. In accordance with the notion of "indirect rule" national courts too become Community courts and those not accustomed to adopting functions of constitutional review are elevated into that role. The British experience provides a striking example of the shifts that follow this revolution. The approach taken in recent years by the House of Lords suggests that the function of constitutional adjudication is becoming steadily more capable of digestion by the English system. As Chapter 11 observes, a "creative response" is called for and it is increasingly perceptible.[64]

The bulk of caselaw concerns negative law; cases in which commercial interests have relied on Community law to achieve a deregulation of national markets, thereby providing a commercial opportunity to exploit a wider market for goods and services. Because Community law concerns protection of individuals as well as the facilitation of trade, a duality observed in several of the Chapters of this book, it is possible to identify decisions in which private rights to protection have been successfully vindicated through litigation before national courts. Positive law too may be

---

[62] Mancini and Keeling, "Democracy and the European Court of Justice" (1994) 57 MLR 175, 183.

[63] Cases C-6/90 and C-9/90 [1991] ECR I-5357. See text at Chapter 3, section 4(iv) and Chapter 4, text accompanying n 13.

[64] Most strikingly in *Equal Opportunities Commission* v *Secretary of State for Employment* [1994] 1 All ER 910. See Chapter 10, section 2(i)(a).

enforceable by virtue of the principle of direct effect. Much of the relevant litigation arises in the area of sex discrimination where Article 119 and supporting directives have a long pedigree. In 1976 the Court in *Defrenne* v *SABENA*[65] seized the opportunity to emphasise the dual function of harmonisation. It insisted that Article 119's requirement of equal pay for equal work "pursues a double aim", both equalisation of competitive conditions and social progress.[66] The *Francovich* ruling is the most striking example of recent years of the Court's determination to ensure effective protection of such Community law rights – in that instance even where the rights in question were not directly effective. Individual rights to a regulated market commonly arise in directives and it is accordingly regrettable that the Court has declined to make directives horizontally directly effective. That extension in the reach of directives would have secured effective protection of rights in the spheres of worker protection, anti-discrimination and consumer protection arising in the private sector even where a State had defaulted on its implementation obligation. The refusal to countenance the horizontal direct effect of directives, stated in *Marshall* v *Southampton AHA*[67] and confirmed in the July 1994 ruling in *Dori* v *Recreb*[68], represents a dent in the equality of the Citizen of the Union before the law.

(g) *Some pressures for the development of Community rules*

It is important to appreciate the nuanced objectives and expectations of individual litigants and, more generally, of those involved in arguments for or against Community rules.[69] It would be misleading to portray negative law as the law of traders and positive law as the law of the individual citizen. The individual citizen gains much from enhanced choice in an integrated market through the application of negative law. Commercial interests may welcome positive law as a means of clarifying opportunities for constructing an integrated marketing strategy. Once negative law fails to come to the aid of traders – whether because of lawful barriers to trade, but also where it is simply too costly to challenge rules which might theoretically be unlawful – they may be supportive of positive law, in order to secure Community-wide market access. They may also support Community rule making in order secure evenness in standards Community-wide so they are not at a competitive disadvantage compared to traders

---

[65] Case 43/75 [1976] ECR 455.
[66] Paras. 8–10 of the ruling.
[67] Case 152/84 [1986] ECR 723.
[68] Case C-91/92 Judgment of 14 July 1994. The motivation for the Court's reluctance may lie in fear that horizontal direct effect would not be accepted by some national judiciaries – a further aspect of the national implementation of EC law. *Cf.* Section 1(iv) above.
[69] *Cf.* Matthews, *The Evolution of Rules*, paper presented to the ESRC Single European Market Programme/COST A7 Action Conference, University of Exeter, 8–11 September 1994.

in other Community States where rules are less strict.[70] Precisely this perception would tend to induce traders to support equalisation of enforcement practice so they do not lose out to competitors in States where application of the rules is lax or, at least, is perceived to be lax. Pressure for Community rules is an issue also in the sphere of external trade policy. Commercial pressure for Community standards may form part of a strategy of raising entry barriers to non-Community operators, or a strategy for improving the position of Community producers in global markets, or both.[71]

A central theme of this book is that a number of interests are affected by the development and the implementation of Community legislation. The varying pressures mentioned above may be identified in the case studies pursued within the framework of this project. It is particularly evident that there are differing perceptions of the function of Community initiatives. Chapter 5, on beer labelling, explains that there is a perception of the measure as concerned with matters other than trade liberalisation (doubtless in part because of the unintegrated nature of the market). In Chapter 6, which deals with food safety, the Institute of Environmental Health Officers perceive measures as directed towards achieving free trade, not consumer protection. In Chapter 7 on the free movement of persons, not only labour mobility but also issues of civil liberties are at stake. Chapter 8 places the market for broadcasting in the context of general market integration and the opportunity to realise economies of scale, but there is also a whiff of an interest in promoting or, at least, protecting European culture.

These varying perceptions about the function of measures may in part account for the persisting concern about uneven and ineffective enforcement at national level which is seen in several case studies. A measure is judged against a different yardstick by different people with different interests and expectations. An unusually rigorous enforcement policy in State *A* may be welcomed by those in that State concerned to see regulatory protection, but deplored by those in that State who are concerned to avoid loss of competitive advantage; vice versa, an unusually lax enforcement policy. The perception will be influenced by what is occurring (or thought to be occurring) in other Member States.

---

[70] This suggests a call for Community rule making to counteract the "Delaware effect" (regulatory competition toward the lowering of regulatory standards) by firms that do not operate out of Delaware and do not want to move there (see Fischel, "The 'Race to the Bottom' Revisited: Reflections on Recent Developments in Delaware's Corporation Law" (1982) 76 Nw.U.L.Rev. 913. See also Chapter 6, text at n 98). More geographically apposite, disquiet from non-UK firms may be expected to increase as UK firms are able to avoid costs of complying with laws made under the Treaty on European Union Social Policy arrangements; section 1(iv) above.

[71] September 1994 saw newspaper criticism of Community plans to set standards for bananas; the Commission rushed to insist that such intervention was prompted by commercial interest in the establishment of consistency – "Responding to demands from the trade, a new classification system for bananas was put forward by the Commission. . .": European Commission (London Office), Release WE/31/94, 22 September 1994.

The problem of varying perception of the scope of intended EC initiatives, from trade facilitation to market regulation, may not be helped by the distribution of functions among different Directorates General in the Commission, nor by distribution of functions among different departments in the United Kingdom. The choice of lead department will affect negotiating tactic pre-adoption and, very probably, implementation strategy post-adoption. The 1993 DTI *Review of the Implementation and Enforcement of EC Law in the United Kingdom* attempts to address some of these issues. This is of value, although it seems extraordinary that appreciation of the issues has come so late.[72]

The legal system has a role to play in shaping the capacity of individuals to express and enforce their perceptions of the function of EC measures. The more willing the system to permit the involvement of a wide range of interested parties, the more multi-dimensional the impact of the measure within the national structure will become. In this sense the scope of individual enforcement becomes a key determinant in the nature of the implementation process.

The point may be illustrated with reference to *Francovich*. Italian failure to implement Directive 80/987 on guarantee funds for workers in the event of employer insolvency led to the claim for compensation against Italy in the case. The European Court's support for the individual claim at national level gave practical impact to the purpose of the Directive in laying a base level of social protection. The Directive had a dual function; it was also designed to equalise competitive conditions. Firms outside Italy suffered a competitive disadvantage as a result of non-implementation. Such firms would not have access to the legal system to challenge Italy's non-implementation. This weakens the function of the Directive as an equaliser of regulation. Commission action would be required.[73] Francovich's vindication of his own interest served indirectly to support the interests of non-Italian commercial interests in equalisation of competitive conditions. Community law's recognition of individual rights at national level affects the process of implementation. Direct effect is the cornerstone of this legal development; *Francovich* moves beyond direct effect; *Dori*, by contrast, restricts the scope of direct effect.[74]

Chapter 10 explores how the capacity of a national legal system to recognise enforceable rights affects the implementation of Community law. For example, the availability of collective redress or representative actions would significantly affect the national perception of the purpose of a directive where such collective or representative opportunities enable access to the courts of interested parties who, individually, would have no standing or no practical possibility of bringing an action before the

---

[72] See generally Chapter 3.
[73] And, in fact, had occurred; Case 22/87 *Commission* v *Italy* [1989] ECR 143.
[74] Section 1(iv)(f) above.

courts. For the United Kingdom, the decision of the House of Lords in *EOC*[75] is important for such reasons.[76]

The wider the opportunity granted to individuals to enforce Community rules, the more interests find expression in the implementation process and the deeper the infeasibility of confining a Community measure to a single objective. Whereas if the Member State retained sole power to enforce and implement a Directive it could choose for itself the objective, the objectives become more varied as different interests become involved. This is part of the modern multi-functionalism of EC law. Its depth and breadth is not simply attributable to the spread of substantive law beyond market integration into market (re)regulation, but is also drawn from the constitutional pattern involving the creation of individual opportunities for enforcement by parties with diffuse interests. Such creeping developments are an important practical aspect of the constitutional shaping of the Union.

2 Implications internal to Member States

(i) Introduction

The impact of European market integration on the constitutional patterns of the Member States has been widely discussed in the context of the relationship between the Community and the "State" as a monolith. It is well understood that market integration demands an adjustment of the functions of public authorities responsible for regulating the market. The more hidden issue, which is a focus of this book, concerns the implications of the Community's evolution for the distribution of powers within a State. If anything, a trace of a constitutional blueprint is even less easy to discern. The Community is based on a transfer of power from the State to the Community. There is nothing in the Treaty which exerts direct impact on the internal distribution of powers within individual Member States. True, where the powers transferred from State to Community were previously held at local level within the State, they are lost to that local level, but that is not a question of redistributing powers among the internal organs of the State. The Community accepts federal States as it accepts unitary States and membership of the Community does not, as such, require internal constitutional change.

Likewise, the Treaty has no explicit rules on the permissible scope of the public or the private sector. Article 222 of the EC Treaty declares

---

[75] *Op. cit.* n 64.

[76] At Community level, the Court of First Instance's decision in Case T-37/92 *BEUC* v *Commission*, Judgment of 18 May 1994, regarding the involvement of consumer groups in competition investigations seems likely to affect the Commission's own "implementation" of the competition rules.

that "This Treaty shall in no way prejudice the rules in Member States governing the system of property ownership." A policy of privatisation or of nationalisation would, of itself, be untouched by Community law. It is true that rules forbidding nationality discrimination would have to be observed. Compliance with the competition rules governing, for example, state monopolies and state aids, would have to be ensured. But choices about public or private property ownership rest in principle with the Member State.

(ii) **Within the State – the range of influences on the pattern of central/local relations**

There are elements in the formal structure of Community law which suggest that Community membership might induce a tightening of the grip of the central State on its component parts. All organs of the State are bound by the obligations of, for example, Article 30 dealing with the free movement of goods. Yet even where a local authority acts in a manner incompatible with the obligation to respect the free movement rules, it is the State which would be the defendant in Article 169 infringement proceedings instituted by the European Commission.[77] It may be that liability in damages for violation of Community law rests with the central State alone even where default has occurred at local level, although this is not settled.[78]

The terms of Article 189 declare that the Directive shall be addressed to the Member State. It is envisaged that the State shall be permitted to make its own choice about how to digest the Community measure within the domestic legal order.[79] States may rely on local or regional authorities. However, it is no defence to a charge of non-implementation of a directive to claim that internal power distribution renders the central authorities impotent to secure observance of the obligations undertaken in a directive.[80] This is a doctrine well established in public international law and its role is understandable in that context, as in EC law, as a means of depriving States of a defence which, if recognised, could empty obligations undertaken on the international plane of any useful content.

However, this approach assumes, indeed requires, that States will put in place certain centralised chains of command. Accordingly the obli-

---

[77] E.g. Case 45/87 *Commission* v *Ireland* [1989] ECR 4929, violation of Article 30 by Dundalk Council.

[78] This is the view of Lord Goff in *Kirklees* v *Wickes* [1992] 3 All ER 717, 734 and that of Hessel and Mortelmans, "Decentralised Government and Community Law: Conflicting Institutional Developments?" (1993) 30 *Comm. Mkt. L. Rev.* 905, 929. The contrary argument draws on the obligation cast on *all* limbs of the State by Article 5 of the EC Treaty to respect Community law; *cf.* Szyszczak, (1994) 19 E. L. Rev. 214, 220.

[79] On the United Kingdom's choices, see Chapter 4.

[80] E.g. Case 1/86 *Commission* v *Belgium* [1987] ECR 2797; Case 73/81, *Commission* v *Belgium* [1982] ECR 189.

gation to implement may induce, indeed require, a State to do more than simply empower a local level of government. The State is obliged to have at its disposal an effective means of ensuring compliance. In federal states, the fact that the subject matter of a duly adopted directive may fall within the competence of the regional authorities cannot absolve the Member State of responsibility for Treaty violation should those regional authorities misapply the measures derived from the Community directive.

This pattern offers a strong inducement to the central State to tighten its grip on the discretion exercised at local levels. This suggests an "upward" redistribution of internal State functions dictated by the Treaty obligations of the (central) State. Caselaw in the European Court offers examples of this process. In *Commission* v *Germany* the Court ruled that Germany was in violation of its obligations under the Treaty in failing to require *Länder* to notify derogations permitted under Directive 80/778 relating to the quality of water intended for human consumption.[81] Within Member States, such issues can cause acute tensions. In Germany, for example, "Länder" have been prepared to initiate legal challenges in an attempt to control the Federal Government's activities in the Community legislative process.[82]

In this vein, the case studies in this book reflect the concern of central government to standardise local authority enforcement practice, or at the very least to improve co-ordination between local enforcement authorities. This theme may be seen in relation to beer labelling, food safety and toy safety. In part this process is driven by the current preoccupation with reducing the burdens on business which are caused by uneven approaches to enforcement adopted in different geographical areas. However, the aspect of Community membership has a role to play in reinforcing this trend.

The Chapters on food and toy safety show a preference to implement relevant directives through absorption into existing structures of control. Entirely new structures have not been devised. There has been no attempt to harmonise practice with other Member States. However, in the Chapter on toy safety it is explained that the DTI has begun to require local authorities to communicate to it information about action taken against toys at local level. That information is then sent on to the Commission. The central institution, in discharging Community obligations, is obliged to add an extra requirement to the internal system. The same issue arises in the Chapter on food safety, where the central department is Ministry of Agriculture, Food and Fisheries (MAFF). In relation to beer labelling, the requirement that local authorities pass on information about investi-

[81] Case 237/90 Judgment of 24 November 1992.
[82] *E.g.* the case brought by Bavaria against the Federal Government, decided by the German Constitutional Court in April 1989, English translation at [1990] 1 CMLR 649. Some discussion of these issues can be found in Schwarze, Govaere, Hélin, Van den Bossche (eds), *The 1992 Challenge at National Level: Report and Conference Proceedings 1989* (1990) pp 171–316.

gations and infringements of food labelling regulations, in the past abandoned, has now been restored, apparently in part as a consequence of the EC dimension.

These are pointers towards a centralisation of regulatory control induced by the obligations imposed on the State by the fact of Community membership. At the very least, it seems that the central State/Community axis contains elements which inhibit a policy of decentralisation within the State from central to local level.

However there are other aspects of the influence of Community law that work in a different direction. Although the centralisation discussed above may be one element, the overall picture is significantly more complex. The process of market integration through law affects all elements in the State. All must come to terms with the discharge of their functions in an economic environment which is border-free. Local authorities must develop a strategy for dealing with Community law. In practice the formal legal point that any violation may not lead them to be in receipt of an Article 169 letter from the Commission does not mean that they can or wish to keep Community law at arm's length. Community law has a significant impact. All organs of the State are bound by Community law, including local authorities. They are accordingly bound by Community law and, in the event of violation, they may be the subject of challenges instituted before national courts by private parties relying on directly effective Community law. This route may cause a local authority to find its practices before the Luxembourg Court via the Article 177 preliminary reference procedure. This has occurred, for example, in relation to failure to observe provisions of directives[83] and in relation to disrespect for the fundamental prohibition on nationality discrimination.[84] The root of this all-embracing obligation of loyalty cast on State bodies is Article 5 of the EC Treaty. This binds the State to the observance of Community law. The 'State' in this context covers the central institutions of the State, the judiciary, whose obligations under Article 5 effectively to protect Community law rights are becoming increasingly well defined[85], and local authorities too.

In response to the impact of Community law, local levels of government endeavour to establish vertical relations with the Community institutions. This is most apparent in relations with the Commission, where local authorities are increasingly concerned to have a presence in Brussels.[86] The Committee of the Regions established by the Treaty on European Union may reflect a broader concern to establish a formal place in the legislative process for regional influence.[87]

---

[83] Case 103/88 *Fratelli Costanzo* v *Milano* [1989] ECR 1839.
[84] Case 197/84 *Steinhauser* v *Biarritz* [1985] ECR 1819.
[85] See Chapters 3 and 11.
[86] Discussed by Preston (Chapter 13) in *The United Kingdom and EC Membership Evaluated* (Bulmer *et al*, 1992).
[87] Article 198a of the EC Treaty.

Both vertical and horizontal aspects of the interest of local authorities in engaging in dialogue prompted by Community membership may be seen in the work of the Institute of Environmental Health Officers (IEHO) in the Chapter on food safety. The Chapter on toy safety also reveals such developments. In both areas, the Local Authorities Co-ordinating Body on Trading Standards (LACOTS) has played a major role in the coordination of the efforts of the local authorities to take seriously the cross-border dimension to their work which is the inevitable consequence of market integration. LACOTS, it should be noted, is the creature of the local level of government. It is not accountable to central government, although much of its work draws it into co-operative contact with central government departments.

The fact that Community law affects local levels of government invites a bypassing of Westminster in a way which could profoundly affect traditional structures of British government. This is plainly capable of exerting a sensitive impact on local/central State relations in the United Kingdom Both the Chapters on food safety and toy safety reflect a sharp awareness on the part of the central departments that, from their perspective, the process needs to be "controlled." Examples of this tension surface with an increasing frequency that suggests that the deepening efforts of local and regional authorities to engage in dialogue with power sources in Brussels is matched by a rising eagerness of the central organs of the State to retain oversight. For example, the efforts of the Welsh Development Agency to establish its own profile in dealing with Brussels and in dealing with outside investors led to concern by the Welsh Secretary of State, John Redwood, about the presentation of Wales as distinct from the United Kingdom.[88] The message is that Community membership injects a set of potentially conflicting impulses into the central/local relationship within Member States. For the United Kingdom, these dynamic processes occur against a background absence of a constitutionally defined distribution of power within the state. At Community level too the most striking constitutional aspect is the absence of a developed constitutional blueprint.

(iii) **Within the State: limits placed on a policy of reducing the role of public authorities**

Elements of Community law impinge on the capacity of the State to choose for itself how to demarcate public functions from private functions. It is discussed above that, although Community law does not dictate the level within the State at which implementation shall occur, the conferral of enhanced functions on local authorities may cause practical

---

[88] *The Independent*, 28 January 1994, p 3.

problems for the central State in respect of its capacity to secure compliance with Community law. Where regulatory functions are placed in, or transferred into, private hands precisely the same practical issues arise, yet there may arise additional objections about the legality of the process. Although Article 222 of the EC Treaty asserts neutrality about property ownership as a general principle, there are specific areas where State supervision is essential in order properly to discharge Community obligations. A policy of transferring assets into private hands will not of itself violate Community law, but there may be circumstances where the transfer of some supervisory powers over those assets may be incompatible with the demands of Community law. In this manner Community membership may inhibit choices and force a State to retain a larger area of responsibility than it would otherwise choose.

In other areas, attempts to adjust the relationship between public and private sectors may meet European-derived obstacles, not because of a Community objection to the transfer from public to private sector per se, but because Community rules prevent transfer being achieved through a clean break. The rules governing transfer of undertakings provide a good example of the costs which are imposed by Community law on any transfer, whatever the status of the parties.[89] One consequence of such Community rules is to raise the costs of a transfer of functions from public to private sector. The cost implications of Community rules were apparent in the recent rulings that the United Kingdom had failed properly to implement the directives on protection of employees on transfer of undertakings and collective redundancies.[90] The United Kingdom had restricted rights of information and consultation to trade unions that are recognised by employers, but had in place no procedure for obligatory recognition. Employers held the power to recognise, not to recognise or to derecognise and could therefore evade the obligations in question. In the view of the European Court, the worker protection envisaged by the Directive and the equalisation of competitive conditions Community-wide were compromised by the United Kingdom's minimalist implementation in this and other respects. This was held to be an inadequate implementation. The United Kingdom will be obliged to extend the scope of its regulation of transfers of undertakings and collective redundancies (and may face claims for compensation from employees able to rely on the *Francovich* principle).

This saga is directly related to the key question of deregulation or reregulation in the Community. The United Kingdom's belief in the virtues of deregulated labour markets explains its refusal to participate in deeper social policy making after Maastricht.[91] This option is not open to it in respect of existing Community law. One reaction to perceived

---

[89] Directive 77/187, (OJ 1997 L61/26).
[90] Cases C-382/92 and C-383/92, Judgments of 8 June 1994.
[91] Section 1(iv) above.

past over-regulation is to pursue a path of minimalist implementation. Another is to seek repeal, or at least dilution, of existing Community rules, and indeed, during 1994 the United Kingdom and Germany engaged in such attempts relating to the Transfer of Undertakings Directive.

A further thread is found in the scope of application of unimplemented directives at national level. The European Court has held that an unimplemented Directive is capable of direct effect against the State, but not against a private party. This renders crucial the scope of the "State" for these purposes.[92] The European Court has adopted a wide interpretation and one which may not be congruent with national notions of the location of the public/private law divide. In *Foster* v *British Gas* it emphasised that EC law does not look to the legal form of the entity.[93] Directives are capable of enforcement against a body "which has been made responsible, pursuant to a measure adopted by the State, for providing a public service under the control of the State and has for that purpose special powers beyond those which result from the normal rules applicable in relations between individuals". The result is that an entity which is in or has been transferred into the private sector may still count as the "State" for Community law purposes and may be susceptible to a direct challenge before national courts where it fails to comply with obligations contained in a directive. The Community notion of the State for these purposes may be broader than that favoured at national level and accordingly a simple shift from public to private sector under national law may not be so clean-cut for Community law purposes.

In keeping with the nuanced picture observed elsewhere in this account, other elements of Community policy seem to have rather a lot in common with recent British policy trends. The application of Article 90 in *Höfner* v *Macrotron*[94] provides a good example of reliance on EC law permitting private parties to penetrate a market characterised by State-conferred exclusive rights, in that instance even where there was no interstate aspect to the activities of the party making use of Article 90. This is a decision which seems to conform to the United Kingdom's interest over the last 15 years in deregulating product and service markets.

The New Approach as a technique is inspired by the desire to impose a much lighter regulatory touch. The New Approach is based on the belief that Community intervention should be limited to the least intrusive style necessary to achieve the objectives of harmonisation.[95] So rules should be pitched at a general target level and supporting standards are developed by private actors, who, after all possess expertise in the area unavailable to the regulator without incurring significant cost. This is not

---

[92] Curtin, "The Province of Government" (1990) 15 E. L. Rev. 195.
[93] Case C-188/89 [1990] ECR I-3133.
[94] Case C-41/90 [1991] ECR I-1979.
[95] The New Approach is discussed further in Chapter 2, section 5(i).

self-regulation because the required level is set by the directive in the shape of the essential safety requirements. However the practical application of that notion is dependent on private sector inputs. More generally, the "New Approach" is built on the objective of releasing private parties from detailed regulatory straitjackets. Moreover, the self-certification procedures, seen in, for example, Chapter 9 on toy safety, involves producers aligning themselves to the legal requirements without the intervention of third-party certification.

It is here that examples may be seen of the EC approach, following on from, and reinforcing, the United Kingdom approach. In the product safety sector, the General Safety Requirement introduced into United Kingdom law in 1987 by Part II of the Consumer Protection Act closely resembles the General Directive adopted by the Community in 1992, the deadline for implementation of which fell in June 1994.[96] Both measures use a broadly phrased general duty, coupled to amplification-by-standards. Public authorities no longer set detailed technical rules governing the sector. More is allowed, and expected, of the private sector.

3 Administrative partnership and indirect rule

(i) The future of administrative co-operation

The message of the preceding analysis is that Community membership brings to bear a number of pressures on the internal distribution of powers within a State. These pressures are to some extent competing. They are not the subject of planned constitutional arrangements. The pattern is dynamic, the future rather unpredictable.

More generally this book has revealed many shifts in domestic practice as a result of the attempts to come to terms with the requirements of the Community system. All this seems likely to deepen as the process of integration and regulation in the border free market progresses. Implementation is a dynamic process.

Since the end of 1992 there has been an increasing appreciation of the significance of administrative co-ordination as an indispensable element in achieving effective market integration in the Community. The focus of Commission activity has switched from preparation of new initiatives to the management of the internal market on the terms of the rules agreed and, in the main, implemented in law if not always in practice in the Member States. Questions about the 'effectiveness' of Community law are prominent. Chapter 3 elaborates the notion that effectiveness in this context encompasses not simply formal implementation, but also enforcement and practical compliance.

---

[96] Directive 92/59 (OJ 1992 I.228/24).

There is accordingly an emphasis on the development of patterns of common strategies for the application and enforcement of the package of internal market legislation. There are elements which suggest that the tension between centralised national State and border-free market may intensify. The Sutherland Report of 1992 is strongly motivated by the need to achieve effective administrative enforcement of the rules.[97] It portrays "horizontal" enforcement, between agencies at the same administrative level in different Member States, as efficient and envisages it as essential. This indicates that some of the central/local State pressures portrayed in this book seem likely to increase.[98]

(ii) Solving disputes about the operation of the internal market – the Court

The Court has a role to play in clarification of some issues. Several of the Chapters in this book pick out points of dispute where a legal interpretation seems necessary and may be sought, whether in the context of Article 169 or Article 177.

For example, in Chapter 8, dealing with broadcasting, we note the making of a reference, to the European Court by the English High Court, on the compatibility of British suppression of transmissions with Directive 89/552. In both Chapters 9 and 6, dealing with toys and food, reference is made to the uncertainty over the compatibility of the "due diligence" defence typically available under British consumer protection law with obligations effectively to enforce directives.[99] More generally, it remains unclear what "effectiveness" means in the context of the enforcement of Community law at national level. How far from national legal traditions should national systems depart in ensuring effective application of Community law? Chapters 3, 10 and 11 all reflect this critically important issue.

Chapter 3 considers the question of the extent to which soft law is justiciable in the Community legal order. In Chapter 8, on broadcasting, there are examples of deliberately vague phrases included in the relevant Directive. This presents problems for the Court in drawing legal implications from vague commitments. The subsidiarity principle is perhaps the most prominent of all the current issues which concern questionable justiciability. These are all areas of potential difficulty for the Court.

---

[97] *The Internal Market after 1992: Meeting the Challenge*, the Sutherland Report to the EEC Commission by the High Level Group on the Operation of Internal Market, October 1992.
[98] *Cf.* Section 2(ii) above.
[99] *Cf.* comparable problems in determining the leeway allowed to Member States in implementing directives in the health and safety field, Baldwin and Daintith, *Harmonization and Hazard* (1992), pp 242–243.

(iii) **Solving disputes about the operation of the internal market – administrative co-operation**

It is self-evident that recourse to judicial interpretation cannot solve every-day problems in the administration of the internal market. Article 169 is cumbersome and inappropriate for the resolution of matters of detail. Article 177 is more flexible, but there are some areas where judicially-inspired harmonisation is not likely to be helpful. Chapter 3 concludes with some scepticism about the role of the European Court in developing a common liability system. Much of the task ahead in the management of the internal market lies not in questions of "hard law", but instead in practical implementation. What is really needed is an institutional pattern of enforcement which will be sufficiently transparent, even and effective to ensure the realisation of the benefits of market integration.

The Sutherland Report, published in October 1992[100], is designed to prepare the Community for the task of devising a strategy for securing the advantages of the internal market once the symbolically important but legally ambiguous[101] deadline of end 1992 is passed. The Report declares itself concerned with practical problems in the operation of the internal market. It seeks to identify practical solutions. It has as an objective that the rules of the internal market shall have equivalent effect throughout the Community. It places great faith on the construction of a "partnership" between Commission and Member States. National officials should be aware that in the border-free market they apply Community law as part of a pattern of Community-wide responsibilities owed to citizens throughout the internal market. Officials of Member States include not only the administration but also the judiciary.

The Report proposes a permanent framework for administrative partnership between Member States and Commission to deal with the application of internal market rules. The Commission has responded to the Sutherland Report. It is engaged on a process of creating such a framework. In June 1993 the Commission published *Reinforcing the effectiveness of the internal market* and the accompanying working document *Towards a strategic programme for the internal market.*[102] This explicitly adopts the language of partnership: "a partnership between the Commission and the Member States in the application and the effective management of the rules". This was followed by further discussion. The Commission refined its thoughts in a communication to the Council, *Making the Most of the Internal Market.*[103] The Commission's programme was welcomed by the Internal Market Council in December 1993.

The Commission plans to develop a framework for improving adminis-

---

[100] Note 97 above.
[101] Section 1(ii) above.
[102] Document COM(93)256.
[103] Document COM(93)632.

trative co-operation between the authorities of the Member States and the Commission and between the authorities of the Member States themselves. A Communication from the Commission to the Council, the European Parliament and the Economic and Social Committee on the handling of urgent situations in the context of implementation of Community rules is explicitly presented as a follow-up to the Sutherland Report.[104] Existing systems of co-operation and communication are reviewed and improvements are suggested.

In this book, the Chapters on toy safety and food in particular demonstrate that horizontal links between enforcement bodies have developed spontaneously in the internal market. This may also be observed in the July 1993 DTI Review in connection with the Institute of Trading Standards Administration's work in relation to Textiles.[105] The Commission has now plainly embarked on a process of securing an intensification. The expectation is that national systems will be receptive to such developing cross-border patterns.

Early in 1994 the Commission published a Communication to the Council and the European Parliament on the development of administrative co-operation in the implementation and enforcement of Community legislation in the Internal Market.[106] This reveals a plan to drive towards a framework for co-operation between Member States and between Commission and Member States. Cumbersome procedures are to be avoided. Discussions between Commission and Member States are to be arranged. Progress in this direction is seen in this book in the Chapters on toy safety and broadcasting and is analysed in Chapter 3.

The Commission has also been active in attempting to make the law more transparent by issuing its own interpretation in particular areas. An example may be observed in Chapter 5 on beer labelling, where the Commission chose to issue a Communication on the use of languages in the marketing of foodstuffs in the light of the judgment in *Piageme* v *Peeters*.[107] Chapter 3 discusses the role of soft law. The value of such communications in the process of implementation is the subject of extensive existing research.[108] The notion of partnership is fruitful as an indication of a co-operative rather than hierarchical relationship. This is in tune with current political interpretations placed upon the principle of subsidiarity. In *the Overall Approach to the Application by the Council of the Subsidiarity Principle and Article 3b of the Treaty on European Union*, a paper annexed to the Conclusions of the Presidency which emerged from the Edinburgh European Council of December 1992, it is explicitly stated that:

---

[104] Document COM(93)430.
[105] *Review of the Implementation and Enforcement of EC Law in the United Kingdom*, p 188.
[106] Document COM(94)29.
[107] OJ 1993 C345/3. See Chapter 5, text at n 4.
[108] *Cf.* especially Schwarze, Govaere, Hélin, Van den Bossche (eds), *op. cit.*, n 82.

"Where appropriate under the Treaty, and provided this is sufficient to achieve its objectives, preference in choosing the type of Community action should be given to encouraging cooperation between Member States, coordinating national action or to complementing, supplementing or supporting such action."

The value of "indirect rule" is thus recognised as an aspect of the subsidiarity debate. From the perspective of the issue of deregulation/reregulation, the critical question asks how much institutional support at Community level is a required for genuine integration.

Partnership is also a keystone of current policymaking applicable to the Structural Funds, where the partners are Community and Member States at national, regional and local level.[109]

(iv) The way ahead

The Commission has been careful to present its proposals as inspired by the need to establish and to maintain an integrated market. It has explicitly denied any intention to create new and cumbersome bureaucratic structures.[110] However, these developments touch on the sensitive debate about the relationship between deregulation and reregulation in the evolving market. This is, once more, "the paradox of regulating in order to deregulate".[111]

For all its claim to be limited to practical suggestions only, the Sutherland Report in fact raises fundamentally important political and constitutional questions about the shape of the internal market. The rules are in place; but how are they to be enforced? The Commission appears to assume *sub silentio* that private litigation based on the application of Community law before national courts is not enough of itself to secure effective application of the rules of market integration. Firmer institutional control is required. The Commission wants to make more transparent the working of national administrations. This suggests that it will seek to impose, at least, obligations on Member States to notify to it action taken which impedes cross-border trade. The Commission will then be able to consider a response. This immediately suggests a potential deeper intrusion by the Commission into national practice. The sensitive political implications are obvious. Even though the Commission can present this as simply a part of securing trade liberalisation, the increase in its own formal powers carries with it a vulnerability to allegations of overregul-

---

[109] Discussed in Hessel and Mortelmans, "Decentralised Government and Community Law: Conflicting Institutional Developments?" (1993) 30 *Common Market Law Review* 905. See also Chapter 2.

[110] *E.g.* Document COM(94)29, *op. cit.*, n 106.

[111] Chapter 1, section 2(i).

ation. This focuses directly on the questionable adequacy of "indirect rule" – can a market be shaped at European level without public intervention at European level?

The July 1993 DTI *Review* is already sensitive to precisely this issue.[112] It expresses fears about the construction of an overly bureaucratic centralised administrative structure. It seems plain that the United Kingdom will closely monitor Commission ambitions in this area. The future promises an intensification of the problems exposed in this book.

"Indirect rule" remains, politically, highly attractive. Direct rule is not politically feasible. However, the political value of indirect rule can be linked to successful implementation of the mass of Community laws only with a level of institutional support at Community level. There is a strong case to be made for the development of a general implementation supervisory agency. It would operate in all areas and would be designed to tackle broadly applicable issues of effective and even enforcement.[113] Such issues of implementation strategy are linked to the examination in sections 1 and 2 of this Chapter. The establishment of such an agency raises questions of Community competence[114] (sections 1(iv)(a) and 1(iv)(b) above). The appropriate legal bases conferring competence to set up agencies that are not sector-specific seem to lie in Article 235 or, possibly, in Article 100a. Perhaps some indication that the European Court is receptive to the use of Article 100a to confer at least limited competence on the Commission may be gleaned from its rejection of Germany's application for annulment of Article 9 of the Directive on General Product Safety.[115] The control of unsafe products under the Directive is largely to be achieved by "indirect rule", *via* national methods, but the conferral of limited powers on the Commission to act in emergency situations has been upheld. It seems, however, that empowering the Commission in this way is likely to remain a potential constitutional flashpoint. The application of the subsidiarity principle to such questions of agency development reveals Article 3b's flexibility (section 1(iv)(c)). On one view, development of such entities at Community level is a classic manifestation of over-regulation and intrusion into matters best organised at national or sub-national level. From another perspective – that of, *inter alia*, the Sutherland Report – fragmented national markets cannot be welded together into a workable European market without support at

---

[112] DTI, *op. cit.*, n 105.
[113] *Cf.* Baldwin and Daintith, *op. cit.*, n 99, discussing the possibility "of stronger centralized control using the main European institutions to oversee practical implementation" (p 243). This passage astutely considers resource problems in achieving a systematic overview and at p 246 pushes more for a practical approach involving coordination, consultation and information sharing by the Commission. It airs the possibility of a European Agency for Health and Safety at Work (now, in fact, in course of establishment at Bilbao in Spain). See Chapter 1, n 44.
[114] For general discussion see Dehousse, Joerges, Majone, Snyder and Everson, *Europe after 1992: New Regulatory Strategies*, Florence, EUI Working Papers in Law, 92/31; Lenaerts, "Regulating the Regulatory Process: 'Delegation of Powers' in the European Community" (1993) E. L. Rev. 23.
[115] Case C-359/92 Judgment of 9 August 1994.

transnational level. Subsidiarity thus dictates a need for Community action. Whatever occurs at Community level does not blot out the need for action at national level (section 1(iv)(d)) nor for the appropriate and fruitful relationships between local, national and Community agencies whose construction, as discussed in section 2 of this Chapter, necessarily implicates the internal ordering of Member States.

The message of this book is that such an agency must be multi-functional to be effective. It must take full account of the wide range of interests that are affected by the implementation of EC law. It must be transparent and receptive to all influences. Implementation strategies focussed on market integration alone will not do justice to the pattern of the modern Community and will be ineffective when they confront wider aspects of Community activities. Allied to this pragmatic consideration is the issue of locating effective democratic accountability for decisions taken on behalf of the Citizens of the individual Member States, who are simultaneously Citizens of the European Union.

These are key issues for the constitutional reordering that seems likely to occur in 1996[116], but in advance of that event the continuing practical processes examined in this book are of great significance for the pattern of the European market and the European Union.

STEPHEN WEATHERILL

---

[116] Section 1(iv) above.

Index

361

.